6   ð

80x86 Assembly Language
and Computer Architecture

RICHARD C. DETMER
Middle Tennessee State University

JONES AND BARTLETT PUBLISHERS
Sudbury, Massachusetts
BOSTON   TORONTO   LONDON   SINGAPORE

World Headquarters
Jones and Bartlett Publishers
40 Tall Pine Drive
Sudbury, MA 01776
978-443-5000
info@jbpub.com
www.jbpub.com

Jones and Bartlett Publishers
Canada
2406 Nikanna Road
Mississauga, ON L5C 2W6
CANADA

Jones and Bartlett Publishers
International
Barb House, Barb Mews
London W6 7PA
UK

Cover Image © Stone/Peter Poulides

Library of Congress Cataloging-in-Publication Data
Detmer, Richard C.
        Introduction to 80x86 Assembly Language and Computer Architecture / Richard Detmer.
            p.   cm.
        Includes index.
        ISBN 0-7637-1773-8
        1. Computer architecture.   2. Assembler language (Computer program language) I.
Title.

QA76.9.A73 D48 2001
004.2'2—dc21   00-069028

Senior Acquisitions Editor: Michael Stranz
Development and Product Manager: Amy Rose
Production Assistant: Tara McCormick
Production Coordination: Trillium Project Management
Composition: Northeast Compositors, Inc.
Copyeditor: Sarah Corey
Text Design: Dartmouth Publishing, Inc.
Cover Design: Kristin Ohlin
Printing and Binding: Courier Westford
Cover printing: John Pow Company

This book was typeset in Quark 4.1 on a Macintosh G4. The font families used were Serifa, Frutiger, and
Courier. The first printing was printed on 50# Decision 94 Opaque.

Printed in the United States of America
05 04 03 02   10 9 8 7 6 5 4 3 2

Dedicated to

my mother, Emma Langenhop Detmer Baldwin Toombs
and my uncle, Carl E. Langenhop
both of whom encouraged me to become a scholar.

PREFACE

A computer can be viewed from many different levels. Many people are interested only in using applications such as word processing or games. A computer programmer, however, often sees the computer as an instrument to create new applications software. A high-level language programmer's image of the computer is provided by the language compiler, which gives the impression that the computer stores object types like `integer`, `real`, and `array of char` in named memory locations, calculates values of expressions, calls procedures, executes `while` loops, and so forth.

However, an actual computer works at even lower levels. This book emphasizes the architectural level, that is, the level defined by the machine instructions that the processor can execute. Assembly-language instructions translate directly into machine-language instructions, so that when you write an assembly-language program, you gain an understanding of how the computer works at the machine-language level.

Although this book emphasizes the assembly-language/machine-language level of computer operations, it also looks at other levels. For instance, it describes how high-level language concepts such as `if` statements are realized at the machine level. It discusses some of the functions of the operating system. It briefly describes the logic gates that are used at the hardware level. It also looks at how assembly language is translated into machine language.

To program effectively at any level, programmers must understand certain fundamental principles at the machine level. These apply to most computer architectures. *Introduction to 80x86 Assembly Language and Computer Architecture* teaches these fundamental concepts:

- memory addressing, CPU registers and their uses
- representation of data in a computer in numeric formats and as character strings
- instructions to operate on 2's complement integers
- instructions to operate on individual bits
- instructions to handle strings of characters

- instructions for branching and looping
- coding of procedures: transfer of control, parameter passing, local variables, and preserving the environment for the calling program

The primary architecture covered is the Intel 80x86 CPU family used in many personal computers. However, almost every chapter includes information about other architectures, or about different computer levels. Programming in assembly language and studying related concepts in *Introduction to 80x86 Assembly Language and Computer Architecture* prepares the student to program effectively in any programming language, to pursue advanced studies in computer design and architecture, or to learn more about system details for specific computers.

Text Organization and Content

Much of the material in this book is based on my previous book, *Fundamentals of Assembly Language Programming Using the IBM PC and Compatibles*. While teaching this material through the years, I have increasingly come to the conclusion that an assembly language course is the best place to introduce computer architecture to most students. This book reflects a stronger emphasis on architecture than on programming. It also concentrates on general concepts as opposed to the details of a particular computer system.

The minimal prerequisite for my assembly language class is a good understanding of a structured high-level language. Chapters 3 through 6 and Chapter 8 form the core of my one-semester course. I normally cover Chapters 1–8 thoroughly, Chapter 9 quickly, and then choose topics from Chapters 10–12 depending on time and resources available. For instance, I sometimes introduce floating-point operations via in-line assembly statements in a C++ program.

Style and Pedagogy

The text primarily teaches by example. A complete assembly-language program is presented very early, in Chapter 3, and its components are carefully examined at a level that the student is able to understand. Subsequent chapters include many examples of assembly language code along with appropriate explanations of new or difficult concepts.

The text uses numerous figures and examples. Many series of "before" and "after" examples are given for instructions. Examples are included that illustrate the use of a debugger. These examples give the student a stronger sense of what is happening inside the computer.

Exercises appear at the end of each section. Short-answer exercises reinforce understanding of the material just covered, and programming exercises offer an opportunity to apply the material to assembly-language programs.

Software Environment

The "standard" 80x86 assembler is Microsoft's Macro Assembler (MASM), version 6.11. Although this assembler can produce code for 32-bit flat memory model programming appropriate to a Windows 95, Windows NT, or other 32-bit Microsoft operating system environment, the linker and debugger that come with this software package are not suitable for use in such an environment. This book comes with a CD containing the assembler program from MASM (ML), a more recent Microsoft linker, the 32-bit full-screen debugger WinDbg (also from Microsoft), and necessary supporting files. This software package provides a good environment for producing and debugging console applications.

The CD included with the book also contains a package designed to simplify input/output for the student, so that the emphasis remains on architecture rather than operating system details. This I/O package is used extensively through most of the book. Finally, the CD contains source code for each program that appears as a figure in the book.

Instructor's Support

Supplementary materials for this book include an Instructor's Guide that contains some teaching tips and solutions to many exercises. In addition, the author can be contacted at rdetmer@mtsu.edu with questions or comments.

Acknowledgments

I would like to thank my students who suffered through preliminary versions of this text, often getting materials that were duplicated "just in time." These students were very good at catching errors. I also want to thank Hong Shi Yuan, who used a preliminary version of this text in his assembly language class and who offered valuable feedback.

Many thanks to the following people who took the time to review the manuscript: Dennis Bouvier, University of Houston–Clear Lake; Barry Fagin, US Air Force Academy; Glynis Hamel, Worcester Polytechnic Institute; Dennis Fairclough, Utah Valley State College; Thomas Higginbotham, Southeastern Louisiana University; Clifford Nadler, Worcester Polytechnic Institute.

My wife, Carol, deserves credit for her understanding during the many hours that I ignored her and word-processed at my computer.

Richard C. Detmer

CONTENTS

CHAPTER 1

Representing Data in a Computer

When programming in a high-level language like Java or C++, you use variables of different types (such as integer, float, or character). Once you have declared variables, you don't have to worry about how the data are represented in the computer. When you deal with a computer at the machine level, however, you must be more concerned with how data are stored. Often you have the job of converting data from one representation to another. This chapter covers some common ways that data are represented in a microcomputer. Chapter 2 gives an overview of microcomputer hardware and software. Chapter 3 illustrates how to write an assembly language program that directly controls execution of the computer's native instructions.

1.1 Binary and Hexadecimal Numbers

A computer uses **bits** (binary digits, each an electronic state representing zero or one) to denote values. We represent such **binary** numbers using the digits 0 and 1 and a base 2 place-value system. This binary number system is like the decimal system except that the positions (right to left) are 1's, 2's, 4's, 8's, 16's (and higher powers of 2) instead of 1's, 10's, 100's, 1000's, 10000's (powers of 10). For example, the binary number 1101 can be interpreted as the decimal number 13,

1		1		0		1		
one 8	+	one 4	+	no 2	+	one 1	=	13

Binary numbers are so long that they are awkward to read and write. For instance, it takes the eight bits 11111010 to represent the decimal number 250, or the fifteen bits 111010100110000 to represent the decimal number 30000. The **hexadecimal** (base 16) number system represents numbers using about one-fourth as many digits as the binary system. Conversions between hexadecimal and binary are so easy that **hex** can be thought of as shorthand for binary. The hexadecimal system requires sixteen digits. The digits 0, 1, 2, 3, 4, 5, 6, 7, 8, and 9 are used just as in the decimal system; A, B, C, D, E, and F are used for the decimal numbers 10, 11, 12, 13, 14, and 15, respectively. Either uppercase or lowercase letters can be used for the new digits.

The positions in hexadecimal numbers correspond to powers of 16. From right to left, they are 1's, 16's, 256's, etc. The value of the hex number 9D7A is 40314 in decimal since

$$
\begin{array}{rclcll}
9 & \times & 4096 & & 36864 & [\ 4096\ =\ 16^3\ ] \\
+\ 13 & \times & 256 & & 3328 & [\ D\ is\ 13,\ 256\ =\ 16^2\ ] \\
+\ 7 & \times & 16 & & 112 & \\
+\ 10 & \times & 1 & & 10 & [\ A\ is\ 10\ ] \\
& & & = & 40314 &
\end{array}
$$

Figure 1.1 shows small numbers expressed in decimal, hexadecimal, and binary systems. It is worthwhile to memorize this table or to be able to construct it very quickly.

You have seen above how to convert binary or hexadecimal numbers to decimal. How can you convert numbers from decimal to hex? From decimal to binary? From binary to hex? From hex to binary? We'll show how to do these conversions manually, but often the easiest way is to use a calculator that allows numbers to be entered in deci-

Decimal	Hexadecimal	Binary
0	0	0
1	1	1
2	2	10
3	3	11
4	4	100
5	5	101
6	6	110
7	7	111
8	8	1000
9	9	1001
10	A	1010
11	B	1011
12	C	1100
13	D	1101
14	E	1110
15	F	1111

Figure 1.1 Decimal, hexadecimal, and binary numbers

mal, hexadecimal, or binary. Conversion between bases is normally a matter of pressing a key or two. These calculators can do arithmetic directly in binary or hex as well as decimal and often have a full range of other functions available. One warning: Many of these calculators use seven segment displays and display the lowercase letter b so that it looks almost like the numeral 6. Other characters may also be difficult to read.

A calculator isn't needed to convert a hexadecimal number to its equivalent binary form. In fact, many binary numbers are too long to be displayed on a typical calculator. Instead, simply substitute four bits for each hex digit. The bits are those found in the third column of Fig. 1.1, padded with leading zeros as needed. For example,

$$3B8E2_{16} = 11\ 1011\ 1000\ 1110\ 0010_{2}$$

The subscripts 16 and 2 are used to indicate the base of the system in which a number is written; they are usually omitted when there is little chance of confusion. The extra spaces in the binary number are just to make it more readable. Note that the rightmost hex digit 2 was converted to 0010, including leading zeros. While it's not necessary to convert the leading 3 to 0011, the conversion would have been correct since leading zeros do not change the value of a binary number.

To convert binary numbers to hexadecimal format, reverse the above steps: Break the binary number into groups of four bits, starting from the right, and substitute the corresponding hex digit for each group of four bits. For example,

$$1011011101001101111 = 101\ 1011\ 1010\ 0110\ 1111 = 5BA6F$$

You have seen how to convert a binary number to an equivalent decimal number. However, instead of converting a long binary number directly to decimal, it is faster to convert it to hex, and then convert the hex number to decimal. Again, using the above 19-bit-long number,

$$1011011101001101111_2$$
$$= 101\ 1011\ 1010\ 0110\ 1111$$
$$= 5BA6F_{16}$$
$$= 5 \times 65536 + 11 \times 4096 + 10 \times 256 + 6 \times 16 + 15 \times 1$$
$$= 375407_{10}$$

The following is an algorithm for converting a decimal number to its hex equivalent. It produces the hex digits of the answer right to left. The algorithm is expressed in pseudocode, which is the way that algorithms and program designs will be written in this book.

---

until DecimalNumber = 0 loop
    divide DecimalNumber by 16, getting Quotient and Remainder;
    Remainder (in hex) is the next digit (right to left);
    DecimalNumber := Quotient;
end until;

Example

As an example, the decimal-to-hex algorithm is traced for the decimal number 5876:

- Since this is an until loop, the controlling condition is not checked until after the body has been executed the first time.

- Divide 16 into 5876 (DecimalNumber).

        367 Quotient   the new value for DecimalNumber
    16)5876
        5872
           4 Remainder the rightmost digit of the answer
                         Result so far: 4

- 367 is not zero. Divide it by 16.

        22 Quotient   the new value for DecimalNumber
    16)367
        352
          15 Remainder the second digit of the answer
                         Result so far: F4

- 22 is not zero. Divide it by 16.

         1 Quotient   the new value for DecimalNumber
    16)22
        16
         6 Remainder the next digit of the answer
                       Result so far: 6F4

- 1 is not zero. Divide it by 16.

         0 Quotient   the new value for DecimalNumber
    16)1
         0
         1 Remainder the next digit of the answer
                       Result so far: 16F4

- 0 is zero, so the until loop terminates. The answer is $16F4_{16}$

The **octal** (base 8) number system is used with some computer systems. Octal numbers are written using digits 0 through 7. Most calculators that do hex arithmetic also handle octal values. It is easy to convert a binary number to octal by writing the octal equivalent for each group of three bits, or to convert from octal to binary by replacing each octal digit by three bits. To convert from decimal to octal, one can use an algorithm that is the same as the decimal to hex scheme except that you divide by 8 instead of 16 at each step.

Exercises 1.1

Complete the table below by supplying the missing two forms for each number.

	Binary	Hexadecimal	Decimal
1.	100	_____	_____
2.	10101101	_____	_____
3.	1101110101	_____	_____
4.	11111011110	_____	_____
5.	10000000001	_____	_____
6.	_____	8EF	_____
7.	_____	10	_____
8.	_____	A52E	_____
9.	_____	70C	_____
10.	_____	6BD3	_____
11.	_____	_____	100
12.	_____	_____	527
13.	_____	_____	4128
14.	_____	_____	11947
15.	_____	_____	59020

1.2 Character Codes

Letters, numerals, punctuation marks, and other characters are represented in a computer by assigning a numeric value to each character. Several schemes for assigning these numeric values have been used. The system commonly used with microcomputers is the American Standard Code for Information Interchange (abbreviated **ASCII** and pronounced ASK-ee).

The ASCII system uses seven bits to represent characters, so that values from 000 0000 to 111 1111 are assigned to characters. This means that 128 different characters can be represented using ASCII codes. The ASCII codes are usually given as hex numbers from 00 to 7F or as decimal numbers from 0 to 127.[1] Appendix A has a complete listing of ASCII codes. Using this table, you can check that the message

        Computers are fun.

---

1 Some computers, including the IBM PC and compatible systems, use an extended character set, additionally assigning characters to hex numbers 80 to FF (decimal 128 to 255). Extended character sets will not be used in this book.

can be coded in ASCII, using hex numbers, as

43	6F	6D	70	75	74	65	72	73	20	61	72	65	20	66	75	6E	2E
C	o	m	p	u	t	e	r	s		a	r	e		f	u	n	.

Note that a space, even though it is invisible, has a character code (hex 20).

Numbers can be represented using character codes. For example, the ASCII codes for the date October 21, 1976 are

4F	63	74	6F	62	65	72	20	32	31	2C	20	31	39	37	36
O	c	t	o	b	e	r		2	1	,		1	9	7	6

with the number 21 represented using ASCII codes 32 31, and 1976 represented using 31 39 37 36. This is very different from the binary representation in the last section, where $21_{10} = 10101_2$ and $1970_{10} = 11110111000_2$. Computers use both of these representations for numbers: ASCII for input and output, and binary for internal computations.

The ASCII code assignments may seem rather arbitrary, but there are certain patterns. The codes for uppercase letters are contiguous, as are the codes for lowercase letters. The codes for an uppercase letter and the corresponding lowercase letter differ by exactly one bit. Bit 5 is 0 for an uppercase letter and 1 for the corresponding lower-case letter while other bits are the same. (Bits in most computer architectures are numbered right to left, starting with 0 for the rightmost bit.) For example,

- uppercase M codes as $4D_{16} = 1001101_2$
- lowercase m codes as $6D_{16} = 1101101_2$

The **printable characters** are grouped together from 20_{16} to $7E_{16}$. (A space is considered a printable character.) Numerals 0, 1, ..., 9 have ASCII codes 30_{16}, 31_{16}, ..., 39_{16}, respectively.

The characters from 00_{16} to $1F_{16}$, along with $7F_{16}$, are known as **control characters**. For example, the ESC key on an ASCII keyboard generates a hex 1B code. The abbreviation ESC stands for extra services control but most people say "escape." The ESC character is often sent in combination with other characters to a peripheral device like a printer to turn on a special feature. Since such character sequences are not standardized, they will not be covered in this book.

The two ASCII control characters that will be used the most frequently in this book are $0D_{16}$ and $0A_{16}$, for carriage return (CR) and line feed (LF). The $0D_{16}$ code is generated by an ASCII keyboard when the Return or Enter key is pressed. When it is sent to an ASCII display, it causes the cursor to move to the beginning of the current line without going down to a new line. When carriage return is sent to an ASCII printer (at least one of older design), it causes the print head to move to the beginning of the line. The line feed code $0A_{16}$ causes an ASCII display to move the cursor straight down, or a printer to roll the paper up one line, in both cases without going to the beginning of the new line. To display a message and move to the beginning of a new line, it is necessary to send the message characters plus CR and LF characters to the screen or printer. This may be annoying sometimes as you program in assembly language, but you will also have the option to not use CR and/or LF when you want to leave the cursor on a line after prompting for input, or to piece together a line using several output instructions.

Lesser-used control characters include form feed ($0C_{16}$), which causes many printers to eject a page; horizontal tab (09_{16}), which is generated by the tab key on the keyboard; backspace (08_{16}) generated by the Backspace key; and delete ($7F_{16}$) generated by the Delete key. Notice that the Backspace and Delete keys do not generate the same codes. The bell character (07_{16}) causes an audible signal when output to the display. Good programming practice is to sound the bell only when really necessary.

Many large computers represent characters using Extended Binary Coded Decimal Information Code (abbreviated EBCDIC and pronounced ib-SEE-dick or eb-SEE-dick). The EBCDIC system will only be used in this book as an example of another coding scheme when translation from one coding system to another is discussed.

Exercises 1.2

1. Each of the following hexadecimal numbers can be interpreted as representing a decimal number or a pair of ASCII codes. Give both interpretations.

   (a) 2A45   (b) 7352   (c) 2036   (d) 106E

2. Find the ASCII codes for the characters in each of the following strings. Don't forget spaces and punctuation. Carriage return and line feed are shown by CR and LF, respectively (written together as CRLF so that it will be clear that there is no space character between them).

   (a) January 1 is New Year's Day.CRLF

(b) George said, "Ouch!"

(c) R2D2 was C3P0's friend.CRLF ["0" is the numeral zero]

(d) Your name? [put two spaces after the question mark]

(e) Enter value: [put two spaces after the colon]

3. What would be displayed if you output each of the following sequences of ASCII codes to a computer's screen?

(a) 62 6C 6F 6F 64 2C 20 73 77 65 61 74 20 61 6E 64 20 74 65 61 72 73

(b) 6E 61 6D 65 0D 0A 61 64 64 72 65 73 73 0D 0A 63 69 74 79 0D 0A

(c) 4A 75 6E 65 20 31 31 2C 20 31 39 34 37 0D 0A

(d) 24 33 38 39 2E 34 35

(e) 49 44 23 3A 20 20 31 32 33 2D 34 35 2D 36 37 38 39

1.3   2's Complement Representation for Signed Integers

It is now time to look more carefully at how numbers are actually represented in a computer. We have looked at two schemes to represent numbers—by using binary integers (often expressed in hex) or by using ASCII codes. However, these methods have two problems: (1) the number of bits available for representing a number is limited, and (2) it is not clear how to represent a negative number.

Chapter 2 will discuss computer hardware, but for now you need to know that memory is divided into **bytes**, each byte containing eight **bits**.[2] Suppose you want to use ASCII codes to represent a number in memory. A single ASCII code is normally stored in a byte. Recall that ASCII codes are seven bits long; the extra (left-hand, or high order) bit is set to 0. To solve the first representation problem mentioned above, you can simply include the code for a minus sign. For example, the ASCII codes for the four characters −817 are 2D, 38, 31, and 37. To solve the first problem, you could always agree to use a fixed number of bytes, perhaps padding on the left with ASCII codes for zeros or spaces. Alternatively, you could use a variable number of bytes, but agree that the number ends with the last ASCII code for a digit, that is, terminating the string with a nondigit.

Suppose you want to use internal representations for numbers corresponding to their binary values. Then you must choose a fixed number of bits for the representation.

---

2 Some early computer systems used byte sizes different than eight bits.

Most central processing units can do arithmetic on binary numbers having a few chosen lengths. For the Intel 80x86 family, these lengths are 8 bits (a byte), 16 bits (a **word**),[3] 32 bits (a **doubleword**), and 64 bits (a **quadword**).

As an example, look at the word-length binary representation of 697.

$$697_{10} = 1010111001_2 = 0000001010111001_2$$

Leading zeros have been added to make 16 bits. Writing this in hex in a word, you have

This illustrated convention will be followed throughout this book. Strips of boxes will represent sequences of bytes. The contents of a single byte will be represented in hex, with two hex digits in each byte since a single hex digit corresponds to four bits. The doubleword representation of 697 simply has more leading zeros.

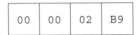

What we now have is a good system of representing nonnegative, or **unsigned**, numbers. This system cannot represent negative numbers. Also, for any given length, there is a largest unsigned number that can represented, for example FF_{16} or 255_{10} for byte length.

The **2's complement** system is similar to the above scheme for unsigned numbers, but it allows representation of negative numbers. Numbers will be a fixed length, so that you might find the "word-length 2's complement representation" of a number. The 2's complement representation for a nonnegative number is almost identical to the unsigned representation; that is, you represent the number in binary with enough leading zeros to fill up the desired length. Only one additional restriction exists—*for a positive number, the leftmost bit must be zero*. This means, for example, that the most positive number that can be represented in word-size 2's complement form is 0111111111111111_2 or $7FFF_{16}$ or 32767_{10}.

As you have probably already guessed, the leftmost bit is always one in the 2's-complement representation of a negative number. You might also guess that the rest of the representation is just the same as for the corresponding positive number, but unfor-

---

3 Other computer architectures use a word size different than 16 bits.

tunately the situation is more complicated than that. That is, you *cannot* simply change the leading bit from 0 to 1 to get the negative version of a number.

A hex calculator makes it easy to convert a negative decimal number to 2's complement form. For instance, if the decimal display shows −565 and the convert-to-hex key is pressed, a typical calculator will display FFFFFFDCB (perhaps with a different number of leading F's). For a word-size representation, ignore all but the last four hex digits; the answer is

or 1111 1101 1100 1011 in binary. (Note the leading 1 bit for a negative number.) The doubleword representation is

which is almost too long to write in binary.

The 2's complement representation of a negative number can also be found without a calculator. One method is to first express the unsigned number in hex, and then subtract this hex number from 10000_{16} to get the word length representation. The number you subtract from is, in hex, a 1 followed by the number of 0's in the length of the representation; for example, 100000000_{16} to get the doubleword length representation. (What would you use for a byte-length 2's complement representation? For a quadword-length 2's complement representation?) In binary, the number of zeros is the length in binary digits. This binary number is a power of two, and subtraction is sometimes called "taking the complement," so this operation is the source of the term "2's complement."

Example

The word-length 2's complement representation of the decimal number −76 is found by first converting the unsigned number 76 to its hex equivalent 4C, then by subtracting 4C from 10000.

```
  1 0 0 0 0
    − 4 C
```

Since you cannot subtract C from 0, you have to borrow 1 from 1000, leaving FFF.

$$
\begin{array}{r}
\text{F F F }^{1}0 \\
-\ \ 4\ \ \text{C} \\
\hline
\text{F F B}\ \ 4
\end{array}
$$

After borrowing, the subtraction is easy. The units digit is

$$10_{16} - C_{16} = 16_{10} - 12_{10} = 4 \text{ (in decimal or hex)},$$

and the 16's position is

$$F_{16} - 4 = 15_{10} - 4_{10} = 11_{10} = B_{16}$$

It is not necessary to convert the hex digits to decimal to subtract them if you learn the addition and subtraction tables for single hex digits.

The operation of subtracting a number from 1 followed by an appropriate number of 0's is called **taking the 2's complement**, or complementing the number. Thus "2's complement" is used both as the name of a representation system and as the name of an operation. The operation of taking the 2's complement corresponds to pressing the change sign key on a hex calculator.

Since a given 2's complement representation is a fixed length, obviously there is a maximum size number that can be stored in it. For a word, the largest positive number stored is 7FFF, since this is the largest 16 bit long number that has a high order bit of 0 when written in binary. The hex number 7FFF is 32767 in decimal. Positive numbers written in hex can be identified by a leading hex digit of 0 through 7. Negative numbers are distinguished by a leading bit of 1, corresponding to hex digits of 8 through F.

How do you convert a 2's complement representation to the corresponding decimal number? First, determine the sign of a 2's complement number. To convert a positive 2's complement number to decimal, just treat it like any unsigned binary number and convert it by hand or with a hex calculator. For example, the word-length 2's complement number 0D43 represents the decimal number 3395.

Dealing with a negative 2's complement number—one starting with a 1 bit or 8 through F in hex—is a little more complicated. Note that any time you take the 2's complement of a number and then take the 2's complement of the result, you get back to the original number. For a word size number N, ordinary algebra gives you

$$N = 10000 - (10000 - N)$$

For example, using the word length 2's complement value F39E

$$10000 - (10000 - F39E) = 10000 - C62 = F39E$$

This says again that the 2's complement operation corresponds to negation. Because of this, if you start with a bit pattern representing a negative number, the 2's complement operation can be used to find the positive (unsigned) number corresponding it.

Example

The word-length 2's complement number E973 represents a negative value since the sign bit (leading bit) is 1 (E = 1110). Taking the complement finds the corresponding positive number.

$10000 - E973 = 168D = 5773_{10}$

This means that the decimal number represented by E973 is -5773.

The word-length 2's complement representations with a leading 1 bit range from 8000 to FFFF. These convert to decimal as follows:

$$10000 - 8000 = 8000 = 32768_{10},$$

so 8000 is the representation of -32768. Similarly,

$$10000 - FFFF = 1,$$

so FFFF is the representation of -1. Recall that the largest positive decimal integer that can be represented as a word-length 2's complement number is 32767; the range of decimal numbers that can be represented in word-length 2's complement form is -32768 to 32767.

Using a calculator to convert a negative 2's complement representation to a decimal number is a little tricky. For example, if you start with the word length representation FF30 and your calculator displays 10 hex digits, you must enter the 10 hex digit long version of the number FFFFFFFF30, with six extra leading F's. Then push the convert to decimal button(s) and your calculator should display −208.

Exercises 1.3

1. Find the word-length 2's complement representation of each of the following decimal numbers:
   (a) 845
   (b) 15000
   (c) 100
   (d) −10
   (e) −923

2. Find the doubleword-length 2's complement representation of each of the following decimal numbers:
   (a) 3874
   (b) 1000000
   (c) −100
   (d) −55555

3. Find the byte-length 2's complement representation of each of the following decimal numbers:
   (a) 23
   (b) 111
   (c) −100
   (d) −55

4. Find the decimal integer that is represented by each of these word-length 2's complement numbers:
   (a) 00 A3
   (b) FF FE
   (c) 6F 20
   (d) B6 4A

5. Find the decimal integer that is represented by each of these doubleword-length 2's complement numbers:
   (a) 00 00 F3 E1
   (b) FF FF FE 03
   (c) 98 C2 41 7D

6. Find the decimal integer that is represented by each of these byte-length 2's complement numbers:
   (a) E1
   (b) 7C
   (c) FF

7. Find the range of decimal integers that can be stored in 2's complement form in a byte.

8. Find the range of decimal integers that can be stored in 2's complement form in a doubleword.

9. This section showed how to take the 2's complement of a number by subtracting it from an appropriate power of 2. An alternative method is to write the number in binary (using the correct number of bits for the length of the representation), change each 0 bit to 1 and each 1 bit to zero (this is called "taking the 1's complement"), and then adding 1 to the result (discarding any carry into an extra bit). Show that these two methods are equivalent.

1.4 Addition and Subtraction of 2's Complement Numbers

One of the reasons that the 2's complement representation scheme is commonly used to store signed integers in computers is that addition and subtraction operations can be easily and efficiently implemented in computer hardware. This section discusses addition and subtraction of 2's complement numbers and introduces the concepts of carry and overflow that will be needed later.

To add two 2's complement numbers, simply add them as if they were unsigned binary numbers. The 80x86 architecture uses the same addition instructions for unsigned and signed numbers. The following examples use word-size representations.

First, 0A07 and 01D3 are added. These numbers are positive whether they are interpreted as unsigned numbers or as 2's complement numbers. The decimal version of the addition problem is given on the right.

```
    0A07            2567
  + 01D3          +  467
    0BDA            3034
```

The answer is correct in this case since $BDA_{16} = 3034_{10}$.

Next, 0206 and FFB0 are added. These are, of course, positive as unsigned numbers, but interpreted as 2's complement signed numbers, 0206 is a positive number and FFB0 is negative. This means that there are two decimal versions of the addition problem. The signed one is given first, then the unsigned version.

```
    0206              518               518
  + FFB0          + (-80)          + 65456
   101B6              438             65974
```

There certainly appears to be a problem since it will not even fit in a word. In fact, since 101B6 is the hex version of 65974, there is no way to represent the correct sum of unsigned numbers in a word. However, if the numbers are interpreted as signed and you ignore the extra 1 on the left, then the word 01B6 is the 2's complement representation of the decimal number 438.

Now FFE7 and FFF6 are added, both negative numbers in a signed interpretation. Again, both signed and unsigned decimal interpretations are shown.

```
    FFE7            (-25)             65511
  + FFF6          + (-10)          + 65526
   1FFDD             -35            131037
```

Again, the sum in hex is too large to fit in two bytes, but if you throw away the extra 1, then FFDD is the correct word-length 2's complement representation of -35.

Each of the last two additions have a **carry** out of the usual high order position into an extra digit. The remaining digits give the correct 2's complement representation. The remaining digits are not always the correct 2's complement sum, however. Consider the addition of the following two positive numbers:

```
    483F            18495
  + 645A          + 25690
    AC99            44185
```

There was no carry out of the high order digit, but the signed interpretation is plainly incorrect since AC99 represents the *negative* number -21351. Intuitively, what went wrong is that the decimal sum 44185 is bigger than the maximal value 32767 that can be stored in the two bytes of a word. However, when these numbers are interpreted as unsigned, the sum is correct.

The following is another example showing a "wrong" answer, this time resulting from adding two numbers that are negative in their signed interpretation.

```
   E9FF              (-5633)             59903
+  8CF0          +  (-29456)         +   36080
  176EF             -35089              95983
```

This time there is a carry, but the remaining four digits 76 EF cannot be the right-signed answer since they represent the *positive* number 30447. Again, intuition tells you that something had to go wrong since -32768 is the most negative number that can be stored in a word.

In the above "incorrect" examples, **overflow** occurred. As a human being, you detect overflow by the incorrect signed answer. Computer hardware can detect overflow as it performs addition, and the signed sum will be correct if there is no overflow. The computer actually performs addition in binary, of course, and the process is logically a right-to-left pairwise addition of bits, very similar to the procedure that humans use for decimal addition. As the computer adds a pair of bits, sometimes a carry (of 1) into the next column to the left is generated. This carry is added to the sum of these two bits, etc. The column of particular interest is the leftmost one: the sign position. There may be a carry *into* this position and/or a carry *out of* this position into the "extra" bit. This "carry out" (into the extra bit) is what was called just "carry" above and was seen as the extra hex 1. Figure 1.2 identifies when overflow does or does not occur. The table can be summarized by saying that overflow occurs when the number of carries into the sign position is different from the number of carries out of the sign position.

Each of the above addition examples is now shown again, this time in binary. Carries are written above the two numbers.

Carry into sign bit?	Carry out of sign bit?	Overflow?
no	no	no
no	yes	yes
yes	no	yes
yes	yes	no

Figure 1.2   Overflow in addition

```
                    111
    0000 1010 0000 0111              0A07
  + 0000 0001 1101 0011            + 01D3
    0000 1011 1101 1010              0BDA
```

This example has no carry into the sign position and no carry out, so there is no overflow.

```
  1 1111 11
    0000 0010 0000 0110               0206
  + 1111 1111 1011 0000            +  FFB0
  1 0000 0001 1011 0110              101B6
```

This example has a carry into the sign position and a carry out, so there is no overflow.

```
  1 1111 1111 11    11
    1111 1111 1110 0111              FFE7
  + 1111 1111 1111 0110            +  FFF6
  1 1111 1111 1101 1101             1FFDD
```

Again, there is both a carry into the sign position and a carry out, so there is no overflow.

```
  1          1111 11
    0100 1000 0011 1111              483F
  + 0110 0100 0101 1010            + 645A
    1010 1100 1001 1001              AC99
```

Overflow does occur in this addition since there is a carry into the sign position, but no carry out.

```
  1    1    11 111
    1110 1001 1111 1111              E9FF
  + 1000 1100 1111 0000            +  8CF0
  1 0111 0110 1110 1111             176EF
```

There is also overflow in this addition since there is a carry out of the sign bit, but no carry in.

In a computer, subtraction $a - b$ of numbers a and b is usually performed by taking the 2's complement of b and adding the result to a. This corresponds to adding the negation of b. For example, for the decimal subtraction $195 - 618 = -423$,

```
   00C3
 - 026A
```

is changed to addition of FD96, the 2's complement of 026A.

```
   00C3
 + FD96
   FE59
```

The hex digits FE59 do represent -423. Looking at the above addition in binary, you have

```
        11          11
   0000 0000 1100 0011
 + 1111 1101 1001 0110
   1111 1110 0101 1001
```

Notice that there was no carry in the addition. However, this subtraction did involve a **borrow**. A borrow occurs in the subtraction $a - b$ when b is larger than a as *unsigned* numbers. Computer hardware can detect a borrow in subtraction by looking at whether on not a carry occurred in the corresponding addition. If there is no carry in the addition, then there is a borrow in the subtraction. If there is a carry in the addition, then there is no borrow in the subtraction. (Remember that "carry" by itself means "carry out.")

Here is one more example. Doing the decimal subtraction $985 - 411 = 574$ using word-length 2's complement representations,

```
   03D9
 - 019B
```

is changed to addition of FE65, the 2's complement of 019B.

```
                1 1111 1111 1          1
   03D9           0000 0011 1101 1001
 + FE65         + 1111 1110 0110 0101
   1023E        1 0000 0010 0011 1110
```

Discarding the extra 1, the hex digits 023E do represent 574. This addition has a carry, so there is no borrow in the corresponding subtraction.

Overflow is also defined for subtraction. When you are thinking like a person, you can detect it by the wrong answer that you will expect when you know that the difference is going to be outside of the range that can be represented in the chosen length for the representation. A computer detects overflow in subtraction by determining whether or not overflow occurs in the corresponding addition problem. If overflow occurs in the addition problem, then it occurs in the original subtraction problem; if it does not occur in the addition, then it does not occur in the original subtraction. There was no overflow in either of the above subtraction examples. Overflow does occur if you use word-length 2's complement representations to attempt the subtraction $-29123 - 15447$. As a human, you know that the correct answer -44570 is outside the range $-32,768$ to $+32,767$. In the computer hardware

```
  8E3D
- 3C57
```

is changed to addition of C3A9, the 2's complement of 3C57.

```
                    1    1   11   111    1
    8E3D          1000 1110 0011 1101
+   C3A9        + 1100 0011 1010 1001
   151E6        1 0101 0001 1110 0110
```

There is a carry out of the sign position, but no carry in, so overflow occurs.

Although examples in this section have use word-size 2's complement representations, the same techniques apply when performing addition or subtraction with byte-size, doubleword-size, or other size 2's complement numbers.

Exercises 1.4

Perform each of the following operations on word-size 2's complement numbers. For each, find the specified sum or difference. Determine whether overflow occurs. For a sum, determine whether there is a carry. For a difference, determine whether there is a borrow. Check your answers by converting the problem to decimal.

1. 003F + 02A4
2. 1B48 + 39E1
3. 6C34 + 5028
4. 7FFE + 0002
5. FF07 + 06BD
6. 2A44 + D9CC

7.   FFE3 + FC70   8.   FE00 + FD2D

9.   FFF1 + 8005   10.   8AD0 + EC78

11.   9E58 − EBBC   12.   EBBC − 9E58

13.   EBBC − 791C   14.   791C − EBBC

1.5   Other Systems for Representing Numbers

Sections 1.2 and 1.3 presented two commonly-used systems for representing numbers in computers, strings of character codes (often ASCII), and 2's complement form. This section introduces three additional schemes, 1's complement, binary coded decimal (BCD), and floating point. The 1's complement system is an alternative scheme for representing signed integers; it is used in a few computer systems, but not the Intel 80x86 family. Binary coded decimal and floating point forms are used in 80x86 computers, as well as many other systems. They will be discussed more fully when appropriate instructions for manipulating data in these forms are covered. The primary reason for introducing them here is to illustrate that there are many alternative representations for numeric data, each valid when used in the correct context.

The **1's complement** system is similar to 2's complement. A fixed length is chosen for the representation and a positive integer is simply the binary form of the number, padded with one or more leading zeros on the left to get the desired length. To take the negative of the number, each bit is "complemented"; that is, each zero is changed to one and each one is changed to zero. This operation is sometimes referred to as taking the 1's complement of a number. Although it is easier to negate an integer using 1's complement than 2's complement, the 1's complement system has several disadvantages, the most significant being that it is harder to design circuitry to add or subtract numbers in this form. There are two representations for zero (why?), an awkward situation. Also, a slightly smaller range of values can be represented; for example, −127 to 127 for an 8 bit length, instead of −128 to 127 in a 2's complement system.

The byte length 1's complement representation of the decimal number 97 is just the value 0110 0001 in binary (61 in hex). Changing each 0 to 1 and each 1 to 0 gives 1001 1110 (9E in hex), the byte length 1's complement representation of −97.

There is a useful connection between taking the 1's complement and taking the 2's complement of a binary number. If you take the 1's complement of a number and then add 1, you get the 2's complement. This is sometimes easier to do by hand than the subtraction method presented in Section 1.3. You were asked to verify the equivalence of these methods in Exercise 1.3.9.

In **binary coded decimal** (BCD) schemes, each decimal digit is coded with a string of bits with fixed length, and these strings are pieced together to form the representation. Most frequently four bits are used for each decimal digit; the choices for bit patterns are shown in Fig. 1.3. Only these ten bit patterns are used.

One BCD representation of the decimal number 926708 is 1001 0010 0110 0111 0000 1000. Using one hex digit as shorthand for four bits, and grouping two hex digits per byte, this BCD representation can be expressed in three bytes as

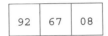

Notice that the BCD representation in hex looks just like the decimal number.

Often BCD numbers are encoded using some fixed number of bytes. For purposes of illustration, assume a four-byte representation. For now, the question of how to represent a sign will be ignored; without leaving room for a sign, eight binary-coded decimal digits can be stored in four bytes. Given these choices, the decimal number 3691 has the BCD representation

| 00 | 00 | 36 | 91 |

Decimal	BCD bit pattern
0	0000
1	0001
2	0010
3	0011
4	0100
5	0101
6	0110
7	0111
8	1000
9	1001

Figure 1.3 Binary coded decimal representation

Notice that the doubleword 2's complement representation for the same number would be 00 00 0E 6B, and that the ASCII codes for the four numerals are 33 36 39 31.

It is not as efficient for a computer to do arithmetic with numbers in a BCD format as with 2's complement numbers. It is usually very inefficient to do arithmetic on numbers represented using ASCII codes. However, ASCII codes are the only method so far for representing a number that is not an integer. For example, 78.375 can be stored as 37 38 2E 33 37 35. Floating point representation systems allow for nonintegers to be represented, or at least closely approximated.

Floating point schemes store numbers in a form that corresponds closely to scientific notation. The following example shows how to convert the decimal number 78.375 into **IEEE single format** that is 32 bits long. (IEEE is the abbreviation for the Institute of Electrical and Electronics Engineers.) This format was one of several sponsored by the Standards Committee of the IEEE Computer Society and approved by the IEEE Standards Board and the American National Standards Institute (ANSI). It is one of the floating point formats used in Intel 80x86 processors.

First, 78.375 must be converted to binary. In binary, the positions to the right of the binary point (it is not appropriate to say *decimal* point for the "." in a binary number) correspond to negative powers of two (1/2, 1/4, 1/8, etc.), just as they correspond to negative powers of 10 (1/10, 1/100, etc.) in a decimal number. Since $0.375 = 3/8 = 1/4 + 1/8 = .01_2 + .001_2$, $0.375_{10} = 0.011_2$. The whole part 78 is 1001110 in binary, so

$$78.375_{10} = 1001110.011_2.$$

Next this is expressed in binary scientific notation with the mantissa written with 1 before the radix point.

$$1001110.011_2 = 1.001110011 \times 2^6$$

The exponent is found exactly as it is in decimal scientific notation, by counting the number of positions the point must be moved to the right or left to produce the mantissa. The notation here is really mixed; it would be more proper to write 2^6 as 10^{110}, but it is more convenient to use the decimal form. Now the floating point number can be pieced together:

- left bit 0 for a positive number (1 means negative)
- 1000 0101 for the exponent. This is the actual exponent of 6, plus a **bias** of 127, with the sum, 133, in 8 bits.
- 00111001100000000000000, the fraction expressed with the leading 1 removed and padded with zeros on the right to make 23 bits

The entire number is then 0 10000101 00111001100000000000000. Regrouping gives 0100 0010 1001 1100 1100 0000 0000 0000, or, in hex

This example worked out easily because 0.375, the noninteger part of the decimal number 78.375, is a sum of negative powers of 2. Most numbers are not as nice, and usually a binary fraction is chosen to closely approximate the decimal fraction. Techniques for choosing such an approximation are not covered in this book.

To summarize, the following steps are used to convert a decimal number to IEEE single format:

1. The leading bit of the floating point format is 0 for a positive number and 1 for a negative number.

2. Write the unsigned number in binary.

3. Write the binary number in binary scientific notation $f_{23}.f_{22} \dots f_0 \times 2^e$, where $f_{23} = 1$. There are 24 fraction bits, but it is not necessary to write trailing 0's.

4. Add a bias of 127_{10} to the exponent e. This sum, in binary form, is the next 8 bits of the answer, following the sign bit. (Adding a bias is an alternative to storing the exponent as a signed number.)

5. The fraction bits $f_{22}f_{21} \dots f_0$ form the last 23 bits of the floating point number. The leading bit f_{23} (which is always 1) is dropped.

Computer arithmetic on floating point numbers is usually much slower than with 2's complement integers. However the advantages of being able to represent non-integral values or very large or small values often outweigh the relative inefficiency of computing with them.

▒▒▒▒▒ **Exercises 1.5**

Express each of the following decimal numbers as a word-length 1's complement number.

1. 175   2. −175
3. −43   4. 43

Use BCD to encode each of the following decimal numbers in four bytes. Express each answer in hex digits, grouped two per byte.

5. 230   6. 1

7. 12348765   8. 17195

Use IEEE single format to encode each of the following decimal numbers in floating point.

9. 175.5   10. −1.25

11. −11.75   12. 45.5

Chapter Summary

All data are represented in a computer using electronic signals. These can be interpreted as patterns of binary digits (bits). These bit patterns can be thought of as binary numbers. Numbers can be written in decimal, hexadecimal, or binary forms.

For representing characters, most microcomputers use ASCII codes. One code is assigned for each character, including nonprintable control characters.

Integer values are represented in a predetermined number of bits in 2's complement form; a positive number is stored as a binary number (with at least one leading zero to make the required length), and the pattern for a negative number can be obtained by subtracting the positive form from a 1 followed by as many 0's as are used in the length. A 2's complement negative number always has a leading 1 bit. A hex calculator, used with care, can simplify working with 2's complement numbers.

Addition and subtraction are easy with 2's complement numbers. Since the length of a 2's complement number is limited, there is the possibility of a carry, a borrow, or overflow.

Other formats in which numbers are stored are 1's complement, binary coded decimal (BCD), and floating point.

CHAPTER 2

Parts of a Computer System

A practical computer system consists of hardware and software. The major hardware components of a typical microcomputer system are a central processing unit (CPU), memory circuits, a keyboard for input, a monitor or some other display device, specialized input/output devices like a mouse, a modem, or a sound card, and one or more disk drives to store programs and data. Software refers to the programs that the hardware executes, including system software and application software.

These basic components vary from one computer system to another. This chapter discusses how the memory and CPU look to the assembly language programmer for a particular class of microcomputers, the IBM PC and compatible systems. These computers have an Intel 80x86 CPU; that is, an 8086 or 8088, an 80286, an 80386, an 80486, or a Pentium processor.[1] This book assumes a system that has an 80386 or higher processor and a 32-bit operating system such as Windows 95 or Windows NT. The remainder of the book is concerned with using assembly language to program these systems, with the intent of showing how such systems work at the hardware level.

---

1 Intel produced an 80186 CPU, but it was rarely used in commercial microcomputers.

2.1   PC Hardware: Memory

The memory in an IBM PC or compatible microcomputer is logically a collection of "slots," each of which can store one byte of instructions or data. Each memory byte has a 32-bit numeric label called its **physical address**. A physical address can always be expressed as eight hex digits. The first address is 00000000_{16} and the last address can be as large as the unsigned number $FFFFFFFF_{16}$. Figure 2.1 shows a logical picture of the possible memory in a PC. Since $FFFFFFFF_{16} = 4,294,967,295$, a PC can contain up to 4,294,967,296 bytes of memory, or four gigabytes. In practice, the user memory in most PCs is smaller than this.

Figure 2.1   **Logical picture of PC memory**

Prior to the 80386 chip, the Intel 80x86 family of processors could only directly address 2^{20} bytes of memory. They used 20-bit physical addresses, often expressed as 5-hex-digit addresses ranging from 00000 to FFFFF.

Physically a PC's memory consists of integrated circuits (ICs). Many of these chips provide **random access memory (RAM)**, which can be written to or read from by program instructions. The contents of RAM chips are lost when the computer's power is turned off. Other ICs are **read-only memory (ROM)** chips, which permanently retain their contents and can be read from but not written to.

The assembly language programs in this book will use a **flat memory** model. This means that the programs will actually encode 32-bit addresses to logically reference locations in a single memory space where data and instructions are stored.

The Intel 80x86 architecture also provides for a **segmented memory** model. In the original 8086/8088 CPU, this memory model was the only one available. With the 8086/8088, the PC's memory is visualized as a collection of segments, each segment 64 Kbytes long, starting on an address that is a multiple of 16. This means that one segment starts at address 00000, another (overlapping the first) starts at address 16 (00010_{16}), another starts at address 32 (00020_{16}), etc. Notice that the starting address of a segment ends in 0 when written in hex. The **segment number** of a segment consists of the first four hex digits of its physical address.

A program written for the 8086/8088 does not encode a five-hex-digit address. Instead, each memory reference depends on its segment number and a 16-bit **offset** from the beginning of the segment. Normally only the offset is encoded, and the segment number is deduced from context. The offset is the distance from the first byte of the segment to the byte being addressed. In hex, an offset is between 0000 and $FFFF_{16}$. The notation for a segment-offset address is the four-hex-digit segment number followed by a colon (:) followed by the four-hex-digit offset.

As an example, 18A3:5B27 refers to the byte that is 5B27 bytes from the beginning of the segment starting at address 18A30. Add the starting address and the offset to get the five-hex-digit address.

```
  18A30      starting address of segment 18A3
+ 5B27       offset
  1E557      five-hex-digit address
```

From the 80386 on, 80x86 processors have had both 16-bit and 32-bit segmented memory models available. Segment numbers are still 16-bits long, but they do not directly reference a segment in memory. Instead, a segment number is used as an index into a table that contains the actual 32-bit starting address of the segment. In the 32-bit segmented model, a 32-bit offset is added to that starting address to compute the actual address of the memory operand. Segments can be logically useful to a programmer: In the segmented Intel model, the programmer normally assigns different memory segments to code, data, and a system stack. The 80x86 flat memory model is really a 32-bit segmented model with all segment registers containing the same value.

In reality, the 32-bit address generated by a program is not necessarily the physical address at which an operand is stored as the program executes. There is an additional layer of memory management performed by the operating system and the Intel 80x86 CPU. A **paging** mechanism is used to map the program's 32-bit addresses into physical addresses. Paging is useful when a logical address generated by a program exceeds the physical memory actually installed in a computer. It can also be used to swap parts of a program from disk as needed when the program is too large to fit into physical memory. The paging mechanism will be transparent to us as we program in assembly language.

1. Suppose that you buy a PC with 32 MBytes of RAM. What is the 8-hex-digit address of the "last" byte?

2. Suppose that you discover that RAM addresses 000C0000 to 000C7FFF are reserved for a PC's video adapter. How many bytes of memory is this?

3. Suppose that you have an Intel 8086. Find the five-hex-digit address that corresponds to each of these segment:offset pairs:
   (a) 2B8C:8D21   (b) 059A:7A04   (c) 1234:5678

2.2   PC Hardware: The CPU

The original 8086/8088 CPU could execute over 200 different instructions. This instruction set has been extended as the 80x86 processor family has expanded to include the 80286, 80386, 80486, and Pentium processors. Much of this book will be concerned with using these instructions to implement programs so that you understand the machine-level computer capabilities. Other manufacturers make CPUs that execute essentially the same instruction set, so that a program written for an Intel 80x86 runs without change on such CPUs. Many other processor families execute different instruction sets. However, most have a similar architecture, so that the basic principles you learn about the 80x86 CPUs also apply to these systems.

A CPU contains **registers**, each an internal storage location that can be accessed much more rapidly than a location in RAM. The application registers are of most concern to the programmer. An 80x86 CPU (from 80386 on) has 16 application registers. Typical instructions transfer data between these registers and memory or perform operations on data stored in the registers or in memory. All of these registers have names, and some of them have special purposes. Their names are given below and some of their special purposes are described. You will learn more special purposes later.

The EAX, EBX, ECX, and EDX registers are called **data registers** or **general registers**. The EAX register is sometimes known as the **accumulator** since it is the destination for many arithmetic results. An example of an instruction using the EAX register is

```
add eax, 158
```

which adds the decimal number 158 (converted to doubleword length 2's complement form) to the number already in EAX, replacing the number originally in EAX by the sum.

(Full descriptions of the add instruction and others mentioned below will appear in Chapter 4.)

Each of EAX, EBX, ECX, and EDX is 32 bits long. The Intel convention is to number bits right to left starting with 0 for the low-order bit, so that if you view one of these registers as four bytes, then the bits are numbered like this

```
31    24 23   16 15    8 7        0
┌──────┬──────┬──────┬──────────┐
│ EAX  │      │      │          │
└──────┴──────┴──────┴──────────┘
```

Parts of the EAX register can be addressed separately from the whole. The low-order word, bits 0–15, is known as AX.

```
        31    24 23   16 15           0
      ┌──────┬──────┬───────────────┐
EAX   │      │      │      AX       │
      └──────┴──────┴───────────────┘
```

The instruction

```
        sub ax, 10
```

subtracts 10 from the word stored in AX, without changing any of the high-order bits (16–31) of EAX.

Similarly, the low-order byte (bits 0–7) and the high-order byte (bits 8–15) of AX are known as AL and AH, respectively.

```
        31    24 23   16 15    8 7        0
      ┌──────┬──────┬──────┬──────────┐
EAX   │      │      │  AH  │    AL    │
      └──────┴──────┴──────┴──────────┘
```

The instruction

```
        mov ah, '*'
```

copies 2A, the ASCII code for an asterisk, to bits 8–15, without changing any of the other bits of EAX.

The EBX, ECX, and EDX registers also have low-order words BX, CX, and DX, which are divided into high-order and low-order bytes BH and BL, CH and CL, and DH and DL. Each of these parts can be changed without altering other bits. It may be a surprise that there are *no* comparable names for the high-order words in EAX, EBX, ECX, and EDX—you cannot reference bits 16–31 independently by name.

The 8086 through 80286 processors had four 16-bit general registers called AX, BX, CX, and DX. The "E" was added for "extended" with the 32-bit 80386 registers. However, the 80386 and later architectures effectively include the older 16-bit architecture.

There are four additional 32-bit registers that Intel also calls general, ESI, EDI, ESP, and EBP. In fact, you can use these registers for operations like arithmetic, but normally you should save them for their special purposes. The ESI and EDI registers are **index registers**, where SI stands for source index and DI stands for destination index. One of their uses is to indicate memory addresses of the source and destination when strings of characters are moved from one place to another in memory. They can also be used to implement array indexes. The names SI and DI can be used for the low-order words of ESI and EDI, respectively, but we will have little occasion to do this.

The ESP register is the **stack pointer** for the system stack. It is rarely changed directly by a program, but is changed when data is pushed onto the stack or popped from the stack. One use for the stack is in procedure (subroutine) calls. The address of the instruction following the procedure call instruction is stored on the stack. When it is time to return, this address is retrieved from the stack. You will learn much more about the stack and the stack pointer register in Chapter 6. The name SP can be used for the low-order word of ESP, but this will not be done in this book.

The EBP register is the **base pointer** register. Normally the only data item accessed in the stack is the one that is at the top of the stack. However, the EBP register is often used to mark a fixed point in the stack other than the stack top, so that data near this point can be accessed. This is also used with procedure calls, particularly when parameters are involved.

There are six 16-bit **segment registers**: CS, DS, ES, FS, GS, and SS. In the older 16-bit segmented memory model, the CS register contains the segment number of the code segment, the area of memory where the instructions currently being executed are stored. Since a segment is 64K long, the length of a program's collection of instructions is often limited to 64K; a longer program requires that the contents of CS be changed while the program is running. Similarly DS contains the segment number of the data segment, the area of memory where most data is stored. The SS register contains the segment number of the stack segment, where the stack is maintained. The ES register contains the segment number of the extra data segment that could have multiple uses. The FS and GS registers were added with the 80386 and make possible easy access to two additional data segments.

With the flat 32-bit memory model we will use, the segment registers become essentially irrelevant to the programmer. The operating system will give each of CS, DS, ES, and SS the same value. Recall that this is a pointer to table entry that includes the actual starting address of the segment. That table also includes the size of your program, so that the operating system can indicate an error if your program accidentally or deliberately attempts to write in another area. However, all of this is transparent to the programmer who can just think in terms of 32-bit addresses.

The 32-bit **instruction pointer**, or EIP register, cannot be directly accessed by an assembly language programmer. The CPU has to fetch instructions to be executed from memory, and EIP keeps track of the address of the next instruction to be fetched. If this were a older, simpler computer architecture, the next instruction to be fetched would also be the next instruction to be executed. However, an 80x86 CPU actually fetches instructions to be executed later while it is still executing prior instructions, making the assumption (usually correct) that the instructions to be executed next will follow sequentially in memory. If this assumption turns out to be wrong, for example if a procedure call is executed, then the CPU throws out the instructions it has stored, sets EIP to contain the offset of the procedure, and then fetches its next instruction from the new address.

In addition to prefetching instructions, an 80x86 CPU actually starts execution of an instruction before it finishes execution of prior instructions. This use of **pipelining** increases effective processor speed.

The final register is called the **flags register**. The name EFLAGS refers to this register, but this mnemonic is not used in instructions. Some of its 32 bits are used to set some characteristic of the 80x86 processor. Other bits, called **status flags**, indicate the outcome of execution of an instruction. Some of the flag register's 32 bits are named, and the names we will use most frequently are given in Fig. 2.2.

Bit 11 is the overflow flag (OF). It is set to 0 following an addition in which no overflow occurred, and to 1 if overflow did occur. Similarly, bit 0, the carry flag (CF), indicates the absence or presence of a carry out from the sign position after an addition. Bit 7, the sign flag, contains the left bit of the result after some operations. Since the left bit is 0 for a nonnegative two's complement number and 1 for a negative number, SF indicates the sign. Bit 6, the zero flag (ZF) is set to 1 if the result of some operation is zero,

Bit	Mnemonic	Usage
0	CF	carry flag
2	PF	parity flag
6	ZF	zero flag
7	SF	sign flag
10	DF	direction flag
11	OF	overflow flag

Figure 2.2   Selected EFLAGS bits

and to 0 if the result is nonzero (positive or negative). Bit 2, the parity flag, is set to 1 if the number of 1 bits in a result is even and to 0 if the number of 1 bits in the result is odd. Other flags will be described later when their uses will be clearer.

As an example of how flags are set by instructions, consider again the instruction

```
add eax, 158
```

This instruction affects CF, OF, PF, SF, and ZF. Suppose that EAX contains the word FF FF FF F3 prior to execution of the instruction. Since 158_{10} corresponds to the word 00 00 00 9E, this instruction adds FF FF FF F3 and 00 00 00 9E, putting the sum 00 00 00 91 in the EAX register. It sets the carry flag CF to 1 since there is a carry, the overflow flag OF to 0 since there is no overflow, the sign flag SF to 0 (the leftmost bit of the sum 00 00 00 91), and the zero flag ZF to 0 since the sum is not zero. The parity flag PF is set to 0 since 0000 0000 0000 0000 0000 0000 1001 0001 contains three 1 bits, an odd number.

In summary, the 80x86 CPU executes a variety of instructions, using its 16 internal registers for operands and results of operations, and for keeping track of segment selectors and addresses. The registers are summarized in Fig. 2.3.

Exercises 2.2

1. For each add instruction below, assume that EAX contains the given contents before the instruction is executed, and give the contents of EAX as well as the values of the CF, OF, SF, and ZF flags after the instruction is executed:

Name	Length (bits)	Use/comments
EAX	32	accumulator, general use;
		low-order-word AX, divided into bytes AH and AL
EBX	32	general use;
		low-order-word BX, divided into bytes BH and BL
ECX	32	general use;
		low-order-word CX, divided into bytes CH and CL
EDX	32	general use;
		low-order-word DX, divided into bytes DH and DL
ESI	32	source index; source address in string moves, array index
EDI	32	destination index; address of destination, array index
ESP	32	stack pointer; address of top of stack
EBP	32	base pointer; address of reference point in the stack
CS	16	holds selector for code segment
DS	16	holds selector for data segment
ES	16	holds selector for extra segment
SS	16	holds selector for stack segment
FS	16	holds selector for additional segment
GS	16	holds selector for additional segment
EIP	32	instruction pointer; address of next instruction to be fetched
EFLAGS	32	collection of flags, or status bits

Figure 2.3   80x86 registers

	EAX before	*Instruction*
(a)	00 00 00 45	add eax, 45
(b)	FF FF FF 45	add eax, 45
(c)	00 00 00 45	add eax, −45
(d)	FF FF FF 45	add eax, −45
(e)	FF FF FF FF	add eax, 1
(f)	7F FF FF FF	add eax, 100

2. In an 8086 program, suppose that the data segment register DS contains the segment number 23D1 and that an instruction fetches a word at offset 7B86 in the data segment. What is the five-hex-digit address of the word that is fetched?

3. In an 8086 program, suppose that the code segment register CS contains the segment number 014C and that the instruction pointer IP contains 15FE. What is the five-hex-digit address of the next instruction to be fetched?

2.3 PC Hardware: Input/Output Devices

A CPU and memory make a computer, but without input devices to get data or output devices to display or write data, the computer is not usable for many purposes. Typical **input/output (I/O) devices** include a keyboard or a mouse for input, a monitor to display output, and a disk drive for data and program storage.

An assembly language programmer has multiple ways to look at I/O devices. At the lowest level, each device uses a collection of addresses or **ports** in the I/O address space. The 80x86 architecture has 64K port addresses, and a typical I/O device uses three to eight ports. These addresses are distinct from ordinary memory addresses. The programmer uses instructions that output data or commands to these ports or that input data or status information from them. Such programming is very tedious and the resulting programs are difficult to reuse with different computer systems.

Instead of using separate port addresses, a computer system can be designed to use addresses in the regular memory address space for I/O device access. Such a design is said to use **memory-mapped input/output**. Although memory-mapped I/O is possible with the 80x86, it is not used with most PCs.

Because of the difficulty of low-level programming of I/O devices, a common approach is to use procedures that do the busywork of communicating with the devices, while allowing the programmer a higher-level, more logical view of the devices. Many such routines are still fairly low-level; examples are procedures to display a single character on the CRT or get a single character from the keyboard. A higher-level procedure might print a string of characters on a printer.

An assembly language programmer may write input/output procedures, using knowledge of input/output ports and devices. Some computers have input/output procedures built into ROM. Many operating systems (see Section 2.4) also provide input/output procedures.

Exercises 2.3

The previous discussion states that there are 64K port addresses.

1. How many addresses is this (in decimal)?

2. Assuming that the first address is 0, what is the last address?

3. Express the range of port addresses in hex.

2.4 PC Software

Without software, computer hardware is virtually useless. **Software** refers to the programs or procedures executed by the hardware. This section discusses different types of software.

PC Software: The Operating System

A general-purpose computer system needs an operating system to enable it to run other programs. The original IBM PC usually ran the operating system known as PC-DOS; compatible systems used the very similar operating systems called MS-DOS. DOS stands for **disk operating system**. All of these operating systems were developed by Microsoft Corporation; PC-DOS was customized by IBM to work on the IBM PC, and the versions of MS-DOS that ran on other computer systems were sometimes customized by their hardware manufacturers. Later versions of PC-DOS were produced solely by IBM.

The DOS operating systems provide the user a **command line interface**. DOS displays a prompt (such as C:\>) and waits for the user to type a command. When the user presses the Enter (or Return) key, DOS interprets the command. The command may be to perform a function that DOS knows how to do (such as displaying the directory of file names on a disk), or it may be the name of a program to be loaded and executed.

Many users prefer a **graphical user interface** that displays icons representing tasks or files, so that the user can make a selection by clicking on an icon with a mouse. Microsoft Windows provided a graphical user interface for PCs. The versions through Windows 3.1 enhanced the operating environment, but still required DOS to run. Windows 95 included a major revision of the operating system, which was no longer sold separately from the graphical user interface. In Windows 95 the graphical user interface became the primary user interface, although a command line interface was still available.

PC Software: Text Editors

A text editor is a program that allows the user to create or modify text files that are stored on disk. A text file is a collection of ASCII codes. The text files of most interest in this book will be assembly language source code files, files that contain assembly language statements. An editor is sometimes useful to prepare a data file as well.

Later versions of MS-DOS and Windows 95 provide a **text editor** called Edit. Edit is invoked from the command line prompt. This full-screen editor uses all or part of the monitor display as a window into the file. The user can move the window up or down (or left or right) to display different portions of the file. To make changes to the file, cursor control keys or the mouse are used to move the cursor to the place to be modified, and the changes are entered.

Microsoft Windows includes a text editor called Notepad. It is also a full-screen editor. Either Edit or Notepad work well for writing assembly language source programs.

Word processors are text editors that provide extra services for formatting and printing documents. For example, when one uses a text editor, usually the Enter key must be pressed at the end of each line. However, a word processor usually wraps words automatically to the next line as they are typed, so that Enter or some other key is used only at the end of a paragraph. The word processor takes care of putting the words on each line within specified margins. A word processor can sometimes be used as an editor to prepare an assembly language source code file, but some word processors store formatting information with the file along with the ASCII codes for the text. Such extra information may make the file unsuitable as an assembly language source code file, so it is safest to avoid a word processor when creating an assembly language source program.

PC Software: Language Translators and the Linker

Language translators are programs that translate a programmer's source code into a form that can be executed by the computer. These are usually not provided with an operating system. Language translators can be classified as interpreters, compilers, or assemblers.

Interpreters directly decipher a source program. To execute a program, an interpreter looks at a line of source code and follows the instructions of that line. Basic or Lisp language programs are often executed by an interpreter. Although the interpreter itself may be a very efficient program, interpreted programs sometimes execute relatively slowly. An interpreter is generally convenient since it allows a program to be quickly changed and run. The interpreter itself is often a very large program.

Compilers start with source code and produce object code that consists mostly of instructions to be executed by the intended CPU. High-level languages such as Pascal, Fortran, Cobol, C, and C++ are commonly compiled. The object code produced by a compiler must often be **linked** or combined with other object code to make a program that can be loaded and executed. This requires a utility called a **linker**, usually provided with a compiler.

A **debugger** allows a programmer to control execution of a program, pausing after each instruction or at a preset breakpoint. When the program is paused, the programmer can examine the contents of variables in a high-level language or registers or memory in assembly language. A debugger is useful both to find errors and to "see inside" a computer to find out how it executes programs.

Integrated development environments use a single interface to access an editor, a compiler, and a linker. They also initiate execution of the program being developed and frequently provide other utilities, such as a debugger. An integrated development environment is convenient, but may not always be available for a particular programming language.

An **assembler** is used much like a compiler, but translates assembly language rather than a high-level language into machine code. The resulting files must normally be linked to prepare them for execution. Because assembly language is closer to machine code than a high-level language, the job of an assembler is somewhat simpler than the job of a compiler. Assemblers historically existed before compilers.

Using again the assembly language instruction cited in Section 2.2,

```
add eax, 158
```

is translated by the assembler into the five bytes 05 00 00 00 9E. The first byte 05 is the **op code** (operation code), which says to add the number contained in the next four bytes to the doubleword already in the EAX register. The doubleword 00 00 00 9E is the 2's complement representation of 158_{10}.

Chapter Summary

This chapter has discussed the hardware and software components that make up a PC microcomputer system.

The major hardware components are the CPU and memory. The CPU executes instructions and uses its internal registers for instruction operands and results and to determine addresses of data and instructions stored in memory. Objects in memory can be addressed by 32-bit addresses. In a flat memory model, such addresses are effectively actual addresses. In a segmented memory model, addresses are calculated from a starting address determined from a segment number and an offset within the segment.

Input/output at the hardware level uses a separate collection of addresses called ports. Input/output is often done through operating systems utilities.

An operating system is a vital software component. Through a command line or a graphical user interface, it interprets the user's requests to carry out commands or to load and execute programs.

A text editor, an assembler, and a linker are necessary software tools for the assembly language programmer. These may be separate programs or available as part of an integrated development environment. A debugger is also a useful programmer's tool.

CHAPTER 3

Elements of Assembly Language

Chapter 3 explains how to write assembly language programs. The first part describes the types and formats of statements that are accepted by MASM, the Microsoft Macro Assembler. Then follows an example of a complete assembly language program, with instructions on how to assemble, link, and execute this and other programs. The last portion of the chapter fills in details about constructs that have been illustrated in the example, laying the groundwork for programs in future chapters.

3.1   Assembly Language Statements

An assembly language source code file consists of a collection of **statements**. Most statements fit easily on an 80-character line, a good limit to observe so that source code can easily be printed or displayed on a monitor. However, MASM 6.1 accepts statements up to 512 characters long; these can be extended over more than one physical line using backslash (\) characters at the end of each line except the last.

Because assembly language programs are far from self-documenting, it is important to use an adequate number of **comments**. Comments can be used with any statement. A semicolon (;) begins the comment, and the comment then extends until the end of the line. An entire line is a comment if the semicolon is in column 1 or if a comment can follow working parts of a statement. In those rare cases where you use a backslash character to break a statement into multiple lines, a comment can follow the backslash.

There are three types of functional assembly language statements: instructions, directives, and macros. An **instruction** is translated by the assembler into one or more bytes of object code (machine code), which will be executed at run time. Each instruction corresponds to one of the operations that can be executed by the 80x86 CPU. The instruction

```
add   eax, 158
```

was used as an example in Chapter 2.

A **directive** tells the assembler to take some action. Such an action does not result in machine instructions and often has no effect on the object code. For example, the assembler can produce a listing file showing the original source code, the object code, and other information. The directive

```
.NOLIST
```

anywhere in the source file tells the assembler to stop displaying source statements in the listing file. The object code produced is the same with or without the .NOLIST directive. (There is a .LIST directive to resume listing source statements.) These directives and many others start with a period, but others do not.

A **macro** is "shorthand" for a sequence of other statements, be they instructions, directives, or even other macros. The assembler expands a macro to the statements it represents and then assembles these new statements. Several macros will appear in the example program later in this chapter.

A statement that is more than just a comment almost always contains a mnemonic that identifies the purpose of the statement, and may have three other fields: name, operand, and comment. These components must be in the following order:

```
name   mnemonic   operand(s)   ;comment
```

For example, a program might contain the statement

```
ZeroCount:   mov   ecx, 0     ; initialize count to zero
```

The name field always ends with a colon (:) when used with an instruction. When used with a directive, the name field has no colon. The mnemonic in a statement indicates a specific instruction, directive, or macro. Some statements have no operand, others have one, others have more. If there is more than one operand, they are separated by commas; spaces can also be added. Sometimes a single operand has several components with spaces between them, making it look like more than one operand.

In the instruction

```
add   eax, 158
```

the mnemonic is add and the operands are eax and 158. The assembler recognizes add as a mnemonic for an instruction that will perform some sort of addition. The operands provide the rest of the information that the assembler needs. The first operand eax tells the assembler that the doubleword in the EAX register is to be one of the values added, and that the EAX register will be the destination of the sum. Since the second operand is a number (as opposed to another register designation or a memory designation), the assembler knows that it is the actual value to be added to the doubleword in the EAX register. The resulting object code is 05 00 00 00 9E, where 05 stands for "add the doubleword immediately following this byte in memory to the doubleword already in EAX." The assembler takes care of converting the decimal number 158 to its doubleword length 2's complement representation 0000009E. The bytes of this doubleword are actually stored backwards in the object code, a fact that we can almost always ignore.

One use for the name field is to label what will be symbolically, following assembly and linking of the program, an address in memory for an instruction. Other instructions can then easily refer to the labeled instruction. If the above add instruction needs to be repeatedly executed in a program loop, then it could be coded

```
addLoop:   add   eax, 158
```

The instruction can then be the destination of a jmp (jump) instruction, the assembly language version of a *goto:*

```
jmp    addLoop      ; repeat addition
```

Notice that the colon does not appear at the end of the name addLoop in the jmp instruction. High-level language loop structures like *while* or *for* are not available in machine language although they can be implemented using jmp or other instructions.

It is sometimes useful to have a line of source code consisting of just a name, for example

```
EndIfBlank:
```

Such a label might be used as the last line of code implementing an if-then-else-endif structure. This name effectively becomes a label for whatever instruction follows it, but it is convenient to implement a structure without worrying about what comes afterwards.

It is considered good coding practice to make labels descriptive. The label addLoop might help to clarify the assembly language code, identifying the first instruction of a program loop that includes an addition. Other labels, like EndIfBlank above, may parallel key words in a pseudocode design.

Names and other identifiers used in assembly language are formed from letters, digits, and special characters. The allowable special characters are underscore (_), question mark (?), dollar sign ($), and at sign (@). In this book, the special characters will be rarely used. A name may not begin with a digit. An identifier may have up to 247 characters, so that it is easy to form meaningful names. The Microsoft Macro Assembler will not allow instruction mnemonics, directive mnemonics, register designations, and other words that have a special meaning to the assembler to be used as names. Appendix C contains a list of such reserved identifiers.

The assembler will accept code that is almost impossible for a human to read. However, since your programs must also be read by other people, you should make them as readable as possible. Two things that help are good program formatting and use of lowercase letters.

Recall that assembly language statements can contain name, mnemonic, operand, and comment fields. A well-formatted program has these fields aligned as you read down the program. Always put names in column 1. Mnemonics might all start in column 12, operands might all start in column 18, and comments might all start in column 30—the particular columns are not as important as being consistent. Blank lines are allowed in an assembly language source file. Use blank lines to visually separate sections of assembly language code, just like breaking a written narrative into paragraphs.

Assembly language statements can be entered using either uppercase or lowercase letters. Normally the assembler does not distinguish between uppercase and lowercase. It can be instructed to distinguish within identifiers, but this is only needed when you are communicating with a program written in a language that is case-sensitive. Mixed-case code is easier for people to read than code written all in uppercase or lowercase. All uppercase code is especially difficult to read. One convention is to use mostly lowercase source code except for uppercase directives. This is the convention that will be followed for programs in this book.

Exercises 3.1

1. Name and describe the three types of assembly language statements.

2. For each combination of characters below, determine whether or not it is an allowable label (name). If not, give a reason.
   - (a) repeat
   - (b) exit
   - (c) more
   - (d) EndIf
   - (e) 2much
   - (f) add
   - (g) if
   - (h) add2
   - (i)   EndOfProcessLoop

3.2   A Complete Example

This section presents a complete example of an assembly language program. We start with a pseudocode design for the program. It is easy to get lost in the details of assembly language, so your programming job will be much easier if you make a design first and then implement the design in assembly language code. This program will prompt for two numbers and then find and display their sum. The algorithm implemented by this program is

> prompt for the first number;
> input ASCII characters representing the first number;
> convert the characters to a 2's complement doubleword;
> store the first number in memory;
> prompt for the second number;

input ASCII characters representing the second number;

convert the characters to a 2's complement doubleword;

add the first number to the second number;

convert the sum to a string of ASCII characters;

display a label and the characters representing the sum;

Figure 3.1 lists the complete program which implements this design. The parts are explained below.

The example program begins with comments identifying the purpose of the program, the author, and the date the program was written. This is minimal documentation for any program; most organizations require much more. In the interest of saving space, the program documentation in this book will be relatively brief, although most lines of code will include comments.

The statements

```
.386
.MODEL FLAT
```

are both directives. Without the directive .386, MASM accepts only 8086/8088 instructions; with it, the assembler accepts the additional instructions that are executed by 80186, 80286, and 80386 processors. The .486 and .586 directives enable use of even more instructions, but we will not be programming with these instructions. There is also a .386P directive that allows the assembler to recognize privileged 80386 instructions; we will not use these instructions. The directive .MODEL FLAT tells the assembler to generate 32-bit code using a flat memory model. With MASM 6.1, this directive must follow the .386 directive.

The next statement

```
ExitProcess PROTO NEAR32 stdcall, dwExitCode:DWORD
```

is another directive. The PROTO directive is used to prototype a function. In this instance, the name of the function is ExitProcess, a system function used to terminate a program. It has one parameter, a doubleword symbolically called dwExitCode.

The next statement

```
INCLUDE io.h
```

is yet another directive. (In spite of the way it looks at this point, a program doesn't consist of only directives!) It instructs the assembler to copy the file IO.H into your program as the program is assembled.[1] The source file is not modified: It still contains just the

---

1 The files IO.H, IO.OBJ, and IO.ASM are written by the author of this book and are available to the user.

```
; Example assembly language program — adds two numbers
; Author:   R. Detmer
; Date:     revised 7/97

.386
.MODEL FLAT

ExitProcess PROTO NEAR32 stdcall, dwExitCode:DWORD

INCLUDE io.h                 ; header file for input/output

cr      EQU     0dh     ; carriage return character
Lf      EQU     0ah     ; line feed

.STACK  4096             ; reserve 4096-byte stack

.DATA                        ; reserve storage for data
number1 DWORD    ?
number2 DWORD    ?
prompt1 BYTE     "Enter first number:  ", 0
prompt2 BYTE     "Enter second number:  ", 0
string  BYTE     40 DUP (?)
label1  BYTE     cr, Lf, "The sum is "
sum     BYTE     11 DUP (?)
        BYTE     cr, Lf, 0

.CODE                             ; start of main program code
_start:
        output  prompt1          ; prompt for first number
        input   string, 40       ; read ASCII characters
        atod    string           ; convert to integer
        mov     number1, eax     ; store in memory

        output  prompt2          ; repeat for second number
        input   string, 40
        atod    string
        mov     number2, eax

        mov     eax, number1     ; first number to EAX
        add     eax, number2     ; add second number
        dtoa    sum, eax         ; convert to ASCII characters
        output  label1           ; output label and sum

        INVOKE  ExitProcess, 0   ; exit with return code 0

PUBLIC _start                     ; make entry point public

END                               ; end of source code
```

Figure 3.1   A complete assembly language program

INCLUDE directive, but for purposes of the assembly, the lines of IO.H are inserted at the point of the INCLUDE directive. In order to be included, this file should be in the same directory/folder as your source program when the assembler is invoked.

The file IO.H contains mostly definitions for macros that are described in Section 3.7. There are also several directives. The only statements from IO.H that you will see in your listing file are .NOLIST, .LIST, and a few comments. The .NOLIST directive, described above, suppresses listing most of the lines from IO.H. The last statement in IO.H is the directive .LIST that instructs the assembler to resume listing source statements. Another directive in IO.H tells the assembler to suppress listings of the statements into which a macro expands. This results in a shorter program listing.

The next two statements

```
cr          EQU     0dh     ; carriage return character
Lf          EQU     0ah     ; linefeed character
```

use the directive EQU to equate symbols to values. Following an EQU directive, the symbol can be used as a synonym for the value in subsequent source code. Using names rather than numbers can make clearer source code. In this example, cr is being equated to the hexadecimal number 0D, which is the ASCII code for a carriage return character; Lf is given the hex value 0A, the ASCII code for a linefeed character. An uppercase L has been used to avoid confusion with the number 1. Carriage return and linefeed characters are needed to move down to a new output line, and are frequently used in defining data to be displayed on a monitor or printed.

In these EQU directives the assembler recognizes the values 0dh and 0ah as hexadecimal because each has a trailing h. Numeric values in assembly language statements are in decimal unless otherwise indicated in the source code. Suffixes that indicate types of values other than hex will be introduced in Section 3.5. A hexadecimal value must start with a digit, not one of the hex digits "a" through "f" so that the assembler can distinguish it from a name.

The .STACK directive tells the assembler how many bytes to reserve for a runtime stack—4096 bytes is generous for the programs we will be writing. The stack is used primarily for procedure calls. Each macro in IO.H generates a procedure call to an associated procedure that actually does the task, and some of these procedures in turn call other procedures.

The directive .DATA starts the data segment of the program, the portion of the code where memory space for variables is reserved. In this program, the BYTE and DWORD directives are used to reserve bytes and doublewords of storage, respectively.

The directive

```
number1 DWORD    ?
```

reserves a single doubleword of storage, associating the symbolic name `number1` with the address 00000000 since it is the first data item. The question mark (?) indicates that this doubleword will have no designated initial value, although actually MASM 6.1 will initialize it to zero. The statement

```
number2 DWORD    ?
```

reserves another doubleword of storage, associating the symbolic name `number2` with the next available address, 00000004, since it follows the doubleword already reserved. The run-time addresses for `number1` and `number2` will be different than 00000000 and 00000004, but these doublewords will be stored consecutively in memory.

The directive

```
prompt1 BYTE     "Enter first number:  ", 0
```

has two operands, the string `"Enter first number"` and the number 0. It reserves one byte for each character inside the quotation marks and one byte for the number 0. For each character, the byte reserved is the ASCII code of the letter. For the number, it is simply its byte-length 2's complement representation. This directive thus reserves 22 bytes of memory containing 45 6E 74 65 72 20 66 69 72 73 74 20 6E 75 6D 62 65 72 3A 20 20 00. The name `prompt1` is associated with the address 00000008 since eight previous bytes have been allocated.

The next `BYTE` directive reserves 23 bytes of memory, with the name `prompt2` associated with address 0000001E. Then the directive

```
string  BYTE     40 DUP (?)
```

reserves 40 uninitialized bytes of memory that will have the symbolic address `string`. The `DUP` operator says to repeat the item(s) in parentheses. The directive

```
label1  BYTE     cr, Lf, "The sum is "
```

has three operands and reserves 13 bytes of storage. The first two bytes contain 0D and 0A since these are the values to which `cr` and `Lf` are equated. The next 11 bytes are the ASCII codes of the characters in quotation marks. Notice that there is no trailing 0 operand for this `BYTE` directive or the next, so there will be no trailing 00 byte generated. The next-to-last `BYTE` directive reserves 11 uninitialized bytes with address associated with the name sum. Even though the last BYTE directive has no label, it reserves three initialized bytes of memory immediately following the 11 for sum.

The next segment of the program contains executable statements. It begins with the directive

```
.CODE
```

The line of code with only the label

```
_start:
```

marks the entry point of the program, the address of the first statement to be executed. The name used is the programmer's choice, but we will consistently use _start for this purpose.

Finally we come to the statements that really do something! Since this program performs mostly input and output, the bulk of its statements are macros to perform these functions. The macro

```
output    prompt1
```

displays characters stored at the address referenced by prompt1, using a null (00) byte to terminate the display. In this program, the user will be prompted to enter the first number. Since there is no carriage return or line feed character at the end of the prompt, the cursor will remain on the line following the colon and the two blanks. The statement

```
input    string, 40          ; read ASCII characters
```

is a macro that functionally causes the computer to pause and wait for characters to be entered at the keyboard until the user presses the Enter key to terminate the input. The first operand (string) identifies where the ASCII codes for these characters will be stored. The second operand (40) identifies the maximum number of characters that can be entered. Notice that 40 uninitialized bytes were reserved at address string. More details about the input macro are in Section 3.6, but for now just note that you want to be fairly generous with the number of bytes you reserve in an input area.

The input macro inputs ASCII codes, but the CPU does arithmetic with numbers in 2's complement form. The atod (for "ASCII to double") macro scans memory at the address specified by its single operand and converts the ASCII codes there to the corresponding 2's complement doubleword; the result is stored in EAX. In this program

```
atod    string              ; convert to integer
```

scans memory starting at `string`, skips leading blanks, notes any plus (+) or minus (−) sign, and builds a number from ASCII codes for digits. The scan stops when any non-digit is encountered.

The statement

```
mov     number1, eax     ; store in memory
```

is an instruction. The mnemonic mov stands for "move" but the instruction really performs a copy operation like an assignment statement in a high-level language. This particular instruction copies the value in the EAX register to the doubleword of memory at address `number1`.

The next four statements

```
output  prompt2              ; repeat for second number
        input   string, 40
        atod    string
        mov     number2, eax
```

repeat the tasks just performed: prompt for the second number; input ASCII codes; convert the ASCII codes to a 2's complement doubleword; and copy the doubleword to memory. Note that the input area is reused.

The next two instructions add the numbers. Addition must be done in a register, so the first number is copied to the EAX register with the instruction

```
mov     eax, number1     ; first number to AX
```

and then the second is added to the first with the instruction

```
add     eax, number2     ; add second number
```

(Do you see a more efficient way to get the sum in EAX?)

The sum is now in the EAX register in 2's complement form. For display purposes we need a sequence of ASCII characters that represent this value. The dtoa ("double to ASCII") macro takes the doubleword specified by its second operand and converts it to a string exactly 11 bytes long at the destination specified by the first operand. In this program, the macro

```
dtoa    sum, eax              ; convert to ASCII characters
```

uses the contents of EAX as the source, and fills in the 11 bytes at sum with ASCII codes corresponding to this value. For a typical small number, leading space characters are used fill a total of 11 bytes. The macro

```
output   label1               ; output label and sum
```

will display bytes of memory, starting at label1 and continuing until a null byte (00) is encountered. Since the undefined bytes at sum have been replaced by ASCII codes, the first null byte in memory will be the one following the carriage return and line feed codes in the unlabeled BYTE directive—a total of 26 characters will be displayed.

The statement

```
INVOKE   ExitProcess, 0  ; exit with return code 0
```

is a directive that generates code to call the procedure ExitProcess with the value 0 for the parameter symbolically called dwExitCode in the prototype. Functionally this terminates the program, with exit code value 0 telling the operating system that the program terminated normally. (Nonzero values can be used to indicate error conditions.)

Normally the names used inside a file are visible only inside the file. The directive

```
PUBLIC _start                        ; make entry point public
```

makes the entry point address visible outside this file, so that the linker can identify the first instruction to be executed as it constructs an executable program file. We will later use this directive to make names of separately assembled procedures visible.

The final statement in an assembly language source file is the directive END. This marks the physical end of the program. There should be no statement following END.

Exercises 3.2

1. Identify three directives that appear in the example program.

2. Identify three macros that appear in the example program.

3. Identify three instructions that appear in the example program.

4. In the example program, why is prompt2 associated with address 0000001E? What are the contents of the 23 bytes reserved by this directive?

3.3 How to Assemble, Link, and Run a Program

This book includes a CD with software to assemble and link a program. This software should be installed on your computer.

The source code for a program is entered using any standard text editor such as Notepad or Edit; no text editor is included on the CD. Assembly language source code is normally stored in a file with a .ASM type. For this section, we will assume that the source program from Fig. 3.1 is stored in the file EXAMPLE.ASM.

We will use the ML assembler from MASM 6.1 to assemble programs. To assemble EXAMPLE.ASM, you enter

```
ml /c /coff example.asm
```

at a DOS prompt in a MS-DOS window. Assuming there is no error in your program, you will see a display like

```
Microsoft (R) Macro Assembler Version 6.11
Copyright (C) Microsoft Corp 1981-1993. All rights reserved.

Assembling: example.asm
```

followed by a DOS prompt. The file EXAMPLE.OBJ will be added to your directory. If your program contains errors, error messages are displayed and no .OBJ file is produced.

There are two switches, /c and /coff, in this invocation of the assembler. The ML product is capable of both assembly and linking, and the switch /c says to assemble only. The /coff switch says to generate common object file format. *ML switches are case-sensitive: They must be entered exactly as shown—these are in lowercase.*

The linker we will use is named LINK. For this example, invoke it at the DOS prompt with

```
link /subsystem:console /entry:start /out:example.exe
                        example.obj io.obj kernel32.lib
```

This is entered as a single command, although it may wrap to a new line as you type. Again, assuming no errors, you will see

```
Microsoft (R) 32-Bit Incremental Linker Version 5.10.7303
Copyright (C) Microsoft Corp 1992-1997. All rights reserved.
```

followed by a DOS prompt. This LINK command links together EXAMPLE.OBJ, IO.OBJ, and KERNEL32.LIB to produce the output file EXAMPLE.EXE. The switch /subsystem:console tells LINK to produce a console application, one that runs in a DOS window. The switch /entry:start identifies the label of the program entry point; notice that you do *not* use an underscore here even though _start was the actual label for the entry point.

A program is executed by simply typing its name at the DOS prompt. Figure 3.2 shows a sample run of EXAMPLE.EXE, with user input underlined. Once the executable file has been produced, you can run the program as many times as you wish without assembling or linking it again.

This book's software package includes Microsoft's Windbg, a symbolic debugger that can be used to trace execution of an assembly language program. This is a useful tool for finding errors and for seeing how the computer works at the machine level.

To use Windbg, you must add the /Zi switch (uppercase Z, lowercase i) to the assembly with ML. This causes the assembler to add debug information to its output. The assembly command now looks like

```
ml /c /coff /Zi example.asm
```

```
C:\AsmFiles>example
Enter first number:   98
Enter second number:  -35

The sum is           63

C:\AsmFiles>
```

Figure 3.2   Execution of EXAMPLE.EXE

Linking is changed to add one new switch, /debug, giving

```
link /debug /subsystem:console /entry:start /out:example.exe
                          example.obj io.obj kernel32.lib
```

Start the debugger by typing Windbg at the DOS prompt. You will be see a window similar to the one shown in Fig. 3.3. From the menu bar choose File, then Open Executable... Select **example.exe** or the name of your executable file, and click OK to get back to a window that looks almost like the opening screen shown in Fig. 3.3 except that **example.exe** appears in its title bar and a few lines appear in the Command window.

Now press the step into button

Click OK in the information window and then press the step into button again. Your source code now appears in a Windbg child window behind the Command window. Minimize the Command window. Next select View and then Registers to open a

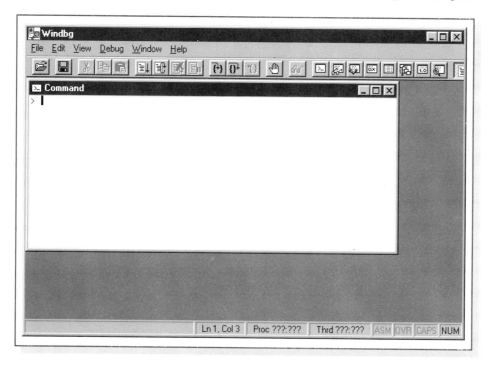

Figure 3.3   Windbg opening screen

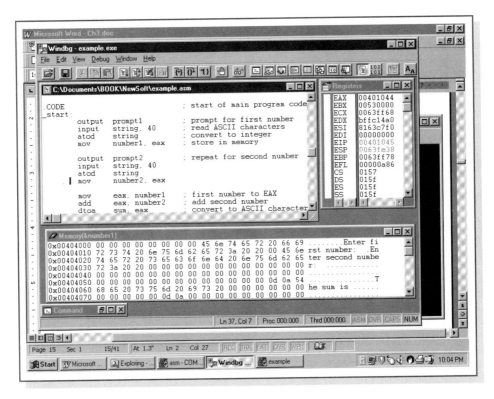

Figure 3.4 Windbg ready for tracing a program

window that shows contents of the 80x86 registers. Then select View and Memory... to open a window that shows contents of memory. For this window you must enter the starting memory address; for the example program, use &number1 as the starting address—the C/C++ address-of operator (&) is used to indicate the address of number1, the first item in the data section. Finally size and rearrange windows until your screen looks something like the screen shown in Fig. 3.4. Notice that the right edge of the example program's output window is visible under the Windbg window. The rest of the desktop is covered by the window in which the assembler and linker were run, as well as a small strip of Microsoft Word that the author was also using.

The first statement of the example program is highlighted. Clicking the step into button causes this statement to be executed. Although this statement is a macro, it is executed as a single instruction, and Enter first number: appears on the output screen. (You can click on the edge of the output screen to put it on top.) Clicking step

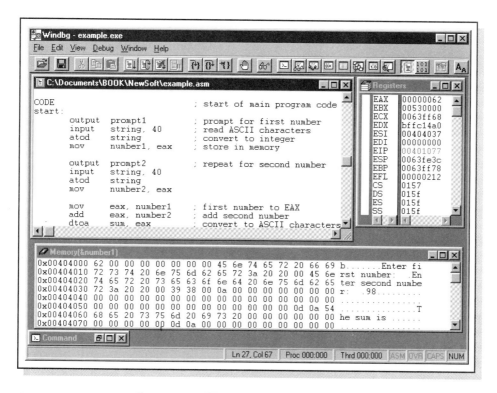

Figure 3.5 Windbg tracing a program

into again causes the input macro to be executed. When you enter a number and press return, Windbg returns to the debugger screen with the third statement highlighted. Two more clicks of the step into button causes the ASCII to double the macro to be executed, and the first mov instruction to be executed. The Windbg window now looks like the one shown in Fig. 3.5.

At this point, the Registers window shows that EAX contains 00000062, the 2's complement doubleword version of 98. The number 98 was entered in response to the prompt. You can see its ASCII codes stored in memory on the fourth line of the Memory window. Each line of the Memory window has three parts: its starting address, hex values for the bytes stored at that address, and printable characters that correspond to those bytes, if any. The first five characters of the fourth line are the end of prompt2, ASCII codes for r and colon, two spaces, and a null byte. The 40 bytes reserved for string come next in memory, and the first four have been replaced by 39, 38, 00, and 0A, ASCII codes for 98, a null byte, and a line feed. When 98 and Enter were pressed, the

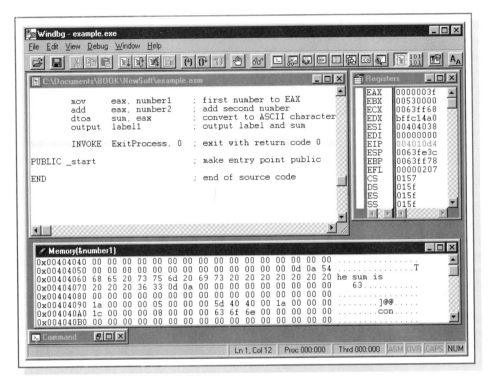

Figure 3.6   Windbg before program termination

operating system stored 39 and 38 plus a carriage return character and a line feed character. The input macro replaced the carriage return by a null byte, but you can still see the line feed in memory. The atod macro scanned these ASCII codes to produce the value in EAX. The Memory window also shows a value of 62 00 00 00 for number1, the bytes of the number stored backwards, copied there by the mov instruction.

The rest of the program is traced similarly. Figure 3.6 shows Windbg just before program termination. The Memory window has been scrolled to show the part containing the output label. At this point, −35 has been entered for the second number, the sum 98 + (−35) has been calculated as a 2's complement number still visible in EAX, and this sum has been converted to an 11-byte-long string by the dtoa macro. You can see ten ASCII space characters (20) in memory prior to the codes for 6 and 3, 36 and 33.

Exercises 3.3

1. Suppose that EXAMPLE.ASM is assembled and linked according to the first instructions (non-debugging) in this section. What additional files are generated by the assembler? By the linker?

2. Suppose that EXAMPLE.ASM is assembled and linked according to the second instructions (debugging) in this section. What additional files are generated by the assembler? By the linker?

Programming Exercises 3.3

1. Run the example program given in this section. Use a text editor to create the source code file EXAMPLE.ASM or copy it from the book's CD. Assemble, link, and execute it without generating debugging code. Run the program several times with different data.

2. Trace the example program given in this section. Use a text editor to create the source code file EXAMPLE.ASM or copy it from the book's CD. Assemble, link, and execute it, generating debugging code. Trace the program several times with different data.

3. Modify the example program given in this section to prompt for, input, and add three numbers. Call the source code file ADD3.ASM. Follow steps parallel to those of this section to assemble and link the program, producing ADD3.EXE. Run ADD3 several times with different data. Use the debugger if you have any trouble or if you want to trace the execution.

4. The instruction

    ```
    sub    eax, label
    ```

    will subtract the word at *label* from the word already in the EAX register. Modify the example program given in this section to prompt for and input two numbers, and then subtract the second number from the first. Call the source code file SUBTRACT.ASM. Follow steps parallel to those of this section to assemble and link the program, producing SUB-TRACT.EXE. Run SUBTRACT several times with different data.

3.4 The Assembler Listing File

The ML assembler can produce a listing file as part of the assembly process. This .LST file shows the source code, the object code to which it is translated, and additional information. Examination of the listing file can help you understand the assembly process. When your source file contains errors, this .LST file displays error messages at the points of the errors, helping to locate the offending statements.

Suppose that we modify the example program EXAMPLE.ASM from Fig. 3.1, changing

```
atod    string        ; convert to integer
mov     number1, eax  ; store in memory
```

to

```
atod    eax, string   ; convert to integer
mov     number1, ax   ; store in memory
```

This introduces two errors: The atod macro only allows one operand, and the source and destination operands for the mov instruction are different sizes. Suppose that this revised file is stored in EXAMPLE1.ASM.

An additional switch, /Fl (uppercase F, lowercase letter l), is needed to generate a listing file during assembly

```
ml /c /coff /Fl example1.asm
```

When this command is entered at a DOS prompt, the console shows

```
        Assembling: example1.asm
example1.asm(32): error A2022: instruction operands must be the
same size
example1.asm(31): error A2052: forced error : extra operand(s) in
ATOD
  atod(7): Macro Called From
          example1.asm(31): Main Line Code
```

These error messages are fairly helpful—they indicate errors on lines 32 and 31 of the source file and describe the errors. However, if you look at the corresponding part of EXAMPLE1.LST, you see

```
00000000                        _start:

                                output   prompt1        ; prompt for first number
                                input    string, 40     ; read ASCII characters
                                atod     eax, string     ; convert to integer
                    1                  .ERR <extra operand(s) in ATOD>
example1.asm(31): error A2052: forced error : extra operand(s) in ATOD
 atod(7): Macro Called From
  example1.asm(31): Main Line Code

                                mov      number1, ax    ; store in memory
example1.asm(32): error A2022: instruction operands must be the same size


                                output   prompt2        ; repeat for second number
```

with the error messages under the statements with the errors. Viewing the listing file frequently makes it easier to find errors in source code.

Figure 3.7 shows a listing file for EXAMPLE.ASM, the original example program without errors. Parts of this file will be examined to better understand the assembly process.

The listing begins by echoing comments and directives at the beginning of the source code file. Following the INCLUDE directive, several lines from IO.H are shown. These lines are marked with the letter C to show they come from an included file. In particular, you see the .NOLIST directive that suppressed listing of most of IO.H, and the .LIST directive that resumed listing of the rest of the source file.

For each EQU directive the assembler shows the value to which the symbol is equated as eight hex digits. This listing shows 0000000D for cr and 0000000A for Lf.

The leftmost column for the rest of the listing shows the offset (distance) of each directive or instruction from the beginning of the segment that contains it. This offset is in bytes. The line

```
00000000 00000000              number1 DWORD    ?
```

shows an offset of 00000000 since this statement is the first in the data segment. The assembler then shows the object code, a doubleword with value 00000000. Since this DWORD directive reserves four bytes, the assembler uses 00000004 for the offset of the next statement.

```
00000004 00000000              number2 DWORD    ?
```

Again four bytes are reserved with contents 00000000.

```
Microsoft (R) Macro Assembler Version 6.11                    08/04/97 21:21:16
example.asm                                                   Page 1 - 1


                        ; Example assembly language program -- adds two numbers
                        ; Author:  R. Detmer
                        ; Date:    revised 7/97

                        .386
                        .MODEL FLAT

                        ExitProcess PROTO NEAR32 stdcall, dwExitCode:DWORD

                        INCLUDE io.h        ; header file for input/output
                    C ; IO.H -- header file for I/O macros
                    C ; 32-bit version for flat memory model
                    C ; R. Detmer   July 1997
                    C  .NOLIST   ; turn off listing
                    C  .LIST     ; begin listing
                    C

= 0000000D              cr      EQU     0dh        ; carriage return character
= 0000000A              Lf      EQU     0ah        ; line feed

00000000                        .STACK  4096               ; reserve 4096-byte stack

00000000                        .DATA                      ; reserve storage for data
00000000 00000000       number1 DWORD   ?
00000004 00000000       number2 DWORD   ?
00000008 45 6E 74 65 72 prompt1 BYTE    "Enter first number:  ", 0
         20 66 69 72 73
         74 20 6E 75 6D
         62 65 72 3A 20
         20 00
```

Figure 3.7 EXAMPLE.LST listing file

```
0000001E  45 6E 74 65 72 20    prompt2  BYTE    "Enter second number:  ", 0
          73 65 63 6F 6E 64
          6E 64 62 65 20 75
          6D 62 65 72 72 3A
          20 20 00
00000035  00000028 [           string   BYTE    40 DUP (?)
          00
          ]
0000005D  0D 0A 54 68 65 65    label1   BYTE    cr, Lf, "The sum is "
          20 73 75 6D 6D 20
          69 73 20
0000006A  0000000B [           sum      BYTE    11 DUP (?)
          00
          ]
00000075  0D 0A 00             BYTE    cr, Lf, 0

                               .CODE
00000000                       _start:                          ; start of main program code
00000000
                                        output  prompt1          ; prompt for first number
                                        input   string, 40       ; read ASCII characters
                                        atod    string           ; convert to integer
0000002E  A3 00000000 R                 mov     number1, eax     ; store in memory

                                        output  prompt2          ; repeat for second number
                                        input   string, 40
                                        atod    string
00000061  A3 00000004 R                 mov     number2, eax

00000066  A1 00000000 R                 mov     eax, number1     ; first number to EAX
0000006B  03 05 00000004 R             add     eax, number2     ; add second number
                                        dtoa    sum, eax         ; convert to ASCII characters
                                        output  label1           ; output label and sum

                                        INVOKE  ExitProcess, 0   ; exit with return code 0

                               PUBLIC  _start                    ; make entry point public

                               END                               ; end of source code
```

Figure 3.7 (continued)

```
Microsoft (R) Macro Assembler Version 6.11          08/04/97 21:21:16
example.asm                                         Symbols 2 - 1


Macros:

                N a m e                 Type

atod . . . . . . . . . . .               Proc
atoi . . . . . . . . . . .               Proc
dtoa . . . . . . . . . . .               Proc
input . . . . . . . . . . .              Proc
itoa . . . . . . . . . . .               Proc
output . . . . . . . . . . .             Proc


Segments and Groups:

                N a m e              Size     Length    Align   Combine Class

FLAT . . . . . . . . . . .           GROUP
STACK . . . . . . . . . . .          32 Bit   00001000  Dword   Stack   'STACK'
_DATA . . . . . . . . . . .          32 Bit   00000078  Dword   Public  'DATA'
_TEXT . . . . . . . . . . .          32 Bit   00000097  Dword   Public  'CODE'


Procedures, parameters and locals:

                N a m e              Type     Value    Attr

ExitProcess . . . . . . . .          P Near   00000000 FLAT   Length= 00000000 External STDCALL
```

Figure 3.7 (continued)

Symbols:

N a m e	Type	Value	Attr	
@CodeSize	Number	00000000h		
@DataSize	Number	00000000h		
@Interface	Number	00000000h		
@Model	Number	00000007h		
@code . . .	Text	_TEXT		
@data . . .	Text	FLAT		
@fardata? . .	Text	FLAT		
@fardata . .	Text	FLAT		
@stack . .	Text	FLAT		
Lf . . .	Number	0000000Ah		
_start . .	L Near	00000000	_TEXT	Public
atodproc . .	L Near	00000000	FLAT	External
atoiproc . .	L Near	00000000	FLAT	External
cr . . .	Number	0000000Dh		
dtoaproc . .	L Near	00000000	FLAT	External
inproc . .	L Near	00000000	FLAT	External
itoaproc . .	L Near	00000000	FLAT	External
label1 . .	Byte	0000005D	_DATA	
number1 . .	Dword	00000000	_DATA	
number2 . .	Dword	00000004	_DATA	
outproc . .	L Near	00000000	FLAT	External
prompt1 . .	Byte	00000008	_DATA	
prompt2 . .	Byte	0000001E	_DATA	
string . . .	Byte	00000035	_DATA	
sum . . .	Byte	0000006A	_DATA	

0 Warnings
0 Errors

Figure 3.7 (continued)

Now eight bytes have been reserved, so the offset of the next item is 00000008. The next two entries show the initial values assigned by the BYTE directives at prompt1 and prompt2.

```
00000008 45 6E 74 65 72       prompt1 BYTE    "Enter first"
         20 66 69 72 73
         74 20 6E 75 6D
         62 65 72 3A 20
         20 00
0000001E 45 6E 74 65 72       prompt2 BYTE    "Enter second"
         20 73 65 63 6F
         6E 64 20 6E 75
         6D 62 65 72 3A
         20 20 00
```

The offset for prompt2 can be calculated by taking the offset 00000008 of prompt1 plus the number of bytes reserved for prompt1, 22 (16_{16}); and finding the sum 0000001E. Similarly, the offset of the statement following prompt2 will be at 0000001E + 17 = 00000035 since there are 23 (17_{16}) bytes generated in the second prompt.

The notation

```
00000035  00000028 [      string  BYTE    40 DUP (?)
          00
          ]
```

shows that this BYTE directive generates 28_{16} (40_{10}) bytes of storage, each initialized to 00. The remaining statements in the data segment illustrate no new concepts.

The assembly listing for the code segment shows, in hex, the offset and the object code of each instruction. Some assemblers may also show the offset for a macro, that is, the address of the first instruction to which it expands. The first byte of the machine code for each instruction is called its **opcode** (operation code). By looking at an opcode as the program executes, the 80x86 knows what kind of operation is to be done and whether or not there are more bytes of the instruction. The object code for a single instruction can be from one to 16 bytes long.

The line

```
0000002E  A3 00000000 R          mov     number1, eax
```

shows that this instruction starts at an offset of 0000002E and has five bytes of object code, beginning with the opcode A3. The opcode A3 tells the 80x86 to copy the contents of the EAX register to the address given in the next four bytes of the instruction. The notation R indicates that the address is **relocatable**, that is, the linker and loader will determine the run-time address, substituting it for 00000000 in this instruction in the code that is actually executed at run time. Figure 3.5 showed that address as 00404000 for one run of the program—it may be different every time the program is executed.

The add instruction

```
0000006B   03 05 00000004 R      add      eax, number2
```

starts at an offset of 0000006B and has an opcode of 03, one of several opcodes used for different add instructions. The 03 opcode itself is used for add instructions with several different formats, and the CPU must also look at the next byte to determine what the operands are. The 05 byte tells the 80x86 that the EAX register is the destination for the sum (and one source) and that the other source is in memory at the address given in the next four bytes. Chapter 9 provides more details about formats of 80x86 instructions and how they are assembled.

The final part of the assembly listing shows all the symbols that are used in the program. The first few lines show the macro names that are defined by including IO.H even though not all are used in this program. After listing segment and procedure names, the assembler shows the remaining symbols. This list includes familiar symbols such as Lf, number2, and _start. It also shows several symbols starting with an at sign (@); these give information about the assembly process. Some of the remaining symbols are names of procedures that are called by the macros in IO.H; for instance, *atoiproc* is called by the atod macro.

Exercises 3.4

Answer the following questions by looking at the assembly listing in Fig. 3.7.

1. What are the ASCII codes for characters in the string "The sum is"?

2. What is the offset of the label sum in the data section?

3. If the following statements were added at the end of the data section (just before .CODE), what offsets and values would appear for them in the assembly listing?

```
extra      DWORD 999
label2     BYTE   "The End", cr, Lf, 0
```

(Hint: An ASCII/hexadecimal conversion chart is useful for this problem.)

4. How many bytes of object code are generated by the first three statements in the example program (the `output`, `input`, and `atod` macros)?

3.5 Constant Operands

This section discusses formats of constant operands used in BYTE, DWORD, and WORD directives. The information also applies to instructions since constants are written the same way in directives and in instructions.

Numeric operands can be expressed in decimal, hexadecimal, binary, or octal notations. The assembler assumes that a number is decimal unless the number has a suffix indicating another base or a .RADIX directive (not used in this book) changes the default number base. The suffixes that may be used are

Suffix	Base	Number System
H	16	hexadecimal
B	2	binary
O or Q	8	octal
none	10	decimal

Any of these suffixes can be coded in uppercase or lowercase. Octal is not used often, but when it is used, Q is easier to read than O, although either letter will designate that the number is octal.

The directive

```
mask      BYTE      01111101b
```

reserves one byte of memory and initializes it to 7D. This is equivalent to any of the following directives

```
mask      BYTE    7dh
mask      BYTE    125
mask      BYTE    175q
```

since $1111101_2 = 7D_{16} = 125_{10} = 175_8$. The choice of number systems often depends on the use planned for the constant. A binary value is appropriate when you need to think of the value as a sequence of eight separate bits, for instance in a logical operation (covered in Chapter 8).

A BYTE directive reserves storage for one or more bytes of data. If a data value is numeric, it can be thought of as signed or unsigned. The decimal range of unsigned values that can be stored in a single byte is 0 to 255. The decimal range of signed values that can be stored in a single byte is −128 to 127. Although the assembler will allow larger or smaller values, normally you restrict numeric operands for BYTE directives to −128 to 255. The comments in the following examples indicate the initial values of the bytes that are reserved.

```
byte1    BYTE    255       ; value is FF
byte2    BYTE    127       ; value is 7F
byte3    BYTE    91        ; value is 5B
byte4    BYTE    0         ; value is 00
byte5    BYTE    -1        ; value is FF
byte6    BYTE    -91       ; value is A5
byte7    BYTE    -128      ; value is 80
```

The situation for DWORD and WORD directives is similar. A DWORD directive reserves a doubleword of storage; since eight bytes can store a signed number in the range −2,147,483,648 to 2,147,483,647 or an unsigned number from 0 to 4,294,967,295, it makes sense to restrict operand values to the range −2,147,483,648 to 4,294,967,295. Similarly, operands for a WORD directive should be restricted to the range −32,768 to 65,535. The examples below give the initial values reserved for a few doublewords and words.

```
double1    DWORD    4294967295    ; value is FFFFFFFF
double2    DWORD    4294966296    ; value is FFFFFC18
double3    DWORD    0             ; value is 00000000
double4    DWORD    -1            ; value is FFFFFFFF
double5    DWORD    -1000         ; value is FFFFFC18
double6    DWORD    -2147483648   ; value is 80000000

word1      WORD     65535         ; value is FFFF
word2      WORD     32767         ; value is 7FFF
word3      WORD     1000          ; value is 03E8
word4      WORD     0             ; value is 0000
word5      WORD     -1            ; value is FFFF
word6      WORD     -1000         ; value is FC18
word7      WORD     -32768        ; value is 8000
```

One of the points of the previous examples is that different operands can result in the same stored value. For instance, note that the WORD directives with operands 65535 and −1 both generate words containing FFFF. This value can be thought of as either the unsigned number 65,535 or the signed number −1, depending on the context in which it is used.

As previously stated, the bytes of a word or doubleword are actually stored backwards so that, for example, the initial value of word6 previous is actually 18FC. This book will concentrate on the logical values rather than the way that they are stored.

The BYTE directive allows character operands with a single character or string operands with many characters. Either apostrophes (') or quotation marks (") can be used to designate characters or delimit strings. They must be in pairs; you can not put an apostrophe on the left and a quotation mark on the right. A string delimited with apostrophes can contain quotation marks, and one delimited with quotation marks can contain apostrophes, making it possible to have strings containing these special characters. Unless there is reason to do otherwise, this book will follow the convention of putting single characters between apostrophes and strings of characters between quotation marks.

Each of the following BYTE directives is allowable.

```
char1      BYTE    'm'      ; value is 6D
char2      BYTE    6dh      ; value is 6D
string1    BYTE    "Joe"    ; value is 4A 6F 65
string2    BYTE    "Joe's"  ; value is 4A 6F 65 27 73
```

If you are trying to store the letter m rather than the number $6D_{16}$, then there is no reason to look up the ASCII code and enter it as in char2—the assembler has a built-in ASCII chart! Notice that the delimiters, the apostrophes or quotation marks on the ends of the character or string, are not themselves stored.

The assembler allows restricted usage of character operands in DWORD or WORD directives. However, there is little reason to do this.

You have already seen examples of BYTE directives with multiple operands separated by commas. DWORD and WORD directives also allows multiple operands. The directive

```
words      WORD    10, 20, 30, 40
```

reserves four words of storage with initial values 000A, 0014, 001E, and 0028. The DUP operator can be used to generate multiple bytes or words with known values as well as uninitialized values. Its use is limited to BYTE, DWORD, WORD, and other directives that reserve storage. The directive

```
DblArray   DWORD   100 DUP(999)
```

reserves 100 doublewords of storage, each initialized to 000003E7. This is an effective way to initialize elements of an array. If one needs a string of 50 asterisks, then

```
stars       BYTE    50 DUP('*')
```

will do the job. If one wants 25 asterisks, separated by spaces,

```
starsAndSpaces BYTE 24 DUP("* "), '*'
```

reserves these 49 bytes and assigns the desired initial values.

An operand of a BYTE, DWORD, WORD, or other statement can be an expression involving arithmetic or other operators. These expressions are evaluated by the assembler at assembly time, not at run time, with the resulting value used for assembly. It is usually not helpful to use an expression instead of the constant of equivalent value, but sometimes it can contribute to clearer code. The following directives are equivalent, each reserving a word with an initial hex value of 0090.

```
gross       WORD    144
gross       WORD    12*12
gross       WORD    10*15 - 7 + 1
```

Each symbol defined by a BYTE, DWORD, or WORD directive is associated with a length. The assembler notes this length and checks to be sure that symbols are used appropriately in instructions. For example, the assembler will generate an error message if

```
char        BYTE    'x'
```

is used in the data segment and

```
mov  ax, char
```

appears in the code segment—the AX register is a word long, but `char` is associated with a single byte of storage.

The Microsoft assembler recognizes several additional directives for reserving storage. These include QWORD for reserving a quadword, TBYTE for a 10-byte integer, REAL4, for reserving a 4-byte floating point number, REAL8 for 8-byte floating point, and REAL10 for 10-byte floating point. It also has directives to distinguish signed bytes, words, and doublewords from unsigned. We will rarely use these directives.

▨▨▨▨▨ **Exercises 3.5**

Find the initial values that the assembler will generate for each directive below.

1.	byte1	BYTE	10110111b
2.	byte2	BYTE	33q
3.	byte3	BYTE	0B7h
4.	byte4	BYTE	253
5.	byte5	BYTE	108
6.	byte6	BYTE	−73
7.	byte7	BYTE	'D'
8.	byte8	BYTE	'd'
9.	byte9	BYTE	"John's program"
10.	byte10	BYTE	5 DUP("<>")
11.	byte11	BYTE	61 + 1
12.	byte12	BYTE	'c' − 1
13.	dword1	DWORD	1000000
14.	dword2	DWORD	1000000b
15.	dword3	DWORD	1000000h
16.	dword4	DWORD	1000000q
17.	dword5	DWORD	−1000000
18.	dword6	DWORD	−2
19.	dword7	DWORD	−10
20.	dword8	DWORD	23B8C9A5h
21.	dword9	DWORD	0, 1, 2, 3
22.	dword10	DWORD	5 DUP(0)
23.	word1	WORD	1010001001011001b
24.	word2	WORD	2274q
25.	word3	WORD	2274h
26.	word4	WORD	0ffffh
27.	word5	WORD	5000
28.	word6	WORD	−5000
29.	word7	WORD	−5, −4, −3, −2, −1
30.	word8	WORD	8 DUP(1)
31.	word9	WORD	6 DUP(−999)
32.	word10	WORD	100/2

3.6 Instruction Operands

There are three basic types of instruction operands; some are constants, some designate CPU registers, and some reference memory locations. There are several ways of referencing memory; two simpler ways will be discussed in this section, and more complex methods will be introduced as needed later in the book.

Many instructions have two operands. In general, the first operand gives the destination of the operation, although it may also designate one of the sources. The second operand gives the source (or a source) for the operation, never the destination. For example, when

```
mov    al, '/'
```

is executed, the byte 2F (the ASCII code for the slash /) will be loaded into the AL register, replacing the previous byte. The second operand '/' specifies the constant source. When

```
add    eax, number1
```

is executed, EAX gets the sum of the doubleword designated by `number1` and the old contents of EAX. The first operand `EAX` specifies the source for one doubleword as well as the destination for the sum; the second operand `number1` specifies the source for the other of the two doublewords that are added together.

Figure 3.8 lists the addressing modes used by the Intel 80x86 microprocessor, giving the location of the data for each mode. Memory addresses can be calculated several ways; Fig. 3.9 lists the two most common.

Mode	Location of data
immediate	in the instruction itself
register	in a register
memory	at some address in memory

Figure 3.8 80x86 addressing modes

Memory mode	Location of data
direct	at a memory location whose address (offset) is built into the instruction
register indirect	at a memory location whose address is in a register

Figure 3.9   Two 80x86 memory addressing modes

For an **immediate mode** operand, the data to be used is built into the instruction before it is executed; once there it is constant.[2] Normally the data is placed there by the assembler, although it can be inserted by the linker or loader, depending on the stage at which the value can be determined. The programmer writes an instruction including an actual value, or a symbol standing for a constant value. For a **register mode** operand, the data to be used is in a register. To indicate a register mode operand, the programmer simply codes the name of the register. A register mode operand can also specify a register as a destination, but an immediate mode operand cannot be a destination.

In each of the following examples, the first operand is register mode and the second operand is immediate mode. The object code (taken from the assembler listing file) is shown as a comment. For the instruction

```
mov   al, '/'   ; B0 2F
```

the ASCII code 2F for the slash is the second byte of the instruction, and is placed there by the assembler. For the instruction

```
add   eax, 135  ; 05 00000087
```

the doubleword length 2's complement version of 135 is assembled into the last four bytes of the instruction.

Any memory mode operand specifies using data in memory or specifies a destination in memory. A **direct mode** operand has the 32-bit address built into the instruction. Usually the programmer will code a symbol that is associated with a BYTE,

---

2 One can write **self-modifying code**; that is, code that changes its own instructions as it executes. This is considered a very poor programming practice.

DWORD, or WORD directive in the data segment or with an instruction in the code segment. The location corresponding to such a symbol will be relocatable so that the assembler listing shows an assembly-time address that may be adjusted later. In the statement

```
add     eax, number2    ; 05 00000004
```

from the example program in Fig. 3.1, the first operand is register mode and the second operand is direct mode. The memory operand has been encoded as the 32-bit address 00000004, the offset of `number2` in the data segment.

The first operand of the instruction

```
add     eax, [edx]      ; 03 02
```

is register mode, and the second operand is **register indirect mode**. We will later discuss how the assembler gets the object code 03 02 for this instruction, but for now notice that it is not long enough to contain a 32-bit memory address. Instead, it contains bits that say to use the *address* in the EDX register to locate a doubleword in memory to add to the doubleword already in EAX. In other words, the second number is not in EDX, but its address is. The square bracket notation ([]) indicates indirect addressing with MASM 6.11. Figure 3.10 illustrates how register indirect addressing works in this example.

Any of the general registers EAX, EBX, ECX, and EDX or the index registers ESI and EDI can be used for register indirect addressing. The base pointer EBP can also be used, but for an address in the stack rather than for an address in the data segment. Although the stack pointer ESP can be used for register indirect addressing in certain special circumstances, we will have no need to do so.

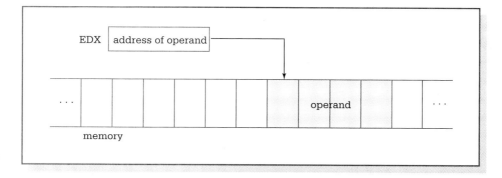

Figure 3.10   **Register indirect addressing**

With register indirect mode, the register serves like a pointer variable in a high-level language. The register contains the location of the data to be used in the instruction, not the data itself. When the size of the memory operand is ambiguous, the PTR operator must be used to give the size to the assembler. For example, the assembler will give an error message for

```
mov   [ebx], 0
```

since it cannot tell whether the destination is a byte, word, or doubleword. If it is a byte, you can use

```
mov   BYTE PTR [ebx], 0
```

For a word or doubleword destination, use WORD PTR or DWORD PTR, respectively. In an instruction like

```
add     eax, [edx]
```

it is not necessary to use DWORD PTR [edx] since the assembler assumes that the source will be a doubleword, the size of the destination EAX.

A few instructions have no operands. Many have a single operand. Sometimes an instruction with no operands requires no data to operate on or an instruction with one operand needs only one value. Other times the location of one or more operands is implied by the instruction and is not coded. For example, one 80x86 instruction for multiplication is mul; it might be coded

```
mul    bh
```

Only one operand is given for this instruction; the other value to be multiplied is always in the AL register. (This instruction will be explained more fully in the next chapter.)

Exercises 3.6

Identify the mode of each operand in the following instructions. Assume that the instructions are in a program also containing the code

```
cr       EQU        0dh
.DATA
value    DWORD      ?
char     BYTE       ?
```

```
1.  mov    value, 100

2.  mov    ecx, value

3.  mov    ah, cr

4.  mov    eax, [esi]

5.  mov    [ebx], ecx

6.  mov    char, '*'

7.  add    value, 1

8.  add    WORD PTR [ecx], 10
```

3.7 Input/Output Using Macros Defined in IO.H

In order to write useful programs, you need to be able to input and output data. Operating systems provide routines to aid in these tasks. A typical input routine might wait for a character to be pressed on the keyboard, and then return the ASCII code for that character in a register. An output routine might display at the terminal the characters in a string up to some terminating character like a dollar sign.

High-level languages usually provide for input or output of numeric data in addition to character or string data. A numeric input routine in a high-level language accepts a string of character codes representing a number, converts the characters to a 2's complement or floating point form, and stores the value in a memory location associated with some variable name. Conversely, output routines of high-level languages start with a 2's complement or floating point number in some memory location, convert it to a string of characters that represent the number, and then output the string. Operating systems usually do not provide these services, so the assembly language programmer must code them.

The file IO.H provides a set of macro definitions that make it possible to do input, output, and numeric conversion fairly easily. Each macro looks much like an 80x86 instruction, but actually expands to several instructions, including a call to an external procedure to do most of the work. The source code for these external procedures is in the file IO.ASM; the assembled version of this file is IO.OBJ. We will examine the code in IO.ASM in later chapters of this book.

Figure 3.11 lists the macros defined in IO.H and briefly describes them. Additional explanation then follows. The macros will be used in programs in subsequent chapters.

The `output` macro is used to output a string of characters to the monitor. Its *source* operand references a location in the data segment, usually the name on a BYTE directive. Characters starting at this address are displayed until a null character is reached; the null character terminates the output. It is important that source string contains ASCII codes for characters that can be displayed. Most of these will be printable characters, although it makes sense to include carriage return, line feed, and a few other special characters. If you attempt to use the output macro to display non-

Name	Parameter(s)	Action	Flags affected
dtoa	*destination, source*	Converts the doubleword at *source* (register or memory) to an eleven-byte-long ASCII string at *destination*.	None
atod	*source*	Scans the string starting at *source* for + or − followed by digits, interpreting these characters as an integer. The corresponding 2's complement number is put in EAX. The offset of the terminating nondigit character is put in ESI. For input error, 0 is put in EAX. Input error occurs if the number has no digits or is out of the range −2,147,483,647 to 2,147,483,647.	OF = 1 for input error; OF = 0 otherwise. Other flag values correspond to the result in EAX.
itoa	*destination, source*	Converts the word at *source* (register or memory) to a six-byte-long ASCII string at *destination*.	None
atoi	*source*	Similar to `atod`, except that the resulting number is placed in AX. The range accepted is −32,768 to 32,767.	similar to `atod`
output	*source*	Displays the string starting at *source*. The string must be null-terminated.	None
input	*destination, length*	Inputs a string up to *length* characters long and stores it at *destination*.	None

Figure 3.11 Macros in IO.H

ASCII data (such as a doubleword integer in 2's complement form), there will be strange results.

The `output` macro does not change any register contents, including the flag register.

The `input` macro is used to input a string of characters from the keyboard. It has two parameters, *destination* and *length*. The destination operand references a string of bytes in the data segment and the length operand references the number of bytes reserved in that string. The destination string should be at least two bytes longer than the actual number of characters to be entered; this allows for the operating system to add carriage return and linefeed characters when you press Enter. The input macro replaces the carriage return character by a null byte, so that the result is a null-terminated string stored at *destination*.

The `input` macro changes only memory at the specified destination. It does not change any register contents, including the flag register.

The name `dtoa` (<u>d</u>ouble <u>to</u> <u>A</u>SCII) describes the function of this macro. It takes a doubleword length `source` containing a 2's complement integer, and produces a string of exactly 11 ASCII characters representing the same integer in the decimal number system. The source operand is normally a register or memory operand. The destination will always be a 11-byte area of storage in the data segment reserved with a BYTE directive. The string of characters produced will have leading blanks if the number is shorter than 11 characters. If the number is negative, a minus sign will immediately precede the digits. Since the decimal range for a word-length 2's complement number is -2147483648 to 2147483647, there is no danger of generating too many characters to fit in a 11-byte-long field. A positive number will always have at least one leading blank.

The `dtoa` macro alters only the 11-byte area of memory that is the destination for the ASCII codes. No registers are changed, including the flag register.

The `atod` (<u>A</u>SCII <u>to</u> <u>d</u>ouble) macro is in many ways the inverse of the `dtoa` macro. It has only a single operand, the address of a string of ASCII character codes in storage, and it scans this area of memory for characters that represent a decimal number. If it finds characters for a decimal number in the range $-2,147,483,648$ to $2,147,483,647$, then the doubleword-length 2's complement form of the number is placed in the EAX register.

The *source* string may contain any number of leading blanks. These are skipped by `atod`. There may then be the ASCII code for $-$ (minus) or the ASCII code for + (plus). A number is assumed positive if there is no leading sign. Codes for digits 0 through 9 must immediately follow the optional sign. Once a digit code is encountered, `atod` continues scanning until any character other than a digit is encountered. Such a character terminates the scan.

Problems may arise when the atod macro is used. The macro may find no digit code; this would be the case if a space character were between a minus sign and the first digit of a number, or if the source string began with the code for a letter. The decimal number could be too large to store in doubleword-length 2's complement form. If any of these things occurs, a value of 00000000 is placed in EAX and the overflow flag OF is set to 1.

If atod is able to successfully convert a string of ASCII characters, then the overflow flag OF is set to 0. In all cases, the SF, ZF, and PF flags are set according to the value returned in EAX as follows:

- SF is 1 if the number is negative, and 0 otherwise
- ZF is 1 if the number is 0, and 0 if the number is nonzero
- PF reflects the parity of the number returned in EAX

In addition, CF is 0 and DF is unchanged. No registers other than EAX and the flag register are changed.

The atod macro will typically be used immediately after the input macro. The input macro produces a string of ASCII codes, including a trailing null character. When atod is applied to this string, the null character serves as a terminating character for the scan. If atod is applied to a string that comes from some source other than input, the programmer must ensure that it has some trailing nondigit character to prevent atod from scanning too far.

The atoi (ASCII to integer) and itoa (integer to ASCII) macros are the word-length versions of atod and dtoa. The atoi macro scans a string of characters and produces the corresponding word-length 2's complement value in AX. The itoa macro takes the 2's complement value stored in a word-length source and produces a string of exactly six characters representing this value in decimal. These macros are useful if you are dealing with values in the range −32,768 to 32,767.

Exercises 3.7

1. Why wasn't the dtoa macro designed to produce a smaller number of ASCII codes? What is important about the number 11?

2. Why wasn't the itoa macro designed to produce a smaller number of ASCII codes? What is important about the number six?

3. Given the data segment definition

```
response1 BYTE    10 DUP(?)
```

and the code segment macro

```
input      response1, 10
```

(a) What ASCII codes will be stored in the data segment if

```
-578<Enter>
```

is typed at run time?

(b) If the macro

```
atod       response1
```

follows the above `input` macro, what will be in the EAX register and what will be the values of the OF, SF, and ZF flags?

4. Given the data segment definition

```
response2 BYTE      10 DUP(?)
```

and the code segment macro

```
input      response2, 10
```

(a) what ASCII codes will be stored in the data segment if

```
123456<Enter>
```

is typed at run time?

(b) If the macro

```
atoi       response2
```

follows the above `input` macro, what will be in the AX register and what will be the values of the OF, SF, and ZF flags?

5. Suppose a program contains the data segment definitions

```
value1     DWORD      ?
result1    BYTE       11 DUP(?)
           BYTE       ' sum', 0dh, 0ah, 0
```

and the code segment macro

```
dtoa       result1, value1
```

(a) Assuming that at run time the doubleword referenced by `value1` contains FFFFFF1A, what codes will be placed in storage at `result1` by the `dtoa` macro?

(b) If the `dtoa` macro is followed by

```
output     result1
```

what will be displayed on the monitor?

6. Suppose a program contains the data segment definitions

```
result2   BYTE      6 DUP(?)
          BYTE      ' total', 0dh, 0ah, 0
```

and the code segment macro

```
itoa      result2, BX
```

(a) Assuming that at run time the BX register contains 1AFF, what codes will be placed in storage at `result2` by the `itoa` macro?

(b) If the `itoa` macro is followed by

```
output     result5
```

what will be displayed on the monitor?

Chapter Summary

Chapter 3 introduced 80x86 assembly language as translated by the Microsoft MASM assembler.

An assembly language comment always starts with a semicolon. Other statements have the format

```
name   mnemonic   operand(s)   ;comment
```

where some of these fields may be optional.

The three types of assembly language statements are:

- instructions—each corresponds to a CPU instruction
- directives—tell the assembler what to do
- macros—expand into additional statements

An assembly language program consists mainly of a data segment in which variables are defined and a code segment that contains statements to be executed at run time. To get an executable program, one must translate the program to object code using an assembler and then link the program using a linker. An executable program can be traced with a debugger like Windbg.

BYTE, DWORD, or WORD directives reserve bytes, doublewords, or words of storage and optionally assign initial values.

Instruction operands have three modes:

- immediate—data built into the instruction
- register—data in a register
- memory—data in storage

Memory mode operands come in several formats, two of which are

- direct—at an address in the instruction
- register indirect—data at an address in a register

Several macros for input and output are defined in the file IO.H. They call procedures whose assembled versions are in the file IO.OBJ. The macros are:

- output—to display a string on the monitor
- input—to input a string from the keyboard
- atod—to convert a string to a doubleword-length 2's complement number
- dtoa—to convert a doubleword-length 2's complement number to a string
- atoi—to convert a string to a word-length 2's complement number
- itoa—to convert a word-length 2's complement number to a string

CHAPTER 4

Basic Instructions

This chapter covers instructions used to copy data from one location to another and instructions used for integer arithmetic. It specifies what types of operands are allowed for the various instructions. The concepts of time and space efficiency are introduced. Finally, some methods are given for accomplishing equivalent operations even when the desired operand types are not allowed. After studying this chapter you will know how to copy data between memory and CPU registers, and between two registers. You will also know how to use 80x86 addition, subtraction, multiplication, and division instructions, and how execution of these instructions affects flags.

4.1 Copying Data

Most computer programs copy data from one location to another. With 80x86 machine language, this copying job is done by mov (move) instructions. Each mov instruction has the form

        mov   *destination, source*

and copies a byte, word, or doubleword value from the source operand location to the destination operand location. The value stored at the source location is not changed. The destination location must be the same size as the source. A mov instruction is similar to a simple assignment statement in a high-level language. For example, the Pascal or Ada assignment statement

        Count := Number

might correspond directly to the assembly language instruction

        mov Count, ecx   ; Count := Number

assuming that the ECX register contains the value of Number and that Count references a doubleword in memory. The analogy between high-level language assignment statements and mov instructions cannot be carried too far. For example, the assignment statement

        Count := 3*Number + 1

cannot be coded with a single mov instruction. Multiple instructions are required to evaluate the right-hand expression before the resulting value is copied to the destination location.

One limitation of the 80x86 architecture is that not all "logical" combinations of source and destination operands are allowed. In particular, *you cannot have both source and destination in memory*. The instruction

        mov Count, Number   ; illegal for two memory operands

is not allowed if both Count and Number reference memory locations.

All 80x86 mov instructions are coded with the same mnemonic. The assembler selects the correct opcode and other bytes of the machine code by looking at the operands as well as the mnemonic.

Figure 4.1 lists mov instructions that have an immediate source operand and a register destination operand. The number of clock cycles it takes to execute each instruction is given for 80386, 80486, and Pentium processors. Although little production programming is actually done in assembly language, some assembly language code is written in the interest of obtaining very efficient procedures. **Time efficiency** is often measured by the length of time it takes to execute a program, and this depends on the number of clock cycles it takes to execute its instructions. **Space efficiency** refers to the size of the code—a small executable file may be important if the program must be stored in ROM, for example. Figure 4.1 also shows the number of bytes for each instruction.

Destination Operand	Source Operand	Clock Cycles 386	486	Pentium	Number of Bytes	Opcode
register 8	immediate byte	2	1	1	2	
AL						B0
CL						B1
DL						B2
BL						B3
AH						B4
CH						B5
DH						B6
BH						B7
register 16	immediate word	2	1	1	3 (plus prefix byte)	
AX						B8
CX						B9
DX						BA
BX						BB
SP						BC
BP						BD
SI						BE
DI						BF
register 32	immediate doubleword	2	1	1	5	
EAX						B8
ECX						B9
EDX						BA
EBX						BB
ESP						BC
EBP						BD
ESI						BE
EDI						BF

Figure 4.1 Immediate-to-register mov instructions

The length of time an instruction takes to execute is measured in clock cycles. To determine the actual time, you must know the clock speed of the processor. The Intel 8088 in the original IBM PC had a clock speed of 4.77 MHz; that is, 4,770,000 cycles per second. Many 80x86 personal computers now operate at speeds higher than 200 MHz; that is, 200,000,000 cycles per second. These rates translate into about 210 ns (ns = nanosecond, 10^{-9} seconds) per clock cycle for the original IBM PC or 5 ns per clock cycle for a 200 MHz machine. Microcomputers have gotten faster not only because of faster clock speeds, but because the same instructions often execute in fewer clock cycles for later members of the same processor family.

The number of bytes for each instruction is the same for the Intel 80386, 80486, and Pentium processors, which is because the object code is identical. It would also be the same for 8086, 8088, 80186, and 80286 processors except that no 32-bit registers were available, so the last third of Fig. 4.1 would not apply.

It may be surprising that the op codes for word and doubleword immediate-to-register mov instructions are identical. The 80x86 processor maintains a **segment descriptor** for each active segment. One bit of this descriptor determines whether operands are 16-bit or 32-bit length by default. With the assembler directives and link options used in this book, this bit is set to 1 to indicate 32-bit operands. Therefore, the B8 opcode means, for instance, to copy the immediate doubleword following the opcode to EAX, not an immediate word to AX. If you code the 16-bit instruction

```
mov   ax, 0
```

then the assembler inserts the **prefix byte** 66 in front of the object code B8 0000, so that the code generated is actually 66 B8 0000. In general, the prefix byte 66 tells the assembler to switch from the default operand size (32-bit or 16-bit) to the alternative size (16-bit or 32-bit) for the single instruction that follows the prefix byte.

As was discussed in Chapter 2, instructions sometimes affect various flag bits in the EFLAGS register. In general, an instruction may have one of three effects:

- no flags are altered
- specific flags are given values depending on the results of the instruction
- some flags may be altered, but their settings cannot be predicted

All mov instructions fall in the first category: *No* mov *instruction changes any flag.*

Figure 4.2 lists the mov instructions that have an immediate source and a memory destination. Again, the 80486 and Pentium processors execute these instructions in a single clock cycle, while the 80386 takes two clock cycles. This is a relatively minor improvement compared to the original 8088, which took at least 14 clock cycles for each of these instructions.

The number of bytes taken by a memory operand depends on the type of operand. A direct operand must be encoded as a 32-bit address, four bytes. A register indirect operand is encoded as three bits in the second object code byte. We will later examine encodings of other types of memory operands. The 66 prefix byte is again required for 16-bit operands; it is not shown in the table since it is technically not part of the instruction.

The C6 and C7 opcodes listed in Fig. 4.2 for immediate-to-memory moves can also be used for immediate-to-register moves. However, these forms require an extra byte of object code, and an assembler normally chooses the shorter form given in Fig. 4.1.

Figure 4.3 lists most of the remaining 80x86 mov instructions. This table introduces some new terminology. **Register 32** refers to one of the 32-bit registers EAX, EBX, ECX, EDX, EBP, ESI, EDI, or ESP. Similarly **register 16** refers to one of the 16 bit registers AX, BX, CX, DX, SP, BP, SI or DI, and **register 8** refers to an eight bit register, AL, AH, BL, BH, CL, CH, DL, or DH.

Destination Operand	Source Operand	386	Clock Cycles 486	Pentium	Number of Bytes	Opcode
memory byte	*immediate byte*	2	1	1		C6
direct					7	
register indirect					3	
other					3–8	
memory word	*immediate word*	2	1	1		C7
direct					8	
register indirect					4	
other					4–9	
memory doubleword	*immediate doubleword*	2	1	1		C7
direct					10	
register indirect					6	
other					6–11	

Figure 4.2 Immediate-to-memory mov instructions

Note that sometimes the same opcode is used for what appear to be distinct instructions, for example for a register 8 to register 8 move and for a memory byte to register 8 move. In these cases the second byte of the instruction determines not only the destination register, it also encodes the source register or indicates the mode of a memory source byte. The structure of this byte will be considered more in Chapter 9.

Two distinct instructions copy a memory operand to the accumulator. For example, either of opcodes A1 and 8B could be used to encode the instruction mov eax, Number. The difference is that the 8B instruction opcode can also be used to copy doublewords to other destination registers, while the A1 opcode is specific to the accumulator. An assembler normally uses the A1 version since it is one byte shorter.

It is important to realize that, particularly with older processors, instructions that access memory are slower than instructions that use data in registers. It should also be

Destination Operand	Source Operand	Clock Cycles 386	Clock Cycles 486	Clock Cycles Pentium	Number of Bytes	Opcode
register 8	register 8	2	1	1	2	8A
register 16	register 16	2	1	1	2	8B
register 32	register 32	2	1	1	2	8B
register 8	memory byte	4	1	1	2–7	8A
register 16	memory word	4	1	1	2–7	8B
register 32	memory doubleword	4	1	1	2–7	8B
AL	direct memory byte	4	1	1	5	A0
AX	direct word	4	1	1	5	A1
EAX	direct doubleword	4	1	1	5	A1
memory byte	register 8	2	1	1	2–7	88
memory word	register 16	2	1	1	2–7	89
memory doubleword	register 32	2	1	1	2–7	89
direct memory byte	AL	2	1	1	5	A2
direct word	AX	2	1	1	5	A3
direct doubleword	EAX	2	1	1	5	A3
segment register	register 16	2	3	1	2	8E
register 16	segment register	2	3	1	2	8C
segment register	memory word	2	3+	2+	2–7	8E
memory word	segment register	2	3	1	2–7	8C

Figure 4.3 Additional mov instructions

noted that instructions that access memory may require more than the number of clock cycles listed. One reason this can occur is memory that does not respond rapidly enough; in this case **wait states**, wasted clock cycles, are inserted until the memory responds. Even with fast memory, extra cycles can be required to access a word or doubleword that is not aligned in memory—that is, stored on an address that is a multiple of two or four, respectively. A programmer should plan to keep frequently-used data in registers when possible.

This book does not discuss mov instructions that copy data to and from special registers used primarily in systems programming.

When you first look at all the mov instructions summarized in Figs. 4.1–4.3, you may think that you can use them to copy any source value to any destination location. However, many seemingly logical combinations are not available. These include

- a move with both source and destination in memory
- immediate source to segment register destination
- any move to or from the flag register
- any move to the instruction pointer register
- a move from one segment register to another segment register
- any move where the operands are not the same size
- a move of several objects

You may need to do some of these operations. We describe below how to accomplish some of them.

Although there is no mov instruction to copy from a memory source to a memory destination, two moves using an intermediate register can accomplish the same thing. For doubleword length data referenced by Count and Number, the illegal instruction

```
mov   Count, Number      ; illegal for two memory operands
```

can be replaced by

```
mov   eax, Number        ; Count := Number
mov   Count, eax
```

each using the accumulator EAX and one direct memory operand. Some register other than EAX could be used, but each of these instructions using the accumulator requires five bytes, while each of the corresponding instructions using some other register takes six bytes—EAX is chosen in the interest of space efficiency.

To load an immediate value into a segment register, one can use an immediate to register 16 move, followed by a register 16 to segment register move. This sequence is needed to initialize the data segment register DS when coding with segmented memory models.

Although the flag register and the instruction pointer cannot be set by mov instructions, other instructions do change their values. The instruction pointer register is routinely updated as new instructions are fetched and it is automatically changed by jump, call, and return instructions. Individual flags are set by a variety of instructions, and it is possible and occasionally desirable to set all bits in the flag register to specified values; some techniques will be covered later.

To change the size of data from a word to a byte, it is legal, for example, to transfer a word to a register 16, and then move out just the high-order or low-order byte to a destination. Going the other way, one can piece together two bytes in the high and low bytes of a 16-bit register and then copy the resulting word to some destination. These techniques are occasionally useful, and others will be discussed in Chapter 8. It is sometimes necessary to extend a byte-length number to word or doubleword length, or a word length number to four bytes; instructions for doing this are covered in Section 4.4.

Suppose that you have source and destination locations declared as

```
source      DWORD  4  DUP(?)
dest        DWORD  4  DUP(?)
```

and that you want to copy all four doublewords from the source to the destination. One way to do this is with four instructions

```
mov   eax, source          ; copy first doubleword
mov   dest, eax
mov   eax, source+4        ; copy second doubleword
mov   dest+4, eax
mov   eax, source+8        ; copy third doubleword
mov   dest+8, eax
mov   eax, source+12       ; copy fourth doubleword
mov   dest+12, eax
```

An address like source+4 refers to the location four bytes (one doubleword) after the address of source. Since the four doublewords reserved at source are contiguous in memory, source+4 refers to the second doubleword. This code clearly would not be space efficient if you needed to copy 40 or 400 doublewords. In Chapter 5 you will learn how to set up a loop to copy multiple objects and in Chapter 7 you will learn how to use string operations to copy large blocks of data.

The 80x86 has a very useful xchg instruction that exchanges data in one location with data in another location. It accomplishes in a single instruction the operation that often requires three high-level language instructions. Suppose Value1 and Value2 are being exchanged. In a design or a high-level language, this might be done using

```
Temp := Value1;      { swap Value1 and Value2 }
Value1 := Value2;
Value2 := Temp;
```

Assuming that `Value1` is stored in the EAX register and `Value2` is stored in the EBX register, the above swap can be coded as

```
xchg    eax, ebx        ; swap Value1 and Value2
```

Instead of using the `xchg` instruction, one could code

```
mov     ecx, eax        ; swap Value1 and Value2
mov     eax, ebx
mov     ebx, ecx
```

However, each of these `mov` instructions takes one clock cycle and two bytes for a total of three clock cycles and six bytes of code; the `xchg` instruction requires only one byte and two clock cycles (on a Pentium). In addition, it is much easier to write one instruction than three, and the resulting code is easier to understand.

Figure 4.4 lists the various forms of the `xchg` instruction. Since 16-bit and 32-bit instructions are the same, distinguished by a prefix byte, they are shown together in the table. Although the table does not show it, the first operand can be a memory operand when the second operand is a register; the assembler effectively reverses the order of the operands and uses the form shown in the table.

The `xchg` instructions illustrate again that the accumulator sometimes plays a special role in a computer's architecture. There are special instructions for swapping

Operand1	Operand2	386	Clock Cycles 486	Pentium	Number of Bytes	Opcode
register 8	register 8	3	3	3	2	86
register 8	memory byte	5	5	3	2–7	86
EAX/AX	register 32/16	3	3	2	1	
	ECX/CX					91
	EDX/DX					92
	EBX/BX					93
	ESP/SP					94
	EBP/BP					95
	ESI/SI					96
	EDI/DI					97
register 32/16	register 32/16	3	3	3	2	87
register 32/16	memory 32/16	5	5	3	2–7	87

Figure 4.4 `xchg` instructions

another register with the accumulator that are both faster than and require fewer bytes than the corresponding general-use register-to-register exchanges. These instructions can be also be used with the accumulator as the second operand.

Note that you cannot use an xchg instruction to swap two memory operands. In general, 80x86 instructions do not allow two memory operands.

Like mov instructions, xchg instructions do not alter any status flag; that is, after execution of an xchg instruction, the contents of the EFLAGS register remains the same as it was before execution of the instruction.

Exercises 4.1

1. For each part of this problem, assume the "before" values when the given mov instruction is executed. Give the requested "after" values.

	Before	Instruction	After
(a)	BX: FF 75		
	CX: 01 A2	mov bx, cx	BX, CX
(b)	AX: 01 A2	mov ax, 100	AX
(c)	EDX: FF 75 4C 2E		
	Value: DWORD −1	mov edx, Value	EDX, Value
(d)	AX: 01 4B	mov ah, 0	AX
(e)	AL: 64	mov al, −1	AL
(f)	EBX: 00 00 3A 4C		
	Value: DWORD ?	mov Value, ebx	EBX, Value
(g)	ECX: 00 00 00 00	mov ecx, 128	ECX

2. Give the opcode for each instruction in Exercise 1.

3. For each part of this problem, assume the "before" values when the given xchg instruction is executed. Give the requested "after" values.

	Before	Instruction	After
(a)	BX: FF 75		
	CX: 01 A2	xchg bx, cx	BX, CX
(b)	AX: 01 A2		
	Temp: WORD −1	xchg Temp, ax	AX, Temp
(c)	DX: FF 75	xchg dl, dh	DX
(d)	AX: 01 4B		
	BX: 5C D9	xchg ah, bl	AX, BX
(e)	EAX: 12 BC 9A 78	xchg eax, edx	EAX, EDX
	EDX: 56 DE 34 F0		

4. Give the opcode for each instruction in Exercise 3.

5. Suppose that number references a doubleword in the data segment of a program, and you wish to swap the contents of that doubleword with the contents of the EDX register. Two possible methods are

```
xchg    edx, number
```

and

```
mov     eax, edx
mov     edx, number
mov     number, eax
```

   (a) What is the total number of clock cycles and the total number of bytes required by each of these methods assuming you are using a Pentium computer? Assuming you are using a 80386 computer?
   (b) How many nanoseconds would it take to execute each set of instructions using a 166 MHz Pentium computer? Using a 20 MHz 80386 computer?
   (c) What difference would it make in the answers to (a) if the EBX register rather than the accumulator EAX were used in the "three-move" method?

6. Note that xchg cannot swap two values in memory. Write a sequence of mov and/or xchg instructions to swap doublewords stored at Value1 and Value2. Assume that any register 32 you want to use is available, and make your code as time efficient and space efficient as possible.

7. How many clock cycles and how many bytes are required for the following instruction? Assume a Pentium system.

```
mov     dx, [ebx]           ; copy table entry
```

4.2 Integer Addition and Subtraction Instructions

The Intel 80x86 microprocessor has add and sub instructions to perform addition and subtraction using byte, word, or doubleword length operands. The operands can be interpreted as unsigned numbers or 2's complement signed numbers. The 80x86 architecture also has inc and dec instructions to increment (add 1 to) and decrement (subtract 1 from) a single operand, and a neg instruction that negates (takes the 2's complement of) a single operand.

One difference between the instructions covered in this section and the mov and xchg instructions of Section 4.1 is that add, sub, inc, dec, and neg instructions all update flags in the EFLAGS register. The SF, ZF, OF, PF, and AF flags are set according to the value of the result of the operation. For example, if the result is negative, then the sign flag SF will be set to one; if the result is zero, then the zero flag ZF will be set to one. The carry flag CF is also given a value by each of these instructions except inc and dec.

Each add instruction has the form

    add   destination, source

When executed, the integer at *source* is added to the integer at *destination* and the sum replaces the old value at *destination*. The sub instructions all have the form

    sub   destination, source

When a sub instruction is executed, the integer at *source* is subtracted from the integer at *destination* and the difference replaces the old value at *destination*. For subtraction, it is important to remember that the difference calculated is

    destination - source

or "operand 1 minus operand 2." With both add and sub instructions the *source* (second) operand is unchanged. Here are some examples showing how these instructions function at execution time.

Example		
Before	*Instruction executed*	*After*
AX: 00 75	add ax, cx	AX 02 | 17
CX: 01A2		CX 01 | A2
		SF 0 ZF 0 CF 0 OF 0

EAX: 00 00 00 75	sub eax, ecx	EAX	FF	FF	FE	D3
ECX: 00 00 01 A2		ECX	00	00	01	A2

SF 1 ZF 0 CF 0 OF 0

AX: 77 AC	add ax, cx	AX	C2	E1
CX: 4B 35		CX	4B	35

SF 1 ZF 0 CF 0 OF 1

EAX: 00 00 00 75	sub ecx, eax	EAX	00	00	00	75
ECX: 00 00 01 A2		ECX	00	00	01	2D

SF 0 ZF 0 CF 0 OF 0

BL: 4B	add bl, 4	BL	4F

SF 0 ZF 0 CF 0 OF 0

DX: FF 20	sub dx, Value	DX	00	00
word at value: FF 20		Value	FF	20

SF 0 ZF 1 CF 0 OF 0

EAX: 00 00 00 09	add eax, 1	EAX	00	00	00	0A

SF 0 ZF 0 CF 0 OF 0

doubleword at Dbl:	sub Dbl, 1	Dbl	00	00	00	FF
00 00 01 00						

SF 0 ZF 0 CF 0 OF 0

Addition and subtraction instructions set the sign flag SF to be the same as the high-order bit of the result. Thus, when these instructions are used to add or subtract 2's complement integers, SF=1 indicates a negative result. The zero flag ZF is 1 if the result is zero, and 0 if the result is nonzero. The carry flag CF records a carry out of the high order bit with addition or a borrow with subtraction. The overflow flag OF records overflow, as discussed in Chapter 2.

One reason that 2's complement form is used to represent signed numbers is that it does not require special hardware for addition or subtraction; the same circuits can be used to add unsigned numbers and 2's complement numbers. The flag values have different interpretations, though, depending on the operand type. For instance, if you add two large unsigned numbers and the high order bit of the result is 1, then SF will be set to 1, but this does not indicate a negative result, only a relatively large sum. For an add with unsigned operands, CF=1 would indicate that the result was too large to store in the destination, but with signed operands, OF=1 would indicate a size error.

Figure 4.5 gives information for both addition and subtraction instructions. For each add there is a corresponding sub instruction with exactly the same operand types, number of clock cycles, and number of bytes of object code, so that it is redundant to make separate tables for add and sub instructions.

Figure 4.5 makes it easy to see that addition or subtraction operands are the fastest when both operands are in registers and the slowest when the destination operand is in memory. It is interesting to note that it is faster to add an operand in memory to the contents of a register than to add the value in a register to a memory operand; this is true since memory must be accessed twice in the latter case, once to get the first addend and once to store the sum. With the 80x86, only one operand can be in memory. Many computer architectures do not have instructions for arithmetic when the destination is a memory operand. Some other processors allow two memory operands for arithmetic operations.

With add and sub, the accumulator again has special instructions, this time when EAX, AX, or AL is the destination and the source is immediate. These instructions are not any faster than the other immediate-to-register instructions but do take one less byte of object code.

The total number of object code bytes for instructions with "+" entries in Fig. 4.5 can be calculated once you know the memory operand type. In particular, for direct mode, you add four bytes for the 32-bit address. For register indirect mode, no additional byte is required.

Notice that an immediate source can be a single byte even when the destination is a word or doubleword. Since immediate operands are often small, this makes the object code more compact. Byte-size operands are **sign-extended** to word or doubleword size at run time before the addition or subtraction operation. If the original operand is negative (viewed as 2's complement number), then it is extended with one or three FF bytes to get the corresponding word or doubleword-length value. A non-negative

Destination Operand	Source Operand	Clock Cycles			Number of Bytes	Opcode	
		386	486	Pentium		add	sub
register 8	immediate 8	2	1	1	3	80	80
register 16	immediate 8	2	1	1	3	83	83
register 32	immediate 8	2	1	1	3	83	83
register 16	immediate 16	2	1	1	4	81	81
register 32	immediate 32	2	1	1	6	81	81
AL	immediate 8	2	1	1	2	04	2C
AX	immediate 16	2	1	1	3	05	2D
EAX	immediate 32	2	1	1	5	05	2D
memory byte	immediate 8	7	3	3	3+	80	80
memory word	immediate 8	7	3	3	3+	83	83
memory doubleword	immediate 8	7	3	3	3+	83	83
memory word	immediate 16	7	3	3	4+	81	81
memory doubleword	immediate 32	7	3	3	6+	81	81
register 8	register 8	2	1	1	2	02	2A
register 16	register 16	2	1	1	2	03	2B
register 32	register 32	2	1	1	2	03	2B
register 8	memory byte	6	2	2	2+	02	2A
register 16	memory word	6	2	2	2+	03	2B
register 32	memory doubleword	6	2	2	2+	03	2B
memory byte	register 8	7	3	3	2+	00	28
memory word	register 16	7	3	3	2+	01	29
memory doubleword	register 32	7	3	3	2+	01	29

Figure 4.5   add and sub instructions

operand is simply extended with one or three 00 bytes. In both cases this is equivalent to copying the original sign bit to the high order 8 or 24 bit positions.

It may be surprising that some add and sub instructions have the same opcode. In such cases, one of the fields in the second instruction byte distinguishes between addition and subtraction. In fact, these same opcodes are used for additional instructions that are covered later in this book.

The inc (increment) and dec (decrement) instructions are special-purpose addition and subtraction instructions, always using 1 as an implied source. They have the forms

Destination Operand	386	Clock Cycles 486	Pentium	Number of Bytes	Opcode inc	dec
register 8	2	1	1	2	FE	FE
register 16	2	1	1	1		
AX					40	48
CX					41	49
DX					42	4A
BX					43	4B
SP					44	4C
BP					45	4D
SI					46	4E
DI					47	4F
register 32	2	1	1	1		
EAX					40	48
ECX					41	49
EDX					42	4A
EBX					43	4B
ESP					44	4C
EBP					45	4D
ESI					46	4E
EDI					47	4F
memory byte	6	3	3	2+	FE	FE
memory word	6	3	3	2+	FF	FF
memory doubleword	6	3	3	2+	FF	FF

Figure 4.6 inc **and** dec **instructions**

```
inc   destination
```

and

```
dec   destination
```

Like the add and sub instructions, these instructions are paired with respect to allowable operand types, clock cycles, and bytes of object code. They are summarized together in Fig. 4.6.

The inc and dec instructions treat the value of the destination operand as an unsigned integer. They affect the OF, SF, and ZF flags just like addition or subtraction of one, but they do not change the carry flag CF. Here are examples showing the execution of a few increment and decrement instructions:

Example

Before	Instruction executed	After
ECX: 00 00 01 A2	inc ecx	ECX 00 00 01 A3
		SF 0 ZF 0 OF 0
AL: F5	dec al	AL F4
		SF 1 ZF 0 OF 0
word at Count: 00 09	inc Count	Count 00 0A
		SF 0 ZF 0 OF 0
BX: 00 01	dec bx	BX 00 00
		SF 0 ZF 1 OF 0
EDX: 7F FF FF FF	inc edx	EDX 80 00 00 00
		SF 1 ZF 0 OF 1

The inc and dec instructions are especially useful for incrementing and decrementing counters. They sometimes take fewer bytes of code and execute in fewer clock cycles than corresponding addition or subtraction instructions. For example, the instructions

```
add    cx, 1          ; increment loop counter
```

and

```
inc    cx             ; increment loop counter
```

are functionally equivalent. The add instruction requires three bytes (three bytes instead of four since the immediate operand will fit in one byte), while the inc instruction requires one byte. Either executes in two clock cycles on an 80386 machine or in one clock cycle on an 80486 or Pentium, so execution times are identical.

In Fig. 4.6, note the fast, single-byte inc and dec instructions for word or doubleword-size operands stored in registers. A register is the best place to keep a counter, if one can be reserved for this purpose.

A neg instruction negates, or finds the 2's complement of, its single operand. When a positive value is negated the result is negative; a negative value will become positive. Zero remains zero. Each neg instruction has the form

```
neg    destination
```

Figure 4.7 shows allowable operands for neg instructions.

Following are four examples illustrating how the neg instructions operate. In each case the "after" value is the 2's complement of the "before" value.

Destination Operand	Clock Cycles			Number of Bytes	Opcode
	386	486	Pentium		
register 8	2	1	1	2	F6
register 16	2	1	1	2	F7
register 32	2	1	1	2	F7
memory byte	6	3	3	2 +	F6
memory word	6	3	3	2 +	F7
memory doubleword	6	3	3	2 +	F7

Figure 4.7 neg instructions

Example

Before	Instruction executed	After

Before   *Instruction executed*   *After*

BX: 01 A2   neg bx   BX | FE | 5E |

SF 1 ZF 0

DH: F5   neg dh   DH | 0B |

SF 0 ZF 0

word at Flag: 00 01   neg Flag   Flag | FF | FF |

SF 1 ZF 0

EAX: 00 00 00 00   neg eax   EAX | 00 | 00 | 00 | 00 |

SF 0 ZF 1

This section ends with an example of a complete, if unexciting, program that uses these new instructions. The program inputs values for three numbers, x, y and z, evaluates the expression $-(x + y - 2z + 1)$ and displays the result. The design implemented is

```
prompt for and input value for x;
convert x from ASCII to 2's complement form;
expression := x;
prompt for and input value for y;
convert y from ASCII to 2's complement form;
add y to expression, giving x + y;
prompt for and input value for z;
convert z from ASCII to 2's complement form;
calculate 2*z as (z + z);
subtract 2*z from expression, giving x + y − 2*z;
```

add 1 to expression, giving x + y − 2*z + 1;

negate expression, giving − (x + y − 2*z + 1);

convert the result from 2's complement to ASCII;

display the result;

To write an assembly language program, you need to plan how registers and memory will be used. In this program the values of x, y, and z are not needed after they are incorporated into the expression. Therefore they are not stored in memory. We will assume that the numbers are not very large, so that values can be stored in words. A logical place to keep the expression value would be the accumulator AX since some operations are faster with it, but this choice is impossible since the `atoi` macro always uses AX as its destination. This leaves the general registers BX, CX, and DX; this program will use DX. It is very easy to run out of registers when designing assembly language programs. Memory must often be used for values even though operations are slower. Sometimes values must be moved back and forth between registers and memory.

Figure 4.8 shows the source program listing. This program follows the same general pattern of the example in Fig. 3.1. In the prompts, note the use of `cr,Lf,Lf` to

```
; program to input values for x, y and z
; and evaluate the expression - (x + y - 2z + 1)
; author:  R. Detmer
; date:  revised 8/97


.386
.MODEL FLAT


ExitProcess PROTO NEAR32 stdcall, dwExitCode:DWORD


include io.h              ; header file for input/output


cr        equ    0dh      ; carriage return character
Lf        equ    0ah      ; line feed


.STACK  4096               ; reserve 4096-byte stack
```

(continued)

Figure 4.8   **Program to evaluate − (x + y − 2z + 1)**

```
.DATA                        ; reserve storage for data
Prompt1     BYTE    "This program will evaluate the expression",cr,Lf,Lf
            BYTE    "    - (x + y - 2z + 1)",cr,Lf,Lf
            BYTE    "for your choice of integer values.",cr,Lf,Lf
            BYTE    "Enter value for x:  ",0
Prompt2     BYTE    "Enter value for y:  ",0
Prompt3     BYTE    "Enter value for z:  ",0
Value       BYTE    16 DUP (?)
Answer      BYTE    cr,Lf,"The result is "
Result      BYTE    6 DUP (?)
            BYTE    cr,Lf,0


.CODE                             ; start of main program code
_start:
            output  Prompt1       ; prompt for x
            input   Value,16      ; read ASCII characters
            atoi    Value         ; convert to integer
            mov     dx,ax         ; x

            output  Prompt2       ; prompt for y
            input   Value,16      ; read ASCII characters
            atoi    Value         ; convert to integer
            add     dx,ax         ; x + y

            output  Prompt3       ; prompt for z
            input   Value,16      ; read ASCII characters
            atoi    Value         ; convert to integer
            add     ax,ax         ; 2*z
            sub     dx,ax         ; x + y - 2*z

            inc     dx            ; x + y - 2*z + 1
            neg     dx            ; - (x + y - 2*z + 1)

            itoa    Result,dx     ; convert to ASCII characters

            output  Answer        ; output label and result

            INVOKE  ExitProcess, 0  ; exit with return code 0

PUBLIC _start                      ; make entry point public
END                                ; end of source code
```

Figure 4.8   (continued)

```
This program will evaluate the expression

    - (x + y - 2z + 1)

for your choice of integer values.

Enter value for x:  10
Enter value for y:  3
Enter value for z:  5


The result is      -4
```

Figure 4.9   Sample run of program

skip to a new line and to leave an extra blank line; it is not necessary to put in a second cr since the cursor will already be at the beginning of the new line after one carriage return character is displayed. The value of 2*z is found by adding z to itself; multiplication will be covered in the next section, but it is more efficient to compute 2*z by addition. Finally, note that the comments in this program do not simply repeat the instruction mnemonics; they help the human reader figure out what is really going on.

Figure 4.9 illustrates a sample run of this program. As in the previous example, user input is underlined.

Exercises 4.2

1. For each instruction, give the opcode, the number of bytes of object code, and the number of clock cycles required for execution on a Pentium system. Assume that *Value* references a word in memory and that *Double* references a doubleword.

(a)	add	ax, Value	(b) sub	Value, ax
(c)	sub	eax, 10	(d) add	Double, 10
(e)	add	eax, [ebx]	(f) sub	[ebx], eax
(g)	sub	dl, ch	(h) add	bl, 5
(i)	inc	bx	(j) dec	al
(k)	dec	Double	(l) inc	BYTE PTR [esi]
(m)	neg	eax	(n) neg	bh
(o)	neg	Double	(p) neg	WORD PTR [ebx]

2. For each part of this problem, assume the "before" values when the given instruction is executed. Give the requested "after" values.

	Before	*Instruction*	*After*
(a)	EBX: FF FF FF 75		
	ECX: 00 00 01 A2	add ebx,ecx	EBX, ECX, SF, ZF, CF, OF
(b)	EBX: FF FF FF 75		
	ECX: 00 00 01 A2	sub ebx,ecx	EBX, ECX, SF, ZF, CF, OF
(c)	BX: FF 75		
	CX: 01 A2	sub cx,bx	BX, CX, SF, ZF, CF, OF
(d)	DX: 01 4B	add dx,40h	DX, SF, ZF, CF, OF
(e)	EAX: 00 00 00 64	sub eax,100	EAX, SF, ZF, CF, OF
(f)	AX: 0A 20		word at Value,
	word at Value: FF 20	add ax,Value	AX, SF, ZF, CF, OF
(g)	AX: 0A 20		word at Value,
	word at Value: FF 20	sub Value,ax	AX, SF, ZF, CF, OF
(h)	CX: 03 1A	inc cx	CX, SF, ZF
(i)	EAX: 00 00 00 01	dec eax	EAX, SF, ZF
(j)	word at Count: 00 99	inc Count	word at Count, SF, ZF
(k)	word at Count: 00 99	dec count	word at Count, SF, ZF
(l)	EBX: FF FF FF FF	neg ebx	EBX, SF, ZF
(m)	CL: 5F	neg cl	CL, SF, ZF
(n)	word at Value: FB 3C	neg Value	word at Value, SF, ZF

Programming Exercises 4.2

For complete programs, prompts for input must make it clear what is to be entered, and output must be appropriately labeled.

1. Write a complete 80x86 assembly language program to prompt for values of x, y, and z and display the value of the expression $x - 2y + 4z$. Allow for 16-bit integer values.

2. Write a complete 80x86 assembly language program to prompt for values of x, y, and z and display the value of the expression $2(-x + y - 1) + z$. Allow for 32-bit integer values.

3. Write a complete 80x86 assembly language program to prompt for the length and width of a rectangle and to display its perimeter (2*length + 2*width).

4.3 Multiplication Instructions

The 80x86 architecture has two multiplication instruction mnemonics. Any imul instruction treats its operands as signed numbers; the sign of the product is determined by the usual rules for multiplying signed numbers. A mul instruction treats its operands as unsigned binary numbers; the product is also unsigned. If only non-negative numbers are to be multiplied, mul should usually be chosen instead of imul since it is a little faster.

There are fewer variants of mul than of imul, so we consider it first. The mul instruction has a single operand; its format is

```
mul     source
```

The source operand may be byte, word, or doubleword-length, and it may be in a register or in memory. The location of the other number to be multiplied is always the accumulator—AL for a byte source, AX for a word source, and EAX for a doubleword source. If *source* has byte length, then it is multiplied by the byte in AL; the product is 16 bits long, with a destination of the AX register. If *source* has word length, then it is multiplied by the word in AX; the product is 32 bits long, with its low order 16 bits going to the AX register and its high order 16 bits going to the DX register. If *source* is a doubleword, then it is multiplied by the doubleword in EAX; the product is 64 bits long, with its low order 32 bits in the EAX register and its high order 32 bits in the EDX register. For byte multiplication, the original value in AX is replaced. For word multiplication, the original values in AX and DX are both wiped out. Similarly, for doubleword multiplication the values in EAX and EDX are replaced by the product. In each case the source operand is unchanged unless it is half of the destination location.

At first glance, it may seem strange that the product is twice the length of its two factors. However, this also occurs in ordinary decimal multiplication; if, for example, two four-digit numbers are multiplied, the product will be seven or eight digits long. Computers that have multiplication operations often put the product in double-length locations so that there is no danger that the destination location will be too small.

Even when provision is made for double-length products, it is useful to be able to tell whether the product is the same size as the source; that is, if the high-order half is zero. With mul instructions, the carry flag CF and overflow flag OF are set to 1 if the high

| Operand | Clock Cycles | | | Number | |
	386	486	Pentium	of Bytes	Opcode
register 8	9–14	13–18	11	2	F6
register 16	9–22	13–26	11	2	F7
register 32	9–38	13–42	10	2	F7
memory byte	12–17	13–18	11	2 +	F6
memory word	12–25	13–26	11	2 +	F7
memory doubleword	12–41	13–42	10	2 +	F7

Figure 4.10 mul **instructions**

order half of the product is not zero, but are cleared to 0 if the high order half of the product is zero. These are the only meaningful flag values following multiplication operations; previously set values of AF, PF, SF, and ZF flags may be destroyed. In Chapter 5, instructions checking flag values will be covered; it is possible to check that the high order half of the product can be safely ignored.

Figure 4.10 summarizes the allowable operand types for mul instructions. No immediate operand is allowed in a mul. Note the number of clock cycles required is appreciably larger than for addition or subtraction instructions. The actual number of clock cycles for the 80386 and 80486 depends on the numbers being multiplied.

Here are some examples to illustrate how the mul instructions work.

Example

Before	Instruction executed	After		
AX: 00 05	mul bx	DX	00	00
BX: 00 02				
DX: ?? ??		AX	00	0A

CF, OF 0

EAX: 00 00 00 0A	mul eax	EDX	00	00	00	00
EDX: ?? ?? ?? ??						
		EAX	00	00	00	64

CF, OF 0

AX: ?? 05   mul Factor   AX | 04 | FB

byte at Factor: FF

CF, OF 1

The first example shows multiplication of words in AX and BX. The contents of DX are not used in the multiplication but are replaced by the high-order 16 bits of the 32-bit product 0000000A. The carry and overflow flags are cleared to 0 since DX contains 0000. The second example shows multiplication of EAX by itself, illustrating that the explicit source for the multiplication can be the same as the other implicit factor. The final example shows multiplication of the byte in AL by a byte at *Factor* in memory with value equivalent to the unsigned number 255_{10}. The product is the unsigned 16-bit number 04 FB, and since the high-order half is not zero, both CF and OF are set to 1.

The signed multiplication instructions use mnemonic `imul`. There are three formats, each with a different number of operands. The first format is

```
imul    source
```

the same as for `mul`, with *source* containing one factor and the accumulator the other. Again, the source operand cannot be immediate. The destination is AX, DX:AX, or EDX:EAX, depending on the size of the source operand. The carry and overflow flags are set to 1 if the bits in the high-order half are significant, and cleared to 0 otherwise. Notice the high-order half may contain all 1 bits for a negative product. Single-operand `imul` instructions are summarized in Fig. 4.11. Notice that this table is identical to Fig.

Operand	Clock Cycles			Number of Bytes	Opcode
	386	486	Pentium		
register 8	9–14	13–18	11	2	F6
register 16	9–22	13–26	11	2	F7
register 32	9–38	13–42	10	2	F7
memory byte	12–17	13–18	11	2 +	F6
memory word	12–25	13–26	11	2 +	F7
memory doubleword	12–41	13–42	10	2 +	F7

Figure 4.11 `imul` instructions (single-operand format)

4.10. Even the opcodes are the same for `mul` and single-operand `imul` instructions, with a field in the second byte of the instruction distinguishing the two.

The second `imul` format is

```
imul    register, source
```

Here the source operand can be in a register, in memory, or immediate. The other factor is in the register, which also serves as the destination. Operands must be words or doublewords, not bytes. The product must "fit" in same size as the factors; if it does, CF and OF are cleared to 0, if not they are set to 1.

Figure 4.12 summarizes two-operand `imul` instructions. Note that some of these instructions have two byte long opcodes. Immediate operands can be either the size of the destination register or a single byte. Single-byte operands are sign-extended before multiplication—that is, the sign bit is copied to leading bit positions, giving a 16 or 32-bit value that represents the same signed integer as the original 8-bit operand.

The third `imul` format is

```
imul    register, source, immediate
```

With this version, the first operand, a register, is only the destination for the product; the two factors are the contents of the register or memory location given by *source* and the immediate value. Operands *register* and *source* are the same size, both 16-bit or both

| | | Clock Cycles | | | Number | |
Operand 1	Operand 2	386	486	Pentium	of Bytes	Opcode
register 16	register 16	9–22	13–26	11	3	0F AF
register 32	register 32	9–38	13–42	10	3	0F AF
register 16	memory word	12–25	13–26	11	3 +	0F AF
register 32	memory doubleword	12–41	13–42	10	3 +	0F AF
register 16	immediate byte	9–14	13–18	11	3	6B
register 16	immediate word	9–22	13–26	11	4	69
register 32	immediate byte	9–14	13–18	11	3	6B
register 32	immediate doubleword	9–38	13–42	10	6	69

Figure 4.12   `imul` **instructions (two-operand format)**

32-bit. If the product will fit in the destination register, then CF and OF are cleared to 0; if not, they are set to 1. The three-operand imul instructions are summarized in Fig. 4.13. Some examples will help show how the imul instructions work.

Example

Before	Instruction executed	After
AX: 00 05	imul bx	DX 00 00
BX: 00 02		
DX: ?? ??		AX 00 0A
		CF, OF 0
AX: ?? 05	imul Factor	AX FF FB
byte at Factor: FF		CF, OF 0
EBX: 00 00 00 0A	imul ebx, 10	EBX 00 00 00 64
		CF, OF 0

Register Destination	Source	Immediate Operand	Clock Cycles 386	486	Pentium	Number of Bytes	Opcode
register 16	register 16	byte	9–14	13–18	10	3	6B
register 16	register 16	word	9–22	13–26	10	4	69
register 16	memory 16	byte	12–17	13–18	10	3+	6B
register 16	memory 16	word	12–25	13–26	10	4+	69
register 32	register 32	byte	9–14	13–18	10	3	6B
register 32	register 32	doubleword	9–38	13–42	10	6	69
register 32	memory 32	byte	12–17	13–18	10	3+	6B
register 32	memory 32	doubleword	12–41	13–42	10	6+	69

Figure 4.13   imul Instructions (three-operand format)

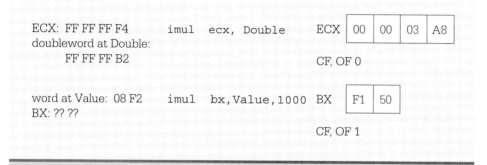

The first two examples are the single-operand format and the products are twice the length of the operands. The first example shows words in AX (the implied operand) and BX being multiplied, with the result in DX:AX. The second example shows 5 in AL being multiplied by −1 in the memory byte at Factor, giving a word-size product equivalent to −5 in AX. The third example shows the two-operand format, with 10 in EBX multiplied by the immediate operand 10, and the result of 100 in EBX. In the fourth example, two negative numbers are multiplied, giving a positive result. In the last example, the product is $22F150_{16}$, too large to fit in BX. The flags CF and OF are set to 1 to indicate that the result was too large, and the low-order digits are saved in BX.

Earlier, the discussion with the example program in Fig. 4.8 stated that it was faster to calculate $2z$ by adding z to itself than by using a multiplication instruction. In that situation, z was in the AX register, so

```
add     ax, ax      ; compute 2z
```

did the job. This instruction is two bytes long, and on an 80486 or Pentium system takes one clock cycle. To do the same task using multiplication, you can code

```
imul    ax, 2       ; compute 2z
```

This instruction (from Fig. 4.12) is three bytes long since the immediate operand 2 is short enough to fit in a single byte; it takes 13–18 clock cycles on an 80486 or 10 clock cycles on a Pentium, much longer than the addition instruction.

This section concludes with an example of a program that will input the length and width of a rectangle and calculate its area (length*width). (Admittedly, this is a job much better suited for a hand calculator than for a computer program in assembly language or any other language.) Figure 4.14 shows the source code for the program. Note

```
; program to find the area of a rectangle
; author:  R. Detmer
; date:  revised 9/97

.386
.MODEL FLAT

ExitProcess PROTO NEAR32 stdcall, dwExitCode:DWORD

INCLUDE io.h

cr          EQU     0dh    ; carriage return character
LF          EQU     0ah    ; linefeed character

.STACK  4096                    ; reserve 4096-byte stack

.DATA                           ; reserve storage for data
prompt1     BYTE    "This program will find the area of a
                    rectangle",cr,Lf,Lf
            BYTE    "Width of rectangle?  ",0
prompt2     BYTE    "Length of rectangle?  ",0
value       BYTE    16 DUP (?)
answer      BYTE    cr,Lf,"The area of the rectangle is "
area        BYTE    11 DUP (?)
            BYTE    cr,Lf,0

.CODE                                   ; start of main program code
_start:
Prompt:     output prompt1              ; prompt for width
            input  value,16             ; read ASCII characters
            atod   value                ; convert to integer
            mov    ebx,eax              ; width

            output prompt2              ; prompt for length
            input  value,16             ; read ASCII characters
            atod   value                ; convert to integer
            mul    ebx                  ; length * width

            dtoa   area,eax             ; convert to ASCII characters
            output answer               ; output label and result

            INVOKE ExitProcess, 0       ; exit with return code 0
PUBLIC _start                           ; make entry point public
            END
```

Figure 4.14 Program to find the area of a rectangle

that the program uses `mul` rather than `imul` for finding the product; lengths and widths are positive numbers. Interesting errors occur in this program if a negative length or width is entered, or if a large width and length (say 200 and 300) are entered. Why? Such errors are unfortunately common in software.

As you have seen in this section, the 80x86 architecture includes multiplication instructions in three formats. You may have noted that the destination of the product cannot be a memory operand. This may sound restrictive, but some processors have even greater limitations. In fact, most 8-bit microprocessors, including the Intel 8080, had no multiplication instruction; any multiplication had to be done using a software routine.

Exercises 4.3

1. For each part of this problem, assume the "before" values when the given instruction is executed. Give the requested "after" values.

	Before	*Instruction*		*After*
(a)	EAX: FF FF FF E4			
	EBX: 00 00 00 02	mul	ebx	EAX, EDX, CF, OF
(b)	AX: FF E4			
	word at Value: FF 3A	mul	Value	AX, DX, CF, OF
(c)	AX: FF FF	mul	ax	AX, DX, CF, OF
(d)	AL: 0F			
	BH: 4C	mul	bh	AX, CF, OF
(e)	AL: F0			
	BH: C4	mul	bh	AX, CF, OF
(f)	AX: 00 17			
	CX: 00 B2	imul	cx	AX, DX, CF, OF
(g)	EAX: FF FF FF E4			
	EBX: 00 00 04 C2	imul	ebx	EAX, EDX, CF, OF
(h)	AX: FF E4			
	word at Value: FF 3A	imul	Value	AX, DX, CF, OF
(i)	EAX: FF FF FF FF	imul	eax	EAX, EDX, CF, OF
(j)	AL: 0F			
	BH: 4C	imul	bh	AX, CF, OF
(k)	AL: F0			
	BH: C4	imul	bh	AX, CF, OF

2. Give the opcode for each instruction in Exercise 1.

3. For each part of this problem, assume the "before" values when the given instruction is executed. Give the requested "after" values.

Before	Instruction	After
(a) BX: 00 17		
CX: 00 B2	`imul bx,cx`	BX, CF, OF
(b) EAX: FF FF FF E4		
EBX: 00 00 04 C2	`imul eax,ebx`	EAX, CF, OF
(c) AX: 0F B2	`imul ax, 15`	AX, CF, OF
(d) ECX: 00 00 7C E4		
doubleword at Mult:	`imul ecx,Mult`	ECX, CF, OF
00 00 65 ED		
(e) DX: 7C E4		
BX: 49 30	`imul dx,bx`	DX, CF, OF
(f) DX: 0F E4		
word at Value: 04 C2	`imul dx,Value`	DX, CF, OF
(g) EBX: 00 00 04 C2	`imul ebx,-10`	EBX, CF, OF
(h) ECX: FF FF FF E4	`imul ebx,ecx,5`	EBX, CF, OF
(i) DX: 00 64	`imul ax,dx,10`	AX, CF, OF

4. Give the opcode for each instruction in Exercise 3.

5. Suppose that the value for x is in the AX register and you need the value of $5x$ in AX. Compare the number of clock cycles for execution on a Pentium system and the number of bytes of object code for each of the following schemes.

```
mov     bx,ax       ; copy value of x
add     ax,ax       ; x + x gives 2x
add     ax,ax       ; 2x + 2x gives 4x
add     ax,bx       ; 4x + x gives 5x
```

and

```
imul    ax,5        ; 5x
```

6. Suppose you need to evaluate the polynomial

$$p(x) = 5x^3 - 7x^2 + 3x - 10$$

for some value of x. If this is done in the obvious way, as

$$5*x*x*x - 7*x*x + 3*x - 10$$

there are six multiplications and three additions/subtractions. An equivalent form, based on Horner's scheme for evaluation of polynomials, is

$$((5*x - 7)*x + 3)*x - 10$$

This has only three multiplications.

Suppose that the value of x is in the EAX register.

(a) Write 80x86 assembly language statements that will evaluate $p(x)$ the "obvious" way, putting the result in EAX.

(b) Write 80x86 assembly language statements that will evaluate $p(x)$ using Horner's scheme, again putting the result in EAX.

(c) Assuming a Pentium system, compare the number of clock cycles for execution and the number of bytes of object code required for the code fragments in (a) and in (b) above.

7. The 80x86 architecture has distinct instructions for multiplication of signed and unsigned numbers. It does not have separate instructions for addition of signed and unsigned numbers. Why are different instructions needed for multiplication but not for addition?

Programming Exercises 4.3

1. Write a complete 80x86 assembly language program to prompt for the length, width, and height of a box and to display its volume (length * width * height).

2. Write a complete 80x86 assembly language program to prompt for the length, width, and height of a box and to display its surface area

   2*(length*width + length*height + width*height).

3. Suppose that someone has a certain number of coins (pennies, nickels, dimes, quarters, fifty-cent pieces, and dollar coins) and wants to know the total value of the coins, as well as how many coins there are. Write a program to help. Specifically, follow the design below.

   prompt for and input the number of pennies;
   total := number of pennies;
   numberOfCoins := number of pennies;
   prompt for and input the number of nickels;
   total := total + 5 * number of nickels;
   add number of nickels to numberOfCoins;

prompt for and input the number of dimes;

total := total + 10 * number of dimes;

add number of dimes to numberOfCoins;

prompt for and input the number of quarters;

total := total + 25 * number of quarters;

add number of quarters to numberOfCoins;

prompt for and input the number of fifty-cent pieces;

total := total + 50 * number of fifty-cent pieces;

add number of fifty-cent pieces to numberOfCoins;

prompt for and input the number of dollars;

total := total + 100 * number of dollars;

add number of dollars to numberOfCoins;

display "There are ", numberOfCoins, " coins worth";

display total div 100, " dollars and", total mod 100," cents";

Note that you are displaying dollars and cents for the total. Assume that all values will fit in doublewords.

4.4 Division Instructions

The Intel 80x86 instructions for division parallel those of the single-operand multiplication instructions; `idiv` is for division of signed 2's complement integers and `div` is for division of unsigned integers. Recall that the single-operand multiplication instructions start with a multiplier and multiplicand and produce a double-length product. Division instructions start with a double-length dividend and a single-length divisor, and produce a single-length quotient *and* a single-length remainder. The 80x86 has instructions that can be used to produce a double-length dividend prior to division.

The division instructions have formats

```
idiv    source
```

and

```
div     source
```

source (divisor) size	other operand (dividend)	quotient	remainder
byte	AX	AL	AH
word	DX:AX	AX	DX
doubleword	EDX:EAX	EAX	EDX

Figure 4.15 Operands and results for 80x86 division instructions

The source operand identifies the divisor. The divisor can be in a register or memory, but not immediate. Both `div` and `idiv` use an implicit dividend (the operand you are dividing into). If *source* is byte length, then the double-length dividend is word size and is assumed to be in the AX register. If *source* is word length, then the dividend is a doubleword and is assumed to have its low order 16 bits in the AX register and its high order 16 bits in the DX register. If *source* is doubleword length, then the dividend is a quadword (64 bits) and is assumed to have its low order 32 bits in the EAX register and its high order 32 bits in the EDX register.

The table in Fig. 4.15 summarizes the locations of the dividend, divisor, quotient, and remainder for 80x86 division instructions.

The source operand (the divisor) is not changed by a division instruction. After a word in AX is divided by a byte length divisor, the quotient will be in the AL register half and the remainder will be in the AH register half. After a doubleword in DX and AX is divided by a word length divisor, the quotient will be in the AX register and the remainder will be in the DX register. After a quadword in EDX and EAX is divided by a doubleword length divisor, the quotient will be in the EAX register and the remainder will be in the EDX register.

For all division operations, the dividend, divisor, quotient, and remainder must satisfy the equation

dividend = quotient*divisor + remainder

For unsigned `div` operations, the dividend, divisor, quotient, and remainder are all treated as non-negative numbers. For signed `idiv` operations, the sign of the quotient is determined by the signs of the dividend and divisor using the ordinary rules of signs; the sign of the remainder is always the same as the sign of the dividend.

The division instructions do not set flags to any significant values. They may destroy previously set values of AF, CF, OF, PF, SF, and ZF flags.

Some examples show how the division instructions work.

Example

Before	Instruction executed	After				
EDX: 00 00 00 00	div ebx	EDX	00	00	00	09
EAX: 00 00 00 64						
EBX: 00 00 00 0D		EAX	00	00	00	07
DX: 00 00	idiv cx	DX	00	09		
AX: 00 64						
CX: 00 0D		AX	00	07		
AX: 00 64	div Divisor	AX	09	07		
byte at Divisor: 0D						

In each of these examples, the decimal number 100 is divided by 13. Since

```
100 = 7 * 13 + 9
```

the quotient is 7 and the remainder is 9. For the doubleword length divisor, the quotient is in EAX and the remainder is in EDX. For the word length divisor, the quotient is in AX and the remainder is in DX. For the byte length divisor, the quotient is in AL and the remainder is in AH.

For operations where the dividend or divisor is negative, equations analogous to the one above are

$$100 = (-7) * (-13) + 9$$
$$-100 = (-7) * 13 + (-9)$$
$$-100 = 7 * (-13) + (-9)$$

Note that in each case the sign of the remainder is the same as the sign of the dividend. The following examples reflect these equations for word size divisors of 13 or −13.

Example

Before	Instruction executed	After		
DX: 00 00	idiv cx	DX	00	09
AX: 00 64				
CX: FF F3		AX	FF	F9

DX: FF FF	idiv cx	DX	FF	F7
AX: FF 9C				
CX: 00 0D				
		AX	FF	F9
DX: FF FF	idiv cx	DX	FF	F7
AX: FF 9C				
CX: FF F3				
		AX	00	07

In the second and third examples, the dividend −100 is represented as the 32 bit number FF FF FF 9C in the DX and AX registers.

Finally, here are two examples to help illustrate the difference between signed and unsigned division.

Example

Before	Instruction executed	After		
AX: FE 01	idiv bl	AX	E1	0F
BL: E0				
AX: FE 01	div bl	AX	00	FF
BL: FF				

With the signed division, −511 is divided by −32, giving a quotient of 15 and a remainder of −31. With the unsigned division, 65025 is divided by 255, giving a quotient of 255 and a remainder of 0.

With multiplication, the double length destination in each single-operand format guarantees that the product will fit in the destination location—nothing can go wrong during a single-operand multiplication operation. There can be errors during division. One obvious cause is an attempt to divide by zero. A less obvious reason is a quotient that is too large to fit in the single-length destination; if, say, 00 02 46 8A is divided

Operand	Clock Cycles			Number of Bytes	Opcode
	386	486	Pentium		
register 8	19	19	22	2	F6
register 16	27	27	30	2	F7
register 32	43	43	48	2	F7
memory byte	22	20	22	2 +	F6
memory word	30	28	30	2 +	F7
memory doubleword	46	44	48	2 +	F7

Figure 4.16 `idiv` **instructions**

by 2, the quotient 1 23 45 is too large to fit in the AX register. If an error occurs during the division operation, the 80x86 generates an **exception**. The routine, or interrupt handler, that services this exception may vary from system to system. Windows 95 on the author's Pentium system pops up a window with the message "This program has performed an illegal operation and will be shut down." When the Details button is pressed, it displays "TEST caused a divide error..." The 80x86 leaves the destination registers undefined following a division error.

Figure 4.16 lists the allowable operand types for `idiv` instructions and Fig. 4.17 lists the allowable operand types for `div` instructions. The only differences in the two tables are in the number of clock cycles columns; `div` operations are slightly faster than `idiv` operations.

Operand	Clock Cycles			Number of Bytes	Opcode
	386	486	Pentium		
register 8	14	16	17	2	F6
register 16	22	24	25	2	F7
register 32	38	40	41	2	F7
memory byte	17	16	17	2 +	F6
memory word	25	24	25	2 +	F7
memory doubleword	41	40	41	2 +	F7

Figure 4.17 `div` **instructions**

When arithmetic is being done with operands of a given length, the dividend must be converted to double length before a division operation is executed. For unsigned division, a doubleword-size dividend must be converted to quadword size with leading zero bits in the EDX register. This can be accomplished many ways, two of which are

```
mov    edx, 0
```

and

```
sub    edx, edx
```

Similar instructions can be used to put a zero in DX prior to unsigned division by a word operand or to put a zero in AH prior to unsigned division by a byte operand.

The situation is more complicated for signed division. A positive dividend must be extended with leading 0 bits, but a negative dividend must be extended with leading 1 bits. The 80x86 has three instructions for this task. The cbw, cwd, and cdq instructions are different from the instructions covered before in that these instructions have no operands. The cbw instruction always has AL as its source and AX as its destination, cwd always has AX as its source and DX and AX as its destination, and cdq always has EAX as its source and EDX and EAX as its destination. The source register is not changed, but is extended as a signed number into AH, DX, or EDX. These instructions are summarized together in Fig. 4.18, which also includes the cwde instruction that extends the word in AX to its signed equivalent in EAX, paralleling the job that cbw does.

The cbw (convert byte to word) instruction extends the 2's complement number in the AL register half to word length in AX. The cwd (convert word to double) instruction extends the word in AX to a doubleword in DX and AX. The cdq (convert double to quadword) instruction extends the word in EAX to a quadword in EDX and EAX. The

Instruction	Clock Cycles			Number of Bytes	Opcode
	386	486	Pentium		
cbw	3	3	3	1	98
cwd	2	3	2	1	99
cdq	2	3	2	1	99
cwde	3	3	3	1	98

Figure 4.18 cbw and cwd instructions

cwde (convert word to double extended) instruction extends the word in AX to a double-word in EAX; this is not an instruction that would normally be used to prepare for division. Each instruction copies the sign bit of the original number to each bit of the high order half of the result. None of these instructions affect flags. Some examples are

Example

Before	Instruction executed	After
AX: 07 0D DX: ?? ??	cwd	DX `00` `00` AX `07` `0D`
EAX: FF FF FA 13 EDX: ?? ?? ?? ??	cdq	EDX `FF` `FF` `FF` `FF` EAX `FF` `FF` `FF` `13`
AL: 53	cbw	AX `00` `53`
AL: C6	cbw	AX `FF` `C6`
AX: FF 2A	cwde	EAX `FF` `FF` `FF` `2A`

Two "move" instructions are somewhat similar to the above "convert" instructions. These instructions copy an 8-bit or 16-bit source operand to a 16-bit or 32-bit destination, extending the source value. The movzx instruction always extends the source value with zero bits. It has the format

        movzx   register, source

The movsx instruction extends the source value with copies of the sign bit. It has a similar format

        movsx   register, source

		Clock Cycles			Number	Opcode	
Destination	Source	386	486	Pentium	of Bytes	movsx	movzx
register 16	register 8	3	3	3	3	0F BE	0F B6
register 32	register 8	3	3	3	3	0F BE	0F B6
register 32	register 16	3	3	3	3	0F BF	0F B7
register 16	memory byte	6	3	3	3+	0F BE	0F B6
register 32	memory byte	6	3	3	3+	0F BE	0F B6
register 32	memory word	6	3	3	3+	0F BF	0F B7

Figure 4.19   movsx and movzx instructions

Data about these instructions is in Fig. 4.19. With either instruction the source operand can be in a register or in memory. Neither instruction changes any flag value.

Here are a few examples showing how these instructions work.

Example

Before	*Instruction executed*	*After*

word at value: 07 0D   movsx ecx,value   ECX | 00 | 00 | 07 | 0D |

word at Value: F7 0D   movsx ecx,value   ECX | FF | FF | F7 | 0D |

word at Value: 07 0D   movzx ecx,value   ECX | 00 | 00 | 07 | 0D |

word at Value: F7 0D   movzx ecx,value   ECX | 00 | 00 | F7 | 0D |

This section concludes with another simple program, this one to convert Celsius (centigrade) temperatures to Fahrenheit. Figure 4.20 gives the source code. The formula implemented is

$$F = (9/5) * C + 32$$

```
; program to convert Celsius temperature to Fahrenheit
; uses formula  F = (9/5)*C + 32
; author:  R. Detmer
; date:  revised 9/97

.386
.MODEL FLAT

ExitProcess PROTO NEAR32 stdcall, dwExitCode:DWORD

INCLUDE io.h

cr          EQU     0dh    ; carriage return character
Lf          EQU     0ah    ; linefeed character

.STACK  4096                  ; reserve 4096-byte stack

.DATA                        ; reserve storage for data
Prompt1     BYTE    CR,LF,"This program will convert a Celsius "
            BYTE    "temperature to the Fahrenheit scale",cr,Lf,Lf
            BYTE    "Enter Celsius temperature:  ",0
Value       BYTE    10 DUP (?)
Answer      BYTE    CR,LF,"The temperature is"
Temperature BYTE    6 DUP (?)
            BYTE    "  Fahrenheit",cr,Lf,0

.CODE                            ; start of main program code
_start:
Prompt:     output  Prompt1      ; prompt for Celsius temperature
            input   Value,10     ; read ASCII characters
            atoi    Value        ; convert to integer

            imul    ax,9         ; C*9
            add     ax,2         ; rounding factor for division
            mov     bx,5         ; divisor
            cwd                  ; prepare for division
            idiv    bx           ; C*9/5
            add     ax,32        ; C*9/5 + 32

            itoa    Temperature,ax ; convert to ASCII characters
            output  Answer       ; output label and result

            INVOKE ExitProcess, 0 ; exit with return code 0
PUBLIC _start                    ; make entry point public
            END
```

Figure 4.20   Convert Celsius temperature to Fahrenheit

where F is the Fahrenheit temperature and C is the Celsius temperature. Since the arithmetic instructions covered so far perform only integer arithmetic, the program gives the integer to which the fractional answer would round. It is important to multiply 9 and C before dividing by 5; the integer quotient 9/5 would be simply 1. Dividing C by 5 before multiplying by 9 produces larger errors than if the multiplication is done first. Why? To get a rounded answer, half the divisor is added to the dividend before dividing. Since the divisor in this formula is 5, the number 2 is added for rounding. Notice that the cwd instruction is used to extend the partial result before division.

Exercises 4.4

1. For each part of this problem, assume the "before" values when the given instruction is executed. Give the requested "after" values. Some of these instructions will cause division errors; identify such instructions.

	Before	*Instruction*	*After*
(a)	EDX: 00 00 00 00		
	EAX: 00 00 00 9A		
	EBX: 00 00 00 0F	idiv ebx	EDX, EAX
(b)	AX: FF 75		
	byte at Count: FC	idiv Count	AX
(c)	AX: FF 75		
	byte at Count: FC	div Count	AX
(d)	DX: FF FF		
	AX: FF 9A		
	CX: 00 00	idiv cx	DX, AX
(e)	EDX: FF FF FF FF		
	EAX: FF FF FF 9A		
	ECX: FF FF FF C7	idiv ecx	EDX, EAX
(f)	DX: 00 00		
	AX: 05 9A		
	CX: FF C7	idiv cx	DX, AX
(g)	DX: 00 00		
	AX: 05 9A		
	CX: 00 00	idiv cx	DX, AX
(h)	EDX: 00 00 00 00		
	EAX: 00 00 01 5D		
	EBX: 00 00 00 08	idiv ebx	EDX, EAX

2. Give the opcode for each instruction in Exercise 1.

3. This section mentioned two methods of zeroing EDX prior to unsigned division, using

```
mov   edx, 0
```

or

```
sub   edx, edx
```

Which instruction would give more compact code? Which instruction would execute in fewer clock cycles on a Pentium?

4. The Celsius to Fahrenheit temperature conversion program (Fig. 4.20) works for Celsius temperatures that have fairly large magnitude and are either positive or negative. Suppose that you limit the Celsius temperature to the range 0–100 degrees, yielding Fahrenheit temperatures from 32–212. How can the program be modified to take advantage of these limited numeric ranges?

Programming Exercises 4.4

1. The formula for converting a Fahrenheit to a Celsius temperature is

$$C = (5/9) * (F - 32)$$

Write a complete 80x86 assembly language program to prompt for a Fahrenheit temperature and display the corresponding Celsius temperature.

2. Write a complete 80x86 assembly language program to prompt for four grades and then display the sum and the average (sum/4) of the grades.

3. Write a complete 80x86 assembly language program to prompt for four grades. Suppose that the last grade is a final exam grade that counts twice as much as the other three. Display the sum (adding the last grade twice) and the average (sum/5).

4. Write a complete 80x86 assembly language program to prompt for four pairs of grades and weighting factors. Each weighting factor indicates how many times the corresponding grade is to be counted in the sum. The weighted sum is

    WeightedSum = Grade1 * Weight1
                        + Grade2 * Weight2
                        + Grade3 * Weight3
                        + Grade4 * Weight4

    and the sum of the weights is

    SumOfWeights = Weight1 + Weight2 + Weight3 + Weight4

    Display the weighted sum, the sum of the weights, and the weighted average (WeightedSum/SumOfWeights).

    A sample run might look like

    ```
    grade 1?   88
    weight 1?   1

    grade 2?   77
    weight 2?   2

    grade 3?   94
    weight 3?   1

    grade 4?   85
    weight 4?   3

    weighted sum:    591
    sum of weights:      7
    weighted average:     84
    ```

5. Write a complete 80x86 assembly language program to prompt for four grades, and then display the sum and the average (sum/4) of the grades in ddd.dd format (exactly three digits before and two digits after a decimal point).

6. Write a short program that causes a division by zero to discover how the interrupt handler in your 80x86 system responds.

4.5   Addition and Subtraction of Larger Numbers

The add and sub instructions covered in Section 4.2 work with byte-length, word-length, or doubleword-length operands. Although the range of values that can be stored in a doubleword is large, $-2{,}147{,}483{,}648$ (80000000_{16}) to $2{,}147{,}483{,}647$ ($7FFFFFFF_{16}$), it is sometimes necessary to do arithmetic with even larger numbers. Very large numbers can be added or subtracted a group of bits at a time.

We will illustrate the technique for adding large numbers by adding two 64-bit long numbers. The idea is to start with the low-order 32 bits from each number and add them using an ordinary add instruction. This operation sets the carry flag CF to 1 if there is a carry out of the high order bit and to 0 otherwise. Now the next 32 bits are added using a special addition instruction adc (add with carry). The two high-order 32-bit numbers are added as usual, but if CF is set to 1 from the prior addition, then 1 is added to their sum before it is sent to the destination location. The adc instruction also sets CF, so this process could be continued for as additional groups of bits.

Assume that the two numbers to be added are in four doublewords in the data segment.

```
Nbr1Hi   DWORD   ?      ; High order 32 bits of Nbr1
Nbr1Lo   DWORD   ?      ; Low order 32 bits of Nbr1
Nbr2Hi   DWORD   ?      ; High order 32 bits of Nbr2
Nbr2Lo   DWORD   ?      ; Low order 32 bits of Nbr2
```

The following code fragment adds Nbr2 to Nbr1, storing the sum at the doublewords reserved for Nbr1.

```
mov   eax, Nbr1Lo      ; Low order 32 bits of Nbr1
add   eax, Nbr2Lo      ; add Low order 32 bits of Nbr2
mov   Nbr1Lo, eax      ; sum to destination
mov   eax, Nbr1Hi      ; High order 32 bits of Nbr1
adc   eax, Nbr2Hi      ; add High order 32 bits of Nbr2 & carry
mov   Nbr1Hi, eax      ; sum to destination
```

One thing making this code work is that the mov instructions that come between the add and adc instructions do not alter the carry flag. If an intervening instruction did change CF, then the sum could be incorrect.

The adc instructions are identical to corresponding add instructions except that the extra 1 is added if CF is set to 1. For subtraction, sbb (subtract with borrow) instructions function like sub instructions except that if CF is set to 1, an extra 1 is subtracted from the difference. Large numbers can be subtracted in groups of bits, working right to left. Figure 4.21 lists the allowable operand types for adc and sbb instructions. This table is identical to Fig. 4.5 except for a few opcodes.

To apply similar techniques to longer numbers, often a loop of identical instructions is used. If CF is known to be 0 before the loop begins, even the first addition can be done using adc. The 80x86 architecture has three instructions that let the programmer manipulate the carry flag. They are summarized in Fig. 4.22. There are no separate

Destination Operand	Source Operand	Clock Cycles			Number of Bytes	Opcode	
		386	486	Pentium		adc	sbb
register 8	immediate 8	2	1	1	3	80	80
register 16	immediate 8	2	1	1	3	83	83
register 32	immediate 8	2	1	1	3	83	83
register 16	immediate 16	2	1	1	4	81	81
register 32	immediate 32	2	1	1	6	81	81
AL	immediate 8	2	1	1	2	14	1C
AX	immediate 16	2	1	1	3	15	1D
EAX	immediate 32	2	1	1	5	15	1D
memory byte	immediate 8	7	3	3	3+	80	80
memory word	immediate 8	7	3	3	3+	83	83
memory doubleword	immediate 8	7	3	3	3+	83	83
memory word	immediate 16	7	3	3	4+	81	81
memory doubleword	immediate 32	7	3	3	6+	81	81
register 8	register 8	2	1	1	2	12	1A
register 16	register 16	2	1	1	2	13	1B
register 32	register 32	2	1	1	2	13	1B
register 8	memory byte	6	2	2	2+	12	1A
register 16	memory word	6	2	2	2+	13	1B
register 32	memory doubleword	6	2	2	2+	13	1B
memory byte	register 8	7	3	3	2+	10	18
memory word	register 16	7	3	3	2+	11	19
memory doubleword	register 32	7	3	3	2+	11	19

Figure 4.21   adc **and** sbb **instructions**

Instruction	Operation	Clock Cycles	Number of Bytes	Opcode
clc	clear carry flag (CF := 0)	2	1	F8
stc	set carry flag (CF := 1)	2	1	F9
cmc	complement carry flag (if CF = 0 then CF := 1 else CF := 0)	2	1	F5

Figure 4.22 Control of carry flag CF

columns for the number of clock cycles on different processors since these instructions take two clock cycles on each of 30386, 80486, and Pentium processors.

Multiplication and division operations with longer numbers are even more involved than addition and subtraction. Often techniques for adding and subtracting longer numbers are used to implement algorithms that are similar to grade school multiplication and division procedures for decimal numbers.

If one really needs to use longer numbers, it takes more than a set of arithmetic procedures. One may also need procedures like itoa and atoi in order to convert long numbers to and from ASCII character format.

Exercises 4.5

1. Suppose that two 96 bit long numbers are to be added.
   (a) Show how storage for three such numbers can be reserved in the data segment of a program.
   (b) Give a fragment of 80x86 code that will add the second number to the first, storing the sum at the locations reserved for the first number.
   (c) Give a fragment of 80x86 code that will add the second number to the first, storing the sum at the locations reserved for the third number.

2. Suppose that two 64 bit numbers are stored as shown in the example in this section. Give a fragment of 80x86 code that will subtract Nbr2 from Nbr1, storing the difference at the locations reserved for Nbr1.

3. For each part of this problem, assume the "before" values when the given instruction is executed. Give the requested "after" values.

	Before	*Instruction*	*After*
(a)	EAX: 00 00 03 7D		
	ECX: 00 00 01 A2		
	CF: 0	adc eax,ecx	EAX, CF
(b)	EAX: 00 00 03 7D		
	ECX: 00 00 01 A2		
	CF: 1	adc eax,ecx	EAX, CF
(c)	EAX: FF 49 00 00		
	ECX: 03 68 00 00		
	CF: 0	adc eax,ecx	EAX, CF
(d)	EAX: FF 4900 00		
	ECX: 03 6800 00		
	CF: 1	adc eax,ecx	EAX, CF
(e)	EAX: 00 00 03 7D		
	ECX: 00 00 01 A2		
	CF: 0	sbb eax,ecx	EAX, CF
(f)	EAX: 00 00 01 A2		
	ECX: 00 00 03 7D		
	CF: 1	sbb eax,ecx	EAX, CF

4.6   Something Extra: Levels of Abstraction and Microcode

In computer science, we look at computers and computation at many levels. When using an application program like a word processing package or a game, we just want its various features to work and we typically do not care how it is written. When we are writing programs in a high-level language, we tend to view the computer as say, an Ada machine or a C++ machine, and often do not think about how various language constructs are implemented. The **application level** and the **high-level language level** are two **levels of abstraction**. As used here, the word "abstraction" can be thought of as "ignoring the details."

This book deals primarily with the **machine-language level** of abstraction. One of the book's primary objectives is to relate this level to the high-level language level of abstraction. To a hardware designer, it is even more important to relate the machine-language level to lower levels of abstraction.

What lower levels are there? Obviously the hardware of the computer somehow has to execute an instruction like `add` or `imul`. The hardware level of a machine is often viewed as a collection of logic circuits, although you can take an even lower view of these as constructed with transistors, etc. For relatively simple architectures, electronic circuits can be designed to implement each possible instruction directly.

For more complex instruction sets, there is usually another level of abstraction between the machine language that the user sees and the digital circuitry of the machine. This **microcode level** consists of a collection of routines that actually implement the instructions. The microinstructions are normally stored in permanent memory in the CPU itself. A CPU that uses microcode has a collection of internal scratchpad registers that are not directly accessible to the user and simple circuitry such as an adder. A machine language instruction is implemented by a series of microinstructions that do have access to these scratchpad registers. Microcode resembles machine language. However, there are many differences. Microinstructions typically have bits that directly control circuits. Often there is no program counter—each instruction contains the address of the next instruction. In general, microprogramming is more complex than assembly language programming.

Chapter Summary

The Intel 80x86 `mov` instruction is used to copy data from one location to another. All but a few combinations of source and destination locations are allowed. The `xchg` instruction swaps the data stored at two locations.

The 80x86 architecture has a full set of instructions for arithmetic with byte-length, word-length, and doubleword-length integers. The `add` and `sub` instructions perform addition and subtraction; `inc` and `dec` add and subtract 1, respectively. The `neg` instruction negates its operand.

There are two multiplication and two division mnemonics. The `imul` and `idiv` instructions assume that their operands are signed 2's complement numbers; `mul` and `div` assume that their operands are unsigned. Many multiplication instructions start with single-length operands and produce double-length products; other formats form a product the same length as the factors. Division instructions always start with a double-length dividend and single-length divisor; the outcome is a single-length quotient and a single-length remainder. The cbw, cwd, and cdq instructions aid in producing a double-length dividend before signed division. Flag settings indicate possible errors during multiplication; an error during division produces a hardware exception that invokes a procedure to handle the error.

Instructions that have operands in registers are generally faster than those that reference memory locations. Multiplication and division instructions are slower than addition and subtraction instructions.

The adc and sbb instructions make it possible to add numbers longer than doublewords a group of bits at a time, incorporating a carry or borrow from one group into the addition or subtraction of the next group to the left. The carry or borrow is recorded in the carry flag CF. The 80x86 clc, stc, and cmc instructions enable the programmer to clear, set, and complement the carry flag when necessary.

The machine language level is just one level of abstraction at which a computer can be viewed. Above this level are the high-level language level and the application level. Below the machine language level are the microcode level and the hardware level.

CHAPTER 5

Branching and Looping

Computers derive much of their power from their ability to execute code selectively and from the speed at which they execute repetitive algorithms. Programs in high-level languages like Ada, C++, or Pascal use **if-then**, **if-then-else**, and **case** structures to execute code and loop structures selectively, such as **while** (pre-test) loops, **until** (post-test) loops, and **for** (counter-controlled) loops to repetitively execute code. Some high-level languages have a **goto** statement for unconditional branching. Somewhat more primitive languages (like older versions of BASIC) depend on fairly simple **if** statements and an abundance of **goto** statements for both selective execution and looping.

The 80x86 assembly language programmer's job is similar to the old BASIC programmer's job. The 80x86 microprocessor can execute some instructions that are roughly comparable to **for** statements, but most branching and looping is done with 80x86 statements that are similar to, but even more primitive than, simple **if** and **goto** statements. The objective of this chapter is to describe the machine implementation of language structures such as **if-then**, **if-then-else**, **while**, **until**, and **for**.

5.1 Unconditional Jumps

The 80x86 `jmp` (jump) instruction corresponds to **goto** in a high-level language. As coded in assembly language, `jmp` usually has the form

```
jmp     StatementLabel
```

where *StatementLabel* corresponds to the name field of some other assembly language statement. Recall that the name field is followed by a colon (:) when used to label an executable statement. The colon is not used in the `jmp` statement itself. As an example, if there were alternative conditions under which a program should be terminated, the code might contain

```
jmp     quit                    ; exit from program
        .
        .

quit:   INVOKE ExitProcess, 0   ; exit with return code 0
        .
        .
```

Figure 5.1 shows a complete example: a program that will input numbers repeatedly and, after each number is entered, display the count of the numbers so far, the cumulative sum, and the average. The program implements the following pseudocode design.

display instructions;
sum := 0;
count := 0;
forever loop
    prompt for number;
    input ASCII characters for number;
    convert number to 2's complement form;
    add number to sum;
    add 1 to count;
    convert count to ASCII;
    display label and count;
    convert sum to ASCII;
    display label and sum;
    average := sum / count;
    display label and average;
end loop;

```
; program to input numbers and display running average and sum
; author:  R. Detmer
; date:  revised 9/97


.386
.MODEL FLAT


INCLUDE io.h


cr          EQU    0dh    ; carriage return character
Lf          EQU    0ah    ; linefeed character


.STACK  4096               ; reserve 4096-byte stack


.DATA                      ; reserve storage for data
sum         DWORD    ?
explain     BYTE     cr,Lf,"As you input numbers one at a time, this",cr,Lf
            BYTE     "program will report the count of numbers so far,",cr,Lf
            BYTE     "the sum so far, and the average.",cr,Lf,Lf,0
prompt      BYTE     "number?  ",0
number      BYTE     16 DUP (?)
countLabel  BYTE     "count",0
sumLabel    BYTE     "      sum",0
avgLabel    BYTE     "        average",0
value       BYTE     11 DUP (?), 0
nextPrompt  BYTE     cr,Lf,Lf,"next ",0


.CODE                              ; start of main program code
_start:
            output explain         ; initial instructions
            mov    sum,0           ; sum := 0
            mov    ebx,0           ; count := 0


forever:    output prompt          ; prompt for number
            input  number,16       ; read ASCII characters
            atod   number          ; convert to integer

            add    sum,eax         ; add number to sum
            inc    ebx             ; add 1 to count
```

(continued)

Figure 5.1   Program with forever loop

```
            dtoa    value,ebx          ; convert count to ASCII
            output  countLabel         ; display label for count
            output  value              ; display count

            dtoa    value,sum          ; convert sum to ASCII
            output  sumLabel           ; display label for sum
            output  value              ; display sum

            mov     eax,sum            ; get sum
            cdq                        ; extend sum to 64 bits
            idiv    ebx                ; sum / count
            dtoa    value,eax          ; convert average to ASCII
            output  avgLabel           ; display label for average
            output  value              ; output average

            output  nextPrompt         ; skip down, start next prompt
            jmp     forever            ; repeat

PUBLIC _start                          ; make entry point public
            END
```

Figure 5.1   (continued)

This program must store values for *count* and *sum*, and all registers except EBX and ECX are used by the input/output macros and/or the division instruction. The value of *count* is kept in EBX, and *sum* is stored in a doubleword reserved in the data segment. Note that *sum* could have been initialized to zero by the DWORD directive instead of by the mov statement; as implemented, the code is more consistent with the design, but is slightly wasteful of time and space since *sum* only needs to be initialized once.

This program has several faults. One slight shortcoming is that it does not round the average. The major fault, however, is that it contains a **forever** loop with no way to get out. In fact, the usual termination code for a program is not even included since it could not be reached anyway. Fortunately there is a way to stop this program without turning off or resetting the computer; simply press control-C when the prompt for a number appears. This works because the input macro uses a Kernel32 service for input, and this function gives special treatment to control-C. Figure 5.2 shows a sample run of this program.

The one jmp in the program in Fig. 5.1 transfers control to a point that precedes the jmp statement itself. This is called a **backward reference**. The code

```
As you input numbers one at a time, this
program will report the count of numbers so far,
the sum so far, and the average.

number?   75
count          1        sum         75      average        75

next number?   93
count          2        sum        168      average        84

next number?   78
count          3        sum        246      average        82

next number?   (control-C pressed)
```

Figure 5.2 **Sample run of program**

```
        jmp     quit                    ; exit from program
                  .
                  .
        quit:   INVOKE ExitProcess, 0   ; exit with return code 0
```

illustrates a **forward reference**.

There are several 80x86 jmp instructions, in two major groups. All work by changing the value in the instruction pointer register EIP, so that the next instruction to be executed comes from a new address rather than from the address immediately following the current instruction. Jumps can be **intersegment**, changing the code segment register CS as well as EIP. However, this does not happen with flat memory model programming, so these instructions will not be covered. The **intrasegment** jumps are summarized in Fig. 5.3; the first two are the most commonly used.

Each relative jump instruction contains the displacement of the target from the jmp statement itself. This displacement is added to the address of the next instruction to find the address of the target. The displacement is a signed number, positive for a forward reference and negative for a backward reference. For the relative short version of the instruction, only a single byte of displacement is stored; this is changed to a sign-extended to a doubleword before the addition. The relative near format includes a 32-bit displacement.

Type	Clock Cycles 386	486	Pentium	Number of Bytes	Opcode
relative near	7+	3	1	5	E9
relative short	7+	3	1	2	EB
register indirect	10+	5	2	2	FF
memory indirect	10+	5	2	2+	FF

Figure 5.3 `jmp` **instructions**

The 8-bit displacement in an relative short jump can serve for a target statement up to 128 bytes before or 127 bytes after the `jmp` instruction. This displacement is measured from the byte following the object code of the `jmp` itself since at the time an instruction is being executed, EIP logically contains the address of the *next* instruction to be executed. The 32-bit displacement in a relative near jump instruction can serve for a target statement up to 2,147,483,648 bytes before or 2,147,483,647 bytes after the `jmp` instruction.

There is no difference in the coding for a relative short jump and for a relative near jump. The assembler uses a short jump if the target is within the small range in order to generate more compact code. A near jump is used automatically if the target is more than 128 bytes away.

The indirect jump instructions use a 32-bit address for the target rather than a displacement. However, this address is not encoded in the instruction itself. Instead, it is either in a register or in a memory doubleword. Thus the format

```
jmp    edx
```

means to jump to the address stored in EDX. The memory indirect format can use any valid reference to a doubleword of memory. If `Target` is declared as a DWORD in the data section, then

```
jmp    Target
```

jumps to the address stored in that doubleword, not to that point in the data section. Using register indirect addressing, you could have

```
jmp    DWORD PTR [ebx]
```

that causes a jump to the address stored at the doubleword whose address is in EBX!
Fortunately, these indirect forms are rarely needed.

Exercises 5.1

1. If the statement

   ```
   hardLoop:   jmp    hardLoop
   ```

   is executed, it continues to execute "forever." What is the object code
   for this statement?

2. Identify the type (relative near, relative short, register indirect, or memory indirect) of each jmp instruction in the following code fragment.

   ```
   .DATA
               . . .
   addrStore DWORD   ?
               . . .
   .CODE
               . . .
   doAgain:
               . . . (3 instructions)
               jmp  doAgain
               . . . (200 instructions)
               jmp  doAgain
               . . .
               jmp  addrStore
               . . .
               jmp  eax
               . . .
               jmp  [edi]
   ```

Programming Exercise 5.1

1. Modify the program in Fig. 5.1 so that the prompt rather than the
   response to it tells which number is being entered. That is, the sample
   run in Fig. 5.2 would be changed to

   ```
   As you input numbers one at a time, this program
   will report the sum so far and the average.
   ```

```
number          1 ?   10
sum       10          average        10


number          2 ?   50
sum       60          average        30
```

and so forth.

5.2 Conditional Jumps, Compare Instructions, and if Structures

Conditional jump instructions make it possible to implement `if` structures, other selection structures, and loop structures in 80x86 machine language. There are many of these instructions. Each has the format

```
j—      targetStatement
```

where the last part of the mnemonic identifies the condition under which the jump is to be executed. If the condition holds, then the jump takes place; otherwise, the next instruction (the one following the conditional jump) is executed.

With one exception (the `jcxz/jecxz` instruction, covered in Section 5.4), the "conditions" considered by the conditional jump instructions are settings of various flags in the flag registers. For example, the instruction

```
jz      endWhile
```

means to jump to the statement with label `endWhile` if the zero flag ZF is set to 1; otherwise fall through to the next statement.

Conditional jump instructions do not modify the flags; they only react to previously set flag values. Recall how the flags in the flag register get values in the first place. Some instructions (like `mov`) leave some or all flags unchanged, some (like `add`) explicitly set some flags according to the value of a result, and still others (like `div`) unpredictably alter some flags, leaving them with unknown values.

Suppose, for example, that the value in the EAX register is added to a sum representing an account balance, and three distinct treatments are needed, depending on whether the new balance is negative, zero, or positive. A pseudocode design for this could be

---

add value to balance;

if balance < 0
then
... { design for negative balance }
elseif balance = 0
then
... { design for zero balance }
else
... { design for positive balance }
end if;

The following 80x86 code fragment implements this design.

```
              add    balance,eax  ; add value to balance
              jns    elseIfZero   ; jump if balance not negative
              ...                 ; code for negative balance
              jmp    endBalanceCheck
elseIfZero:   jnz    elsePos      ; jump if balance not zero
              ...                 ; code for zero balance
              jmp    endBalanceCheck
elsePos:      ...                 ;code for positive balance

endBalanceCheck:
```

Appropriate flags are set or cleared by the add instruction. No other instruction shown in the above code fragment changes the flags. The design checks first for (balance < 0). The code does this with the instruction

```
    jns    elseIfZero
```

which says to jump to elseIfZero if the sign flag is not set; that is, if (balance < 0) is *not* true. The code following this instruction corresponds to statements following the first **then** in the design. The statement

```
    jmp    endBalanceCheck
```

at the end of this block of statements is necessary so that the CPU skips the statements that correspond to the other cases. If the first conditional jump transfers control to `elseIfZero`, then the balance must be non-negative. The design checks to see if the balance is zero; the instruction

```
elseIfZero: jnz    elsePos
```

jumps to `elsePos` if the zero flag ZF=0. The last instruction that set flags is the `add` at the beginning, so the jump occurs of the balance was not zero. The code for the (balance=0) case must again end with an unconditional jump to `endBalanceCheck`. Finally, the code that corresponds to the **else** in the design is at elsePos. This last block of code does not need a jump to `endBalanceCheck` since execution will fall through to this point.

The 80x86 code above directly corresponds to the order of statements in the design. If you are actually doing production coding in assembly language, a good technique is to initially code following a careful design and then reexamine the code to see if there are places where you can make it more efficient if there is a need to do so. This corresponds to what happens in many high-level language compilers. Most initially produce machine language that corresponds to the order of the high-level language statements being translated. Some compilers may then optimize the code, rearranging some statements for efficiency.

In the previous code, the label `endBalanceCheck` is on a line by itself. Technically this label will reference the address of whatever statement follows it, but it is far simpler to treat it as the part of the current design structure without worrying about what comes next. If what comes after this structure is changed, the code for this structure can remain the same. If the next statement requires another label, that is perfectly okay—multiple labels can reference the same spot in memory. Labels are not part of object code, so extra labels do not add to the length of object code or to execution time.

When writing code to mirror a design, one often wants to use labels like **if**, **then**, **else**, and **endif**. Unfortunately, **IF**, **ELSE**, and **ENDIF** are MASM directives, so they cannot be used as labels. In addition, **IF1**, **IF2**, and several other desirable labels are also reserved for use as directives. One solution is to use long descriptive labels like `elseIfZero` in the above example. Since no reserved word contains an underscore, another solution is to use labels like `if_1` and `endif_2` that parallel keywords in the original design.

The terms **set** a flag and **reset** a flag are often used to mean "give the value 1" to a flag and "give the value 0" to a flag, respectively. (Sometimes the word **clear** is used instead of reset.) As you have seen, many instructions set or reset flags. However, the `cmp` (compare) instructions are probably the most common way to establish flag values.

Each `cmp` instruction compares two operands and sets or resets AF, CF, OF, PF, SF, and ZF. The *only* job of a `cmp` instruction is to fix flag values; this is not just a side effect of some other function. Each has the form

```
cmp     operand1, operand2
```

A cmp executes by calculating *operand1* minus *operand2*, exactly like a sub instruction; the value of the difference and what happens in doing the subtraction determines the flag settings. A cmp instruction is unlike sub in that the value at the *operand1* location is not changed. The flags that are of most interest in this book are CF, OF, SF, and ZF. The carry flag CF is set if there is a borrow for the subtraction and reset if no borrow is required. The overflow flag OF is set if there is an overflow and reset otherwise. The sign flag SF is set if the difference represents a negative 2's complement number (the leading bit is one) and is reset if the number is zero or positive. Finally, the zero flag ZF is set if the difference is zero and is reset if it is nonzero.

Here are a few examples showing how the flags are set or reset when some representative byte length numbers are compared. Recall that the subtraction operation is the same for unsigned and signed (2's complement) values. Just as a single bit pattern can be interpreted as a unsigned number or a signed number, flag values have different interpretations after comparison of unsigned or signed values. The "interpretation" columns below show the relationship of the operands under both signed and unsigned interpretations.

What flag values characterize the relations equal, less than, and greater than? Equality is easy; the ZF flag is set if and only if *operand1* has the same value as *operand2* no matter whether the numbers are interpreted as signed or unsigned. This is illustrated by Example 1 below. Less than and greater than take a bit more analysis.

	operand1	operand2	difference	flags				interpretation	
				CF	OF	SF	ZF	signed	unsigned
1	3B	3B	00	0	0	0	1	*op1=op2*	*op1=op2*
2	3B	15	26	0	0	0	0	*op1>op2*	*op1>op2*
3	15	3B	DA	1	0	1	0	*op1<op2*	*op1<op2*
4	F9	F6	03	0	0	0	0	*op1>op2*	*op1>op2*
5	F6	F9	FD	1	0	1	0	*op1<op2*	*op1<op2*
6	15	F6	1F	1	0	0	0	*op1>op2*	*op1<op2*
7	F6	15	E1	0	0	1	0	*op1<op2*	*op1>op2*
8	68	A5	C3	1	1	1	0	*op1>op2*	*op1<op2*
9	A5	68	3D	0	1	0	0	*op1<op2*	*op1>op2*

When one first thinks about less than, it seems as if the carry flag should be set for a borrow whenever *operand1* is less than *operand2*. This logic is correct if one interprets the operands as unsigned numbers. Examples 3, 5, 6, and 8 all have *operand1* < *operand2* as unsigned numbers, and these are exactly the examples where CF=1. Therefore, for unsigned numbers, CF=0 means that *operand1* ≥ *operand2*. Strict inequality for unsigned numbers is characterized by CF=0 *and* ZF=0, that is *operand1* ≥ *operand2* and *operand1* ≠ *operand2*.

Examples 3, 5, 7, and 9 have *operand1* < *operand2* as signed numbers. What characterizes this situation is that SF≠OF. In the remaining examples, SF=OF, and *operand1* ≥ *operand2* are signed numbers. Strict inequality for unsigned numbers is characterized by SF=OF *and* ZF=0, that is *operand1* ≥ *operand2* and *operand1* ≠ *operand2*.

The cmp instructions are listed in Fig. 5.4. Looking back at Fig. 4.5, one sees that the entries in the various columns are almost all the same as for sub instructions. When the first operand is in memory, the cmp instructions require fewer clock cycles than corre-

Destination Operand	Source Operand	Clock Cycles			Number of Bytes	Opcode
		386	486	Pentium		
register 8	immediate 8	2	1	1	3	80
register 16	immediate 8	2	1	1	3	83
register 32	immediate 8	2	1	1	3	83
register 16	immediate 16	2	1	1	4	81
register 32	immediate 32	2	1	1	6	81
AL	immediate 8	2	1	1	2	3C
AX	immediate 16	2	1	1	3	3D
EAX	immediate 32	2	1	1	5	3D
memory byte	immediate 8	5	2	2	3+	80
memory word	immediate 8	5	2	2	3+	83
memory doubleword	immediate 8	5	2	2	3+	83
memory word	immediate 16	5	2	2	4+	81
memory doubleword	immediate 32	5	2	2	6+	81
register 8	register 8	2	1	1	2	38
register 16	register 16	2	1	1	2	3B
register 32	register 32	2	1	1	2	3B
register 8	memory byte	6	2	2	2+	3A
register 16	memory word	6	2	2	2+	3B
register 32	memory doubleword	6	2	2	2+	3B
memory byte	register 8	5	2	2	2+	38
memory word	register 16	5	2	2	2+	39
memory doubleword	register 32	5	2	2	2+	39

Figure 5.4 cmp instructions

sponding `sub` instructions since the result need not be stored. There are alternative opcodes for some operand combinations—the ones listed are those chosen by MASM 6.11.

A few reminders are in order about immediate operands. These can be coded in your choice of bases or as characters. Assuming that *pattern* references a word in the data segment, each of the following is allowable.

```
cmp     eax, 356
cmp     pattern, 0d3a6h
cmp     bh, '$'
```

Note that an immediate operand must be the second operand. The instruction

```
cmp     100, total      ; illegal
```

is not acceptable since the first operand is immediate.

Finally it is time to list the conditional jump instructions; they are shown in Fig. 5.5. Many of these have alternative mnemonics that generate exactly the same machine code; these describe the same set of conditions a different way. Often one mnemonic is more natural than the other for implementation of a given design.

Conditional jump instructions always compare the first operand to the second operand. For example, for the instruction `jg`, "jump if greater" means to jump if operand1 > operand2.

Appropriate for use after comparison of unsigned operands				
			opcode	
mnemonic	**description**	**flags to jump**	**short**	**near**
ja jnbe	jump if above jump if not below or equal	CF=0 and ZF=0	77	0F 87
jae jnb	jump if above or equal jump if not below	CF=0	73	0F 83
jb jnae	jump if below jump if not above or equal	CF=1	72	0F 82
jbe jna	jump if below or equal jump if not above	CF=1 or ZF=1	76	0F 86

(continued)

Figure 5.5   Conditional jump instructions

Appropriate for use after comparison of signed operands

			opcode	
mnemonic	description	flags to jump	short	near
jg	jump if greater	SF=OF and ZF=0	7F	OF 8F
jnle	jump if not less or equal			
jge	jump if greater or equal	SF=OF	7D	OF 8D
jnl	jump if not less			
jl	jump if less	SF≠OF	7C	OF 8C
jnge	jump if not greater or equal			
jle	jump if less or equal	SF≠OF or ZF=1	7E	OF 8E
jng	jump if not greater			

Other conditional jumps

			opcode	
mnemonic	description	flags to jump	short	near
je	jump if equal	ZF=1	74	OF 84
jz	jump if zero			
jne	jump if not equal	ZF=0	75	OF 85
jnz	jump if not zero			
js	jump if sign	SF=1	78	OF 88
jns	jump if not sign	SF=0	79	OF 89
jc	jump if carry	CF=1	72	OF 82
jnc	jump if not carry	CF=0	73	OF 83
jp	jump if parity	PF=1	7A	OF 8A
jpe	jump if parity even			
jnp	jump if not parity	PF=0	7B	OF 8B
jpo	jump if parity odd			
jo	jump if overflow	OF=1	70	OF 80
jno	jump if not overflow	OF=0	71	OF 81

Figure 5.5   (continued)

Each conditional jump instruction takes a single clock cycle for execution.

No conditional jump instruction changes any flag value. Each instruction has a short version and a near version. Just as with short unconditional jump instructions, a short conditional jump encodes a single-byte displacement and can transfer control 128 bytes before or 127 bytes after the address of the byte following the instruction itself. A short conditional jump requires two bytes of object code, one for the opcode and one for the displacement. A near conditional jump encodes a 32-bit displacement in addition to a two-byte opcode, giving a total length of six bytes. It can transfer control up to 2,147,483,648 bytes backward or 2,147,483,647 forward. The number of bytes and number of clock cycles for conditional jump instructions is summarized in Fig. 5.6.

One more pair of examples will illustrate the difference between the conditional jumps appropriate after comparison of signed and unsigned numbers. Suppose a value is stored in EAX and some action needs to be taken when that value is larger than 100. If the value is unsigned, one might code

```
cmp     eax, 100
ja      bigger
```

The jump would be chosen for any value bigger than 00000064_{16}, including values between 80000000_{16} and $FFFFFFFF_{16}$, which represent both large unsigned numbers and negative 2's complement numbers. If the value in EAX is interpreted as signed, then the instructions

```
cmp     ax,100
jg      bigger
```

	Clock Cycles			Number
	386	486	Pentium	of Bytes
short conditional jump	7+, 3	3, 1	1	2
near conditional jump	7+, 3	3, 1	1	6

For the 80386 and 80486 the longer time is when the jump is executed; the shorter time is for no jump.

Figure 5.6 Timing and size of conditional jump instructions

are appropriate. The jump will only be taken for values between 00000064 and 7FFFFFFF, not for those bit patterns that represent negative 2's complement numbers.

We now look at three examples showing implementation of **if** structures. The implementations are consistent with what a high-level language compiler would use. First consider the design

```
if value < 10
then
        add 1 to smallCount;
else
        add 1 to largeCount;
end if;
```

Suppose that *value* is stored in the EBX register and that *smallCount* and *largeCount* reference words in memory. The following 80x86 code implements this design.

```
            cmp   ebx, 10          ; value < 10 ?
            jnl   elseLarge
            inc   smallCount        ; add 1 to small_count
            jmp   endValueCheck
elseLarge:  inc   largeCount        ; add 1 to large_count
endValueCheck:
```

Note that this code is completely self-contained; you do not need to know what comes before or after in the overall design to implement this portion. You must have a plan for making labels, though, to avoid duplicates and reserved words. A compiler often produces a label consisting of a letter followed by a sequence number, but most of the time we can do better as humans writing code.

Now consider the design

```
if (total ≥ 100) or (count = 10)
then
        add value to total;
end if;
```

Assume that *total* and *value* reference doublewords in memory and that *count* is stored in the CX register. Here is assembly language code to implement this design.

```
            cmp   total, 100      ; total >= 100 ?
            jge   addValue
            cmp   cx, 10          ; count = 10 ?
            jne   endAddCheck
addValue:   mov   ebx, value      ; copy value
            add   total, ebx      ; add value to total
endAddCheck:
```

Notice that the design's **or** requires two cmp instructions. If either of the corresponding tests is passed, then the addition is performed. (Why was the addition done with two statements? Why not use add total,value?) This code implements a *short-cut or* — if the first condition is true, then the second is not checked at all. The code implemented for some languages always checks both operands of an **or** operation, even if the first is true.

Finally consider the design

---

if (count > 0) and (ch = backspace)
then
        subtract 1 from count;
end if;

For this third example, assume that *count* is in the CX register, *ch* is in the AL register and that *backspace* has been equated to 08_{16}, the ASCII backspace character. This design can be implemented as follows.

```
            cmp   cx, 0           ; count > 0 ?
            jng   endCheckCh
            cmp   al, backspace   ; ch a backspace?
            jne   endCheckCh
            dec   count           ; subtract 1 from count
endCheckCh:
```

This compound condition uses **and**, so both parts must be true in order to execute the action. This code implements a *short-cut and* — if the first condition is false, then the second is not checked at all. The code implemented for some languages always checks both operands of an **and** operation, even if the first is false.

This section ends with an example implementing a simple game program. The computer asks one player to enter a number. After it is typed in, the screen is cleared, and the other player tries to guess the number. After each guess the computer reports "too low," "too high," or "you got it." After the number is finally guessed, the number of attempts is reported, and the players are asked if they want to play another game. The pseudocode design in Fig. 5.7 gives a more precise description.

```
until response='N' or response='n' loop

    prompt first player for target;
    input target and convert to 2's complement form;
    clear screen;
    count := 0;

    until guess=target loop

        add 1 to count;
        prompt second player for guess;
        input guess and convert to 2's complement;

        if guess=target
        then
            display "you got it";
        elseif guess<target
        then
            display "too low";
        else
            display "too high";
        end if;

    end until;  { guess=target }

    convert count to ASCII;
    display count;
    display "Do you want to play again?";
    input response;

end until;  { response= 'N' or response='n' }
```

Figure 5.7   Design for game program

The assembly language source code for the game program is shown in Fig. 5.8. Note that screen is cleared by writing 24 line feed characters. The loop and selection structures in the program faithfully follow the design. Recall that an **until** loop is a

```
; program to implement number guessing game
; author:  R. Detmer
; date:  revised 9/97

.386
.MODEL FLAT

INCLUDE io.h

ExitProcess PROTO NEAR32 stdcall, dwExitCode:DWORD

cr              EQU    0dh    ; carriage return character
Lf              EQU    0ah    ; linefeed character

.STACK  4096                  ; reserve 4096-byte stack

.DATA                         ; reserve storage for data
prompt1       BYTE    cr,Lf,Lf,"Player 1, please enter a number:  ", 0
target        DWORD   ?
clear         BYTE    24 DUP (Lf), 0
prompt2       BYTE    cr,Lf,"Player 2, your guess?   ", 0
stringIn      BYTE    20 DUP (?)
lowOutput     BYTE    "too low", cr, Lf, 0
highOutput    BYTE    "too high", cr, Lf, 0
gotItOutput   BYTE    "you got it", cr, Lf, 0
countLabel    BYTE    Lf, "Number of guesses:"
countOut      BYTE    6 DUP (?)
              BYTE    cr, Lf, Lf, Lf, "Do you want to play again?   ",0

.CODE                                ; start of main program code
_start:

untilDone:  output prompt1          ; ask player 1 for target
            input  stringIn, 20      ; get number
```

(continued)

Figure 5.8   Game program

```
                atod    stringIn            ; convert to integer
                mov     target,eax          ; store target
                output  clear               ; clear screen
                mov     cx, 0               ; zero count

untilMatch: inc     cx                      ; increment count of guesses
                output  prompt2             ; ask player 2 for guess
                input   stringIn, 20        ; get number
                atod    stringIn            ; convert to integer

                cmp     eax, target         ; compare guess and target
                jne     ifLess              ; guess = target ?
equal:          output  gotItOutput         ; display "you got it"
                jmp     endCompare
ifLess:         jnl     isGreater           ; guess < target ?
                output  lowOutput           ; display "too low"
                jmp     endCompare
isGreater:  output  highOutput              ; display "too high"
endCompare:
                cmp     eax, target         ; compare guess and target
                jne     untilMatch          ; ask again if guess not = target

                itoa    countOut, cx        ; convert count to ASCII
                output  countLabel          ; display label, count and prompt
                input   stringIn, 20        ; get response
                cmp     stringIn, 'n'       ; response = 'n' ?
                je      endUntilDone        ; exit if so
                cmp     stringIn, 'N'       ; response = 'N' ?
                jne     untilDone           ; repeat if not
endUntilDone:

                INVOKE ExitProcess, 0       ; exit with return code 0

PUBLIC _start                               ; make entry point public
                END                         ; end of source code
```

Figure 5.8 (continued)

post-test loop. The next section carefully describes how to implement both **until** and **while** loops.

The outside **until** loop in the game program is terminated by either a "N" or "n" response to a query to the players. The input macro is used to get the response in the same input area as used for numbers earlier. Since the address of a multibyte object is the address of its first byte, the instruction

```
cmp     stringIn, 'n'    ; response = 'n' ?
```

is really comparing the first (and probably only) character of input to the letter "n". This is not a comparison of two strings.

Exercises 5.2

1. Assume for each part of this problem that the EAX register contains 00 00 00 4F and the doubleword referenced by *value* contains FF FF FF 38. Determine whether or not each of the conditional jump statements causes a jump to *dest*.

   (a) `cmp     eax, value`
       `jl      dest`

   (b) `cmp     eax, value`
       `jb      dest`

   (c) `cmp     eax, 04fh`
       `je      dest`

   (d) `cmp     eax, 79`
       `jne     dest`

   (e) `cmp     value, 0`
       `jbe     dest`

   (f) `cmp     value, -200`
       `jge     dest`

   (g) `add     eax, 200`
       `js      dest`

   (h) `add     value, 200`
       `jz      dest`

2. Each part of this problem gives a design with an **if** structure and some assumptions about how the variables are stored in an assembly language program. Give a fragment of assembly language code that implements the design.

   (a) design:
       if count = 0
       then
           count := value;
       end if;

   Assumptions: *count* is in ECX; *value* references a doubleword in memory

   (b) design:
       if count > value
       then
           count := 0;
       end if;

Assumptions: *count* is in ECX; *value* references a doubleword in memory

(c) design:

    if a + b = c
    then
        check := 'Y';
    else
        check := 'N';
    end if;

Assumptions: each of *a*, *b*, and *c* references a doubleword in memory; the character *check* is in the AL register

(d) design:

    if (value ≤ −1000) or (value ≥ 1000)
    then
        value := 0;
    end if;

Assumption: *value* is in EDX

(e) design:

    if (ch ≥ 'a') and (ch ≤ 'z')
    then
        add 1 to lowerCount;
    else
        if (ch ≥ 'A') and (ch ≤ 'Z')
        then
            add 1 to upperCount;
        else
            add 1 to otherCount;
        end if;
    end if;

Assumptions: *ch* is in AL; each of *lowerCount*, *upperCount*, and *otherCount* references a doubleword in memory

Programming Exercises 5.2

1. Modify the game program to accept only numbers between 0 and 1000 from either player. A design for the new code section is

```
        until (value ≥ 0) and (value ≤ 1000) loop
            input value and convert to 2's complement;
            if (value < 0) or (value > 1000)
            then
                display "enter value 0 to 1000";
            end if;
        end until;
```

2. Modify the game program so that it only allows Player 2 five attempts at guessing the number entered by Player 1. If the fifth attempt is incorrect, display "Sorry, the number is *value of target*" and proceed to asking the players if they want another game.

5.3   Implementing Loop Structures

Most programs contain loops. Commonly used loop structures include **while**, **until**, and **for** loops. This section describes how to implement all three of these structures in 80x86 assembly language. The next section describes additional instructions that can be used to implement **for** loops.

A **while** loop can be indicated by the following pseudocode design.

```
while continuation condition loop
    ... { body of loop }
end while;
```

The *continuation condition*, a Boolean expression, is checked first. If it is true, then the body of the loop is executed. The continuation condition is then checked again. Whenever the value of the Boolean expression is false, execution continues with the statement following **end while**.

An 80x86 implementation of a **while** loop follows a pattern much like this one.

```
while:          .           ; code to check Boolean expression
                .
                .
body:           .           ; loop body
                .
                .
                jmp  while   ; go check condition again
endWhile:
```

It often takes several statements to check the value of the Boolean expression. If it is determined that the value is false, then there will be a jump to *endWhile*. If it is determined that the continuation condition is true, then the code will either fall through to body or there will be a jump to its label. Notice that the body of the loop ends with a `jmp` to go check the condition again. Two common mistakes are to omit this jump or to jump to the body instead.

The label *while* in this model is not allowed in actual code since `while` is a reserved word in MASM. In fact, MASM 6.11 has a `while` directive that simplifies writing code for **while** loops. It is not used in this book since our main concern is understanding how structures are implemented at the machine language level.

For an example, suppose that the design

```
while (sum < 1000) loop
      ... { body of loop }
end while;
```

is to be coded in 80x86 assembly language. Assuming that *sum* references a doubleword in memory, one possible implementation is

```
whileSum:    cmp    sum, 1000      ; sum < 1000?
             jnl    endWhileSum    ; exit loop if not
              .                    ; body of loop
              .
              .
             jmp    whileSum       ; go check condition again
endWhileSum:
```

The statement

```
        jnl    endWhileSum
```

directly implements the design. An alternative would be to use

```
        jge    endWhileSum
```

which transfers control to the end of the loop if *sum* $\geq$ 1000. This works since the inequality (*sum* $\geq$ 1000) will be true exactly when the (*sum* < 1000) is false, but the `jnl` mnemonic makes it easier to implement the design without having to reverse the inequality.

For a short example showing a complete loop body, suppose that the integer base 2 logarithm of a positive number needs to be determined. The integer base 2 logarithm of a number is the largest integer x such that

$$2^x \leq \text{number}$$

The following design does the job.

---

x := 0;
twoToX := 1;
while twoToX ≤ number
    multiply twoToX by 2;
    add 1 to x;
end while;
subtract 1 from x;

Assuming that *number* references a doubleword in memory, the following 80x86 code implements the design, using the EAX register for *twoToX* and the CX register for *x*.

```
                mov    cx, 0        ; x := 0
                mov    eax, 1       ; twoToX := 1
    whileLE:    cmp    eax, number  ; twoToX <= number?
                jnle   endWhileLE   ; exit if not
    body:       add    eax, eax     ; multiply twoToX by 2
                inc    cx           ; add 1 to x
                jmp    whileLE      ; go check condition again
    endWhileLE:
                dec    cx           ; subtract 1 from x
```

Often the continuation condition in a **while** is compound, having two parts connected by Boolean operators **and** or **or**. Both operands of an **and** must be true for a true conjunction. With an **or**, the only way the disjunction can be false is if both operands are false.

Changing a previous example to include a compound condition, suppose that the following design is to be coded.

---

while (sum < 1000) and (count ≤ 24) loop
    ... { body of loop }
end while;

Assuming that *sum* references a doubleword in memory and the value of *count* is in CX, an implementation is

```
whileSum:    cmp    sum, 1000        ; sum < 1000?
             jnl    endWhileSum      ; exit if not
             cmp    cx, 24           ; count <= 24
             jnle   endWhileSum      ; exit if not
               .                     ; body of loop
               .
               .
             jmp    whileSum         ; go check condition again
endWhileSum:
```

Modifying the example another time, here is a design with an **or** instead of an **and**.

---
while (sum < 1000) or (flag = 1) loop
    ... { body of loop }
end while;

This time, assume that *sum* is in the EAX register and that *flag* is a single byte in the DH register. Here is 80x86 code that implements the design.

```
whileSum:    cmp    eax, 1000        ; sum < 1000?
             jl     body             ; execute body if so
             cmp    dh,1             ; flag = 1?
             jne    endWhileSum      ; exit if not
body:          .                     ; body of loop
               .
               .
             jmp    whileSum         ; go check condition again
endWhileSum:
```

Notice the difference in the previous two examples. For an **and** the loop is *exited* if either operand of the compound condition is *false*. For an **or** the loop body is *executed* if either operand of the compound condition is *true*.

Sometimes processing in a loop is to continue while normal values are encountered and to terminate when some sentinel value is encountered. If data are being entered from the keyboard, this design can be written

```
get value from keyboard;
while (value is not sentinel) loop
      ... { body of loop }
      get value from keyboard;
end while;
```

In some high-level languages, implementation code must exactly parallel this design. One of the advantages of assembly language is that one has more flexibility. An equivalent design is

```
while (value entered from keyboard is not sentinel) loop
      ... { body of loop }
end while;
```

This design does not require two separate instructions to input data. It can be coded in some high-level languages and also in 80x86 assembly language.

For a concrete example illustrating implementation of such a design, suppose that non-negative numbers entered at the keyboard are to be added, with any negative entry serving as a sentinel value. A design looks like

```
sum := 0;
while (number keyed in is not negative) loop
      add number to sum;
end while;
```

Assuming appropriate definitions in the data segment, the 80x86 code could be

```
            mov     ebx, 0          ; sum := 0
whileNotNeg: output prompt          ; prompt for input
            input   number,10       ; get number from keyboard
            atod    number          ; convert to 2's complement
            js      endWhile        ; exit if negative
```

```
                    add     ebx, eax        ; add number to sum
                    jmp     whileNotNeg     ; go get next number
        endWhile:
```

Recall that the `atod` macro affects the sign flag SF, setting it if the ASCII characters are converted to a negative number in the EAX register and clearing it otherwise.

The body of a **for** loop, a counter-controlled loop, is executed once for each value of a loop index (or counter) in a given range. In some high-level languages, the loop index can be some type other than integer; in assembly language the index is usually an integer. A **for** loop can be described by the following pseudocode.

```
for index := initialValue to finalValue loop
        ... { body of loop }
end for;
```

A **for** loop can easily be translated into a **while** structure.

```
index := initialValue;
while index ≤ finalValue loop
        ... { body of loop }
        add 1 to index;
end while;
```

Such a **while** is readily coded in 80x86 assembly language.

As an example, suppose that a collection of numbers needs to be added and no value is convenient as a sentinel. Then one might want to ask a user how many numbers are to be entered and loop for that many entries. The design looks like

```
prompt for tally of numbers;
input tally;
sum := 0
for count := 1 to tally loop
        prompt for number;
        input number;
        add number to sum;
end for;
```

Making straightforward assumptions about definitions in the data segment, here is an 80x86 implementation of the design.

```
            output prompt1         ; prompt for tally
            input  value, 20       ; get tally (ASCII)
            atoi   value           ; convert to 2's complement
            mov    tally, ax       ; store tally

            mov    edx, 0          ; sum := 0
            mov    bx, 1           ; count := 1

forCount:   cmp    bx, tally       ; count <= tally?
            jnle   endFor          ; exit if not
            output prompt2         ; prompt for number
            input  value, 20       ; get number (ASCII)
            atod   value           ; convert to 2's complement
            add    edx, eax        ; add number to sum
            inc    bx              ; add 1 to count
            jmp    forCount        ; repeat
endFor:
```

In a **for** loop implementation where one is sure that the body of the loop will be executed at least once (i.e., *initialValue* ≤ *finalValue*), one can check the index against the final value at the end of the loop body rather than prior to the body. Other variations are also possible. Additional instructions for implementing **for** loops will be covered in Section 5.4.

You have already seen examples of **until** loops. In general, an **until** loop can be expressed as follows in pseudocode.

---
until *termination condition* loop
　　... { body of loop }
end until;

The body of the loop is executed at least once; then the termination condition is checked. If it is false, then the body of the loop is executed again; if true, execution continues with the statement following **end until**.

An 80x86 implementation of an **until** loop usually looks like the following code fragment.

```
until:        .              ; start of loop body
        .             .
        .             .
              .              ; code to check termination condition
endUntil:
```

If the code to check the termination condition determines that the value is *false*, then there will be a jump to *until*. If it is determined that the value is *true*, then the code will either fall through to *endUntil* or there will be a jump to that label.

The game program implemented in Fig. 5.8 contained two simple **until** loops. Here is an example with a compound terminating condition. Given the design

```
count := 0;
until (sum > 1000) or (count = 100) loop
        ... { body of loop }
        add 1 to count;
end until;
```

the following 80x86 code provides an implementation. Assume that *sum* references a word in the data segment and that *count* is stored in CX.

```
              mov    cx, 0        ; count := 0
until:          .                 ; body of loop
                .
                .
              inc    cx           ; add 1 to count
              cmp    sum, 1000    ; sum > 1000 ?
              jg     endUntil     ; exit if sum > 1000
              cmp    cx, 100      ; count = 100 ?
              jne    until        ; continue if count not = 100
endUntil:
```

Other loop structures can also be coded in assembly language. The **forever** loop is frequently useful. As it appears in pseudocode, it almost always has an **exit loop** statement to transfer control to the end of the loop; this is often conditional—that is, in an **if** statement. Here is a fragment of a typical design.

---

forever loop

.

.

.

if (response = 's') or (response = 'S')
then
        exit loop;
end if;

.

.

.

end loop;

Assuming that the value of *response* is in the AL register, this can be implemented as follows in 80x86 assembly language.

```
        forever:      .

                      .

                      .

                cmp   al, 's'        ; response = 's'?
                je    endLoop        ; exit loop if so
                cmp   al, 'S'        ; response = 'S'?
                je    endLoop        ; exit loop if so

                      .

                      .

                      .

                jmp   forever        ; repeat loop body
        endLoop:
```

Exercises 5.3

1. Each part of this problem contains a design with a **while** loop. Assume that *sum* references a doubleword in the data segment and that the value of *count* is in the ECX register. Give a fragment of 80x86 code that implements the design.

    (a) sum := 0;
         count := 1;

```
          while (sum < 1000) loop
             add count to sum;
             add 1 to count;
          end while;
   (b)  sum := 0;
        count := 1;
        while (sum < 1000) and (count ≤ 50) loop
           add count to sum;
           add 1 to count;
        end while;
   (c)  sum := 0;
        count := 100;
        while (sum < 1000) or (count ≥ 0) loop
           add count to sum;
           subtract 1 from count;
        end while;
```

2. Each part of this problem contains a design with a **until** loop. Assume that **sum** references a doubleword in the data segment and that the value of *count* is in the ECX register. Give a fragment of 80x86 code that implements the design.

```
   (a)  sum := 0;
        count := 1;
        until (sum > 5000) loop
           add count to sum;
           add 1 to count;
        end until;
   (b)  sum := 0;
        count := 1;
        until (sum > 5000) or (count = 40) loop
           add count to sum;
           add 1 to count;
        end until;
   (c)  sum := 0;
        count := 1;
        until (sum ≥ 5000) and (count > 40) loop
           add count to sum;
           add 1 to count;
        end until;
```

3. Each part of this problem contains a design with a **for** loop. Assume that *sum* references a doubleword in the data segment and that the value of *count* is in the ECX register. Give a fragment of 80x86 code that implements the design.

(a) sum := 0;
    for count := 1 to 100 loop
      add count to sum;
    end for;

(b) sum := 0;
    for count := –10 to 50 loop
      add count to sum;
    end for;

(c) sum := 1000;
    for count := 100 downto 50 loop
      subtract 2*count from sum;
    end for;

Programming Exercises 5.3

1. Write a complete 80x86 assembly language program that will accept numbers from the keyboard and report the minimum and maximum of the numbers. Implement the following design, adding appropriate labels to output.

```
display "First number?  ";
input number;
minimum := number;
maximum := number;
while (response to "Another number? " is 'Y' or 'y') loop
    input number;
    if (number < minimum)
    then
        minimum := number;
    end if;
    if (number > maximum)
    then
        maximum := number;
    end if;
end while;
```

display the minimum value;
display the maximum value;

2. Write a complete 80x86 assembly language program that will accept numbers from the keyboard and report the sum and average of the numbers. The count of numbers is not known in advance; use the value −999999 as a sentinel to terminate input. Implement the following design, adding appropriate prompts for input and labels for output.

sum := 0;
count := 0;

while (number entered from keyboard ≠ −999999) loop
    add number to sum;
    add 1 to count;
end while;

if (count = 0)
then
    display "No numbers entered";
else
    average := sum/count;
    display sum and average;
end if;

3. Write a complete 80x86 assembly language program to help your overworked instructor analyze examination grades. The program will input an unknown number of examination grades, using any negative grade as a sentinel, and then report the number of As (90–100), Bs (80–89), Cs (70–79), Ds (60–69), and Fs (under 60). Implement the following design. Prompt for input as appropriate.

ACount := 0;
BCount := 0;
CCount := 0;
DCount := 0;
FCount := 0;

while (grade entered at keyboard ≥ 0) loop
    if (grade ≥ 90)

```
    then
        add 1 to ACount;
    elseif (grade ≥ 80)
    then
        add 1 to BCount;
    elseif (grade ≥ 70)
    then
        add 1 to CCount;
    elseif (grade ≥ 60)
    then
        add 1 to DCount;
    else
        add 1 to FCount;
    end if;
end while;

display "Number of As", ACount;
display "Number of Bs", BCount;
display "Number of Cs", CCount;
display "Number of Ds", DCount;
display "Number of Fs", FCount;
```

4. The greatest common divisor of two non-negative integers is the largest integer that evenly divides both numbers. The following algorithm will find the greatest common divisor of *number1* and *number2*.

```
gcd := number1;
remainder := number2;

until (remainder = 0) loop
    dividend := gcd;
    gcd := remainder;
    remainder := dividend mod gcd;
end until;
```

Write a complete 80x86 assembly language program that implements the following design, with appropriate prompts for input and labels for output.

```
until (number1 > 0) loop
    input number1;
```

```
    end until;

    until (number2 > 0) loop
        input number2;
    end until;

    find gcd of number1 and number2;   (see design above)
    display gcd;
```

5. Write a complete 80x86 assembly language program to simulate a simple calculator. The calculator does addition and subtraction operations and also accepts commands to clear the accumulated value or to quit. Implement the following design.

```
total := 0;

forever loop
    display "number? ";
    input number;

    display "action (+, -, c or q) ? ";
    input action;

    if (action = '+')
    then
        add number to total;
    elseif (action = '-')
    then
        subtract number from total;
    elseif (action = 'c') or (action = 'C')
    then
        total := 0;
    elseif (action = 'q') or (action = 'Q')
    then
        exit loop;
    else
        display "Unknown action";
```

```
    end if;

    display "total", total;
end loop;
```

5.4   for Loops in Assembly Language

Often the number of times the body of a loop must be executed is known in advance, either as a constant that can be coded when a program is written, or as the value of a variable that is assigned before the loop is executed. The **for** loop structure is ideal for coding such a loop.

The previous section showed how to translate a **for** loop into a **while** loop. This technique always works and is frequently the best way to code a **for** loop. However, the 80x86 microprocessor has instructions that make coding certain **for** loops very easy.

Consider the following two **for** loops, the first of which counts forward and the second of which counts backward.

```
for index := 1 to count loop
    ... { body of loop }
end for;
```

and

```
for index := count downto 1 loop
    ... { body of loop }
end for;
```

The body of each loop executes *count* times. If the value of *index* is not needed for display or for calculations within the body of the loop, then the loop that counts down is equivalent to the loop that counts up, although the design may not be as natural. Backward **for** loops are very easy to implement in 80x86 assembly language with the `loop` instruction.

The `loop` instruction has the format

```
loop    statementLabel
```

where *statementLabel* is the label of a statement that is a short displacement (128 bytes backward or 127 bytes forward) from the loop instruction. The loop instruction causes the following actions to take place:

- the value in ECX is decremented
- if the new value in ECX is zero, then execution continues with the statement following the loop instruction
- if the new value in ECX is nonzero, then a jump to the instruction at *statementLabel* takes place

In addition to the loop instruction, there are two conditional loop instructions that are less frequently used. Features of all three instructions are summarized in Fig. 5.9. Each requires two bytes of object code; the first byte is the opcode and the second byte is the displacement to the destination statement. Two times are given for 80486 and Pentium instructions, the first showing how many clock cycles are required if the jump is not taken, and the second showing how many clock cycles are required if it is taken. The situation is more complex for the 80386, but it also has two distinct execution times. None of these instructions changes any flag.

Although the ECX register is a general register, it has a special place as a counter in the loop instruction and in several other instructions. No other register can be substituted for ECX in these instructions. In practice this often means that when a loop is coded, either ECX is not used for other purposes or a counter value is put in ECX before a loop instruction is executed but is saved elsewhere to free ECX for other uses for most of the body of the loop.

The backward **for** loop structure

```
for count := 20 downto 1 loop
    ... { body of loop }
end for;
```

Mnemonic	Clock Cycles			Number of Bytes	Opcode
	386	486	Pentium		
loop	11+	6/7	5/6	2	E2
loope/loopz	11+	6/9	7/8	2	E1
loopne/loopnz	11+	6/9	7/8	2	E0

Figure 5.9   loop instructions

can be coded as follows in 80x86 assembly language.

```
              mov    ecx, 20        ; number of iterations
    forCount:    .                  ; body of loop
                 .
                 .
              loop   forCount       ; repeat body 20 times
```

The counter in the ECX register will be 20 the first time the body of the loop is executed and will be decremented to 19 by the `loop` instruction. The value 19 is not zero, so control transfers to the start of the loop body at label `forCount`. The second time the body of the loop is executed, the ECX register will contain 19. The last time the value in ECX will be one; it will be decremented to zero by the loop instruction, and the jump to `forCount` will not be taken.

The obvious label to mark the body of a **for** loop is `for`. Unfortunately this is a reserved word in MASM. It is used for a directive that simplifies coding of **for** loops. Again, our primary interest is in learning how the computer works at the machine level, so this directive will not be used.

Now suppose that the doubleword in memory referenced by *number* contains the number of times a loop is to be executed. The 80x86 code to implement a backward **for** loop could be

```
              mov    ecx, number    ; number of iterations
    forIndex:    .                  ; body of loop
                 .
                 .
              loop   forIndex       ; repeat body number times
```

This is safe code only if the value stored at *number* is not zero. If it is zero, then the loop body is executed, the zero value is decremented to FFFFFFFF (a borrow is required to do the subtraction), the loop body is executed again, the value FFFFFFFF is decremented to FFFFFFFE, and so forth. The body of the loop is executed 4,294,967,296 times before the value in ECX gets back down to zero! To avoid this problem, one could code

```
                 mov    ecx, number    ; number of iterations
                 cmp    ecx, 0         ; number = 0 ?
                 je     endFor         ; skip loop if number = 0
       forIndex:    .                  ; body of loop
                    .
                    .
```

```
                    loop   forIndex      ; repeat body number times
          endFor:
```

If *number* is a signed value and might be negative, then

```
          jle   endFor       ; skip loop if number <= 0
```

is a more appropriate conditional jump.

There is another way to guard a **for** loop so that it is not executed when the value in ECX is zero. The 80x86 instruction set has a jecxz conditional jump instruction that jumps to its destination if the value in the ECX register is zero. Using the jecxz instruction, the example above can be coded as

```
                    mov    ecx, number   ; number of iterations
                    jecxz endFor         ; skip loop if number = 0
          forIndex:      .               ; body of loop
                         .
                         .

                    loop   forIndex      ; repeat body number times
          endFor:
```

There is also a jcxz instruction that checks the CX register rather than the ECX register. Both instructions are two bytes long, the opcode E3 plus a single-byte displacement; the prefix byte 67 distinguishes between the 16-bit size and the 32-bit versions. Like the other conditional jump instructions, jcxz/jecxz affects no flag value. They do take longer to execute, six clock cycles on a Pentium if the jump takes place (if the value in ECX is zero), and five clock cycles to fall through to the next statement otherwise.

The jecxz instruction can be used to code a backward **for** loop when the loop body is longer than 127 bytes, too large for the loop instruction's single-byte displacement. For example, the structure

---

for counter := 50 downto 1 loop
   ... { body of loop }
end for;

---

could be coded as

```
          mov    ecx, 50        ; number of iterations
forCounter:    .                ; body of loop
               .

               .

          dec    ecx            ; decrement loop counter
          jecxz  endFor         ; exit if counter = 0
          jmp    forCounter     ; otherwise repeat body
endFor:
```

However, since the `dec` instruction sets or resets the zero flag ZF, the faster conditional jump

```
jz   endFor
```

can be used instead of the `jecxz` instruction.

It is often convenient to use a `loop` statement to implement a **for** loop, even when the loop index increases and must be used within the body of the loop. The `loop` statement uses ECX to control the number of iterations, while a separate counter serves as the loop index.

For example, to implement the **for** loop

---

for index := 1 to 50 loop
        ...{ loop body using index }
end for;

---

the EBX register might be used to store *index* counting from 1 to 50 while the ECX register counts down from 50 to 1.

```
          mov    ebx, 1      ; index := 1
          mov    ecx, 50     ; number of iterations for loop
forNbr:    .
           .                 ; use value in EBX for index
           .

          inc    ebx         ; add 1 to index
          loop   forNbr      ; repeat
```

Figure 5.9 listed two variants of the `loop` instruction, `loopz/loope` and `loopnz/loopne`. Each of these work like `loop`, decrementing the counter in ECX. However, each examines the value of the zero flag ZF as well as the new value in the ECX register to decide whether or not to jump to the destination location. The `loopz/loope` instruction jumps if the new value in ECX is nonzero and the zero flag is set (ZF=1). The `loopnz/loopne` instruction jumps if the new value in ECX is nonzero and the zero flag is clear (ZF=0).

The `loopz` and `loopnz` instructions are useful in special circumstances. Some programming languages allow loop structures such as

```
for year := 10 downto 1 until balance = 0 loop
    ... { body of loop }
end for;
```

This confusing structure means to terminate loop execution using whichever loop control is satisfied first. That is, the body of the loop is executed 10 times (for year = 10, 9,...,1) unless the condition *balance = 0* is true at the bottom of some execution of the loop body, in which case the loop terminates with fewer than 10 iterations. If the value of balance is in the EBX register, the following 80x86 code could be used.

```
            mov     ecx, 10 ; maximum number of iterations
forYear:    .               ; body of loop

            .

            .

            cmp     ebx, 0  ; balance = 0 ?
            loopne forYear  ; repeat 10 times if balance not 0
```

Exercises 5.4

1. Each part of this problem has a **for** loop implemented with a `loop` statement. How many times is each loop body executed?

    (a)
```
            mov   ecx, 10
forA:       .

            .                       ; body of loop

            .

            loop forA
```

(b)
```
        mov   ecx, 1
   forB:   .
             .              ; body of loop
             .
        loop forB
```

(c)
```
        mov   ecx, 0
   forC:   .
             .              ; body of loop
             .
        loop forC
```

(d)
```
        mov   ecx, -1
   forD:   .
             .              ; body of loop
             .
        loop forD
```

2. Each part of this problem contains a design with a **for** loop. Assume that *sum* references a doubleword in the data segment. Give a fragment of 80x86 code that uses a loop statement to implement the design. Use the dtoa and output macros for display, assuming that the data segment contains

```
ASCIIcount   BYTE   11 DUP (?)
ASCIIsum     BYTE   11 DUP (?)
             BYTE   13, 10, 0    ; carriage return, linefeed
```

(a) sum := 0;
     for count := 50 downto 1 loop
         add count to sum;
         display count, sum;
     end for;

(b) sum := 0;
     for count := 1 to 50 loop
         add count to sum;
         display count, sum;
     end for;

   (c) sum := 0;
        for count := 1 to 50 loop
            add (2*count − 1) to sum;
            display count, sum;
        end for;

Programming Exercises 5.4

1. Write a complete 80x86 program to input a positive integer value N and to display a table of integers from 1 to N and their squares. Use a two-column format such as

```
number       square

   1            1
   2            4
   3            9
   4            16
   5            25
```

2. A Pythagorean triple consists of three positive integers A, B, and C such that $A^2 + B^2 = C^2$. For example, the numbers 3, 4, and 5 form a Pythagorean triple since $9 + 16 = 25$. Write a complete 80x86 program to input a value for C and then display all possible Pythagorean triples with this value for C, if any. For example, if 5 is entered for the value of C, then the output might be

```
A           B           C
3           4           5
4           3           5
```

5.5 Arrays

Programs frequently use arrays to store collections of data values. Loops are commonly used to manipulate the data in arrays. This section shows one way to access 1-dimensional arrays in 80x86 assembly language; other techniques will appear in Chapter 9 with discussion of additional memory addressing modes.

    This section contains a complete program to implement the design below. The program first accepts a collection of positive numbers from the keyboard, counting them and storing them in an array. It then calculates the average of the numbers by going back through the numbers stored in the array, accumulating the total in *sum*. Finally the numbers in the array are scanned again, and this time the numbers larger than the average are displayed. The first two loops could be combined, of course, with the sum being accumulated as the numbers are keyed in. As a general programming philosophy, clearer code results from separating tasks; they should be combined only if there is a real need to save execution time or bytes of object code.

```
nbrElts := 0;              { input numbers into array }
get address of first item of array;

while (number from keyboard > 0) loop
    convert number to 2's complement;
    store number at address in array;
    add 1 to nbrElts;
    get address of next item of array;
end while;

sum := 0;                  { find sum and average }
get address of first item of array;

for count := nbrElts downto 1 loop
    add doubleword at address in array to sum;
    get address of next item of array;
end for;

average := sum/nbrElts;
display average;

get address of first item of array;  { list big numbers }

for count := nbrElts downto 1 loop
    if doubleword of array > average
    then
        convert doubleword to ASCII;
        display value;
    end if;
    get address of next item of array;
end for;
```

This design contains the curious instructions "get address of first item of array" and "get address of next item of array." These reflect the particular assembly language implementation, one which works well if the task at hand involves moving sequentially through an array. The 80x86 feature which makes this possible is register indirect addressing, first discussed in Chapter 3. The example will use the EBX register to contain the address of the word currently being accessed; then [ebx] references the double-word at the address in the EBX register rather than the doubleword in the register itself. In the 80x86 architecture any of the general registers EAX, EBX, ECX, and EDX or the index registers EDI and ESI are appropriate for use as a "pointer." The ESI and EDI registers are often reserved for use with strings, which are usually arrays of characters. String operations are covered in Chapter 7. The program listing appears in Fig. 5.10.

```
; input a collection of numbers
; report their average and the numbers which are above average
; author:  R. Detmer
; date:  revised 9/97


.386
.MODEL FLAT

INCLUDE io.h

ExitProcess PROTO NEAR32 stdcall, dwExitCode:DWORD

cr          EQU    0dh    ; carriage return character
Lf          EQU    0ah    ; linefeed character
maxNbrs     EQU    100    ; size of number array


.STACK      4096

.DATA
directions  BYTE       cr, Lf, 'You may enter up to 100 numbers'
            BYTE       ' one at a time.',cr,Lf
            BYTE       'Use any negative number to terminate
                       input.',cr,Lf,Lf
            BYTE       'This program will then report the average and
                       list',cr,Lf
            BYTE       'those numbers which are above the
                       average.',cr,Lf,Lf,Lf,0
prompt      BYTE       'Number?  ',0
number      BYTE       20 DUP (?)
nbrArray    DWORD      maxNbrs DUP (?)
nbrElts     DWORD      ?
avgLabel    BYTE       cr,Lf,Lf,'The average is'
```

(continued)

Figure 5.10   **Program using array**

```
outValue        BYTE        11 DUP (?), cr,Lf,0
aboveLabel      BYTE        cr,Lf,'Above average:',cr,Lf,Lf,0

.CODE
_start:
; input numbers into array

                output directions     ; display directions
                mov    nbrElts,0      ; nbrElts := 0
                lea    ebx,nbrArray   ; get address of nbrArray

whilePos:       output prompt         ; prompt for number
                input  number,20      ; get number
                atod   number         ; convert to integer
                jng    endWhile       ; exit if not positive
                mov    [ebx],eax      ; store number in array
                inc    nbrElts        ; add 1 to nbrElts
                add    ebx,4          ; get address of next item of array
                jmp    whilePos       ; repeat
endWhile:

; find sum and average

                mov    eax,0          ; sum := 0
                lea    ebx,nbrArray   ; get address of nbrArray
                mov    ecx,nbrElts    ; count := nbrElts

                jecxz  quit           ; quit if no numbers
forCount1:      add    eax,[ebx]      ; add number to sum
                add    ebx,4          ; get address of next item of array
                loop   forCount1      ; repeat nbrElts times

                cdq                   ; extend sum to quadword
                idiv   nbrElts        ; calculate average
                dtoa   outValue,eax   ; convert average to ASCII
                output avgLabel       ; print label and average
                output aboveLabel     ; print label for big numbers

; display numbers above average
                lea    ebx,nbrArray   ; get address of nbrArray
                mov    ecx,nbrElts    ; count := nbrElts
```

(continued)

Figure 5.10 (continued)

```
forCount2:  cmp     [ebx],eax       ; doubleword > average ?
            jng     endIfBig        ; continue if average not less
            dtoa    outValue,[ebx]  ; convert value from array to
                                    ; ASCII
            output  outValue        ; display value
endIfBig:
            add     ebx,4           ; get address of next item of array
            loop    forCount2       ; repeat

quit:       INVOKE ExitProcess, 0   ; exit with return code 0

PUBLIC _start                       ; make entry point public
            END                     ; end of source code
```

Figure 5.10 (continued)

The design statement "get address of first item of array" is implemented by the 80x86 statement

```
lea   ebx, nbrArray
```

The mnemonic lea stands for "load effective address." The lea instruction has the format

```
lea    destination, source
```

The destination will normally be a 32-bit general register; the source is any reference to memory. The *address* of the source is loaded into the register. (Contrast this with mov destination, source where the *value* at the source address is copied to the destination.) The lea instruction has opcode 8D takes one clock cycle on a Pentium, one or two on an 80486, and two on an 80386.

The design statement "get address of next item of array" is implemented using the 80x86 statement

```
add   ebx, 4
```

Since each doubleword occupies four bytes of storage, adding 4 to the address of the current element of an array gives the address of the next element of the array.

If one were planning to code this program in a high-level language, then the design of the first two loops might be

```
nbrElts := 0;              { input numbers into array }
while number from keyboard > 0 loop
    add 1 to nbrElts;
    store number in nbrSrray[nbrElts];
end while;


sum := 0;                  { find sum and average }
for count := 1 to nbrElts loop
    add nbrArray[count] to sum;
end for;
```

This design exploits one of the principal features of arrays, namely that any element can be accessed at any time by simply giving its index; the elements do not have to be accessed sequentially. Such random access can be implemented using register indirect addressing. For example, the design statement "add nbrArray[count] to sum" can be implemented as follows, assuming the same register usage as before—the ECX register for *count* and the EAX register for *sum*.

```
mov    edx,ecx            ; count
dec    edx               ; count-1
add    edx,edx           ; 2*(count-1)
add    edx,edx           ; 4*(count-1)
lea    ebx,nbrArray      ; starting address of array
add    ebx,edx           ; address of nbrArray[count]
add    eax,[ebx]         ; add array[count] to sum
```

The technique here is to calculate the number of bytes in the array prior to the desired element and add this number to the starting address. There are more efficient ways to directly access an array element; these will be covered in later chapters.

Exercises 5.5

1. Modify the program in Fig. 5.10, adding a loop that will display those elements of the array that are smaller than the average. (The numbers that are equal to the average should not be displayed by either loop.)

2. Modify the program in Fig. 5.10, replacing the last loop by one that displays all numbers that are within 5 of the average. Include values equal to *average*–5 or to *average*+5.

3. Modify the program in Fig. 5.10, adding a loop that will display the list of numbers backwards. (Hint: Find the address of *nbrArray[nbrElts]*, display the element at this address first, and subtract 4 repeatedly until all elements are displayed.)

4. Modify the program in Fig. 5.10 to ensure that the user gives at most *maxNbrs* values.

Programming Exercises 5.5

1. It is often necessary to search an array for a given value. Write a complete program that inputs a collection of integers and then sequentially searches for values stored in the array. Implement the following design.

```
nbrElts := 0;
get address of first item of array;
while (number from keyboard > 0) loop
    convert number to 2's complement;
    store number at address in array;
    add 1 to nbrElts;
    get address of next item of array;
end while;
until (response = 'N') or (response = 'n')
    display "Search for?  ";
    input keyValue;
    convert keyValue to 2's complement;
    get address of first item of array;
    count := 1;
    forever loop
        if count > nbrElts
        then
            display keyValue, "not in array";
            exit loop;
        end if;
```

```
            if keyValue = current element of array
            then
                display keyValue, "is element", count;
                exit loop;
            end if;
            add 1 to count;
            get address of next item of array;
        end loop;
        display "Search for another number?  ";
        input response;
    end until;
```

2. Programming Exercise 1 above shows one way to search an array. An alternative way is to put the value you are searching for at the end of the array. A search then always finds the value, and success or failure depends on whether the value was found before or after position *nbrElts*. Write a complete program that uses this technique. The design is the same as in Exercise 1 except for the body of the search loop; it is replaced by the following.

```
until (response = 'N') or (response = 'n')
    display "Search for?  ";
    input keyValue;
    convert keyValue to 2's complement;
    store keyValue at position (nbrElts+1) in array;
    get address of first item of array;
    count := 1;

    while keyValue not equal to current array element loop
        add 1 to count;
        get address of next word of array;
    end while;

    if count > nbrElts
    then
        display keyValue, "not in array";
        exit loop;
```

```
        else
            display keyValue, "is element", count;
            exit loop;
        end if;

        display "Search for another number?  ";
        input response;
    end until;
```

3. There are many ways to determine prime numbers. Here is a design for one way to find the first 100 primes. Implement this design in 80x86 assembly language.

```
prime[1] := 2; { first prime number }
prime[2] := 3; { second prime number }
primeCount := 2;
candidate := 4; { first candidate for a new prime }
while primeCount < 100 loop
   index := 1;
   while (index ≤ primeCount)
            and (prime[index] does not evenly divide candidate) loop
      add 1 to index;
   end while;
   if (index > primeCount)
   then {no existing prime evenly divides the candidate, so it is a new prime}
   add 1 to primeCount;
      prime[primeCount] := candidate;
   end if;
   add 1 to candidate;
end while;

display "Prime Numbers";
for index := 1 to 100 loop {display the numbers 5 per line }
   display prime[index];
   if index is divisible by 5 then skip to a new line;
   end if;
end for;
```

5.6   Something Extra: Pipelining

Chapter 2 discussed the central processing unit's basic operation cycle:

- fetch an instruction from memory
- decode the instruction
- execute the instruction

A CPU must have circuitry to perform each of these functions. One of the things that computer designers have done to speed up CPU operation is to design CPUs with stages that can carry out these (and other) operations almost independently.

The first stage of the CPU might have the job of fetching the next instruction from memory, perhaps doing just enough decoding to recognize the number of bytes the instruction has and update the program counter PC. The first stage passes on information to the second stage whose job might be to finish decoding the instruction, perhaps also computing some operand addresses. Meanwhile the first stage can be fetching the next instruction from memory. The second stage could pass a fully-decoded instruction to the third stage for execution. Meanwhile, the first stage could have passed on its second instruction to stage two, so that the first stage can be fetching a third instruction. This sort of design is called a **pipeline**. If the pipeline is kept full, the resulting throughput of the CPU is three times faster than if it had to finish the complete fetch-decode-execute process for each instruction before proceeding to the next one.

Figure 5.11 illustrates the operation of a pipeline. The instructions being processed are shown as horizontal strips of three boxes labeled with 1, 2, and 3 to indicate stages. The horizontal axis shows time. You can see that at any given time parts of three instructions are being executed.

CPU Stage	Instruction being processed										
1	1	2	3	4	5	6	7	8	9	10	11
2		1	2	3	4	5	6	7	8	9	10
3			1	2	3	4	5	6	7	8	9
Time interval	1	2	3	4	5	6	7	8	9	10	11

Figure 5.11   Instructions in a pipeline

A pipelined CPU is not as simple as illustrated above. One problem may occur if, say, stage 2 needs to compute an address based on the contents of a register modified by stage 3 of the previous instruction; the register might not yet contain the correct address. A CPU can be designed to avoid such problems, usually at the cost of a "hole" in the pipeline.

A more serious problem occurs when the CPU executes a conditional jump instruction. With a conditional jump the CPU cannot tell which of two possible sequences of instructions will be executed next until the condition itself is evaluated by the last stage. Earlier stages may be working on one instruction stream, only to be forced to discard all this work and refill the pipeline from the beginning with instructions from the alternative stream.

Chapter Summary

This chapter introduced 80x86 instructions that can be used to implement many high-level design or language features including **if** statements, various loops structures, and arrays.

The `jmp` instruction unconditionally transfers control to a destination statement. It has several versions, including one that jumps to a short destination 128 bytes before or 127 bytes after the `jmp` and one that jumps to a near destination a 32-bit displacement away. The `jmp` instruction is used in implementing various loop structures, typically transferring control back to the beginning of the loop, and in the **if-then-else** structure at the end of the "then code" to transfer control to **endif** so that the **else** code is not also executed. A `jmp` statement corresponds directly to the **goto** statement that is available in most high-level languages.

Conditional jump instructions examine the settings of one or more flags in the flag register and jump to a destination statement or fall through to the next instruction depending on the flag values. Conditional jump instructions have short and near displacement versions. There is a large collection of conditional jump instructions. They are used in **if** statements and loops, often in combination with compare instructions, to check Boolean conditions.

The `cmp` (compare) instructions have the sole purpose of setting or resetting flags in the EFLAGS register. Each compares two operands and assigns flag values. The comparison is done by subtracting the second operand from the first. The difference is not retained as it is with a `sub` instruction. Compare instructions often precede conditional jump instructions.

Loop structures like **while**, **until**, and **for** loops can be implemented using compare, jump, and conditional jump instructions. The `loop` instruction provides another way to implement many **for** loops. To use the **loop** instruction, a counter is placed in the ECX register prior to the start of the loop. The `loop` instruction itself is at the bottom of the loop body; it decrements the value in ECX and transfers control to a destination (normally the first statement of the body) if the new value in ECX is not zero. This results in the body of the loop being executed the number of times originally placed in the ECX register. The conditional jump `jecxz` instruction can be used to guard against executing such a loop when the initial counter value is zero.

Storage for an array can be reserved using the DUP directive in the data segment of a program. The elements of an array can be sequentially accessed by putting the address of the first element of the array in a register and adding the size of an array element repeatedly to get to the next element. The current element is referenced using register indirect addressing. The `lea` (load effective address) instruction is commonly used to load the initial address of the array.

Pipelining is done by a CPU with multiple stages that work on more than one instruction at a time, doing such tasks as fetching one, while decoding another, while executing a third. This can greatly speed up CPU operation.

6

Procedures

The 80x86 architecture enables implementation of procedures that are similar to those in a high-level language. Procedures use the hardware stack for several purposes. This chapter begins with a discussion of the 80x86 stack and then turns to important procedure concepts—how to call a procedure and return from one, parameter passing, local data, and recursion. The concluding section describes how procedures are implemented in one architecture that does not have a hardware stack.

6.1 The 80x86 Stack

Programs in this book have allocated stacks with the code

```
.STACK    4096
```

This `.STACK` directive tells the assembler to reserve 4096 bytes of uninitialized storage. The operating system initializes ESP to the address of the first byte above the 4096 bytes in the stack. A larger or smaller stack could be allocated, depending on the anticipated usage in the program.

The stack is most often used by **pushing** words or doublewords on it or by **popping** them off it. This pushing or popping is done automatically as part of the execution of call and return instructions (Section 6.2). It is also done manually with push and pop instructions. This section covers the mechanics of push and pop instructions, describing how they affect the contents of the stack.

Source code for a push instruction has the syntax

```
push source
```

The *source* operand can be a register 16, a register 32, a segment register, a word in memory, a doubleword in memory, an immediate byte, an immediate word, or an immediate doubleword. The only byte-size operand is immediate, and as you will see, multiple bytes are pushed on the stack for an immediate byte operand. Figure 6.1 lists the allowable operand types. The usual mnemonic for a push instruction is just push. However, if there is ambiguity about the size of the operand (as would be with a small immediate value), then you can use `pushw` or `pushd` mnemonics to specify word or doubleword-size operands, respectively.

When a push instruction is executed for a word-size operand, the stack pointer ESP is decremented by 2. Recall that initially ESP contains the address of the byte just above the allocated space. Subtracting 2 makes ESP point to the top word in the stack. The operand is then stored at the address in ESP; that is, at the high-memory end of the stack space. Execution is similar for a doubleword-size operand, except that ESP is decremented by 4 before the operand is stored. The immediate byte operand is interesting. Although a single byte is stored in the instruction, it is sign-extended to a doubleword that is actually stored on the stack. The byte-size operand saves three bytes of object code, but no stack space at execution time.

| | Clock Cycles | | | Number | |
Operand	386	486	Pentium	of Bytes	Opcode
register	2	1	1	1	
EAX or AX					50
ECX or CX					51
EDX or DX					52
EBX or BX					53
ESP or SP					54
EBP or BP					55
ESI or SI					56
EDI or DI					57
segment register	2	3	1		
CS				1	0E
DS				1	1E
ES				1	06
SS				1	16
FS				2	0F A0
GS				2	0F A8
memory word	5	4	2	2+	FF
memory doubleword	5	4	2	2+	FF
immediate byte	2	1	1	2	6A
immediate word	2	1	1	3	68
immediate doubleword	2	1	1	5	68

Figure 6.1 push instructions

Example

We now show an example of execution of two push instructions. It assumes that ESP initially contains 00600200. The first push instruction decrements ESP to 006001FE and then stores the contents of AX at that address. Notice that the low and high-order byte are reversed in memory. The second push decrements ESP to 006001FA and stores FFFFFF10 (-240_{10}) at that address.

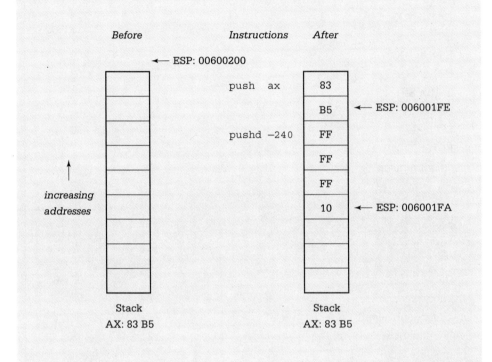

As additional operands are pushed onto the stack, ESP is decremented further and the new values are stored. No push instruction affects any flag bit.

Notice that a stack "grows downward," contrary to the image that you may have of a typical software stack. Also notice that the only value on the stack that is readily available is the last one pushed; it is at the address in ESP. Furthermore, ESP changes frequently as you push values and as procedure calls are made. In Section 6.3 you will learn a way to establish a fixed reference point in the middle of the stack using the EBP register, so that values near that point can be accessed without having to pop off all the intermediate values.

Pop instructions do the opposite job of push instructions. Each pop instruction has the format

pop *destination*

where *destination* can reference a word or doubleword in memory, any register 16, any register 32, or any segment register except CS. (The push instruction does not exclude CS.) The pop instruction gets a word-size value from the stack by copying the word at the address in ESP to the destination, then incrementing ESP by 2. Operation for a doubleword value is similar, except that ESP is incremented by 4. Figure 6.2 gives information about pop instructions for different destination operands.

| | Clock Cycles | | | Number | |
Operand	386	486	Pentium	of Bytes	Opcode
register	4	1	1	1	
EAX or AX					58
ECX or CX					59
EDX or DX					5A
EBX or BX					5B
ESP or SP					5C
EBP or BP					5D
ESI or SI					5E
EDI or DI					5F
segment register	7	3	3		
DS				1	1F
ES				1	07
SS				1	17
FS				2	0F A1
GS				2	0F A9
memory word	5	6	3	2+	8F
memory doubleword	5	6	3	2+	8F

Figure 6.2 pop instructions

Example

This example shows how pop instructions work. The doubleword at the address in ESP is copied to ECX before ESP is incremented by 4. The values popped from the stack are physically still there even though they logically have been removed. Note again that the bytes of a doubleword are stored backward in memory in the 80x86 architecture, but forward in the ECX register.

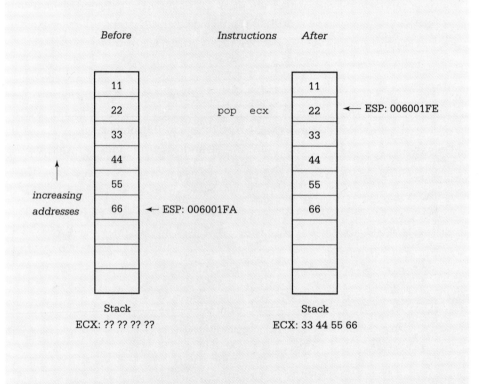

One use of push and pop instructions is to save the contents of a register temporarily on the stack. We have noted previously that registers are a scarce resource when programming. Suppose, for example, that you are using EDX to store some program variable but need to do a division that requires you to extend a dividend into EDX-EAX prior to the operation. One way to avoid losing your value in EDX is to push it on the stack.

```
push   edx       ; save variable
cdq              ; extend dividend to quadword
idiv   Divisor   ; divide
pop    edx       ; restore variable
```

This example assumes that you don't need the remainder the division operation puts in EDX. If you do need the remainder, it could be copied somewhere else before popping the value stored on the stack back to EDX.

As the above example shows, push and pop instructions are often used in pairs. When we examine how the stack is used to pass parameters to procedures, you will see a way to discard values from the stack without copying them to a destination location.

In addition to the ordinary push and pop instructions, special mnemonics push and pop flag registers. These mnemonics are pushf (pushfd for the extended flag register) and popf (popfd for the extended flag register). These are summarized in Fig. 6.3. They are often used in procedure code. Obviously popf and popfd instructions change flag values; these are the only push or pop instructions that change flags.

The 80x86 architecture has instructions that push or pop all general purpose registers with a single instruction. The pushad instruction pushes EAX, ECX, EDX, EBX, ESP, EBP, ESI and EDI, in this order. The value pushed for ESP is the address it contains before any of the registers are pushed. The popad instruction pops the same registers in the opposite order, except that the value for ESP is discarded. Popping the registers in the reverse order ensures that if these instructions are used in a pushad-popad pair, each register (except ESP) will get back its original value. Figure 6.4 shows the push all and pop all instructions, including the pusha and popa instructions that push and pop the 16-bit registers.

Instruction	Clock Cycles			Number of Bytes	Opcode
	386	486	Pentium		
pushf pushfd	4	4	3	1	9C
popf popfd	5	9	4	1	9D

Figure 6.3 pushf **and** popf **instructions**

| | Clock Cycles | | | Number | |
Instruction	386	486	Pentium	of Bytes	Opcode
pusha	18	11	5	1	60
pushad					
popa	24	9	5	1	61
popad					

Figure 6.4   Push all and pop all instructions

Finally, a note of caution. Although the Intel architecture allows 16-bit or 32-bit quantities to be pushed on the stack, some operating systems (including Microsoft Windows NT) require parameters used in system calls to be on doubleword boundaries, that is, a parameter's address must be a multiple of 4. The stack starts on a doubleword boundary, but to maintain this alignment, only doublewords should be pushed on the stack prior to a system call. (See Chapter 12 for examples of system calls.)

Exercises 6.1

1. For each instruction, give the opcode, the number of clock cycles for execution, and the number of bytes of object code. Assume that Double references a doubleword in memory. Assume a Pentium system for the number of clock cycles.

    (a) `push  ax`   (b) `pushd  10`
    (c) `pusha`   (d) `pop  ebx`
    (e) `pop  Double`   (f) `popad`
    (g) `pushf`

2. For each part of this problem, assume the "before" values when the given instructions are executed. Give the requested "after" values. Trace execution of the instructions by drawing a picture of the stack

	Before	*Instructions*	*After*
(a)	ESP: 06 00 10 00	`push  ecx`	ESP, ECX
	ECX: 01 A2 5B 74	`pushw  10`	

(b) ESP: 02 00 0B 7C   pushd 20   ESP, EBX

    EBX: 12 34 56 78   push ebx

(c) ESP: 00 00 F8 3A   push eax   ESP, EAX, BX, ECX

    EAX: 12 34 56 78   pushw 30

                               pop   bx

                               pop   ecx

3. Many microprocessors do not have an instruction equivalent to `xchg`. With such systems, a sequence of instructions like the following can be used to exchange the contents of two registers:

```
push   eax
push   ebx
pop    eax
pop    ebx
```

Explain why this sequence works to exchange the contents of the EAX and EBX registers. Compare the number of bytes of code and clock cycles required to execute this sequence with those required for the instruction `xchg eax,ebx`.

4. Another alternative to the `xchg` instruction is to use

```
push   eax
mov    eax, ebx
pop    ebx
```

Explain why this sequence works to exchange the contents of the EAX and EBX registers. Compare the number of bytes of code and clock cycles required to execute this sequence with those required for the instruction `xchg eax,ebx`.

6.2 Procedure Body, Call and Return

The word *procedure* is used in high-level languages to describe a subprogram that is almost a self-contained unit. The main program or another subprogram can call a procedure by including a statement that consists of the procedure name followed by a parenthesized list of arguments to be associated with the procedure's formal parameters.

Many high-level languages distinguish between a procedure that performs an action and a *function* that returns a value. A function is similar to a procedure except that it is called by using its name and argument list in an expression. It returns a value associated with its name; this value is then used in the expression. All subprograms in the C/C++ language are technically functions in this sense, but the language allows for functions that return no value.

In assembly language and in some high-level languages the term *procedure* is used to describe both types of subprograms, those that return values and those that do not. The term procedure will be used in both senses in this book.

Procedures are valuable in assembly language for the same reasons as in high-level languages. They help divide programs into manageable tasks and they isolate code that can be used multiple times within a single program or that can be saved and reused in several programs.

This section describes how to write 80x86 procedures, as well as how to assemble and link them using Microsoft software. Information is included on how to define a procedure, and how to transfer execution control to a procedure and back to the calling program. We show how the stack is used to save register contents, so that a procedure returns to the caller with almost all registers unchanged. Other important concepts to be considered with procedures are how to pass arguments to a procedure and how to implement local variables in a procedure body; these topics are covered in later sections.

The code for a procedure always follows a `.CODE` directive. The body of each procedure is bracketed by two directives, `PROC` and `ENDP`. Each of these directives has a label that gives the name of the procedure. With the Microsoft Macro Assembler, the `PROC` directive allows several attributes to be specified; we are only going to use one, `NEAR32`. This attribute says that the procedure will be located in the same code segment as the calling code and that 32-bit addresses are being used. These choices are normal for flat 32-bit memory model programming. Figure 6.5 shows relevant parts of a program that incorporates a procedure named Initialize. The job of the procedure is to initialize several variables; the calling program is sketched, but the code for the procedure itself is complete.

In Fig. 6.5 the procedure *Initialize* is bracketed by `PROC` and `ENDP`. The distance attribute `NEAR32` declares this to be a near procedure. Although this example shows the procedure body prior to the main code, it could also have been placed afterwards. Recall that execution of a program does not necessarily begin at the first statement of the code segment; the statement identified by the label `_start` marks the first instruction to be executed.

Most of the statements of procedure *Initialize* are ordinary mov instructions. These could have been used in the main program at the two places that the `call`

```
; procedure structure example
; Author:  R. Detmer
; Date:    revised 10/97

.386
.MODEL FLAT

ExitProcess PROTO NEAR32 stdcall, dwExitCode:DWORD

.STACK  4096              ; reserve 4096-byte stack

.DATA                     ; reserve storage for data
Count1     DWORD    11111111h
Count2     DWORD    22222222h
Total1     DWORD    33333333h
Total2     DWORD    44444444h
;          other data here

.CODE                         ; program code

Initialize  PROC    NEAR32
            mov     Count1,0     ; zero first count
            mov     Count2,0     ; zero second count
            mov     Total1,0     ; zero first total
            mov     Total2,0     ; zero second total
            mov     ebx,0        ; zero balance
            ret                  ; return
Initialize  ENDP

_start:                             ; program entry point
            call    Initialize      ; initialize variables

; — other program tasks here

            call    Initialize      ; reinitialize variables

; — more program tasks here

            INVOKE ExitProcess, 0   ; exit with return code 0
PUBLIC _start                       ; make entry point public

END                                 ; end of source code
```

Figure 6.5 Procedure structure

statements are coded; however, using the procedure makes the main code both shorter and clearer. The procedure affects doublewords defined in the program's data segment and the EBX register; it has no local variables.

When the main program executes, the instruction

```
call   Initialize
```

transfers control from the main code to the procedure. The main program calls the procedure twice; in general, a procedure may be called any number of times. The return instruction

```
ret
```

transfers control from the procedure back to the caller; there is almost always at least one `ret` instruction in a procedure and there can be more than one. If there is only one `ret`, it is ordinarily the last instruction in the procedure since subsequent instructions would be unreachable without "spaghetti code." Although a `call` instruction must identify its destination, the `ret` does not—control will transfer to the instruction following the most recent `call`. The 80x86 uses the stack to store the return address.

When the example program in Fig. 6.5 is assembled, linked, and executed, there is no visible output. However, it is informative to trace execution with a tool like WinDbg. Figure 6.6 show WinDbg's initial display. Note that ESP contains 0063FE3C. The memory window has been opened to start at address 0063FE30, 12 bytes down into the stack. The EIP register contains 0040103E, the address of the first instruction to be executed (the first call). Figure 6.7 shows the new state after this statement is executed. The EIP register now contains 00401010, the address of the first statement in procedure *Initialize*. The ESP register contains 0063FE38, so four bytes have been pushed onto the stack. Looking in memory at this address, you see 43 10 40 00—that is, 00401043, an address five bytes larger than the address of the first call. If you examine the listing file for the program, you see that the each call instruction takes five bytes of object code, so that 00401043 is the address of the instruction *following* the first `call`.

In general, a call instruction pushes the address of the next instruction (the one immediately following the call) onto the stack and then transfers control to the procedure code. A near call instruction works by pushing the EIP to the stack and then changing EIP to contain the address of the first instruction of the procedure.

Return from a procedure is accomplished by reversing the above steps. A `ret` instruction pops EIP, so that the next instruction to be executed is the one at the address that was pushed on the stack.

Recall that 80x86 programming can be done using either a flat memory model or a segmented memory model. With a segmented memory model a procedure may be in a

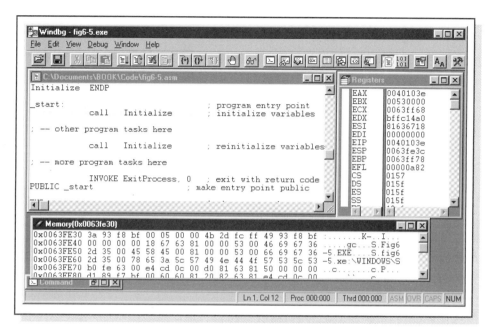

Figure 6.6 State prior to procedure call

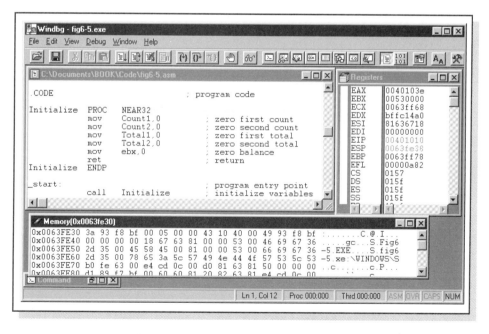

Figure 6.7 State after procedure call

different segment from the calling code. In fact, with 16-bit segmented programming, segments were limited to 65,536 bytes, so procedures were often in separate segments. The 80x86 architecture uses a **far call** to transfer control to a procedure in a different memory segment: A far call pushes both EIP and CS onto the stack. A far return pops both off the stack. With 32-bit flat memory model programming, there is no need for anything other than near calls.

The syntax of the 80x86 `call` statement is

```
call destination
```

Figure 6.8 lists some of the available 80x86 call instructions, omitting 16-bit forms and forms used primarily for systems programming. The "+" notations on the timings for the 80386 processor indicate that there are additional clock cycles that depend on the next instruction. The program in Fig. 6.6 included a near procedure, designated by the PROC operand NEAR32. In general, the assembler determines whether *destination* references a near or far procedure from the PROC directive or from some other directive or operand. No call instruction modifies any flag.

All of the procedures used in this book will be the first type, near relative. For a near relative procedure, the assembler calculates a 32-bit displacement to the destination, and the E8 opcode plus this displacement comprise the five bytes of the instruc-

| | Clock Cycles | | | Number | |
Operand	386	486	Pentium	of Bytes	Opcode
near relative	7+	3	1	5	E8
near indirect					FF
using register	7+	5	2	2	
using memory	10+	5	2	2+	
far direct	17+	18	4	7	9A
far indirect	22+	17	5	6	FF

Figure 6.8 `call` instructions

tion. The transfer of control when a procedure is called is similar to the transfer of a relative jump, except that the old contents of EIP are pushed, of course.

Near indirect calls encode a register 32 or a reference to a doubleword in memory. When the call is executed, the contents of that register or doubleword are used as the address of the procedure. This makes it possible for a `call` instruction to go to different procedures different times.

All far calls must provide both new CS contents and new EIP contents. With far direct calls, both of these are coded in the instruction, adding six bytes to the opcode. With far indirect calls, these are located at a six-byte block in memory, and the address of that block is coded in the instruction.

The return instruction `ret` is used to transfer control from a procedure body back to the calling point. Its basic operation is simple; it pops the address previously stored on the stack and loads it into the instruction pointer EIP. Since the stack contains the address of the instruction following the call, execution will continue at that point. A near return just has to restore EIP. A far return instruction reverses the steps of a far call, restoring both EIP and CS; both of these values are popped from the stack.

There are two formats for the `ret` instruction. The more common form has no operand and is simply coded

```
ret
```

An alternative version has a single operand and is coded

```
ret     count
```

The operand *count* is added to the contents of ESP after completion of the other steps of the return process (restoring EIP and, for a far procedure, CS). This can be useful if other values (parameters in particular) have been saved on the stack just for the procedure call, and can be logically discarded when the procedure is exited. (Parameters are discussed further in the next section.) Figure 6.9 lists the various formats of `ret` instructions.

If a procedure's `PROC` directive has the operand `NEAR32`, then the assembler generates near calls to the procedure and near returns to exit from it. The Microsoft Macro Assembler also has `retn` (return near) and `retf` (return far) mnemonics to force near or far returns; we will not need these mnemonics.

To construct building blocks for large programs, it is often desirable to assemble a procedure or group of procedures separately from the code that calls them; that is, with procedures and calling programs in separate files. There are a few additional steps

Type	Operand	Clock Cycles			Number of Bytes	Opcode
		386	486	Pentium		
near	none	10+	5	2	1	C3
near	immediate	10+	5	3	3	C2
far	none	18+	13	4	1	CB
far	immediate	18+	14	4	3	CA

Figure 6.9 `ret` instructions

required to do this. First, you must assemble the procedures so that their names are visible outside the file containing them. Second, you must let the calling program know necessary information about the external procedures. Finally, you must link the additional .OBJ files to get an executable program.

The `PUBLIC` directive is used to make procedure names visible outside the file containing them. This is the same directive we have been using to make the symbol `_start` visible. In general, its syntax is

        PUBLIC   *symbol1* [, *symbol2*] ...

A file may contain more than one `PUBLIC` directive.

The `EXTRN` directive gives the calling program information about external symbols. It has many options, including

        EXTRN   *symbol1:type* [, *symbol2:type*]

A file may contain more than one `EXTRN` directive. Figure 6.10 outlines how this all fits together for two procedures, Procedure1 and Procedure2, which are assembled in a file separate from the main code. Note that `.386` and `.MODEL FLAT` directives will also be required, and `INCLUDE` directives may be needed.

You assemble each of the above files just as if it were the main program. Each assembly produces a .OBJ file. To link the files, simply list all .OBJ files in the link command—you already have been linking your programs with the separately assembled file IO.OBJ.

We conclude this section with a procedure that will calculate the integer square root of a positive integer *Nbr*; that is, the largest integer *SqRt* such that $SqRt*SqRt \leq Nbr$.

File containing procedure definitions

```
PUBLIC      Procedure1, Procedure2

.CODE

Procedure1  PROC  NEAR32
            ...
Procedure1  ENDP

Procedure2  PROC  NEAR32
            ...
Procedure2  ENDP

            END
```

File containing procedure calls

```
EXTRN Procedure1:NEAR32, Procedure2:NEAR32
            ...
.CODE
            ...
            call  Procedure1
            ...
            call  Procedure2
            ...
            END
```

Figure 6.10   Code for external procedures

The procedure code is in Fig. 6.11. This is not a complete file ready for assembly; the procedure code could be assembled separately with the addition of the directives shown in Fig. 6.10, or it could be included in a file with a calling program.

Procedure Root implements the following design.

```
Sqrt := 0;
while Sqrt*Sqrt ≤ Nbr loop
    add 1 to SqRt;
end while;
subtract 1 from Sqrt;
```

```
; procedure to compute integer square root of number Nbr
; Nbr is passed to the procedure in EAX
; The square root SqRt is returned in EAX
; Other registers are unchanged.
; author:  R. Detmer    revised:  10/97

Root        PROC  NEAR32
            push  ebx              ; save registers
            push  ecx
            mov   ebx, 0           ; SqRt := 0
WhileLE:    mov   ecx, ebx         ; copy SqRt
            imul  ecx, ebx         ; SqRt*SqRt
            cmp   ecx, eax         ; SqRt*SqRt <= Nbr ?
            jnle  EndWhileLE       ; exit if not
            inc   ebx              ; add 1 to SqRt
            jmp   WhileLE          ; repeat
EndWhileLE:
            dec   ebx              ; subtract 1 from SqRt
            mov   eax, ebx         ; return SqRt in AX
            pop   ecx              ; restore registers
            pop   ebx
            ret                  ; return
Root        ENDP
```

Figure 6.11   **Procedure to find integer square root**

This algorithm works by trying larger and larger integer candidates for *SqRt;* after it overshoots the correct value, it backs up one unit. This is not a very efficient technique, but it is easy to code.

The calling program must put the value for *Nbr* in the EAX register; the next section discusses a more common way of passing parameters to procedures. Procedure *Root* will return the value of *SqRt* in the EAX register; functions that return a single integer value frequently use the accumulator for this purpose.

In addition to the code that implements the design, the procedure contains two push instructions at the beginning, with corresponding pops immediately before the return. The purpose of these instructions is to preserve the contents of the EBX and ECX registers; that is, to return to the calling program with the same values in the registers as they had before call Root. This makes the procedure relatively independent of the calling program since someone using procedure *Root* does not have to worry about unexpected side-effects. This technique is extended in the next section.

Exercises 6.2

1. Suppose that the NEAR32 procedure Exercise1 is called by the instruction

   ```
   call  Exercise1
   ```

   If this call statement is at address 00402000 and ESP contains 00406000 before the call, what return address will be on the stack when the first instruction of procedure Exercise1 is executed? What will the value in ESP be?

2. Why is the PUBLIC directive used when procedures are separately compiled? Why is the EXTRN directive used when procedures are separately compiled?

Programming Exercises 6.2

1. Write a main program that will input an integer, call procedure *Root* (Fig. 6.11) to find the integer square root, and display the value of the square root. Include this program in the same file as procedure *Root* and assemble them together.

2. Repeat Exercise 1, except assemble procedure *Root* and your main program in separate files.

3. Write a procedure *GetValue* that prompts for and inputs an integer between 0 and a specified size *MaxValue*. A main program must send *MaxValue* to the procedure in the EAX register. Procedure *GetValue* will return the integer it inputs in EAX. Procedure *GetValue* will repeatedly prompt for input until the user enters a value in the specified range. Write procedure *GetValue* so that EAX is the only register changed upon return to the calling program; even the flags register must be unchanged.

6.3 Parameters and Local Variables

Using a high-level language, a procedure definition often includes parameters or formal parameters that are associated with arguments or actual parameters when the procedure is called. For the procedure's **in** (**pass-by-value**) parameters, values of the arguments, which may be expressions, are copied to the parameters when the procedure is called, and these values are then referenced in the procedure using their local names, which are the identifiers used to define the parameters. **In-out** (**pass-by-location** or **variable**) parameters associate a parameter identifier with an argument that is a single variable and can be used to pass a value either to the procedure from the caller or from the procedure back to the caller. A common technique for passing parameters is discussed in this section. This technique can be used to pass word-size or doubleword-size values for **in** parameters, or addresses of data in the calling program for **in-out** parameters.

Although simple procedures can be written using only registers to pass parameters, most procedures use the stack to pass parameters. The stack is also frequently used to store local variables. As you will see, the techniques for using the stack for parameters and for local variables are closely related.

We start with a simple example to show how the stack is used to pass parameters. Suppose that the job of a NEAR32 procedure *Add2* is to add two doubleword-size integers, returning the sum in EAX. If the calling program passes these parameters by pushing them on the stack, then its code might look like

```
push    Value1      ; first argument value
push    ecx         ; second argument value
call    Add2        ; call procedure to find sum
add     esp,8       ; remove parameters from stack
```

Before we look at how the parameter values are accessed from the stack, notice how they are removed from the stack following the call. There is no need to pop them off the stack to some destination; we simply add eight to the stack pointer to move ESP above the parameters. It is important to remove parameters from the stack since otherwise repeated procedure calls might exhaust the stack space. Even more serious, if procedure calls are nested and the inside call leaves parameters on the stack, then the outside return will not find the correct return address on the stack. An alternative to adding *n* to the stack pointer in the calling program is to use ret *n* in the procedure, the version of the return instruction that adds *n* to ESP after popping the return address. Both forms will be illustrated in this book.

Figure 6.12 shows how the procedure *Add2* can retrieve the two parameter values from the stack. The procedure code uses the **based** addressing mode. In this mode, a memory address is calculated as the sum of the contents of a base register and a displacement built into the instruction. The Microsoft assembler accepts several alternative notations for a based address; this book will use [*register+number*], for example, [ebp+6]. Any general register (e.g., EAX, EBX, ECX, EDX, ESI, EDI, EBP, or ESP) can be used as the base register; EBP is the normal choice for accessing values in the stack.

```
Add2        PROC NEAR32   ; add two words passed on the stack
                          ; return the sum in the EAX register
            push   ebp                ; save EBP
            mov    ebp,esp            ; establish stack frame
            mov    eax,[ebp+8]        ; copy second parameter
                                      ; value
            add    eax,[ebp+12]       ; add first parameter value
            pop    ebp                ; restore EBP
            ret                       ; return
Add2        ENDP
```

Figure 6.12   Using parameter values passed on stack

This method of passing argument values works as follows. Upon entry to the procedure, the stack looks like the left illustration in Fig. 6.13. After the procedure's instructions

```
push   ebp                   ; save EBP
mov    ebp,esp               ; establish stack frame
```

are executed, the stack looks like the right illustration in Fig. 6.13.

Eight bytes are stored between the address stored in EBP (and also ESP) and the second parameter value. Therefore parameter 2 can be referenced by [bp+8]. The first parameter value is four bytes higher on the stack; its reference is [bp+12]. The code

```
mov    eax,[bp+8]            ; copy second parameter
add    eax,[bp+12]           ; add first parameter
```

uses the values from memory locations in the stack to compute the desired sum.

You may wonder why EBP is used at all. Why not just use ESP as a base register? The principal reason is that ESP is likely to change, but the instruction mov ebp,esp loads EBP with a *fixed* reference point in the stack. This fixed reference point will not change as the stack used for other purposes—for example, to push additional registers or to call other procedures.

Some procedures need to allocate stack space for local variables, and most procedures need to save registers as illustrated in Fig. 6.11. Instructions to accomplish these tasks, along with the instructions

```
push   ebp                   ; save EBP
mov    ebp,esp               ; establish stack frame
```

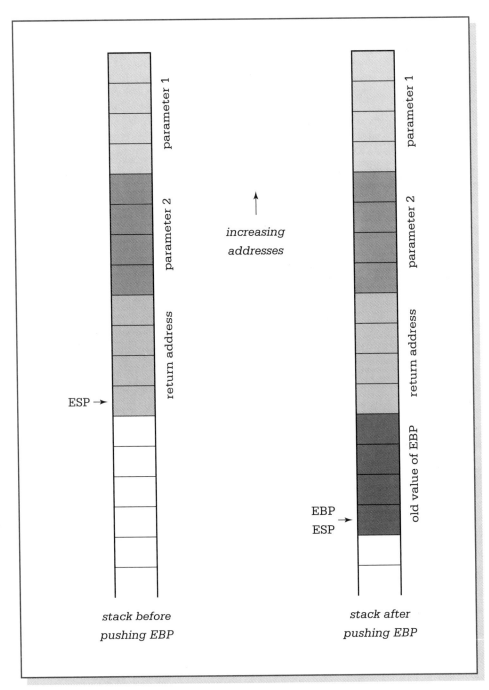

Figure 6.13 Locating parameters in the stack

make up the **entry code** for a procedure. However, the two instructions here are always the first entry code instructions. Because they are, you can count on the last parameter being exactly eight bytes above the reference point stored in EBP. The EBP register itself is always the first pushed and last popped so that upon return to the calling program it has the same value as prior to the call.

We now show how the stack can provide space for local variables. For this purpose, we revisit the algorithm for computing the greatest common divisor of two integers that appeared in Programming Exercises 5.3.

```
gcd := number1;
remainder := number2;

until (remainder = 0) loop
    dividend := gcd;
    gcd := remainder;
    remainder := dividend mod gcd;
end until;
```

Figure 6.14 shows this design implemented as a NEAR32 procedure that computes the greatest common divisor of two doubleword-size integer values passed to the procedure on the stack, returning the GCD in EAX. Figure 6.14 includes more than the procedure itself. It shows a complete file, ready for separate assembly.

In this procedure, *gcd* is stored on the stack until it is time to return the value in EAX. The instruction

```
sub    esp,4      ; space for one local doubleword
```

moves the stack pointer down four bytes, reserving one doubleword of space below where EBP was stored and above where other registers are stored. After EDX and the flags register are pushed, the stack has the contents shown in Fig. 6.15. Now the local variable *gcd* can be accessed as [ebp-4], since it is four bytes below the fixed reference point stored in EBP.

The rest of the procedure is a straightforward implementation of the design. In this example, a register could have been used to store *gcd*, but many procedures have too many local variables to store them all in registers. Within reason, you can reserve as many local variables on the stack as you wish, accessing each by [ebp-*offset*]. Notice that registers are *saved* after local variable space is reserved, so that the number of registers saved does not affect the offset down to a variable. Note also that most

```
PUBLIC GCD
; Procedure to compute the greatest common divisor of two
; doubleword-size integer parameters passed on the stack.
; The GCD is returned in EAX.
; No other register is changed.  Flags are unchanged.
; Author:  R. Detmer     Revised:  10/97


GCD     PROC    NEAR32
        push    ebp             ; establish stack frame
        mov     ebp,esp
        sub     esp,4           ; space for one local doubleword
        push    edx             ; save EDX
        pushf                   ; save flags

        mov     eax,[ebp+8] ; get Number1
        mov     [ebp-4],eax ; GCD := Number1
        mov     edx,[ebp+8] ; Remainder := Number2
until0: mov     eax,[ebp-4] ; Dividend := GCD
        mov     [ebp-4],edx ; GCD := Remainder
        mov     edx,0           ; extend Dividend to doubleword
        div     DWORD PTR [ebp-4]    ; Remainder in EDX
        cmp     edx, 0          ; remainder = 0?
        jnz     until0          ; repeat if not

        mov     eax,[ebp-4] ; copy GCD to EAX
        popf                    ; restore flags
        pop     edx             ; restore EDX
        mov     esp,ebp         ; restore ESP
        pop     ebp             ; restore EBP
        ret     8               ; return, discarding parameters
GCD     ENDP
        END
```

Figure 6.14   Greatest common divisor procedure

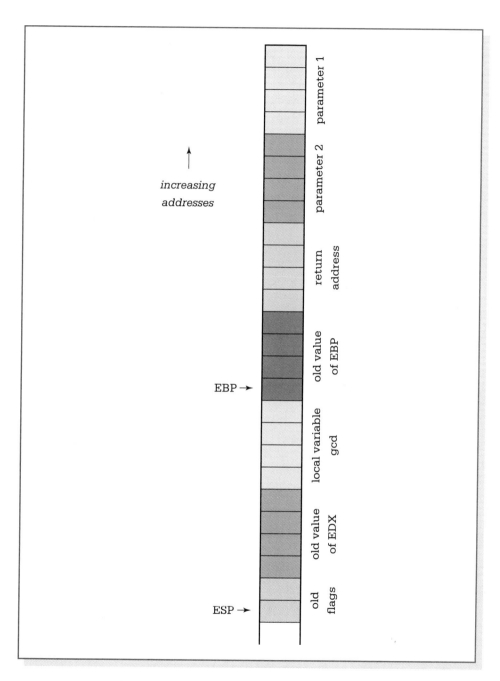

Figure 6.15 Stack usage with local variables

procedures will need to save more than two registers if register contents are to be unchanged upon return to the calling program.

Finally, consider the **exit code** for the procedure.

```
popf                    ; restore flags
pop     edx             ; restore EDX
mov     esp,ebp         ; restore ESP
pop     ebp             ; restore EBP
ret     8               ; return, discarding parameters
```

The first two `pop` instructions simply restore the flag register and EDX; these instructions are popped in the opposite order in which they were pushed. It may seem that the next instruction should be `add  sp,4` to undo the effects of the corresponding subtraction in the entry code. However, the instruction `mov  esp,ebp` accomplishes the same objective more efficiently, working no matter how many bytes of local variable space were allocated, and without changing flags like an add instruction. Finally, we are using the `ret` instruction with operand 8, so that for this procedure the calling program must *not* remove parameters from the stack; this task is accomplished by the procedure.

Figure 6.16 summarizes typical entry code and exit code for a procedure. High-level language compilers generate similar code for subprograms. In fact, you can usually

```
Entry code:

push    ebp             ; establish stack frame
mov     ebp,esp
sub     esp,n           ; n bytes of local variables space
push    ...             ; save registers
...
push    ...
pushf                   ; save flags


Exit code:

popf                    ; restore flags
pop     ...             ; restore registers
...
pop     ...
mov     esp,ebp         ; restore ESP if local variables used
pop     ebp             ; restore EBP
ret                     ; return
```

Figure 6.16   Typical procedure entry and exit code

write an assembly language procedure that is called by a high-level language program with code like this. Check reference materials for the compiler before beginning since there are many variations of these techniques.

How can a high-level language implement variable parameters? How can large parameters such as an array, a character string, or a record be efficiently passed to a procedure? Either of these can be implemented by passing the address of an argument rather than the value of the argument to the procedure. The procedure can then either use the value at the address or store a new value at the address. Figure 6.17 shows a procedure that might implement the Pascal procedure with header

```
PROCEDURE Minimum(A : IntegerArray;
          Count : INTEGER;
          VAR Min : INTEGER);
(* Set Min to smallest value in A[1], A[2], ..., A[Count] *)
```

In this implementation the addresses of arguments corresponding to *A* and *Min* are passed to procedure *Minimum*. The procedure uses register indirect addressing, first to examine each array element, and at the end to store the smallest value.

The instructions `pushad` and `popad` save and restore all general registers. These instructions are convenient, but they cannot be used if the procedure generates a value to be returned in a register. Note that since the Count parameter is word-size, the address of the first parameter is 14 bytes above the fixed base point—four bytes for EBP, four bytes for the return address, four bytes for the address of Min, and two bytes for the value of Count. (Draw the stack picture.)

Calling code for procedure *Minimum* could look like the following.

```
lea     eax, Array      ; Parameter 1:  address of Array
push    eax
push    Count           ; Parameter 2:  value of Count
lea     eax, Min        ; Parameter 3:  address of Min
push    eax
call    Minimum         ; call procedure
add     esp, 10         ; discard parameters
```

After this code is executed, the smallest value from Array will be in the word referenced by Min.

It is perfectly legal for a procedure to store local variables in the data segment. The .DATA directive can be included in a file used for separate assembly of procedures. In fact, a program may have multiple .DATA directives, although this is generally not necessary. You should normally keep variables as local as possible, stored on the stack or

```
; Procedure to find the smallest word in array A[1..Count]
; Parameters:  (1)  address of array A
;              (2)  value of Count (word)
;              (3)  address of Min (destination for smallest)
; No register is changed.  Flags are unchanged
Minimum PROC   NEAR32
        push   ebp            ; establish stack frame
        mov    ebp,esp
        pushad                ; save all registers
        pushf                 ; save flags

        mov    ebx,[ebp+14]   ; get address of array A
        mov    ecx, 0         ; ensure high order 0s in ECX
        mov    cx,[ebp+12]    ; get value of Count
        mov    eax,7fffffffh  ; smallest so far (MaxInt)
        jecxz  endForCount    ; exit when no elements to check
forCount:
        cmp    [ebx],eax      ; element < smallest so far ?
        jnl    endIfLess      ; exit if not
        mov    eax,[ebx]      ; new smallest
endIfLess:
        add    ebx,4          ; address of next array element
        loop   forCount       ; iterate
endForCount:
        mov    ebx,[ebp+8]    ; get address of Min
        mov    [ebx],eax      ; move smallest to Min
        popf                  ; restore flags
        popad                 ; restore registers
        pop    ebp            ; restore EBP
        ret                   ; return
Minimum ENDP
```

Figure 6.17 Procedure using address parameters

in part of the data segment that is visible only during assembly of the file containing the definitions. Even when a procedure and a calling program are assembled in a single file, you should avoid referencing the calling code's variables directly in the procedure.

Because 80x86 instructions are often the output of a compiler, the 80x86 architecture includes additional instructions to facilitate implementation of procedures. The `enter` instruction has syntax

```
enter   localBytes, nestingLevel
```

When *nestingLevel* is zero, this does precisely the job of the following familiar instructions:

```
push    ebp
mov     ebp,esp
sub     esp, localBytes
```

that is, it establishes a stack frame and reserves the requested numbers of local bytes of storage. If *nestingLevel* > 0, the `enter` instruction also pushes the stack frame pointers from *nestingLevel*–1 levels back onto the stack above the new frame pointer. This gives this procedure easy access to the variables of procedures in which it is nested. If used, an `enter` instruction would normally be the first instruction in a procedure.

The `leave` instruction reverses the actions of the enter instruction. Specifically, it does the same thing as the instruction pair

```
mov     esp,ebp      ; restore ESP
pop     ebp          ; restore EBP
```

and normally would be used immediately before a return instruction. We will not use the `enter` or `leave` instructions for procedures in this book.

You have observed that each program we write exits with the statement

```
INVOKE ExitProcess, 0   ; exit with return code 0
```

`INVOKE` is not an instruction—MASM references call it a directive. However, it acts more like a macro. In fact, if the directive `.LISTALL` precedes the above line of code, you see the expansion

```
push    +000000000h
call    ExitProcess
```

This is clearly a call to procedure *ExitProcess* with a single doubleword parameter with value 0.

Exercises 6.3

1. Suppose that a NEAR32 procedure begins with

```
push   ebp        ; save EBP
mov    ebp,esp    ; new base pointer
push   ecx        ; save registers
push   esi
. . .
```

   Assume that this procedure has three parameters passed on the stack, (1) a doubleword, (2) a word, and (3) a second word. Draw a picture of the stack following execution of the above code. Include parameters, return address, and show the bytes to which EBP and ESP point. How can each parameter be referenced?

2. Give entry code (Fig. 6.16) for a NEAR32 procedure that reserves eight bytes of storage on the stack for local variables. Assuming that this space is used for two doublewords, how can each local variable be referenced?

3. Explain why you cannot use pushad and popad in a procedure that returns a value in EAX.

Programming Exercises 6.3

Write a NEAR32 procedure to perform each task specified below. For each procedure, use the stack to pass arguments to the procedure. Except for those problems that explicitly say to return a result in a register, register contents should be unchanged by the procedure; that is, registers, including the flags register, which are used in the procedure should be saved at the beginning of the procedure and restored before returning. Allocate stack space as needed for local variables. Use the ret instruction with no operand. For each problem, write a separately assembled test driver, a simple main program that will input appropriate values, call the procedure, and output results. The main program must remove arguments from the stack. Link and run each complete program.

1. Write a procedure Min2 to find the minimum of two word-size integer parameters. Return the minimum in the AX register.

2. Write a procedure Max3 to find the maximum of three doubleword-size integer parameters. Return the maximum in the EAX register.

3. Write a procedure *Avg* to find the average of collection of doubleword-size integers in an array. Procedure *Avg* will have three parameters:
    (1) the address of the array
    (2) the number of integers in the array (passed as a doubleword)
    (3) the address of a doubleword at which to store the result.

4. Write a procedure *Search* to search an array of doublewords for a specified doubleword value. Procedure *Search* will have three parameters:
    (1) the value for which to search (a doubleword)
    (2) the address of the array
    (3) the number *N* of doublewords in the array (passed as a doubleword)
    Return in **EAX** the position (1,2,...,N) at which the value is found, or return 0 if the value does not appear in the array.

6.4   Recursion

A **recursive** procedure or function is one that calls itself, either directly or indirectly. The best algorithms for manipulating many data structures are recursive. It is frequently very difficult to code certain algorithms in a programming language that does not support recursion.

It is almost as easy to code a recursive procedure in 80x86 assembly language as it is to code a nonrecursive procedure. If parameters are passed on the stack and local variables are stored on the stack, then each call of the procedure gets new storage allocated for its parameters and local variables. There is no danger of the arguments passed to one call of a procedure being confused with those for another call since each call has its own stack frame. If registers are properly saved and restored, then the same registers can be used by each call of the procedure.

This section gives one example of a recursive procedure in 80x86 assembly language. It solves the Towers of Hanoi puzzle, pictured in Fig. 6.18 with four disks. The object of the puzzle is to move all disks from source spindle A to destination spindle B, one at a time, never placing a larger disk on top of a smaller disk. Disks can be moved to spindle C, a spare spindle. For instance, if there are only two disks, the small disk can be moved from spindle A to C, the large one can be moved from A to B, and finally the small one can be moved from C to B.

In general, the Towers of Hanoi puzzle is solved by looking at two cases. If there is only one disk, then the single disk is simply moved from the source spindle to the destination. If the number of disks *NbrDisks* is greater than one, then the top (*NbrDisks*–1)

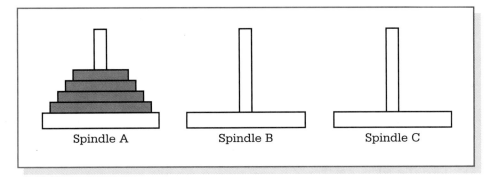

Figure 6.18   Towers of Hanoi puzzle

disks are moved to the spare spindle, the largest one is moved to the destination, and finally the (*NbrDisks*–1) smaller disks are moved from the spare spindle to the destination. Each time (*NbrDisks*–1) disks are moved, exactly the same procedure is followed, except that different spindles have the roles of source, destination, and spare. Figure 6.19 expresses the algorithm in pseudocode.

```
procedure Move(NbrDisks, Source, Destination, Spare);
begin
        if NbrDisks = 1
        then
                display "Move disk from ", Source, " to ", Destination
        else
                Move(NbrDisks – 1, Source, Spare, Destination);
                Move(1, Source, Destination, Spare);
                Move(NbrDisks – 1, Spare, Destination, Source);
        end if;
end procedure Move;
begin {main program}
        prompt for and input Number;
        Move(Number, 'A', 'B', 'C');
end;
```

Figure 6.19   Pseudocode for Towers of Hanoi Solution

Figure 6.20 shows 80x86 code that implements the design. The stack is used to pass parameters to procedure *Move,* which is a NEAR32 procedure referencing the data segment for output only. A standard stack frame is established, and registers used by the procedure are saved and restored. The code is a fairly straightforward translation of the pseudocode design. The operator DWORD PTR is required in the statement

```
cmp     DWORD PTR [bp+14],1
```

so that the assembler knows whether to compare words or byte size operands. Similarly, the pushw mnemonic is used several places so that the assembler knows to push word-size parameters. Notice that the recursive calls are implemented exactly the same way as the main program call, by pushing four parameters on the stack, calling procedure *Move,* then removing the parameters from the stack. However, in the main program the spindle parameters are constants, stored as the low order part of a word since single bytes cannot be pushed on the 80x86 stack.

```
; program to print instructions for "Towers of Hanoi" puzzle
; author:  R. Detmer   revised:  10/97


.386
.MODEL FLAT

ExitProcess PROTO NEAR32 stdcall, dwExitCode:DWORD

include io.h              ; header file for input/output

cr      equ     0dh      ; carriage return character
Lf      equ     0ah      ; line feed

.STACK  4096              ; reserve 4096-byte stack

.DATA                     ; reserve storage for data
prompt      BYTE    cr,Lf,'How many disks?   ',0
number      BYTE    16 DUP (?)
message     BYTE    cr,Lf,'Move disk from spindle '
source      BYTE    ?
            BYTE    ' to spindle '
dest        BYTE    ?
            BYTE    '.',0
```

(continued)

Figure 6.20   Towers of Hanoi solution

```
.CODE
Move          PROC NEAR32
; procedure Move(NbrDisks : integer; { number of disks to move }
;          Source, Dest, Spare : character { spindles to use }  )
; parameters are passed in words on the stack

              push    ebp               ; save base pointer
              mov     ebp,esp           ; copy stack pointer
              push    eax               ; save registers
              push    ebx

              cmp     WORD PTR [ebp+14],1  ; NbrDisks = 1?
              jne     elseMore          ; skip if more than 1
              mov     bx,[ebp+12]       ; Source
              mov     source,bl         ; copy character to output
              mov     bx,[ebp+10]       ; destination
              mov     dest,bl           ; copy character to output
              output  message          ; print line
              jmp     endIfOne          ; return
elseMore:     mov     ax,[ebp+14]       ; get NbrDisks
              dec     ax                ; NbrDisks - 1
              push    ax                ; parameter 1: NbrDisks-1
              pushw   [ebp+12]          ; parameter 2: source does not change
              pushw   [ebp+8]           ; parameter 3: old spare is new destination
              pushw   [ebp+10]          ; parameter 4: old destination is new spare
              call    Move              ; Move(NbrDisks-1,Source,Spare,Destination)
              add     esp,8             ; remove parameters from stack

              pushw   1                 ; parameter 1: 1
              pushw   [ebp+12]          ; parameter 2: source does not change
              pushw   [ebp+10]          ; parameter 3: destination unchanged
              pushw   [ebp+8]           ; parameter 4: spare unchanged
              call    Move              ; Move(1,Source,Destination,Spare)
              add     esp,8             ; remove parameters from stack

              push    ax                ; parameter 1: NbrDisks-1
              pushw   [ebp+8]           ; parameter 2: source is original spare
              pushw   [ebp+10]          ; parameter 3: original destination
              pushw   [ebp+12]          ; parameter 4: original source is spare
              call    Move              ; Move(NbrDisks-1,Spare,Destination,Source)
```

(continued)

Figure 6.20   *(continued)*

```
            add     esp,8           ; remove parameters from stack
endIfOne:
            pop     ebx             ; restore registers
            pop     eax
            pop     ebp             ; restore base pointer
            ret                     ; return
Move        ENDP

_start:     output  prompt          ; ask for number of disks
            input   number,16       ; read ASCII characters
            atoi    number          ; convert to integer
            push    ax              ; argument 1: Number
            mov     al,'A'          ; argument 2: ' A'
            push    ax
            mov     al,'B'          ; argument 3: ' B'
            push    ax
            mov     al,'C'          ; argument 4: ' C'
            push    ax
            call    Move            ; Move(Number,Source,Dest,Spare)
            add     esp,8           ; remove parameters from stack

            INVOKE  ExitProcess, 0  ; exit with return code 0

PUBLIC _start                       ; make entry point public
END                                 ; end of source code
```

Figure 6.20 *(continued)*

Exercises 6.4

1. What will go wrong in the Towers of Hanoi program if EAX is not saved at the beginning of procedure *Move* and restored at the end?

2. Suppose that the Towers of Hanoi program is executed and 2 is entered for the number of disks. Trace the stack contents from the first push in the main program through the instruction add esp,8 in the main program.

Programming Exercises 6.4

1. The factorial function is defined for a non-negative integer argument n by

$$factorial(n) = \begin{cases} 1 \text{ if } n = 0 \\ n \times factorial(n-1) \text{ if } n > 0 \end{cases}$$

Write a recursive assembly language procedure named *Factorial* that implements this recursive definition. Use the stack to pass the single doubleword integer argument; return the value of the function in the EAX register. The calling program should remove the parameter from the stack. Test your function by calling it from a main program that inputs an integer, calls the *Factorial* function, and displays the value returned by the function. Why is it better to use doubleword-size than word-size integers for this function?

2. The greatest common divisor (GCD) of two positive integers m and n can be calculated recursively by the function described below in pseudocode.
   function GCD(m, n : integer) : integer;

   if $n = 0$
   then
       return m;
   else
       Remainder := m mod n;
       return GCD(n, Remainder);
   end if;

   Implement this recursive definition in assembly language. Use the stack to pass the two doubleword-size argument values. Return the value of the function in the EAX register. The procedure should remove the parameters from the stack. Test your function with a main program that inputs two integers, calls the greatest common divisor function GCD, and displays the value returned.

6.5 Other Architectures: Procedures Without a Stack

Not all computer architectures provide a hardware stack. One can always implement a software stack by setting aside a block of memory, thinking of it as a stack, maintaining the stack top in a variable, and pushing or popping data by copying to or from the stack. However, this is much less convenient than having an architecture like the 80x86 that automatically adjusts the stack top for you as you push values, pop values, call procedures, and return from procedures.

Obviously the stack plays a large role in 80x86 procedure implementation. How can you reasonably implement procedures in an architecture that has no stack? This section gives a brief description of one system for doing this. It is based on the conventions commonly used in IBM mainframe computers whose architecture is derived from the System/360 (S/360) systems first introduced in the 1960s.

The S/360 architecture includes sixteen 32-bit *general purpose registers* (GPRs), numbered 0 to 15. Addresses are 24 bits long and an address can be stored in any register. The architecture includes addressing modes comparable to direct, register indirect, and indexed.

A procedure is usually called by loading its address into GPR 15 and then executing a *branch and link* instruction that jumps to the procedure code after copying the address of the next instruction into GPR 14. This makes return easy; simply jump to the address in GPR 14.

Parameter passing is more challenging. Normally GPR 1 is used to pass the address of a *parameter address list*. This is a list of 32-bit storage locations (32 bits is called a *word* in the S/360 architecture), the first word containing the address of the first parameter, the second word containing the address of the second parameter, etc. To retrieve a word-size parameter, one must first get its address from the parameter address list, then copy the word at that address.

Since the same general purpose registers are normally used for the same tasks each time a procedure is called, problems may occur if one procedure calls another. For instance, a second procedure call would put the second return address into GPR 14, wiping out the first return address. To avoid this problem, the main program and each procedure allocates a block of storage for a *register save area* and puts its address in GPR 13 prior to a procedure call. The procedure then saves general purpose registers 0–12, 14, and 15 in the register save area of the calling program and GPR 13 in its own register save area. This system is relatively complicated compared to using a stack, but it works well except for recursive procedure calls. Since there is only one register save area per procedure, recursive procedure calls are impossible without modifying the scheme.

Exercises 6.5

1. If you translate the IBM S/360 parameter passing scheme into 80x86 assembly language, you get code that looks like the following in the calling program.

```
Double1     DWORD   ?
. . .
Value1      DWORD   ?
Value2      DWORD   ?
. . .
```

```
AddrList    DWORD   OFFSET Value1   ; address of parameter 1
            DWORD   OFFSET Value2   ; address of parameter 2
            DWORD   OFFSET Double1  ; address of parameter 3

 . . .

            lea     ebx,AddrList    ; get address of AddrList
            call    Proc1
```

Note that the parameters do not need to be in consecutive storage locations, but their addresses are in consecutive words at AddrList. Give code to show how the values of the three parameters can be accessed from within procedure *Proc1*.

2. Describe what happens if you attempt a recursive procedure call using the system described in this section.

Chapter Summary

This chapter has discussed techniques for implementing procedures in the 80x86 architecture. The stack serves several important purposes in procedure implementation. When a procedure is called, the address of the next instruction is stored on the stack before control transfers to the first instruction of the procedure. A return instruction retrieves this address from the stack in order to transfer control back to the correct point in the calling program. Argument values or their addresses can be pushed onto the stack to pass them to a procedure; when this is done, the base pointer EBP and based addressing provide a convenient mechanism for accessing the values in the procedure. The stack can be used to provide space for a procedure's local variables. The stack is also used to "preserve the environment"—for example, register contents can be pushed onto the stack when a procedure begins and popped off before returning to the calling program so that the calling program does not need to worry about what registers might be altered by the procedure.

Recursive algorithms arise naturally in many computing applications. Recursive procedures are no more difficult than nonrecursive procedures to implement in the 80x86 architecture.

Some computer architectures do not have a hardware stack. Nonrecursive procedures can be implemented using registers to store addresses, and memory to save registers when one procedure calls another.

CHAPTER 7

String Operations

Computers are frequently used to manipulate characters strings as well as numeric data. In data processing applications names, addresses, and so forth must be stored and sometimes rearranged. Text editor and word processor programs must be capable of searching for and moving strings of characters. An assembler must be able to separate assembly language statement elements, identifying those that are reserved mnemonics. Even when computation is primarily numerical, it is often necessary to convert either a character string to an internal numerical format when a number is entered at the keyboard or an internal format to a character string for display purposes.

An 80x86 microprocessor has instructions to manipulate character strings. The same instructions can manipulate strings of doublewords or words. This chapter covers 80x86 instructions that are used to handle strings, with emphasis on character strings. A variety of applications are given, including procedures that are similar to those in some high-level languages and the procedure called by the `dtoa` macro.

7.1   Using String Instructions

Five 80x86 instructions are designed for string manipulation: movs (move string), cmps (compare string), scas (scan string), stos (store string), and lods (load string). The movs instruction is used to copy a string from one memory location to another. The cmps instruction is designed to compare the contents of two strings. The scas instruction can be used to search a string for one particular value. The stos instruction can store a new value in some position of a string. Finally, the lods instruction copies a value out of some position of a string.

A **string** in the 80x86 architecture refers to a contiguous collection of bytes, words, or doublewords in memory. Strings are commonly defined in a program's data segment using such directives as

```
response      BYTE    20 DUP (?)
label1        BYTE    'The results are ', 0
wordString    WORD    50 DUP (?)
arrayD        DWORD   60 DUP (0)
```

Note that strings and arrays are actually the same except for the way we look at them.

Each string instruction applies to a source string, a destination string, or both. The bytes, words, or doublewords of these strings are processed one at a time by the string instruction. Register indirect addressing is used to locate the individual byte, word, or doubleword elements. The 80x86 instructions access elements of the source string using the address in the source index register ESI. Elements in the destination string are accessed using the address in the destination index register EDI. If you program using a segmented memory model, then you also must know that the source element is in the data segment (at address DS:ESI) while the destination element is in the extra segment (at address ES:EDI). With flat memory model programming, both segment registers contain the same segment number and no distinction between segments.

Since the source and destination addresses of string elements are always given by ESI and EDI, respectively, no operands are needed to identify these locations. Without any operand, however, the assembler cannot tell the size of the string element to be used. For example, just movs by itself could say to move a byte, a word, or a doubleword. The Microsoft Macro Assembler offers two ways around this dilemma. The first method is to use destination and source operands; these are ignored except that MASM notes their type (both operands must be the same type) and uses that element size. The second method is to use special versions of the mnemonics that define the element size—

instructions that operate on bytes use a *b* suffix, word string instructions use a *w* suffix, and doubleword string instructions use a *d* suffix. For example, movsb is used to move byte strings, movsw is used to move word strings, and movsd is used to move doubleword strings. Any of these instructions assemble as a movs and none uses an operand since the assembler knows the element size from the mnemonic. This book will use mnemonics with *b*, *w*, and *d* suffixes rather than operands for string instructions.

Although a string instruction operates on only one string element at a time, it always gets ready to operate on the next element. It does this by changing the source index register ESI and/or the destination index register EDI to contain the address of the next element of the string(s). When byte-size elements are being used, the index registers are changed by one; for words, ESI and EDI are changed by two; and for doublewords, the registers are changed by four. The 80x86 can move either forward through a string, from lower to higher addresses, or backward, from higher to lower addresses. The movement direction is determined by the value of the direction flag DF, bit 10 of the EFLAGS register. If DF is set to 1, then the addresses in ESI and EDI are decremented by string instructions, causing right to left string operations. If DF is clear (0), then the values in ESI and EDI are incremented by string instructions, so that strings are processed left to right.

The 80x86 has two instructions whose sole purpose is to reset or set the direction flag DF. The cld instruction clears DF to 0 so that ESI and EDI are incremented by string instructions and strings are processed left to right. The std instruction sets DF to 1 so that strings are processed backward. Neither instruction affects any flag other than DF. Technical data about these instructions appear in Fig. 7.1.

Finally it is time to present all the details about a string instruction. The move string instruction movs transfers one string element (byte, word, or doubleword) from a source string to a destination string. The source element at address DS:ESI is copied to address ES:EDI. After the string element is copied, both index registers are changed by the element size (1, 2, or 4), incremented if the direction flag DF is 0 or decremented if

| Instruction | Clock Cycles | | | Number of Bytes | Opcode |
	386	486	Pentium		
cld	2	2	2	1	FC
std	2	2	2	1	FD

Figure 7.1   cld **and** std **instructions**

Mnemonic	Element size	Clock Cycles 386	486	Pentium	Number of bytes	Opcode
movsb	byte	7	7	4	1	A4
movsw	word	7	7	4	1	A5
movsd	doubleword	7	7	4	1	A5

Figure 7.2   movs instructions (use ESI and EDI)

DF is 1. The movs instruction does not affect any flag. It comes in movsb, movsw, and movsd versions; Fig. 7.2 gives information about each form.

Figure 7.3 gives an example of a program that uses the movs instruction. The important part of the example is the procedure *strcopy*. This procedure has two parameters

```
; test of "strcopy" procedure
; author:  R. Detmer   revised:  10/97

.386
.MODEL FLAT
ExitProcess PROTO NEAR32 stdcall, dwExitCode:DWORD
INCLUDE io.h            ; header file for input/output
cr       equ      0dh    ; carriage return character
Lf       equ      0ah    ; line feed

.STACK  4096             ; reserve 4096-byte stack

.DATA                    ; reserve storage for data
prompt       BYTE    cr, Lf, "Original string?   ",0
stringIn     BYTE    80 DUP (?)
display      BYTE    cr, Lf, "Your string was...", cr, Lf
stringOut    BYTE    80 DUP (?)

.CODE
_start:      output prompt          ; ask for string
             input  stringIn, 80    ; get source string
             lea    eax, stringOut  ; destination address
             push   eax             ; first parameter
```
(continued)

Figure 7.3   String copy program

```
                lea     eax, stringIn      ; source
                push    eax                ; second parameter
                call    strcopy            ; call string copy procedure
                output  display            ; print result
                INVOKE  ExitProcess, 0     ; exit with return code 0
PUBLIC _start                              ; make entry point public

strcopy     PROC NEAR32

; Procedure to copy string until null byte in source is copied.
; It is assumed that destination location is long enough for copy.

; Parameters are passed on the stack:
;     (1)   address of destination
;     (2)   address of source
                push    ebp                ;save base pointer
                mov     ebp,esp            ;copy stack pointer

                push    edi                ;save registers and flags
                push    esi
                pushf

                mov     esi,[ebp+8]        ;initial source address
                mov     edi,[ebp+12]       ;destination
                cld                        ;clear direction flag
whileNoNull:
                cmp     BYTE PTR [esi],0   ;null source byte?
                je      endWhileNoNull     ;stop copying if null
                movsb                      ;copy  one byte
                jmp     whileNoNull        ;go check next byte
endWhileNoNull:
                mov     BYTE PTR [edi],0   ;terminate destination string

                popf                       ;restore flags and registers
                pop     esi
                pop     edi
                pop     ebp
                ret     8                  ;exit procedure, discarding parameters
strcopy     ENDP

                END
```

Figure 7.3   *(continued)*

passed on the stack, which give the destination and source addresses of byte or character strings. The source string is assumed to be null-terminated. Procedure *strcopy* produces an exact copy of the source string at the destination location, terminating the destination string by a null byte.

The procedure only uses registers ESI and EDI. It saves each of these and the flag register on the stack so that the procedure will return with them unchanged. The index registers ESI and EDI must be initialized to the addresses of the first string bytes to be processed. The values for ESI and EDI are the arguments that were pushed on the stack. The direction flag is cleared for left-to-right copying.

After initialization, the procedure executes the following pseudocode design:

---

while next source byte is not null
      copy source byte to destination;
      increment source index;
      increment destination index;
end while;
put null byte at end of destination string;

To check whether the next source byte is null, the statement

```
cmp    BYTE PTR [esi],0  ; null source byte?
```

is used. Recall that the notation [esi] indicates register indirect addressing, so that the element at the address in ESI is used, that is, the current byte of the source string. The operator BYTE PTR is necessary since MASM cannot tell from the operands [esi] and 0 whether byte, word, or doubleword comparison is needed. Copying the source byte and incrementing both index registers is accomplished by the movsb instruction. Finally,

```
mov    BYTE PTR [edi],0  ; terminate destination string
```

serves to move a null byte to the end of the destination string since EDI was incremented after the last byte of the source was copied to the destination. Again, the operator BYTE PTR tells MASM that the destination is a byte rather than a word or doubleword.

The program to test *strcopy* simply inputs a string from the keyboard, calls *strcopy* to copy it somewhere else, and finally displays the string copy. The most interesting part of the code is the collection of instructions needed to call the procedure. The arguments are not removed from the stack since the procedure does that job.

Normally the source string for a movs instruction does not overlap the destination string. However, occasionally this is useful. Suppose that you want to initialize a 80 character-long string at *starSlash* with the pattern */, repeated 40 times. The following code can do this task.

```
starSlash   BYTE   80 DUP (?)

            ...
            mov    starSlash, '*'      ; first *
            mov    starSlash+1, '/'    ; first /
            lea    esi, starSlash      ; source address
            lea    edi, starSlash+2    ; destination
            cld                        ; process left to right
            mov    ecx, 78             ; characters to copy
forCount:   movsb                      ; copy next character
            loop   forCount            ; repeat
```

In this example, the first time movsb is executed, a * from the first string position is copied to the third position. The next iteration, a / is copied from the second to the fourth position. The third time, a * is copied from the third to the fifth position, and so on. The next section introduces an easier way to repeat a movs instruction.

Exercises 7.1

1. What will be the output of the following program?

```
.386
.MODEL FLAT
ExitProcess PROTO NEAR32 stdcall, dwExitCode:DWORD
INCLUDE io.h            ; header file for input/output
cr      equ    0dh      ; carriage return character
Lf      equ    0ah      ; line feed

.STACK  4096            ; reserve 4096-byte stack
.DATA                   ; global data
string  BYTE   'ABCDEFGHIJ'
        BYTE   cr, Lf, 0
```

```
        .CODE
        setup1  PROC NEAR32
                lea    esi, string     ; beginning of string
                lea    edi, string+5   ; address of 'F'
                cld                     ; forward movement
                ret
        setup1  ENDP


        _start: call   setup1    ; set source, destination, direction
                movsb             ; move 4 characters
                movsb
                movsb
                movsb
                output string     ; display modified string
                INVOKE  ExitProcess, 0  ; exit with return code 0
        PUBLIC _start             ; make entry point public
                END
```

2. Repeat Problem 1, replacing the procedure *setup1* by

```
setup2  PROC NEAR32
        lea    esi, string     ; beginning of string
        lea    edi, string+2   ; address of 'C'
        cld                     ; forward movement
        ret
setup2  ENDP
```

3. Repeat Problem 1, replacing the procedure *setup1* by

```
setup3  PROC NEAR32
        lea    esi, string+9   ; end of string
        lea    edi, string+4   ; address of 'E'
        std                     ; backward movement
        ret
setup3  ENDP
```

4. Repeat Problem 1, replacing the procedure *setup1* by

```
setup4   PROC NEAR32
         lea    esi, string+9   ; end of string
         lea    edi, string+7   ; address of 'H'
         std                    ; backward movement
         ret
setup4   ENDP
```

Programming Exercises 7.1

1. Write a program that copies strings read in one at a time from the keyboard into a large storage area for later processing. Specifically, use the input macro to input a string, then copy the string to the first of a 1024 byte block of storage that has been reserved in the data segment. (Recall that the input macro produces a null-terminated string.) Follow the string by a carriage return and a linefeed character in this storage area. Repeat the process with additional strings, copying each subsequent string to the storage area so that it immediately follows the linefeed after the last string. Exit the loop when the first character of the source string is $—do not copy this last string to the storage area. Do, however, place a null byte after the linefeed of the last string in the storage area. Finally, use the output macro to display all the characters in the data area. The result should be the strings that were entered, one per line.

7.2 Repeat Prefixes and More String Instructions

Each 80x86 string instruction operates on one string element at a time. However, the 80x86 architecture includes three repeat prefixes that change the string instructions into versions that repeat automatically either for a fixed number of iterations or until some condition is satisfied. The three repeat prefixes actually correspond to two different single-byte codes; these are not themselves instructions, but supplement machine codes for the primitive string instructions, making new instructions.

Figure 7.4 shows two program fragments, each of which copies a fixed number of characters from *sourceStr* to *destStr*. The number of characters is loaded into the ECX register from *count*. The code in part (a) uses a loop. Since the count of characters might be zero, the loop is guarded by a jecxz instruction. The body of the loop uses movsb to copy one character at a time. The loop instruction takes care of counting loop iterations. The program fragment in part (b) is functionally equivalent to the one

```
            lea     esi, sourceStr   ; source string
            lea     edi, destStr     ; destination
            cld                      ; forward movement
            mov     ecx, count       ; count of characters to copy
            jecxz endCopy            ; skip loop if count is zero
    copy:   movsb                    ; move 1 character
            loop    copy             ; decrement count and continue
    endCopy:
```

(a) movsb iterated in a loop

```
            lea     esi, sourceStr   ; source string
            lea     edi, destStr     ; destination
            cld                      ; forward movement
            mov     ecx, count       ; count of characters to copy
            rep movsb                ; move characters
```

(b) repeat prefix with movsb

Figure 7.4   **Copying a fixed number of characters of a string**

in part (a). After the count is copied into ECX, it uses the repeat prefix rep with a movsb instruction; the rep movsb instruction does the same thing as the last four lines in part (a).

The rep prefix is normally used with the movs instructions and with the stos instruction (discussed below). It causes the following design to be executed:

```
while count in ECX > 0 loop
      perform primitive instruction;
      decrement ECX by 1;
end while;
```

Note that this is a *while* loop. The primitive instruction is not executed at all if ECX contains zero. It is not necessary to guard a repeated string instruction as it often is with an ordinary **for** loop implemented with the loop instruction.

The other two repeat prefixes are repe, with equivalent mnemonic repz, and repne, which is the same as repnz. The mnemonic repe stands for "repeat while

Mnemonic	Loop while	Number of bytes	Opcode
rep	ECX>0	1	F3
repz/repe	ECX>0 and ZF=1	1	F3
repnz/repne	ECX>0 and ZF=0	1	F2

Figure 7.5 **Repeat prefixes**

equal" and `repz` stands for "repeat while zero." Similarly `repne` and `repnz` mean "repeat while not equal" and "repeat while not zero," respectively. Each of these repeat prefixes is appropriate for use with the two string instructions `cmps` and `scas`, which affect the zero flag ZF.

The names of these mnemonics partially describe their actions. Each instruction works the same as `rep`, iterating a primitive instruction while ECX is not zero. However, each also examines ZF after the string instruction is executed. The `repe` and `repz` continue iterating while ZF=1, as it would be following a comparison where two operands were equal. The `repne` and `repnz` continue iterating while ZF=0, as it would be following a comparison where two operands were different. Repeat prefixes themselves do not affect any flag. The three repeat prefixes are summarized in Fig. 7.5. Note that `rep` and `repz` (`repe`) generate exactly the same code.

The `repz` and `repnz` prefixes do not quite produce true *while* loops with the conditions shown in Fig. 7.5. The value in ECX is checked *prior* to the first iteration of the primitive instruction, as it should be with a *while* loop. However, ZF is not checked until *after* the primitive instruction is executed. In practice, this is very convenient since the instruction is skipped for a zero count, but the programmer does not have to do anything special to initialize ZF prior to repeated instructions.

Figure 7.6 shows how the repeat prefix `rep` combines with the `movs` instructions. In the clock cycles columns, there is a "set up" time plus a time for each iteration.

Mnemonic	Element size	Clock Cycles			Number of bytes	Opcode
		386	486	Pentium		
rep movsb	byte	7+4n	12+3n	13+4n	2	F3 A4
rep movsw	word					F3 A5
rep movsd	doubleword					F3 A5

Figure 7.6 `rep movs` **instructions**

Mnemonic	Element size	Clock Cycles 386	486	Pentium	Number of bytes	Opcode
cmpsb	byte	10	8	5	1	A6
cmpsw	word					A7
cmpsd	doubleword					A7
repe cmpsb	byte	$5+9n$	$7+7n$	$9+4n$	2	F3 A6
repe cmpsw	word					F3 A7
repe cmpsd	doubleword					F3 A7
repne cmpsb	byte	$5+9n$	$7+7n$	$9+4n$	2	F2 A6
repne cmpsw	word					F2 A7
repne cmpsd	doubleword					F2 A7

Figure 7.7 cmps **instructions**

The n in the table represents the number of iterations, so that, for example, a rep movsb takes 33 ($13+4\times5$) clock cycles on a Pentium to move five bytes. (The table entries are not strictly accurate since there are special timings for the 486 and Pentium when $n=0$ or $n=1$.)

The cmps instructions, summarized in Fig. 7.7, compare elements of source and destination strings. Chapter 5 explained how a cmp instruction subtracts two operands and sets flags based on the difference. Similarly, cmps subtracts two string elements and sets flags based on the difference; neither operand is changed. If a cmps instruction is used in a loop, it is appropriate to follow cmps by almost any of the conditional jump instructions, depending on the design being implemented.

Repeat prefixes are often used with cmps instructions. In fact, for the task of finding if two strings are identical, the repe prefix is a perfect companion for cmps. Figure 7.7 summarizes all the cmps instructions, including repeated ones. Again, the timings are not strictly accurate for 486 and Pentium CPUs; for rep cmps there are special timings when $n=0$.

It is often necessary to search for one string embedded in another. Suppose that the task at hand is to find the position, if any, at which the string at *key* appears in the string at *target*. One simple algorithm to do this is

```
position := 1;
while position ≤ (targetLength – keyLength + 1) loop
      if key matches the substring of target starting at position
      then
            report success;
            exit process;
      end if;
      add 1 to position;
end while;
report failure;
```

This algorithm checks to see if the key string matches the portion of the target string starting at each possible position. Using 80x86 registers, checking for one match can be done as follows:

```
ESI := address of key;
EDI := address of target + position – 1;
ECX := length of key;

forever loop
      if ECX = 0 then exit loop; end if;
      compare [ESI] and [EDI] setting ZF;
      increment ESI;
      increment EDI;
      decrement ECX;
      if ZF = 0 then exit loop; end if;
end loop;

if ZF = 1
then
      match was found;
end if;
```

The forever loop is exactly what is done by the repeated string instruction repe cmpsb. Since the loop is terminated when either ECX = 0 or when ZF = 0, it is necessary to be sure that the last pair of characters compared were the same; this is the reason for the extra **if** structure at the end of the design. Figure 7.8 shows a complete program that implements this design.

The scan string instruction scas is used to scan a string for the presence or absence of a particular string element. The string that is examined is a destination string; that is, the address of the element being examined is in the destination index register EDI. With a scasb instruction, the element searched for is the byte in the AL register; with a scasw, it is the word in the AX register; and with a scasd, it is the doubleword in the EAX register. The scasb, scasw, and scasd instructions use no

```
; program to search for one string embedded in another
; author:  R. Detmer    revised:  10/97

.386
.MODEL FLAT

ExitProcess PROTO NEAR32 stdcall, dwExitCode:DWORD
INCLUDE io.h

cr          EQU    0dh    ; carriage return character
Lf          EQU    0ah    ; linefeed character


.STACK  4096                ; reserve 4096-byte stack

.DATA
prompt1     BYTE   "String to search?  ", 0
prompt2     BYTE   cr, Lf, "Key to search for?  ", 0
target      BYTE   80 DUP (?)
key         BYTE   80 DUP (?)
trgtLength  DWORD ?
keyLength   DWORD ?
lastPosn    DWORD ?
failure     BYTE   cr,Lf,Lf,"The key does not appear in the string.",cr,Lf,0
success     BYTE   cr,Lf,Lf,'The key appears at position'
```

(continued)

Figure 7.8 **String search program**

```
position    BYTE   11 DUP (?)
            BYTE   "   in the string.", cr, Lf, 0

PUBLIC _start                    ; make entry point public
.CODE

_start:     output prompt1           ; ask for
            input  target,80         ;   and input target string
            lea    eax, target       ; find length of string
            push   eax               ; length parameter
            call   strlen
            mov    trgtLength,eax     ; save length of target
            output prompt2           ; ask for
            input  key,80            ;   and input key string
            lea    eax, key          ; find length of string
            push   eax               ; length parameter
            call   strlen
            mov    keyLength,eax      ; save length of key

; calculate last position of target to check
            mov    eax,trgtLength
            sub    eax,keyLength
            inc    eax               ; trgtLength - keyLength + 1
            mov    lastPosn, eax
            cld                      ; left to right comparison

            mov    eax,1             ; starting position
whilePosn:  cmp    eax,lastPosn      ; position <= last_posn?
            jnle   endWhilePosn      ; exit if past last position

            lea    esi,target        ; address of target string
            add    esi,eax           ; add position
            dec    esi               ; address of position to check
            lea    edi,key           ; address of key
            mov    ecx,keyLength      ; number of positions to check
            repe cmpsb               ; check
            jz     found             ; exit on success
            inc    eax               ; increment position
            jmp    whilePosn         ; repeat
endWhilePosn:
```

(continued)

Figure 7.8   *(continued)*

```
              output failure        ; the search failed
              jmp    quit           ; exit

found:        dtoa   position,eax   ; convert position to ASCII
              output success        ; search succeeded
quit:
              INVOKE ExitProcess, 0 ; exit with return code 0

strlen        PROC   NEAR32
; find length of string whose address is passed on stack
; length returned in EAX
              push   ebp            ; establish stack frame
              mov    ebp, esp
              pushf                 ; save flags
              push   ebx            ; and EBX
              sub    eax, eax       ; length := 0
              mov    ebx, [ebp+8]   ; address of string
whileChar:    cmp    BYTE PTR [ebx], 0  ; null byte?
              je     endWhileChar   ; exit if so
              inc    eax            ; increment length
              inc    ebx            ; point at next character
              jmp    whileChar      ; repeat
endWhileChar:
              pop    ebx            ; restore registers and flags
              popf
              pop    ebp
              ret    4              ; return, discarding parameter
strlen        ENDP

              END
```

Figure 7.8 *(continued)*

operand since the mnemonics tell the element size. Figure 7.9 summarizes the scas instructions; as with the previous repeated instructions, there are special timings for $n=0$ on the 486 and Pentium.

The program shown in Fig. 7.10 inputs a string and a character and uses repne scasb to locate the position of the first occurrence of the character in the string. It then displays the part of the string from the character to the end. The length of the string is calculated using the *strlen* procedure that previously appeared in Fig. 7.8; this time we assume that *strlen* is separately assembled. The lea instruction is used to load the offset of the string to be searched and cld ensures a forward search.

Mnemonic	Element size	Clock Cycles 386	486	Pentium	Number of bytes	Opcode
scasb	byte	7	6	4	1	AE
scasw	word					AF
scasd	doubleword					AF
repe scasb	byte	$5+8n$	$7+5n$	$9+4n$	2	F3 AE
repe scasw	word					F3 AF
repe scasd	doubleword					F3 AF
repne scasb	byte	$5+8n$	$7+5n$	$9+4n$	2	F2 AE
repne scasw	word					F2 AF
repne scasd	doubleword					F2 AF

Figure 7.9   scas instructions (use EDI)

```
; Program to locate a character within a string.
; The string is displayed from the character to the end.
; author:  R. Detmer     revised:  10/97

.386
.MODEL FLAT

ExitProcess PROTO NEAR32 stdcall, dwExitCode:DWORD
INCLUDE io.h
EXTRN strlen:NEAR32
PUBLIC _start

cr          EQU    0dh    ; carriage return character
Lf          EQU    0ah    ; linefeed character

.STACK  4096             ; reserve 4096-byte stack

.DATA
prompt1     BYTE    "String?  ", 0
prompt2     BYTE    cr, Lf, Lf, "Character?  ", 0
string      BYTE    80 DUP (?)
char        BYTE    5 DUP (?)

                                            (continued)
```

Figure 7.10   Program to find character in string

```
label1        BYTE    cr, Lf, Lf, "The rest of the string is—", 0
crlf          BYTE    cr, Lf, 0

.CODE
_start:       output prompt1         ; prompt for string
              input  string,80       ; get string
              lea    eax, string     ; find length of string
              push   eax             ; length parameter
              call   strlen
              mov    ecx, eax         ; save length of string
              inc    ecx              ; include null in string length

              output prompt2         ; prompt for character
              input  char,5          ; get character
              mov    al, char         ; character to AL

              lea    edi, string     ; offset of string
              cld                     ; forward movement
              repne scasb             ; scan while character not found
              dec    edi             ; back up to null or matching character

              output label1          ; print label
              output [edi]           ; output string
              output crlf            ; skip to new line

              INVOKE  ExitProcess, 0  ; exit with return code 0
              END
```

Figure 7.10 *(continued)*

After the search, the destination index EDI will be one greater than desired since a string instruction always increments index registers whether or not flags were set. If the search succeeded, EDI will contain the address of the character following the one that matched with AL, or the address of the character after the end of the string if ECX was decremented to zero. The `dec edi` instruction takes care of both cases, backing up to the position of the matching character if there was one, or to the null byte at the end of the string otherwise. The string length was incremented so that the null character would be included in the search. The `output` macro displays the last portion of the string, whose address is in EDI.

The store string instruction `stos` copies a byte, a word, or a doubleword from AL, AX, or EAX to an element of a destination string. A `stos` instruction affects no flag, so that when it is repeated with `rep`, it copies the same value into consecutive positions of a string. For example, the following code will store spaces in the first 30 bytes of string.

```
mov   ecx,30              ; 30 bytes
mov   al, ' '             ; character to store
lea   edi, string         ; address of string
cld                       ; forward direction
rep stosb                 ; store spaces
```

Information about the `stos` instructions is in Fig. 7.11. As with previous repeated string instructions, the 80486 and Pentium have special timings when $n=0$.

The load string instruction `lods` is the final string instruction. This instruction copies a source string element to the AL, AX, or EAX register, depending on the string element size. A `lods` instruction sets no flag. It is possible to use a `rep` prefix with `lods` but it is not helpful—all values except for the last string element would be replaced as successive values were copied to the destination register. A `lods` instruction is useful in a loop set up with other instructions, making it possible to easily process string elements one at a time. The `lods` instructions are summarized in Fig. 7.12. Repeated versions are not included since they are not used.

Mnemonic	Element size	Clock Cycles			Number of bytes	Opcode
		386	486	Pentium		
stosb	byte	4	5	3	1	AA
stosw	word					AB
stosd	doubleword					AB
rep stosb	byte	5+5n	7+4n	9n	2	F3 A6
rep stosw	word					F3 A7
rep stosd	doubleword					F3 A7

Figure 7.11   `stos` instructions (use EDI)

Mnemonic	Element size	Clock Cycles 386	486	Pentium	Number of bytes	Opcode
lodsb	byte	5	5	2	1	AC
lodsw	word					AD
lodsd	doubleword					AD

Figure 7.12 lods instructions (use ESI)

Exercises 7.2

For each exercise below, assume that the data segment contains

```
source     BYTE     "brown"
dest       BYTE     "brine"
```

1. Suppose that the following instructions are executed:

```
lea    esi, source
lea    edi, dest
cld
mov    ecx, 5
repne cmpsb
```

Assuming that ESI starts at 00010000 and EDI starts at 00010005, what will be the values stored in ESI and EDI following the repne cmpsb instruction? What will be stored in ECX?

2. Suppose that the following instructions are executed:

```
lea    esi, source
lea    edi, dest
cld
mov    ecx, 5
repe cmpsb
```

Assuming that ESI starts at 00010000 and EDI starts at 00010005, what will be the values stored in ESI and EDI following the repe cmpsb instruction? What will be stored in ECX?

3. Suppose that the following instructions are executed:

```
mov   al, 'w'
lea   edi, dest
cld
mov   ecx, 5
repe scasb
```

Assuming that EDI starts at 00010005, what will be the value stored in EDI following the `repe scasb` instruction? What will be stored in ECX?

4. Suppose that the following instructions are executed:

```
mov   al, 'n'
lea   edi, dest
cld
mov   ecx, 5
repne scasb
```

Assuming that EDI starts at 00010005, what will be the value stored in EDI following the `repne scasb` instruction? What will be stored in ECX?

5. Suppose that the following instructions are executed:

```
mov   al, '*'
lea   edi, dest
cld
mov   ecx, 5
rep stosb
```

Assuming that EDI starts at 00010005, what will be the value stored in EDI following the `rep stosb` instruction? What will be stored in ECX? What will be stored in the destination string?

6. Suppose that the following instructions are executed:

```
      lea   esi, source
      lea   edi, dest
      cld
      mov   ecx, 5
for6: lodsb
      inc   al
```

```
                stosb
                loop   for6
      endFor6:
```

Assuming that ESI starts at 00010000 and EDI starts at 00010005, what will be the values stored in ESI and EDI following the for loop? What will be stored in ECX? What will be stored in the destination string?

7. Suppose that the following instructions are executed:

```
lea    esi, source
lea    edi, dest
cld
mov    ecx, 3
rep    movsb
```

Assuming that ESI starts at 00010000 and EDI starts at 00010005, what will be the values stored in ESI and EDI following the rep movsb instruction? What will be stored in ECX? What will be stored in the destination string?

8. Suppose that the following instructions are executed:

```
lea    esi, source+4
lea    edi, dest+4
std
mov    ecx, 3
rep    movsb
```

Assuming that ESI starts at 00010010 and EDI starts at 00010015, what will be the values stored in ESI and EDI following the rep movsb instruction? What will be stored in ECX? What will be stored in the destination string?

Programming Exercises 7.2

1. Write a NEAR32 procedure *index* to find the position of the first occurrence of a character in a null-terminated string. Specifically, the procedure must have two parameters: (1) a character and (2) the address of a string in the data segment. Use the stack to pass the parameters: For the character, use an entire word with the character in the low-order byte.

Use the EAX register to return the position of the character within the string; return zero if the character is not found. No other register should be altered. Procedure *index* will not remove parameters from the stack.

2.   Write a NEAR32 procedure *append* that will append one null-terminated string to the end of another. Specifically, the procedure must have two parameters: (1) the address of *string1* in the data segment and (2) the address of *string2* in the data segment. Use the stack to pass the parameters. The procedure should copy the characters of *string2* to the end of *string1* with the first character of *string2* replacing the null byte at the end of *string1*, and so on. (Warning: In the data section, enough space must be reserved after the null byte of the first string to hold the characters from the second string.) All registers used by the procedure should be saved and restored. Procedure *append* will not remove parameters from the stack.

3.   Write a complete program that prompts for and inputs a person's name in the "*LastName, FirstName*" format and builds a new string with the name in the format "*FirstName LastName.*" A comma and a space separate the names originally and there is no character except the null following *FirstName*; only a space separates the names in the new string. After you generate the new string in memory, display it.

4.   Write a complete program which prompts for and inputs a person's name in the "*LastName, FirstName*" format and builds a new string with the name in the format "*FirstName LastName.*" One or more spaces separate the names originally and there may be spaces following *FirstName*. Only a single space separates the names in the new string. After you generate the new string in memory, display it.

5.   Write a complete program that prompts for and inputs a string and a single character. Construct a new string that is identical to the old one except that it is shortened by removing each occurrence of the character. After you generate the new string in memory, display it.

6.   Write a complete program that prompts for and inputs a sentence and a single word. Construct a new sentence that is identical to the old one except that it is shortened by removing each occurrence of the word. After you generate the new sentence in memory, display it.

7. Write a complete program that prompts for and inputs a sentence and two words. Construct a new sentence that is identical to the old one except that each occurrence of the first word is replaced by the second word. After you generate the new sentence in memory, display it.

7.3 Character Translation

Sometimes character data are available in one format but need to be in another format for processing. One instance of this occurs when characters are transmitted between two computer systems, one normally using ASCII character codes and the other normally using EBCDIC character codes. Another time character codes need to be altered is to transmit them to a device that cannot process all possible codes; it is sometimes easier to replace the unsuitable codes by acceptable codes than to delete them entirely.

The 80x86 instruction set includes the xlat instruction to translate one character to another character. In combination with other string-processing instructions, it can easily translate all the characters in a string.

The xlat instruction requires only one byte of object code, the opcode D7. It takes five clock cycles to execute on an 80386, and four clock cycles on an 80486 or a Pentium. Prior to execution, the character to be translated is in the AL register. The instruction works by using a translation table in the data segment to look up the translation of the byte in AL. This translation table normally contains 256 bytes of data, one for each possible 8-bit value in AL. The byte at offset zero in the table—the first byte—is the character to which 00 is translated. The byte at offset one is the character to which 01 is translated. In general xlat uses the character being translated as an offset into the table, and the byte at that offset then replaces the character in AL.

The xlat instruction has no operand. The EBX register must contain the address of the translation table.

Figure 7.13 illustrates a short program which translates each character of string in place; that is, it replaces each character by its translation using the original location in memory. The heart of the program is the translation table and the sequence of instructions

```
mov     ecx, strLength ; string length
lea     ebx, table      ; address of translation table
lea     esi, string     ; address of string
```

```
            lea     edi, string      ; destination also string
forIndex:   lodsb                    ; copy next character to AL
            xlat                     ; translate character
            stosb                    ; copy character back into string
            loop    forIndex         ; repeat for all characters
```

```
; Translate uppercase letters to lowercase; don't change lower
; case letters and digits.  Translate other characters to spaces.
; author:  R. Detmer    revised: 10/97


.386
.MODEL FLAT

ExitProcess PROTO NEAR32 stdcall, dwExitCode:DWORD
INCLUDE io.h
PUBLIC _start
cr          EQU     0dh    ; carriage return character
Lf          EQU     0ah    ; linefeed character

.STACK  4096               ; reserve 4096-byte stack

.DATA
string      BYTE    'This is a #!$& STRING',0
strLength   EQU     $ - string - 1
label1      BYTE    'Original string   ->',0
label2      BYTE    cr, Lf, 'Translated string ->',0
crlf        BYTE    cr, Lf, 0
table       BYTE    48 DUP (' '), '0123456789', 7 DUP (' ')
            BYTE    'abcdefghijklmnopqrstuvwxyz', 6 DUP (' ')
            BYTE    'abcdefghijklmnopqrstuvwxyz', 133 DUP (' ')

.CODE
_start:     output label1        ; display original string
            output string
            output crlf
```

(continued)

Figure 7.13 Translation program

```
                mov     ecx, strLength  ; string length
                lea     ebx, table      ; address of translation table
                lea     esi, string     ; address of string
                lea     edi, string     ; destination also string
forIndex:       lodsb                   ; copy next character to AL
                xlat                    ; translate character
                stosb                   ; copy character back into string
                loop    forIndex        ; repeat for all characters

                output  label2          ; display altered string
                output  string
                output  crlf

                INVOKE  ExitProcess, 0
                END
```

Figure 7.13 *(continued)*

These instructions implement a **for** loop with the design

---

for index := 1 to stringLength loop
    load source character into AL;
    translate character in AL;
    copy character in AL to destination;
end for;

One new feature in this program is the use of the location counter symbol $. Recall that the assembler calculates addresses as if they start at 00000000, and increments a counter every time it generates bytes of object code. The dollar sign symbol refers to the value of this counter at the time it is encountered in assembly. In this particular program, it will be at the address just beyond the null byte of the string. Since the symbol *string* actually references its address, the expression string $-$ $ is the length of string, including the null byte. The value equated to *strLength* is $ $-$ string $-$ 1, which excludes the null byte. The assembly process will be discussed more in Chapter 9.

Each ASCII code is translated to another ASCII code by this program. Uppercase letters are translated to lowercase, lowercase letters and digits are unchanged, and all other characters are translated to spaces. Construction of such a table involves looking at a table of ASCII codes (see Appendix A). For this program the translation table is defined by

```
table      BYTE    48 DUP (' '), '0123456789', 7 DUP (' ')
           BYTE    'abcdefghijklmnopqrstuvwxyz', 6 DUP (' ')
           BYTE    'abcdefghijklmnopqrstuvwxyz', 133 DUP (' ')
```

Careful counting will show that exactly 256 bytes are defined. Recall that a BYTE directive stores the ASCII code of each character operand. Each of the first 48 bytes of the table will contain the ASCII code for a space (i.e., blank), 20_{16}. Therefore if the code in the AL register represents any of the first 48 ASCII characters—a control character, or one of the printable characters from 20_{16} (space) to $2F_{16}$ (/)—it will be translated to a space.

Note that it is legal to translate a character to itself. Indeed, this is what will happen for digits; the ASCII codes 30_{16} to 39_{16} for digits 0 through 9 appear at offsets 30_{16} to 39_{16}. The codes for the seven characters : through @ are next in an ASCII chart; each of these will be translated to a space. The next ASCII characters are the uppercase letters and the next entries in the table are codes for the lowercase letters. For example, the table contains 61_{16} at offset 41_{16}, so an uppercase A (ASCII code 41_{16}) will be translated to a lower case a (ASCII code 61_{16}). The next six blanks are at the offsets 91_{16} ([) through 96_{16} ('), so that each of these characters is translated to a blank. The ASCII code for each lowercase letter is assembled at an offset equal to its value, so each lowercase letter is translated to itself. Finally, the translation table contains 133 ASCII codes for blanks; these are the destinations for {, |, }, ~, DEL, and each of the 128 bit patterns starting with a one, none of them codes for ASCII characters.

Figure 7.14 shows the output of the program in Fig. 7.13. Notice that "strange" characters are not deleted, they are replaced by blanks.

```
Original string    ->This is a #!$& STRING

Translated string ->this is a       string
```

Figure 7.14 Output from translation program

Exercises 7.3

1. Here is a partial hexadecimal/EBCDIC conversion table:

81 a	C1 A	40 space
82 b	C2 B	4B .
83 c	C3 C	6B ,
84 d	C4 D	
85 e	C5 E	F0 0
86 f	C6 F	F1 1
87 g	C7 G	F2 2
88 h	C8 H	F3 3
89 i	C9 I	F4 4
91 j	D1 J	F5 5
92 k	D2 K	F6 6
93 l	D3 L	F7 7
94 m	D4 M	F8 8
95 n	D5 N	F9 9
96 o	D6 O	
97 p	D7 P	
98 q	D8 Q	
99 r	D9 R	
A2 s	E2 S	
A3 t	E3 T	
A4 u	E4 U	
A5 v	E5 V	
A6 w	E6 W	
A7 x	E7 X	
A8 y	E8 Y	
A9 z	E9 Z	

   Give a translation table that would be suitable for `xlat` translation of EBCDIC codes for letters, digits, space, period, and comma to the corresponding ASCII codes, translating every other EBCDIC code to a null character.

2. Give a translation table that would be suitable for `xlat` translation of ASCII codes for lowercase letters to the corresponding uppercase letters, leaving all other characters unchanged.

3. Here is an alternative to the `xlat` instruction.

```
movzx   eax, al       ; clear high order bits in EAX
mov     al, [ebx+eax] ; copy new character from table to AL
```

Given that `[ebx+eax]` references the memory byte at the address that is the sum of the contents of EBX and EAX, explain why this pair of instructions is equivalent to a single `xlat` instruction.

Programming Exercises 7.3

1. In the United States, decimal numbers are written with a decimal point separating the integral part from the fractional part and with commas every three positions to the left of the decimal point. In many European countries, decimal numbers are written with the roles of commas and decimal points reversed. For example, the number 1,234,567.89 would be written 1.234.567,89. Write a program that will interchange commas and periods, translating a string of characters representing either format of number to the other format. Use the `xlat` instruction with a translation table that translates a period to a comma, a comma to a period, each digit to itself, and any other character to a space. Prompt for and input the number to be translated. Translate the string. Display the new number format with an appropriate label.

7.4   Converting a 2's Complement Integer to an ASCII String

The `dtoa` and `itoa` macros have been used to convert 2's complement integers to strings of ASCII characters for output. The code for these operations is similar. In this section we examine the slightly shorter code for `itoa`.

The `itoa` macro expands into the following sequence of instructions.

```
push    ebx                   ; save EBX
mov     bx, source
push    bx                    ; source parameter
lea     ebx, dest             ; destination address
push    ebx                   ; destination parameter
call    itoaproc              ; call itoaproc(source,dest)
pop     ebx                   ; restore EBX
```

These instructions call procedure *itoaproc* after pushing the source value and the destination address on the stack. The actual source and destination are used in the expanded macro, not the names *source* and *dest*. So that the user does not need to worry about any register contents being altered, EBX is initially saved on the stack and is restored at the end of the sequence. The parameters are removed from the stack by procedure *itoaproc* since the alternative add esp, 6 following the call instruction potentially changes the flags.

The real work of 2's complement integer to ASCII conversion is done by the procedure *itoaproc*. The assembled version of this procedure is contained in the file IO.OBJ. The source code from file IO.ASM is shown in Fig. 7.15. The procedure begins by saving all of the registers that it alters on the stack; the flag register is also saved so that the procedure call to *itoaproc* will not change flag settings. The flag register and other registers are restored immediately before returning from the procedure.

The basic idea of the procedure is to build a string of characters right to left by repeatedly dividing the number by 10, using the remainder to determine the rightmost

```
; itoaproc(source, dest)
; convert integer (source) to string of 6 characters at destination address

itoaproc    PROC    NEAR32
            push    ebp                 ; save base pointer
            mov     ebp, esp            ; establish stack frame
            push    eax                 ; Save registers
            push    ebx                 ;    used by
            push    ecx                 ;    procedure
            push    edx
            push    edi
            pushf                       ; save flags

            mov     ax, [ebp+12]        ; first parameter (source integer)
            mov     edi, [ebp+8]        ; second parameter (dest address)
ifSpecial:  cmp     ax,8000h            ; special case -32,768?
            jne     EndIfSpecial        ; if not, then normal case
            mov     BYTE PTR [edi],'-'  ; manually put in ASCII codes
            mov     BYTE PTR [edi+1],'3' ;   for -32,768

                                                            (continued)
```

Figure 7.15 Integer to ASCII conversion procedure

```
            mov    BYTE PTR [edi+2],'2'
            mov    BYTE PTR [edi+3],'7'
            mov    BYTE PTR [edi+4],'6'
            mov    BYTE PTR [edi+5],'8'
            jmp    ExitIToA               ; done with special case
EndIfSpecial:

            mov    dx, ax                 ; save source number

            mov    al,' '                 ; put blanks in
            mov    ecx,5                  ;    first five
            cld                           ;    bytes of
            rep stosb                     ;    destination field

            mov    ax, dx                 ; copy source number
            mov    cl,' '                 ; default sign (blank for +)
IfNeg:      cmp    ax,0                   ; check sign of number
            jge    EndIfNeg               ; skip if not negative
            mov    cl,'-'                 ; sign for negative number
            neg    ax                     ; number in AX now >= 0
EndIfNeg:

            mov    bx,10                  ; divisor
WhileMore:  mov    dx,0                   ; extend number to doubleword
            div    bx                     ; divide by 10
            add    dl,30h                 ; convert remainder to character
            mov    [edi],dl               ; put character in string
            dec    edi                    ; move forward to next position
            cmp    ax,0                   ; check quotient
            jnz    WhileMore              ; continue if quotient not zero

            mov    [edi],cl               ; insert blank or "-" for sign
ExitIToA:   popf                          ; restore flags and registers
            pop    edi
            pop    edx
            pop    ecx
            pop    ebx
            pop    eax
            pop    ebp
            ret    6                      ;exit, discarding parameters
itoaproc    ENDP
```

Figure 7.15 (continued)

character. For instance, dividing the number 2895 ($0B4F_{16}$) by 10 gives a remainder of 5 and a quotient of 289 (0121_{16}), the last digit of the number and a new number with which to repeat the process. This scheme works nicely for positive numbers, but a negative number must be changed to its absolute value before starting the division loop. To complicate things further, the bit pattern 8000_{16} represents the negative number $-32,768_{10}$, but $+32,768$ cannot be represented in 2's complement form in a 16-bit word.

After standard entry code, the value parameter is copied to AX and the destination address to EDI. The procedure then checks for the special case 8000_{16}. If this is the value, then the ASCII codes for -32768 are moved one at a time to the destination, using the fact that the destination address is in EDI. The location for the minus sign is in the EDI register, so register indirect addressing can be used to put this character in the correct memory byte. The location for the character 3 is one byte beyond the address contained in EDI; this address is referenced by `[edi+1]`. The remaining four characters are similarly put in place, and the procedure is exited.

The next step of the procedure is to put five leading blanks in the six-byte-long destination field. The procedure does this with a `rep stosb`, which uses EDI to point to successive bytes in destination field. Note that EDI is left pointing at the last byte of the destination field.

The procedure next stores the correct "sign" in the CL register. A blank is used for a number greater than or equal to zero, and minus character ($-$) is used for a negative number. A negative number is also negated, giving its absolute value for subsequent processing.

Finally the main idea is executed. The divisor 10 is placed in the BX register. The non-negative number is extended to a doubleword by moving zeros to DX. Division by 10 in BX gives a remainder from 0 to 9 in DX, the last decimal digit of the number. This is converted to the corresponding ASCII code by adding 30_{16}; recall that the ASCII codes for digits 0 through 9 are 30_{16} through 39_{16}. A `mov` using register indirect addressing puts the character in place in the destination string, and EDI is decremented to point at the next position to the left.

This process is repeated until the quotient is zero. Finally the "sign" stored in CL (blank or $-$) is copied to the immediate left of the last code for a digit. Other positions to the left, if any, were previously filled with blanks.

Exercises 7.4

1. Why does *itoaproc* use a destination string six bytes long?

2. Suppose that negative numbers are not changed before the division loop of *itoaproc* begins and that an `idiv` instruction is used rather than

a `div` instruction in this loop. Recall that when a negative number is divided by a positive number, both quotient and remainder will be negative. For instance, $-1273 = 10*(-127) + (-3)$. How could the rest of the division loop be modified to produce the correct ASCII codes for both positive and negative numbers?

Programming Exercises 7.4

1. Rewrite *itoaproc*, adding a length parameter. Specifically, the new *itoaNew* will be a `NEAR32` procedure with three parameters, passed on the stack:

   (1) the 2's complement number to convert to ASCII characters (a word)

   (2) the address of the ASCII string (a doubleword)

   (3) the desired length of the ASCII string (a word)

   The number will be converted to a string of ASCII characters starting at the offset in the data segment. Do *not* use a blank in front of a positive number. If the length is less than the actual number of characters needed to display the number, fill the entire field with pound signs (#). If the length is larger than needed, pad with extra spaces to the left of the number. The procedure will remove parameters from the stack and must modify no register.

2. Write a `NEAR32` procedure *hexString* that converts a 32-bit integer to a string of exactly eight characters representing its value as a hexadecimal number. (That is, the output characters will be 0–9 and A–F, with no blanks.) The procedure will have two parameters, passed on the stack:

   (1) the number

   (2) the address of the destination string

   The procedure will remove parameters from the stack and must modify no register. (The remainder upon division by 16 produces a decimal value corresponding to the rightmost hex digit.)

3. Write a `NEAR32` procedure *binaryString* that converts a 32-bit integer to a string of exactly 32 characters representing its value as a binary number. The procedure will have two parameters, passed on the stack:

   (1) the number

   (2) the address of the destination string

   The procedure will remove parameters from the stack and must modify no register. (The remainder upon division by 2 gives the rightmost bit.)

7.5   Other Architectures: CISC versus RISC Designs

Early digital computers had very simple instruction sets. When designers began to use microcode to implement instructions in the 1960s, it became possible to have much more complex instructions. At the same time high-level programming languages were becoming popular, but language compilers were fairly primitive. This made it desirable to have machine language statements that almost directly implemented high-level language statements, increasing the pressure to produce computer architectures with many complex instructions.

The Intel 80x86 machines use **complex instruction set computer (CISC)** designs. Instructions such as the string instructions discussed in this chapter would never have appeared in early computers. CISC machines also have a variety of memory addressing modes, and the 80x86 family is typical in this respect, although you have only seen a few of its modes so far. Often CISC instructions take several clock cycles to execute.

Reduced instruction set computer (RISC) designs began to appear in the 1980s. These machines have relatively few instructions and few memory addressing modes. Their instructions are so simple that any one can be executed in a single clock cycle. As compiler technology improved, it became possible to produce efficient code for RISC machines. Of course, it often takes many more instructions to implement a given high-level language statement on a RISC than on a CISC machine, but the overall operation is often faster because of the speed with which individual instructions execute.

In RISC architectures, instructions are all the same format; that is, the same number of bytes are encoded in a common pattern. This is not the case with CISC architectures. If the 80x86 chips were RISC designs, then this book would have no questions asking "How many clock cycles?" or "How many bytes?" When we look at the many 80x86 instruction formats in Chapter 9, you may wish for the simplicity of a RISC machine.

One unusual feature of many RISC designs is a relatively large collection of registers (sometimes over 500), of which only a small number (often 32) are visible at one time. Registers are used to pass parameters to procedures, and the registers that are used to store arguments in the calling program overlap the registers that are used to receive the parameter values in the procedure. This provides a simple but very efficient method of communication between a calling program and a procedure.

There are proponents of both CICS and RISC designs. At this point in time it is not obvious that one is clearly better than the other. However, the popular Intel 80x86 and Motorola 680x0 families are both CISC designs, so we will be dealing with CISC systems at least in the near future.

Chapter Summary

The word string refers to a collection of consecutive bytes, words, or doublewords in memory. The 80x86 instruction set includes five instructions for operating on strings: `movs` (to move or copy a string from a source to a destination location), `cmps` (to compare two strings), `scas` (to scan a string for a particular element), `stos` (to store a given value in a string), and `lods` (to copy a string element into EAX, AX, or AL). Each of these has mnemonic forms ending with *b*, *w*, or *d* to give the size of the string element.

A string instruction operates on one string element at a time. When a source string is involved, the source index register ESI contains the address of the string element. When a destination string is involved, the destination index register EDI contains the address of the string element. An index register is incremented or decremented after the string element is accessed, depending on whether the direction flag DF is reset to zero or set to one; the `cld` and `std` instructions are used to give the direction flag a desired value.

Repeat prefixes `rep`, `repe` (`repz`), and `repne` (`repnz`) are used with some string instructions to cause them to repeat automatically. The number of times to execute a primitive instruction is placed in the ECX register. The conditional repeat forms use the count in ECX but will also terminate instruction execution if the zero flag gets a certain value; these are appropriate for use with the `cmps` and `scas` instructions that set or reset ZF.

The `xlat` instruction is used to translate the characters of a string. It requires a 256-byte-long translation table that starts with the destination byte to which the source byte 00 is translated and ends with the destination byte to which the source byte FF is translated. The `xlat` instruction can be used for such applications as changing ASCII codes to EBCDIC codes or for changing the case of letters within a given character coding system.

The `itoa` macro expands to code that calls a procedure *itoaproc*. Basically this procedure works by repeatedly dividing a non-negative number by 10 and using the remainder to get the rightmost character of the destination string.

The 80x86 chips are examples of complex instruction set computer (CISC) architecture. They include many complex instructions and offer many different addressing modes. Reduced instruction set computer (RISC) architectures implement fewer and simpler instructions and have more limited addressing options. Even though RISC computers take more instructions to accomplish a task, they are usually quite fast since they execute their simple instructions very rapidly.

CHAPTER 8

Bit Manipulation

A computer contains many integrated circuits that enable it to perform its functions. Each chip incorporates from a few to many thousand **logic gates**, each an elementary circuit that performs Boolean **and**, **or**, **exclusive or**, or **not** operations on bits that are represented by electronic states. The CPU is usually the most complex integrated circuit in a PC.

Previous chapters have examined the 80x86 microprocessors' instructions for moving data, performing arithmetic operations, handling strings, branching, and utilizing subroutines. The 80x86 (and most other CPUs) can also execute instructions that perform Boolean operations on multiple pairs of bits at one time. This chapter defines the Boolean operations and describes the 80x86 instructions that implement them. It also covers the instructions that cause bit patterns to shift or rotate in a byte, word, or doubleword, or to shift from one location to another. Although bit manipulation instructions are very primitive, they are widely used in assembly language programming, often because they provide the sort of control that is rarely available in a high-level language. The chapter contains several application examples, including the procedure that is called by the `atoi` macro; this procedure uses bit manipulation instructions in several places.

8.1 Logical Operations

Many high-level languages allow variables of Boolean type; that is, variables that are capable of storing *true* or *false* values. Virtually all high-level languages allow expressions with Boolean values to be used in conditional (**if**) statements. In assembly language the Boolean value *true* is identified with the bit value 1 and the Boolean value *false* is identified with the bit value 0. Figure 8.1 gives the definitions of the Boolean operations using bit values as the operands. The **or** operation is sometimes called "inclusive or" to distinguish it from "exclusive or" (**xor**). The only difference between **or** and **xor** is for two 1 bits; 1 **or** 1 is 1, but 1 **xor** 1 is 0; that is, "exclusive" or corresponds to one operand or the other true, but not both.

bit1	*bit2*	*bit1* **and** *bit2*	(a) **and** operation
0	0	0	
0	1	0	
1	0	0	
1	1	1	

bit1	*bit2*	*bit1* **or** *bit2*	(b) **or** operation
0	0	0	
0	1	1	
1	0	1	
1	1	1	

bit1	*bit2*	*bit1* **xor** *bit2*	(c) **xor** operation
0	0	0	
0	1	1	
1	0	1	
1	1	0	

bit	**not** *bit*	(d) **not** operation
0	1	
1	0	

Figure 8.1 Definitions of logical operations

The 80x86 has and, or, xor, and not instructions that implement the logical operations. The formats of these instructions are

```
and    destination, source
or     destination, source
xor    destination, source
not    destination
```

The first three instructions act on pairs of doublewords, words, or bytes, performing the logical operations on the bits in corresponding positions from the two operands. For example, when the instruction and bx,cx is executed, bit 0 from the BX register is "anded" with bit 0 from the CX register, bit 1 from BX is "anded" with bit 1 from CX, and so forth to bit 15 from BX and bit 15 from CX. The results of these 16 **and** operations are put in the corresponding positions in the destination.

The not instruction has only a single operand. It changes each 0 bit in that operand to 1 and each 1 bit to 0. For example, if the AH register contains 10110110 and the instruction not ah is executed, then the result in AH will be 01001001. This is sometimes called "taking the one's complement" of the operand.

The not instruction does not affect any flag. However, each of the other three Boolean instructions affects CF, OF, PF, SF, ZF, and AF. The carry flag CF and overflow flag OF flags are both reset to 0; the value of the auxiliary carry flag AF may be changed but is undefined. The parity flag PF, the sign flag SF, and the zero flag ZF are set or reset according to the value of the result of the operation. For instance, if the result is a pattern of all 0 bits, then ZF will be set to 1; if any bit of the result is not 0, then ZF will be reset to 0.

The and, or, and xor instructions all accept the same types of operands, use the same number of clock cycles for execution, and require the same number of bytes of object code. They are summarized together in Fig. 8.2. Information about the not instruction is given in Fig. 8.3.

It is interesting to note that Fig. 8.2 is almost identical to Fig. 4.5, which showed add and sub instructions. Also, Fig. 8.3 is almost identical to Fig. 4.7, which showed neg instructions. In both cases, the available operand formats are identical, the timings are identical, and even many of the opcodes are the same. (Recall that when the opcodes are the same, the second byte of the instruction distinguishes between add, sub, and, or, and xor instructions.)

Here are some examples showing how the logical instructions work. To compute the results by hand, it is necessary to expand each hex value to binary, do the logical operations on corresponding pairs of bits, and convert the result back to hex. These

Destination Operand	Source Operand	Clock Cycles			Number of Bytes	Opcode		
		386	486	Pentium		and	or	xor
register 8	immediate 8	2	1	1	3	80	80	80
register 16	immediate 8	2	1	1	3	83	83	83
register 32	immediate 8	2	1	1	3	83	83	83
register 16	immediate 16	2	1	1	4	81	81	81
register 32	immediate 32	2	1	1	6	81	81	81
AL	immediate 8	2	1	1	2	24	0C	34
AX	immediate 16	2	1	1	3	25	0D	35
EAX	immediate 32	2	1	1	5	25	0D	35
memory byte	immediate 8	7	3	3	3+	80	80	80
memory word	immediate 8	7	3	3	3+	83	83	83
memory doubleword	immediate 8	7	3	3	3+	83	83	83
memory word	immediate 16	7	3	3	4+	81	81	81
memory doubleword	immediate 32	7	3	3	6+	81	81	81
register 8	register 8	2	1	1	2	22	0A	32
register 16	register 16	2	1	1	2	23	0B	33
register 32	register 32	2	1	1	2	23	0B	33
register 8	memory byte	6	2	2	2+	22	0A	32
register 16	memory word	6	2	2	2+	23	0B	33
register 32	memory doubleword	6	2	2	2+	23	0B	33
memory byte	register 8	7	3	3	2+	20	08	30
memory word	register 16	7	3	3	2+	21	09	31
memory doubleword	register 32	7	3	3	2+	21	09	31

Figure 8.2 and, or, and xor instructions

Destination Operand	Clock Cycles			Number of Bytes	Opcode
	386	486	Pentium		
register 8	2	1	1	2	F6
register 16	2	1	1	2	F7
register 32	2	1	1	2	F7
memory byte	6	3	3	2 +	F6
memory word	6	3	3	2 +	F7
memory doubleword	6	3	3	2 +	F7

Figure 8.3 not instruction

expansions are shown in the examples. Most hex calculators perform the logical operations directly.

Example

Before	Instruction	Bitwise Operation	After		
AX: E2 75	and ax,cx	1110 0010 0111 0101	AX	A0	55
CX: A9 D7		1010 1001 1101 0111			
		1010 0000 0101 0101	SF 1	ZF 0	

DX: E2 75	or dx,value	1110 0010 0111 0101	DX	EB	F7
value: A9 D7		1010 1001 1101 0111			
		1110 1011 1111 0111	SF 1	ZF 0	

BX: E2 75	xor bx,0a9d7h	1110 0010 0111 0101	BX	4B	A2
		1010 1001 1101 0111			
		0100 1011 1010 0010	SF 0	ZF 0	

AX: E2 75	not ax	1110 0010 0111 0101	AX	1D	8A
		0001 1101 1000 1010			

Each of the logical instructions has a variety of uses. One application of the and instruction is to clear selected bits in a destination. Note that if any bit value is "anded" with 1, the result is the original bit. On the other hand, if any bit value is "anded" with 0, the result is 0. Because of this, selected bits in a byte or word can be cleared by "anding" the destination with a bit pattern that has 1s in positions that are not to be changed and 0s in positions that are to be cleared.

For example, to clear all but the last four bits in the EAX register, the following instruction can be used.

```
and    eax, 0000000fh      ; clear first 28 bits of EAX
```

If EAX originally contained 4C881D7B, this and operation would yield 0000000B:

```
0100 1100 1000 1000 0001 1101 0111 1011 4C881D7B
0000 0000 0000 0000 0000 0000 0000 1111 0000000F
0000 0000 0000 0000 0000 0000 0000 1011 0000000B
```

Only one of the leading zeros is needed in 0000000fh, but coding seven zeros helps clarify the purpose of this operand. The trailing hex digit f corresponds to 1111 in binary, providing the four 1s that will leave the last four bits in EAX unchanged.

A value that is used with a logical instruction to alter bit values is often called a **mask**. The Microsoft assembler MASM accepts numeric values in decimal, hexadecimal, binary, and octal formats. Hex and binary are preferred for constants used as masks since the bit pattern is obvious for binary values or easy to figure out for hex values.

As illustrated above, the and instruction is useful when selected bits of a byte or word need to be cleared. The or instruction is useful when selected bits of a byte or word need to be set to 1 without changing other bits. Observe that if the value 1 is combined with either a 0 or 1 using the **or** operation, then the result is 1. However, if the value 0 is used as one operand, then the result of an **or** operation is the other operand.

The exclusive or instruction will complement selected bits of a byte or word without changing other bits. This works since 0 **xor** 1 is 1 and 1 **xor** 1 is 0; that is, combining any operand with 1 using an **xor** operation results in the opposite of the operand value.

A second use of logical instructions is to implement high-level language Boolean operations. One byte in memory could be used to store eight Boolean values. If such a byte is at *flags*, then the statement

```
and    flags, 11011101b    ; flag5 := false;  flag1 := false
```

assigns value *false* to bits 1 and 5, leaving the other values unchanged. (Recall that bits are numbered from right to left, starting with zero for the rightmost bit.)

If the byte in memory at *flags* is being used to store eight Boolean values, then an or instruction can assign *true* values to any selected bits. For instance, the instruction

```
or    flags, 00001100b    ; flag3 := true;  flag2 := true
```

assigns true values to bits 2 and 3 without changing the other bits.

If the byte in memory at *flags* is being used to store eight Boolean values, then an xor instruction can negate selected values. For instance, the design statement

```
flag6 := NOT flag6;
```

can be implemented as

```
xor   flags, 01000000b       ; flag6 := not flag6
```

A third application of logical instructions is to perform certain arithmetic operations. Suppose that the value in the EAX register is interpreted as an unsigned integer. The expression (*value* mod 32) could be computed using the following sequence of instructions.

```
mov   edx,0       ; extend value to quadword
mov   ebx,32      ; divisor
div   ebx         ; divide value by 32
```

Following these instructions, the remainder (value mod 32) will be in the EDX register. The following alternative sequence leaves the same result in the EDX register without, however, putting the quotient in EAX.

```
mov   edx,eax        ; copy value to DX
and   edx,0000001fh  ; compute value mod 32
```

This choice is much more efficient than the first one (see Exercise 2). It works because the value in EDX is a binary number; as a sum it is

$$\text{bit31}*2^{31} + \text{bit30}*2^{30} + \ldots + \text{bit2}*2^2 + \text{bit1}*2 + \text{bit0}$$

Since each of these terms from $\text{bit31}*2^{31}$ down to $\text{bit5}*2^5$ is divisible by 32 (2^5), the remainder upon division by 32 is the bit pattern represented by the trailing five bits, those left after masking by 0000001F. Similar instructions will work whenever the second operand of mod is a power of 2.

A fourth use of logical instructions is to manipulate ASCII codes. Recall that the ASCII codes for digits are 30_{16} for 0, 31_{16} for 1, and so forth, to 39_{16} for 9. Suppose that the AL register contains the ASCII code for a digit, and that the corresponding integer value is needed in EAX. If the value in the high-order 24 bits in EAX are known to be zero, then the instruction

```
sub   eax, 00000030h       ; convert ASCII code to integer
```

will do the job. If the high-order bits in EAX are unknown, then the instruction

```
and   eax, 0000000fh       ; convert ASCII code to integer
```

is a much safer choice. It ensures that all but the last four bits of EAX are cleared. For example, if the EAX register contains 5C3DF036, junk in the high order bits, and the ASCII code for the character 6 in AL, then `and eax,0000000fh` produces the integer 00000006 in EAX.

The `or` instruction can be used to convert an integer value between 0 and 9 in a register to the corresponding ASCII character code. For example, if the integer is in BL, then the following instruction changes the contents of BL to the ASCII code.

```
or    bl,30h     ; convert digit to ASCII code
```

If BL contains 04, then the `or` instruction will yield 34:

```
0000 0100     04
0011 0000     30
0011 0100     34
```

With the 80x86 processors, the instruction `add bl,30h` does the same job using the same number of clock cycles and object code bytes. However, the `or` operation is more efficient than addition with some CPUs.

An `xor` instruction can be used to change the case of the ASCII code for a letter. Suppose that the CL register contains the ASCII code for some upper- or lowercase letter. The ASCII code for an uppercase letter and the ASCII code for the corresponding lowercase letter differ only in the value of bit 5. For example, the code for the uppercase letter S is 53_{16} (01010011_2) and the code for lowercase s is 73_{16} (01110011_2). The instruction

```
xor    cl, 00100000b     ; change case of letter in CL
```

"flips" the value of bit 5 in the CL register, changing the value to the ASCII code for the other case letter.

The 80x86 instruction set includes `test` instructions that function the same as `and` instructions except that destination operands are not changed. This means that the only job of a `test` instruction is to set flags. (Remember that a `cmp` instruction is essentially a `sub` instruction that sets flags but does not change the destination operand.) One application of a `test` instruction is to examine a particular bit of a byte or word. The following instruction tests bit 13 of the DX register.

```
test    dx, 2000h   ; check bit 13
```

Note that 2000 in hex is the same as 0010 0000 0000 0000 in binary, with bit 13 equal to 1. Often this `test` instruction would be followed by a `jz` or `jnz` instruction, and the effect would be to jump to the destination if bit 13 were 0 or 1, respectively.

The `test` instruction can also be used to get information about a value in a register. For example,

```
test    cx, cx    ; set flags for value in CX
```

"ands" the value in the CX register with itself, resulting in the original value. ("Anding" any bit with itself gives the common value.) The flags are set according to the value in CX. The instruction

```
and     cx, cx    ; set flags for value in CX
```

will accomplish the same goal and is equally efficient. However, using `test` makes it clear that the only purpose of the instruction is testing.

The various forms of the test instruction are listed in Fig. 8.4. They are almost the same as for `and`, `or`, and `xor` instructions. Only the accumulator can be the destination when the source is in memory, but MASM lets you specify any register as the destination and transposes the operands to have the memory operand first, one of the allowable formats.

Destination Operand	Source Operand	Clock Cycles 386	486	Pentium	Number of Bytes	Opcode
register 8	immediate 8	2	1	1	3	F6
register 16	immediate 16	2	1	1	4	F7
register 32	immediate 32	2	1	1	6	F7
AL	immediate 8	2	1	1	2	A8
AX	immediate 16	2	1	1	3	A9
EAX	immediate 32	2	1	1	5	A9
memory byte	immediate 8	5	2	2	3+	F6
memory word	immediate 16	5	2	2	4+	F7
memory doubleword	immediate 32	5	2	2	6+	F7
register 8	register 8	2	1	1	2	84
register 16	register 16	2	1	1	2	85
register 32	register 32	2	1	1	2	85
memory byte	register 8	5	2	2	2+	84
memory word	register 16	5	2	2	2+	85
memory doubleword	register 32	5	2	2	2+	85

Figure 8.4 `test` instructions

Exercises 8.1

1. For each part of this problem, assume the "before" values when the given instruction is executed. Give the requested "after" values.

	Before	Instruction	After
(a)	BX: FA 75		
	CX: 31 02	and bx,cx	BX, SF, ZF
(b)	BX FA 75		
	CX 31 02	or bx,cx	BX, SF, ZF
(c)	BX FA 75		
	CX 31 02	xor bx,cx	BX, SF, ZF
(d)	BX FA 75	not bx	BX
(e)	AX FA 75	and ax,000fh	AX, SF, ZF
(f)	AX FA 75	or ax,0fff0h	AX, SF, ZF
(g)	AX FA 75	xor ax,0ffffh	AX, SF, ZF
(h)	AX FA 75	test ax,0004h	AX, SF, ZF

2. Recall the two methods given in this section for computing (*value* mod 32) when *value* is an unsigned integer in the EAX register:

```
mov   edx,0          ; extend value to quadword
mov   ebx,32         ; divisor
div   ebx            ; divide value by 32
```

and

```
mov   edx,eax        ; copy value to DX
and   edx,0000001fh  ; compute value mod 32
```

Find the total number of clock cycles required for execution on a Pentium and the number of bytes of object code necessary for each of these methods.

3. Suppose that *value* is an unsigned integer in the EAX register. Give appropriate instructions to compute (*value* mod 8) putting the result in the EBX register and leaving EAX unchanged.

4. Suppose that each bit of the doubleword at flags represents a Boolean value, with bit 0 for flag0, and so forth, up to bit 31 for flag31. For each of the following design statements, give a single 80x86 instruction to implement the statement.

(a) `flag2 := true;`

(b) `flag5 := false; flag16 := false; flag19 := false;`

(c) `flag12 := NOT flag12`

5. (a) Suppose that the AL register contains the ASCII code for an upper-case letter. Give a logical instruction (other than `xor`) that will change its contents to the code for the corresponding lowercase letter.

   (b) Suppose that the AL register contains the ASCII code for a lowercase letter. Give a logical instruction (other than `xor`) that will change its contents to the code for the corresponding uppercase letter.

Programming Exercises 8.1

1. The Pascal programming language includes the predefined function *odd*, which has a single doubleword integer parameter and returns true for an odd integer and false for an even integer. Write a `NEAR32` proce-dure that implements this function in assembly language, returning -1 in EAX for true and 0 in EAX for false. The procedure must not change any register other than EAX. Use an appropriate logical instruction to generate the return value. The procedure is responsible for removing the parameter from the stack.

2. In 2-dimensional graphics programming a rectangular region of the plane is mapped to the display; points outside this region are **clipped**. The region, bounded by four lines $x = x_{min}$, $x = x_{max}$, $y = y_{min}$, and $y = y_{max}$, can be pictured

```
0110 │ 0100 │ 0101
     │      │        ── y = y_max
0010 │ 0000 │ 0001
     │      │        ── y = y_min
1010 │ 1000 │ 1001

   x = x_min   x = x_max
```

An **outcode** (or region code) is associated with each point (x,y) of the plane. This 4-bit code is assigned according to the following rules:

- bit 0 (rightmost) is 1 if the point is to the right of the region, that is $x > x_{max}$; it is 0 otherwise
- bit 1 is 1 if the point is left of the region $(x < x_{min})$

- bit 2 is 1 if the point is above the region ($y > y_{max}$)
- bit 3 is 1 if the point is below the region ($y < y_{min}$)

The previous diagram shows the outcodes for each of the nine regions of the plane.

(a) Suppose that the outcode for point (x_1, y_1) is in the low order four bits of AL, that the outcode for point (x_2, y_2) is in the low order four bits of BL, and that other bits of these registers are reset to 0. Give a single 80x86 statement that will set ZF to 1 if the two points are both inside the rectangular region and to 0 otherwise. The value in AL or BL may be changed.

(b) Suppose that the outcode for point (x_1, y_1) is in the low order four bits of AL, that the outcode for point (x_2, y_2) is in the low order four bits of BL, and that other bits of these registers are reset to 0. Give a single 80x86 statement that will set ZF to 0 if the two points are both on the same side of the rectangular region. ("Both on the same side" means both right of $x=x_{max}$, both left of $x=x_{min}$, both above $y=y_{max}$, or both below $y=y_{min}$.) The value in AL or BL may be changed.

(c) Write a NEAR32 procedure setcode that returns the outcode for a point (x, y). Specifically, setcode has six word-size integer parameters: x, y, x_{min}, x_{max}, y_{min}, and y_{max} that are passed on the stack in the order given. Return the outcode in the low order four bits of the AL register, assigning 0 to each of the higher order bits in EAX.

8.2   Shift and Rotate Instructions

The logical instructions introduced in the previous section enable the assembly language programmer to set or clear bits in a word or byte stored in a register or memory. Shift and rotate instructions enable the programmer to change the position of bits within a doubleword, word, or byte. This section describes the shift and rotate instructions and gives examples of some ways they are used.

Shift instructions slide the bits in a location given by the destination operand to the left or to the right. The direction of the shift can be determined from the last character of the mnemonic—sal and shl are left shifts; sar and shr are right shifts. Shifts are also categorized as logical or arithmetic—shl and shr are logical shifts; sal and sar are arithmetic shifts. The difference between arithmetic and logical shifts is explained below. The table in Fig. 8.5 summarizes the mnemonics.

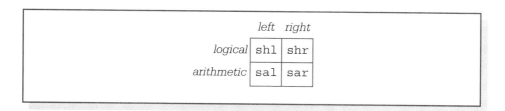

Figure 8.5 **Shift instructions**

The source code format of any shift instruction is

```
s-    destination, count
```

There are three versions of the *count* operand. This operand can be the number 1, another number serving as a byte-size immediate operand, or the register specification CL. The original 8086/8088 CPU had only the first and third of these options.

An instruction having the format

```
s-    destination, 1
```

causes a shift of exactly one position within the destination location. With the format

```
s-    destination, immediate8
```

an immediate operand of 0 to 255 can be coded. However, most of the 80x86 family mask this operand by 00011111_2; that is they reduce it mod 32 before performing the shift. This makes sense because you cannot do over 32 meaningful shift operations to an operand no longer than a doubleword. In the final format,

```
s-    destination, cl
```

the unsigned count operand is in the CL register. Again, most 80x86 CPUs reduce it modulo 32 before beginning the shifts.

Arithmetic and logical left shifts are identical; the mnemonics sal and shl are synonyms that generate the same object code. When a left shift is executed, the bits in the destination slide to the left and 0 bits fill in on the right. The bits that fall off the left are lost except for the very last one shifted off; it is saved in the carry flag CF. The sign flag SF, zero flag ZF, and parity flag PF are assigned values corresponding to the final value in the destination location. The overflow flag OF is undefined for a multiple-bit shift; for a single-bit shift (*count*=1) it is reset to 0 if the sign bit of the result is the same as the sign bit of the original operand value, and set to 1 if they are different. The auxiliary carry flag AF is undefined.

Arithmetic and logical right shifts are not the same. With both, the bits in the destination slide to the right and the bits that fall off the right are lost except for the very last one shifted off, which is saved in CF. For a logical right shift (shr) 0 bits fill in on the left. However, with an arithmetic right shift (sar) the original sign bit is used to fill in on the left. Therefore, for an arithmetic right shift, if the original operand represents a negative 2's complement number, then the new operand will have leading 1 bits for each position shifted and will also be negative. As with left shifts, the values of SF, ZF, and PF depend on the result of the operation, and AF is undefined. The overflow flag OF is undefined for a multiple-bit shift. For a single-bit logical right shift shr, OF is reset to 0 if the sign bit in the result is the same as the sign bit in the original operand value, and set to 1 if they are different. (Notice that this is equivalent to assigning OF the sign bit of the original operand.) With a single-bit arithmetic right shift, sar, OF is always cleared—the sign bits of the original and new value are always the same.

Some hex calculators can directly do shift operations. Hand evaluation requires writing the operand in binary, shifting or regrouping the bits (filling in with 0s or 1s as appropriate), and then translating the new bit pattern back to hex. Things are a little simpler for a multiple-bit shift, which shifts four positions or some multiple of four positions; in this case each group of four bits corresponds to one hex digit, so one can think of shifting hex digits instead of bits. Here are a few examples that illustrate execution of shift instructions; each example begins with a word containing the hex value A9 D7 (1010 1001 1101 0111 in binary). The bit(s) shifted off are separated by a line in the original value. The bit(s) added are in bold in the new value.

Example

Before	Instruction	Operation in binary	After		
CX: A9 D7	sal cx,1	1010 1001 1101 0111	CX	53	AE
		0101 0011 1010 1110	SF 0	ZF 0	
			CF 1	OF 1	
AX: A9 D7	shr ax,1	1010 1001 1101 0111	AX	54	EB
		0101 0100 1110 1011	SF 0	ZF 0	
			CF 1	OF 1	

```
BX: A9 D7      sar bx,1      1010 1001 1101 0111
                                              ──────┘
                             1101 0100 1110 1011
```

BX | D4 | EB

SF 1   ZF 0
CF 1   OF 0

```
ace: A9 D7     sal ace,4     1010 1001 1101 0111
                             ┌───────
                             1001 1101 0111 0000
```

ace | 9D | 70

SF 1   ZF 0
CF 0   OF ?

```
DX: A9 D7      shr dx,4      1010 1001 1101 0111
                                      ──────┘
                             0000 1010 1001 1101
```

DX | 0A | 9D

SF 0   ZF 0
CF 0   OF ?

```
AX: A9 D7      sar ax,cl     1010 1001 1101 0111
CL: 04                                ──────┘
                             1111 1010 1001 1101
```

AX | FA | 9D

SF 1   ZF 0
CF 0   OF ?

Figure 8.6 gives the number of clock cycles and number of bytes required using various operand types in shift instructions. All four types of shifts discussed so far, as well as the rotate instructions discussed below, share opcodes. The size of the destination and the type of the count operand are implied by the opcode. As with some other instructions, the second byte of the object code is used to choose among the different types of shifts and rotates, as well as between register and memory destinations. Notice that the single-bit shifts are faster than the multiple-bit shifts—often it is more time-efficient to use several single-bit shifts than one multiple-bit shift.

The shift instructions are quite primitive, but they have many applications. One of these is to do some multiplication and division operations. In fact, for processors without multiplication instructions, shift instructions are a crucial part of routines to do multiplication. Even with the 80x86 architecture, some products are computed more rapidly with shift operations than with multiplication instructions.

In a multiplication operation where the multiplier is 2, a single-bit left shift of the multiplicand results in the product in the original location. The product will be correct unless the overflow flag OF is set. It is easy to see why this works for unsigned

Destination Operand	Count Operand	Clock Cycles			Number of Bytes	Opcode
		386	486	Pentium		
register 8	1	3	3	1	2	D0
register 16/32	1	3	3	1	2	D1
memory byte	1	7	4	3	2+	D0
memory word/doubleword	1	7	4	3	2+	D1
register 8	immediate 8	3	2	1	3	C0
register 16/32	immediate 8	3	2	1	3	C1
memory byte	immediate 8	7	4	3	3+	C0
memory word/doubleword	immediate 8	7	4	3	3+	C1
register 8	CL	3	3	4	2	D2
register 16/32	CL	3	3	4	2	D3
memory byte	CL	7	4	4	2+	D2
memory word/doubleword	CL	7	4	4	2+	D3

Figure 8.6 **Shift and rotate instructions**

numbers; shifting each bit to the left one position makes it the coefficient of the next higher power of two in the binary representation of the number. A single-bit left shift also correctly doubles a signed operand. In fact, one can use multiplication by 2 on a hex calculator to find the result of any single-bit left shift.

A single-bit right shift can be used to efficiently divide an unsigned operand by 2. Suppose, for example, that the EBX register contains an unsigned operand. Then the logical right shift shr ebx,1 shifts each bit in EBX to the position corresponding to the next lower power of two, resulting in half the original value. The original units bit is copied into the carry flag CF, and is the remainder for the division.

If EBX contains a signed operand, then the arithmetic right shift sar ebx,1 does almost the same job as an idiv instruction with a divisor of 2. The difference is that if the dividend is an odd negative number, then the quotient is rounded down; that is, it is one smaller than it would be using an idiv instruction. For a concrete example, suppose that the DX register contains FFFF and the AX register contains FFF7, so that DX-AX has the doubleword size 2's complement representation for −9. Assume also that CX contains 0002. Then idiv cx gives a result of FFFC in AX and FFFF in DX; that is, a quotient of −4 and a remainder of −1. However, if FFFFFFF7 is in EBX, then sar ebx,1 gives a result of FFFFFFFB in EBX and 1 in CF, a quotient of −5 and a remainder of +1. Both quotient-remainder pairs satisfy the equation

dividend = quotient*divisor + remainder

but with the −5 and +1 combination, the sign of the remainder differs from the sign of the dividend, contrary to the rule followed by `idiv`.

Instead of multiplying an operand by 2, it can be doubled by either adding it to itself or by using a left shift. A shift is sometimes slightly more efficient than addition and either is much more efficient than multiplication. To divide an operand by 2, a right shift is the only alternative to division and is much faster; however, the right shift is not quite the same as division by 2 for a negative dividend. To multiply or divide an operand by 4, 8, or some other small power of two, either repeated single-bit shifts or one multiple-bit shift can be used.

Shifts can be used in combination with other logical instructions to combine distinct groups of bits into a byte or a word or to separate the bits in a byte or word into different groups. The program shown in Fig. 8.7 prompts for an integer, uses the `atod` macro to convert it to 2's complement form in the EAX register, and then displays the word in the EAX register as eight hexadecimal digits. To accomplish this display, eight

```
; program to display integer as 8 hex digits
; Author:   R. Detmer
; Date:     revised 11/97

.386
.MODEL FLAT

ExitProcess PROTO NEAR32 stdcall, dwExitCode:DWORD

include io.h              ; header file for input/output

cr       equ     0dh      ; carriage return character
Lf       equ     0ah      ; line feed

.STACK   4096             ; reserve 4096-byte stack

                                               (continued)
```

Figure 8.7 Program to display an integer in hex

```
.DATA                                ; reserve storage for data
prompt      BYTE    "Enter a number:  ",0
number      BYTE    20 DUP (?)
result      BYTE    cr,Lf,"The 2's complement representation is "
hexOut      BYTE    8 DUP (?),cr,Lf,0

.CODE                                ; start of main program code
_start:
            output prompt            ; prompt for number
            input  number,20         ; read ASCII characters
            atod   number            ; convert to integer

            lea    ebx,hexOut+7       ; address for last character
            mov    ecx,8              ; number of characters
forCount:   mov    edx,eax            ; copy pattern
            and    edx,0000000fh      ; zero all but last hex digit
            cmp    edx,9              ; digit?
            jnle   elseLetter         ; letter if not
            or     edx,30h            ; convert to character
            jmp    endifDigit
elseLetter: add    edx,'A'-10         ; convert to letter
endifDigit:
            mov    BYTE PTR [ebx],dl  ; copy character to memory
            dec    ebx                ; point at next character
            shr    eax,4              ; shift one hex digit right
            loop   forCount           ; repeat

            output result            ; output label and hex value

            INVOKE ExitProcess, 0    ; exit with return code 0
PUBLIC _start                        ; make entry point public
END                                  ; end of source code
```

Figure 8.7 (continued)

groups of four bits must be extracted from the value in EAX. Each group of four bits represents a decimal value from 0 to 15, and each group must be converted to a character for display. This character is a digit 0 through 9 for integer value 0 (0000_2) through 9 (1001_2) or a letter A through F for integer value 10 (1010_2) through 15 (1111_2).

The eight characters are stored right to left in contiguous bytes of memory as they are generated; the EBX register is used to point at the destination byte for each character. The design for the middle of the program is

```
for count := 8 downto 1 loop
      copy EAX to EDX;
      mask off all but last 4 bits in EDX;

      if value in EDX ≤ 9
      then
            convert value in EDX to a character 0 through 9;
      else
            convert value in EDX to a letter A through F;
      end if;

      store character in memory at address in EBX;
      decrement EBX to point at next position to the left;
      shift value in EAX right four bits;
end for;
```

To implement this design, the instruction

```
        and     edx,0000000fh    ; zero all but last hex digit
```

masks off all but the last four bits in EDX. The **if** is implemented by

```
            cmp     edx,9           ; digit?
            jnle    elseLetter      ; letter if not
            or      edx,30h         ; convert to character
            jmp     endifDigit
elseLetter: add     edx,'A'-10      ; convert to letter
endifDigit:
```

A value from 0 to 9 is converted to the ASCII code for a digit using the or instruction; add edx,30h would work just as well here. To convert numbers 0A to 0F to the corresponding ASCII codes 41 to 46 for letters A to F, the value 'A'-10 is added to the number. This actually adds the decimal number 55, but the code used is clearer than add edx,55. The shr instruction shifts the value in EAX right four bits, discarding the hex digit that was just converted to a character.

Programming Exercise 2 of Section 7.4 asked for a procedure to do a job similar to that done by the program in Fig. 8.7. That procedure was to use the remainder upon division by 16 to produce a value corresponding to the rightmost hex digit. Notice that the shr and and instructions used in this example program are both easier to code and more efficient.

The shift instructions discussed above shift the bits of an operand in place, except that one bit affects the carry flag. The 80x86 architecture has two additional double shift instructions, shld and shrd. Each of these instructions has the format

```
sh-d  destination, source, count
```

where the destination may be a word or a doubleword in a register or memory, the source is a word or doubleword in a register, and the count is either immediate or in CL. A shld instruction shifts the destination left exactly like a shl instruction, except that the bits shifted in come from the left end of the source operand. The source operand is not changed. A shrd instruction shifts the destination right exactly like a shr instruction, except that the bits shifted in come from the right end of the source operand. For both double shifts, the last bit shifted out goes to CF, and SF, ZF, and PF are given values corresponding to the result in the destination location. The overflow flag OF is left undefined by a double shift.

The following two examples illustrate double shift instructions. The one with shld shifts off the leading three hex digits (12 bits) of ECX, filling from the right with the leftmost three hex digits from EAX. The carry flag CF is 1 since the last bit shifted off was the rightmost bit of 3 (0011_2). The example using shrd shifts off the trailing two hex digits (8 bits) of ECX, filling from the left with the rightmost two hex digits from EAX. The carry flag CF is 0 since the last bit shifted off was the leftmost bit of 7 (0111_2).

Example

Before	Instruction	After			
ECX: 12 34 56 78	shld ecx,eax,12	ECX	45	67	89	0A
EAX: 90 AB CD EF						
		EAX	90	AB	CD	EF
		CF 1 ZF 0 SF 0				
ECX: 12 34 56 78	shrd ecx,eax,CL	ECX	EF	12	34	56
EAX: 90 AB CD EF						
CL: 08		EAX	90	AB	CD	EF
		CF 0 ZF 0 SF 1				

| | | Clock Cycles | | | Number | Opcode | |
Destination Operand	Count Operand	386	486	Pentium	of Bytes	shld	shrd
register 16/32	immediate 8	3	2	4	4	0F 04	0F AC
memory word/doubleword	immediate 8	7	4	4	4+	0F 04	0F AC
register 16/32	CL	3	3	4	3	0F 05	0F AD
memory word/doubleword	CL	7	4	5	3+	0F 05	0F AD

Figure 8.8 Double shift instructions

Figure 8.8 lists the various double shift instructions. The source operand is not shown since it is always a register 16 or register 32, the same size as the destination.

A double shift instruction can be used to get a slightly cleaner version of the program in Fig. 8.7. The following code generates the hex digits left-to-right instead of right-to-left. Each time through the loop, a shld copies the leading hex digit from EAX into EDX.

```
            lea     ebx,hexOut      ; address for first character
            mov     ecx,8           ; number of characters
forCount:   shld    edx,eax,4       ; get leading hex digit
            and     edx,0000000fh   ; zero all but last hex digit
            cmp     edx,9           ; digit?
            jnle    elseLetter      ; letter if not
            or      edx,30h         ; convert to character
            jmp     endifDigit
elseLetter: add     edx,'A'-10      ; convert to letter
endifDigit:
            mov     BYTE PTR [ebx],dl ; copy character to memory
            inc     ebx             ; point at next character
            shl     eax,4           ; shift one hex digit left
            loop    forCount        ; repeat
```

Rotate instructions are very similar to single shift instructions. With shift instructions the bits that are shifted off one end are discarded while vacated space at the other end is filled by 0s (or 1s for a right arithmetic shift of a negative number). With rotate instructions the bits that are shifted off one end of the destination are used to fill in the vacated space at the other end.

Rotate instruction formats are the same as single shift instruction formats. A single-bit rotate instruction has the format

```
r-   destination, 1
```

and there are two multiple-bit versions

```
r-   destination, immediate8
r-   destination, cl
```

The instructions `rol` (rotate left) and `ror` (rotate right) can be used for byte, word, or doubleword operands in a register or in memory. As each bit "falls off" one end, it is copied to the other end of the destination. In addition, the last bit copied to the other end is also copied to the carry flag CF. The overflow flag OF is the only other flag affected by rotate instructions. It is undefined for multibit rotates, and familiarity with its definition for single-bit rotate instructions is not needed in this book.

As an example, suppose that the DX register contains D25E and the instruction

```
rol   dx, 1
```

is executed. In binary, the operation looks like

```
1 1 0 1   0 0 1 0   0 1 0 1   1 1 1 0
```

resulting in 1010 0100 1011 1101 or A4BD. The carry flag CF is set to 1 since a 1 bit rotated from the left end to the right.

Timings and opcodes for rotate instructions are identical to those for shift instructions. They are given in Fig. 8.6.

A rotate instruction can be used to give yet another version of the program in Fig. 8.7. This one produces the hex digits in a left-to-right order and has the advantage of leaving the value in EAX unchanged at the end since eight rotations, four bits each time, result in all bits being rotated back to their original positions.

```
            lea    ebx,hexOut       ; address for first character
            mov    ecx,8            ; number of characters
forCount:   rol    eax,4            ; rotate first hex digit to end
            mov    edx,eax          ; copy all digits
            and    edx,0000000fh    ; zero all but last hex digit
```

```
        cmp     edx,9               ; digit?
        jnle    elseLetter          ; letter if not
        or      edx,30h             ; convert to character
        jmp     endifDigit
elseLetter: add   edx,'A'-10        ; convert to letter
endifDigit:
        mov     BYTE PTR [ebx],dl ; copy character to memory
        inc     ebx                 ; point at next character
        loop    forCount            ; repeat
```

There is an additional pair of rotate instructions, rcl (rotate through carry left) and rcr (rotate through carry right). Each of these instructions treats the carry flag CF as if it were part of the destination. This means that rcl eax, 1 shifts bits 0 through 30 of EAX left one position, copies the old value of bit 31 into CF and copies the old value of CF into bit 0 of EAX. The rotate through carry instructions obviously alter CF; they also affect OF, but no other flag. The opcodes for rotate through carry instructions are the same as the corresponding shift instructions and can be found in Fig. 8.6. However, the timings are different and are not given in this book.

Exercises 8.2

1. For each part of this problem, assume the "before" values when the given instruction is executed. Give the requested "after" values.

	Before	Instruction	After
(a)	AX: A8 B5	shl ax, 1	AX, CF, OF
(b)	AX: A8 B5	shr ax, 1	AX, CF, OF
(c)	AX: A8 B5	sar ax, 1	AX, CF, OF
(d)	AX: A8 B5	rol ax, 1	AX, CF
(e)	AX: A8 B5	ror ax, 1	AX, CF
(f)	AX: A8 B5		
	CL: 04	sal ax, cl	AX, CF
(g)	AX: A8 B5	shr ax, 4	AX, CF
(h)	AX: A8 B5		
	CL: 04	sar ax, cl	AX, CF
(i)	AX: A8 B5		
	CL: 04	rol ax, cl	AX, CF

(j) AX: A8 B5   ror ax, 4   AX, CF

(k) AX: A8 B5   rcl ax, 1   AX, CF

    CF: 1

(l) AX: A8 B5   rcr ax, 1   AX, CF

    CF: 0

(m) AX: A8 B5

    CX: FE 40   shrd ax, cx, 4   AX, CF

(n) AX: A8 B5

    CX: FE 40   shld ax, cx, 4   AX, CF

2. Using clock cycles for the Pentium, compare the total number of clock cycles and bytes of object code for each of these alternative ways of dividing the unsigned integer in the EAX register by 32:

```
(a) mov   edx,0    ; extend value to doubleword
    mov   ebx,32   ; divisor
    div   ebx      ; value div 32
(b) shr   eax,1    ; divide by 2
    shr   eax,1    ; divide by 2
    shr   eax,1    ; divide by 2
    shr   eax,1    ; divide by 2
    shr   eax,1    ; divide by 2
(c) shr   eax,5    ; divide by 32
```

3. Using clock cycles for the Pentium, compare the total number of clock cycles and bytes of object code for each of these alternative ways of multiplying the value in the EAX register by 32:

```
(a) mov   ebx,32   ; multiplier
    mul   ebx      ; value * 32
(b) imul  eax,32   ; value * 32
(c) shl   eax,1    ; multiply by 2
    shl   eax,1    ; multiply by 2
    shl   eax,1    ; multiply by 2
    shl   eax,1    ; multiply by 2
    shl   eax,1    ; multiply by 2
(d) shl   eax,5    ; multiply by 32
```

4. Suppose that each of *value1*, *value2*, and *value3* references a byte in memory and that an unsigned integer is stored in each byte. Assume

that the first value is no larger than 31 so that it has at most five significant bits and at least three leading 0 bits. Similarly assume that the second value is no larger than 15 (four significant bits) and the third value is no larger than 127 (seven bits).

(a) Give code to pack all three of these numbers into a 16-bit word in the AX register, copying the low order five bits from *value1* to bits 11–15 of AX, the low order four bits from *value2* to bits 7–10 of AX, and the low-order seven bits from *value3* into bits 0–6 of AX.

(b) Give code to unpack the 16 bit number in the AX register into five-bit, four-bit, and seven-bit numbers, padding each value with zeros on the left to make eight bits, and storing the resulting bytes at *value1*, *value2*, and *value3* respectively.

5. The instructions

```
mov    ebx, eax      ; value
shl    eax, 1        ; 2*value
add    eax, ebx      ; 3*value
```

multiplies the value in EAX by 3. Write similar code sequences that use shift and addition instructions to efficiently multiply by 5, 7, 9, and 10.

Programming Exercises 8.2

1. Write a NEAR32 procedure binaryString that converts a 32-bit integer to a string of exactly 32 characters representing its value as a binary number. The procedure will have two parameters, passed on the stack:

(1) the number

(2) the address of the destination string

The procedure will remove parameters from the stack and must modify no register. Use a rotate instruction to extract the bits one at a time, left-to-right, recalling that jc or jnc instructions look at the carry bit. (This exercise is the same as Programming Exercise 3 in Section 7.4 except for the method of producing the bits.)

2. An eight-bit number can be represented using three octal digits. Bits 7 and 6 determine the left octal digit, which is never larger than 4, bits 5, 4, and 3 the middle digit, and bits 2, 1, and 0 the right digit. For instance, 11010110_2 is 11 010 110$_2$ or 326_8. The value of a 16-bit number

is represented in *split octal* by applying the 2–3–3 system to the high-order and low-order bytes separately. Write a NEAR32 procedure split-Octal which converts an 16-bit integer to a string of exactly six characters representing the value of the number in split octal. The procedure will have two parameters, passed on the stack:

(1) the number

(2) the address of the destination string

The procedure will remove parameters from the stack and must modify no register.

8.3 Converting an ASCII String to a 2's Complement Integer

The atoi and atod macros have been used to scan an area of memory containing an ASCII representation of an integer, producing the corresponding word-length 2's complement integer in the EAX register. These macros and the procedures they call are very similar. This section uses atod as an example.

The atod macro expands into the following sequence of instructions.

```
lea     eax,source          ; source address to EAX
push    eax                 ; source parameter on stack
call    atodproc            ; call atodproc(source)
```

These instructions simply call procedure *atodproc* using a single parameter, the address of the string of ASCII characters to be scanned. The EAX register is not saved by the macro code since the result is to be returned in EAX. The actual source identifier is used in the expanded macro, not the name *source*.

The actual ASCII to 2's complement integer conversion is done by the procedure *atodproc*. The assembled version of this procedure is contained in the file IO.OBJ. Source code for *atodproc* is shown in Fig. 8.9. The procedure begins with standard entry code. The flags are saved so that flag values that are not explicitly set or reset as promised in the comments can be returned unchanged. The popf and pop instructions at AToDExit restore these values; however, the word on the stack that is popped by popf will have been altered by the body of the procedure, as discussed below.

The first job of *atodproc* is to skip leading spaces, if any. This is implemented with a straightforward while loop. Note that BYTE PTR [esi] uses register indirect

```
; atodproc(source)
; Procedure to scan data segment starting at source address, interpreting
; ASCII characters as an integer value that is returned in EAX.

; Leading blanks are skipped.  A leading - or + sign is acceptable.
; Digit(s) must immediately follow the sign (if any).
; Memory scan is terminated by any nondigit, and the address of
; the terminating character is in ESI.

; The following flags are affected:
;   AF is undefined
;   PF, SF, and ZF reflect sign of number returned in EAX.
;   CF reset to 0
;   OF set to indicate error.  Possible error conditions are:
;     - no digits in input
;     - value outside range -2,147,483,648 to 2,147,483,647
;   (EAX) will be 0 if OF is set.

atodproc    PROC    NEAR32
            push    ebp                 ; save base pointer
            mov     ebp, esp            ; establish stack frame
            sub     esp, 4              ; local space for sign
            push    ebx                 ; Save registers
            push    ecx
            push    edx
            pushf                       ; save flags

            mov     esi,[ebp+8]         ; get parameter (source addr)

WhileBlankD:cmp     BYTE PTR [esi],' '  ; space?
            jne     EndWhileBlankD      ; exit if not
            inc     esi                 ; increment character pointer
            jmp     WhileBlankD         ; and try again
EndWhileBlankD:

            mov     eax,1               ; default sign multiplier
IfPlusD:    cmp     BYTE PTR [esi],'+'  ; leading + ?
            je      SkipSignD           ; if so, skip over
IfMinusD:   cmp     BYTE PTR [esi],'-'  ; leading - ?
            jne     EndIfSignD          ; if not, save default +
            mov     eax,-1              ; -1 for minus sign
SkipSignD:  inc     esi                 ; move past sign
EndIfSignD:
```

(continued)

Figure 8.9   ASCII to doubleword integer conversion

```
                mov     [ebp-4],eax        ; save sign multiplier
                mov     eax,0              ; number being accumulated
                mov     cx,0               ; count of digits so far

WhileDigitD:cmp BYTE PTR [esi],'0'  ; compare next character to '0'
                jl      EndWhileDigitD     ; not a digit if smaller than '0'
                cmp     BYTE PTR [esi],'9' ; compare to '9'
                jg      EndWhileDigitD     ; not a digit if bigger than '9'
                imul    eax,10             ; multiply old number by 10
                jo      overflowD          ; exit if product too large
                mov     bl,[esi]           ; ASCII character to BL
                and     ebx,0000000Fh      ; convert to single-digit integer
                add     eax,ebx            ; add to sum
                jc      overflowD          ; exit if sum too large
                inc     cx                 ; increment digit count
                inc     esi                ; increment character pointer
                jmp     WhileDigitD        ; go try next character
EndWhileDigitD:

                cmp     cx,0               ; no digits?
                jz      overflowD          ; if so, set overflow error flag
; if value is 80000000h and sign is '-',  want to return 80000000h (-2^32)

                cmp     eax,80000000h      ; 80000000h ?
                jne     TooBigD?
                cmp     DWORD PTR [ebp-4],-1 ; multiplier -1 ?
                je      ok1D               ; if so, return 8000h

TooBigD?:       test    eax,eax            ; check sign flag
                jns     okD                ; will be set if number > 2^32 - 1

overflowD:      pop     ax                 ; get flags
                or      ax,0000100001000100B  ; set overflow, zero & parity flags
                and     ax,1111111101111110B  ; reset sign and carry flags
                push    ax                 ; push new flag values
                mov     eax,0              ; return value of zero
                jmp     AToDExit           ; quit

okD:            imul    DWORD PTR [ebp-4]  ; make signed number
ok1D:           popf                       ; get original flags
                test    eax,eax            ; set flags for new number
                pushf                      ; save flags
```

(continued)

Figure 8.9 (continued)

```
AToDExit:   popf                             ; get flags
            pop     edx                      ; restore registers
            pop     ecx
            pop     ebx
            mov     esp, ebp                 ; delete local variable space
            pop     ebp
            ret     4                        ; exit, removing parameter
atodproc    ENDP
```

Figure 8.9   (continued)

addressing to reference a byte of the source string. Following the while loop, ESI points at some nonblank character.

The main idea of the procedure is to compute the value of the integer by implementing the following left-to-right scanning algorithm.

---

value :=0;
while pointing at code for a digit loop
     multiply value by 10;
     convert ASCII character code to integer;
     add integer to value;
     point at next byte in memory;
end while;

This design works for an unsigned number; a separate multiplier is used to give the correct sign to the final signed result. The second job of the procedure, after skipping blanks, is to store this multiplier, 1 for a positive number or -1 for a negative number. The multiplier, stored in local variable space on the stack, is given the default value 1 and changed to -1 if the first nonblank character is a minus sign. If the first nonblank character is either plus or a minus sign, then the address in ESI is incremented to skip over the sign character.

Now the main design is executed. The value is accumulated in the EAX register. If multiplication by 10 produces an overflow, then the result is too large to represent in EAX. The jc overflowD instruction transfers control to the code at *overflowD* that takes care of all error situations.

To convert a character to a digit, the character is loaded into the BL register and the instruction and ebx,0000000Fh clears all bits except the low-order four in the EBX register. Thus, for example, the ASCII code 37_{16} for 7 becomes 00000007 in the EBX register. If adding the digit to the accumulated value produces a carry, the sum is too large for EAX; the jc instruction transfers control to *overflowD*.

The main loop terminates as soon as ESI points at any character code other than one for a digit. Thus an integer is terminated by a space, comma, letter, null, or *any* nondigit. In order to determine if a valid integer has been entered, the main loop keeps a count of decimal digits in the CX register. When the loop terminates, this count is checked. If it is zero, there was no digit and the jz instruction jumps to *overflowD* for error handling. There is no need to check for too many digits; this would already have been caught by overflow in the main loop.

If the accumulated value in the AX register is larger than 80000000_{16} (2,147,483,648 as an unsigned number), then the magnitude of the number is too great to be represented in doubleword-length 2's complement form. If it is equal to 80000000_{16}, then the multiplier must be -1 since $-2,147,483,648$ can be represented (as 80000000_{16}), but $+2,147,483,648$ is too large. The next section of code checks for 8000000_{16} in EAX and a multiplier of -1; in this case the work is almost done. Otherwise, the instruction test eax,eax is used to see if the accumulated value is larger than 8000000_{16}; the sign bit will be 1 for a value of this magnitude.

If any of the error conditions occur, the instructions starting at *overflowD* are executed. The original flags are popped into the AX register. The bit corresponding to the overflow flag is set to 1 to indicate an error, and a value of 00000000 will be returned in EAX; other flags are set or reset to correspond to the zero value. The instruction

```
or   ax,0000100001000100b  ; set overflow, zero & parity flags
```

sets bit 11 (the position of overflow flag), bit 6 (zero flag), and bit 2 (parity flag). The zero flag is set since the result returned will be zero; the parity flag is set since 00000000_{16} has even parity (an even number of 1 bits). The instruction

```
and    ax,1111111101111110b  ; reset sign and carry flags
```

clears bit 7 (sign flag) since 00000000 is not negative and bit 0 (carry), which is always cleared. The bit pattern resulting from these or and and instructions is pushed back on the stack to be popped into the flags register by popf before exiting the procedure.

When no exceptional condition exists, an imul instruction finds the product of the unsigned value and the multiplier (± 1) giving the correct signed result. Flag values are set in this normal situation by using popf to recover the original flag values; test eax,eax clears CF and OF and assigns appropriate values to PF, SF, and ZF. The new flag values are then pushed back on the stack with another `pushf` to be recovered by the normal `popf` in the exit code. The `test` instruction leaves AF undefined; this is why the comments at the beginning of the procedure mention AF.

Exercises 8.3

1. The code for *atodproc* includes

```
TooBigD?:   test    eax,eax ; check sign flag
            jns     okD     ; will be set if number > 2^32 - 1
```

An alternative sequence would be

```
TooBigD?:   cmp     eax,80000000h     ; EAX < 2,147,483,648
            jb      okD               ; OK if so
```

Compare the number of clock cycles and number of bytes of object code for the `test` and the `cmp` instructions.

2. The procedure *atodproc* checks for zero digits in the number it is converting, but not for too many digits. Show why this is unnecessary by tracing the code for 100,000,000,000, the smallest possible 11-digit number. (Another valid reason not to limit the number of digits is that any number of leading zeros would be valid.)

Programming Exercises 8.3

1. Write a `NEAR32` procedure *hexToInt* that has a single parameter passed on the stack, the address of a string. This procedure will be similar to *atodproc* except that it will convert a string of characters representing an *unsigned* hexadecimal number to a doubleword-length 2's complement integer in EAX. The procedure should skip leading blanks and then accumulate a value until a character that does not represent a hex digit is encountered. (Valid characters are 0 through 9, A through F, and a through f.) If there are no hex digits or the result is too large to fit in EAX, then return 0 and set OF; these are the only possible errors. Clear OF if no error occurs. In all cases set SF, ZF, and PF according to the value returned in EAX and clear CF.

8.4   The Hardware Level—Logic Gates

Digital computers contain many integrated circuits and many of the components on these circuits are *logic gates*. A logic gate performs one of the elementary logical operations described in Section 8.1: **and**, **or**, **xor**, or **not**. Each type of gate has a simple diagram that represents its function. These diagrams are pictured in Fig. 8.10, with inputs shown on the left and output on the right.

These simple circuits operate by getting logic 0 or 1 inputs and putting the correct value on the output. For example, if the two inputs of the **or** circuit are 0 and 1, then the output will be 1. Logic values 0 and 1 are often represented by two distinct voltage levels.

These simple circuits are combined to make the complex circuits that perform a computer's operations. For example, Fig. 8.11 pictures a *half* adder circuit. The logic values at inputs x and y of this circuit can be thought of as two bits to add. The desired results are 0+0=0, 1+0=1, and 0+1=1, each with a carry of 0, and 1+1=0 with a carry of 1. These are exactly the results given by a half adder circuit.

Exercises 8.4

Addition of multibit numbers is performed much like decimal addition learned in grade school; pairs of bits are added starting with the rightmost pair, but after the first pair, you must also add the carry from the previous result. To do this takes a series of *full adder* circuits. One full

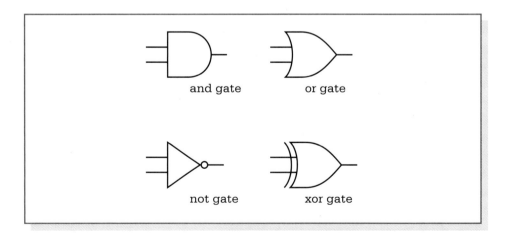

Figure 8.10   Logic Gates

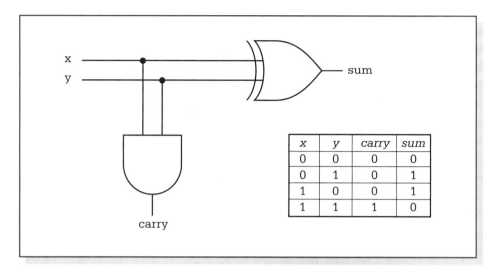

Figure 8.11 Half adder circuit

adder circuit has three inputs x, y, and *carry in*, and two outputs, *sum* and *carry out*.

1. Make a chart similar to the one in Fig. 8.11 showing the inputs and outputs for a full adder. The chart will have five columns (x, y, *carry in*, sum, and *carry out*) and eight rows below the header row.

2. Draw a full adder circuit. Hint: Use two half adders and an **or** gate to combine their *carry* outputs.

3. Use three full adders and a half adder to draw a circuit that can add two four bit numbers. This circuit will have eight inputs (four pairs of bits) and five outputs (four sum bits and a carry bit). For simplicity, you can draw each adder or half adder as a block diagram, without showing all its gates.

Chapter Summary

This chapter has explored the various 80x86 instructions that allow bits in a byte, word, or doubleword destination to be manipulated. The logical instructions and, or, and xor perform Boolean operations using pairs of bits from a source and destination. Applications of these instructions include setting or clearing selected bits in a destination. The `not` instruction takes the one's complement of each bit in its destination operand, changing each 0 to a 1 and each 1 to a 0. The `test` instruction is the same as the `and` instruction except that it only affects flags; the destination operand is unchanged.

Shift instructions move bits left or right within a destination operand. These instructions come in single-bit and multiple-bit versions. Single-bit shifts use 1 for the second operand; multiple-bit versions use CL or an immediate value for the second operand and shift the destination the number of positions specified. Vacated positions are filled by 0 bits in all single shift operations except for the arithmetic right shift of a negative number, for which 1 bits are used. Shift instructions can be used for efficient, convenient multiplication or division by 2, 4, 8 or some higher power of two. Double shift instructions get bits to shift in from a source register.

Rotate instructions are similar to shift instructions. However, the bit that falls off one end of the destination fills the void on the other end. Shift or rotate instructions can be used in combination with logical instructions to extract groups of bits from a location or to pack multiple values into a single byte or word.

The `atod` macro generates code that calls the procedure *atodproc*. This procedure scans a string in memory, skipping leading blanks, noting a sign (if any), and accumulating a doubleword integer value as ASCII codes for digits are encountered. Logical instructions are used in several places in the procedure.

Logic gates are the primitive building blocks for digital computer circuits. Each gate performs one of the elementary Boolean operations.

CHAPTER 9

The Assembly Process

The job of an assembler is to turn assembly language source code into object code. With simpler computer systems this object code is machine language, ready to be loaded into memory and executed. With more complex systems, object code produced by the assembler must be "fixed up" by a linker and/or loader before it can be executed. The first section of this chapter describes the assembly process for a typical assembler and gives some details particular to the Microsoft Macro Assembler. The second section is very specific to the 80x86 microprocessor family; it details the structure of its machine language. The third and fourth sections discuss macros and conditional assembly, respectively. Most assemblers have these capabilities, and these sections describe how MASM implements them. The final section describes the macros in the header file IO.H.

9.1   Two-Pass and One-Pass Assembly

One of the many reasons for writing assembly language rather than machine language is that assemblers allow the use of identifiers or symbols to reference data in the data segment and instructions in the code segment. To code in machine language, a programmer must know run-time addresses for data and instructions. An assembler maintains a **symbol table** that associates each identifier with various attributes. One attribute is a location, typically relative to the beginning of a segment, but sometimes an absolute address to be used at run time. Another attribute is the type of the symbol, where possible types include labels for data or instructions, symbols equated to constants, procedure names, macro names, and segment names. Some assemblers start assembling a source program with a symbol table that includes all the mnemonics for the language, all register names, and other symbols with reserved usage.

The other main job of an assembler is to output object code that is close to the machine language executed when a program is run. A **two-pass assembler** scans the source code once to produce a symbol table and a second time to produce the object code. A **one-pass assembler** only scans the source code one time, but often must patch the object code produced during this scan. A simple example shows why: If the segment

```
        jmp     endLoop
        add     eax, ecx
endLoop:
```

is scanned, the assembler finds a forward reference to *endLoop* in the jmp instruction. At this point the assembler cannot tell the address of *endLoop*, much less whether this destination is short (within 2^7 bytes of the address of the add instruction) or near (within 2^{32} bytes). The first option would use an EB opcode and a single-byte displacement. The second option would use an E9 opcode and a doubleword displacement. Clearly the final code must wait at least until the assembler reaches the source code line with the *endLoop* label.

Typical assemblers use two passes, and some actually use three or more passes. The Microsoft Macro Assembler is a one-pass assembler. This book will not attempt to cover details of how it fixes up object code. You can see part of MASM's symbol table by looking at the end of an assembly listing. The remainder of this section concentrates on a typical symbol table, drawing examples from the program and listing file that appear in Chapter 3.

If a symbol is a label for data, then the symbol table may include the size of the data. For instance, the program in Fig. 3.1 contains the directive

```
number2 DWORD    ?
```

and the corresponding line in the listing file (Fig. 3.7) is

```
number2  . . . . . . . . . . .    Dword    00000004 _DATA
```

This shows that the size of *number2* has been recorded as a doubleword. Having the size recorded enables MASM to detect incorrect usage of a symbol—with this definition of *number2*, MASM would indicate an error for the instruction

```
mov   bh, number2
```

since the BH register is byte size while the symbol table identifies *number2* as double-word size. In addition to the size, if a symbol is associated with multiple objects, a symbol table may contain the number of objects or the total number of bytes associated with the symbol. The MASM symbol listing does not show this.

     If a symbol is equated to a value, then the value is usually stored in the symbol table. When the assembler encounters the symbol in subsequent code, it substitutes the value recorded in the symbol table. In the example program, the source code line

```
cr     EQU     0dh     ; carriage return character
```

is reflected in the listing file line

```
cr . . . . . . . . . . . . . . .    Number    0000000Dh
```

     If a symbol is a label for data or an instruction, then its location is entered in the symbol table. An assembler keeps a location counter to compute this value. With a typical assembler, the location counter is set to zero at the beginning of a program or at the beginning of each major subdivision of the program. The Microsoft Macro Assembler sets the location counter to zero at the beginning of each segment. As an assembler scans source code, the location of each datum or instruction is the value of the location counter *before* the statement is assembled. The number of bytes required by the statement is added to the location counter to give the location of the *next* statement. Again looking at the line

```
number2 DWORD    ?
```

the listing file shows

```
number2  . . . . . . . . . . .    Dword    00000004 _DATA
```

with 00000004 in the *Value* column. This is the value of the location counter at the time *number2* is encountered in the data segment. The value is 00000004 since the only item preceding *number2* was *number1*, and it took four bytes.

The location counter is used the same way when instructions are assembled. Suppose that the location counter has value 0000012E when MASM reaches the code fragment shown in Fig. 9.1. The location for the symbol *while1* will be 0000012E. The cmp instruction requires three bytes of object code. (Section 9.2 details how to determine the object code of an 80x86 instruction.) Therefore the location counter will have value 00000131 when MASM reaches the jnle instruction. The jnle instruction requires two bytes of object code, so the location counter will increase to 00000133 for the first add instruction. The first add instruction takes two bytes of object code, so the location counter is 00000135 when MASM reaches the second add instruction. Three bytes are required for add ebx, 2 so the location counter is 00000138 for the inc instruction. The inc instruction takes a single byte, so the location counter is 00000139 for the jmp instruction. The jmp instruction requires two bytes, making the location counter 0000013B when the assembler reaches the label *endWhile1*. Therefore 0000013B is recorded in the symbol table as the location of *endWhile1*.

The location of a symbol is needed for a variety of purposes. Suppose that MASM encounters the statement

```
mov     eax, number
```

where *number* is the label on a DWORD directive in the data section. Since the addressing mode for *number* is direct, the assembler needs the offset of *number* for the object code; this offset is precisely the location of *number* recorded in the symbol table.

The primary job of an assembler is to generate object code. However, a typical assembler does many other tasks. One duty is to reserve storage. A statement like

```
WORD    20 DUP(?)
```

```
while1: cmp    ecx, 100        ; count <= 100 ?
        jnle endWhile1         ; exit if not
        add    eax, [ebx]      ; add value to sum
        add    ebx, 4          ; address of next value
        inc    ecx             ; add 1 to count
        jmp    while1
endWhile1:
```

Figure 9.1 **Code with forward reference**

sets aside 20 words of storage. This storage reservation is typically done one of two ways:

- the assembler may write 40 bytes with some known value (like 00) to the object file, or
- the assembler may insert a command that ultimately causes the loader to skip 40 bytes when the program is loaded into memory

In the latter case, storage at run time will contain whatever values are left over from execution of other programs.

In addition to reserving storage, assemblers can initialize the reserved memory with specified values. The MASM statement

```
WORD    10, 20, 30
```

not only reserves three words of storage, it initializes the first to 000A, the second to 0014 and the third to 001E. Initial values may be expressed in a variety of ways using MASM and most other assemblers. Numbers may be given in different number systems, often binary, octal, decimal, and hexadecimal. The assembler converts character values to corresponding ASCII or EBCDIC character codes. Assemblers usually allow expressions as initial values. The Microsoft Macro Assembler is typical in accepting expressions that are put together with addition, subtraction, negation, multiplication, division, not, and, or, exclusive or, shift, and relational operators. Such an expression is evaluated *at assembly time*, producing the value that is actually used in the object code.

Most assemblers can produce a listing file that shows the original source code and some sort of representation of the corresponding object code. Another responsibility of an assembler is to produce error messages when there are errors in the source code. Rudimentary assemblers just display a line number and an error code for each error. Slightly less primitive assemblers produce a separate page with line numbers and error messages. Most assemblers can include an error message in the listing file at the point where the error occurs. The Microsoft Macro Assembler includes messages in the optional listing file and also displays them on the console.

In addition to the listing that shows source and object code, an assembler often can generate a listing of symbols used in the program. Such a listing may include information about each symbol's attributes—taken from the assembler's symbol table—as well as cross references that indicate the line where the symbol is defined and each line where it is referenced.

Some assemblers begin assembling instructions with the location counter set to a particular actual memory address and thus generate object code that is ready to be loaded at that address. This is the only way to generate object code with some simpler systems. Generally such code is not linked; it is ready to load and run.

One file can reference objects in another. Recall that the EXTRN directive facilitates this for MASM. A linker combines separate object code files into a single file. If one file references objects in the other, the linker changes the references from "to be determined" to locations in the combined file.

Most assemblers produce object code that is **relocatable**; that is, it can be loaded at any address. One way to do this is to put a map in the object code file that records each place in the program where an address must be modified. Address modifications are usually carried out by the loader. The loader finally produces true machine language, ready for execution.

Another way to get relocatable code is to write it with only relative references; that is, so that each instruction only references an object at some distance from itself, not at a fixed address. In an 80x86 system, most jump instructions are relative, so if a programmer stores data in registers or on the stack, it is fairly easy to produce such a program.

With MASM, a programmer can actually directly reference the location counter using the $ symbol. The code fragment from Fig. 9.1 could be rewritten as

```
cmp   ecx, 100        ; count <= 100 ?
jnle $+10             ; exit if not
add   eax, [ebx]      ; add value to sum
add   ebx, 4          ; address of next value
inc   ecx             ; add 1 to count
jmp   $-11
```

This works since the value of the location counter $ is the location of the *beginning* of the jnle statement as it is assembled. Its two bytes and the eight bytes of the next four statements need to be skipped to exit the loop. Similarly the backward reference must skip the inc statement and the four other statements back through the beginning of the cmp statement, a total of eleven bytes. Although MASM allows use of $ to reference the location counter, obviously this can produce confusing code and should normally be avoided.

Exercises 9.1

1. Describe the differences between object code and machine language.

2. Suppose that every symbol reference in an assembly language program is a backward reference. Would a one-pass assembler ever have to "fix up" the code it produced? Explain your answer.

3. Assemble the following code fragment

```
Array   DWORD   10 DUP(?)
ArrSize EQU     SIZE Array
```

To what value is *ArrSize* equated? What conclusion can you draw about whether or not MASM records an attribute that tracks the number of bytes associated with a variable?

4. This section states that storage reservation with a directive like WORD can work by putting the correct number of some known byte value in the object file or by inserting a command that ultimately causes the loader to skip the correct number of bytes. State one advantage and one disadvantage of each design.

9.2   80x86 Instruction Coding

This section describes the structure of 80x86 machine language. From this information one could almost assemble an 80x86 assembly language program by hand. However, the primary purpose here is to acquire a better understanding of the capabilities and limitations of the 80x86 microprocessor family.

An 80x86 instruction consists of several fields, which are summarized in Fig. 9.2. Some instructions have only an opcode, while others require that other fields be included. Any included fields always appear in this order. Each of these components is discussed below.

The repeat prefixes for string instructions were discussed in Chapter 7. There you learned that adding a **repeat prefix** to one of the basic string instructions effectively changes it into a new instruction that automatically iterates a basic operation. The repeat prefix is coded in the instruction prefix byte, with the opcode of the basic string instruction in the opcode byte. Repeat prefix bytes can be coded only with the basic string instructions.

The LOCK prefix is not illustrated in this book's code. It can be used with a few selected instructions and causes the system bus to be locked during execution of the instruction. Locking the bus guarantees that the 80x86 processor has exclusive use of shared memory.

All the code in this book uses 32-bit memory addresses. In a 32-bit address environment it is possible to have an instruction that only contains a 16-bit address.

Field	Number of bytes	Purpose
instruction prefix	0 or 1	$F3_{16}$ for REP, REPE, or REPZ $F2_{16}$ for REPNE or REPNZ $F0_{16}$ for LOCK
address size	0 or 1	value 67_{16} if present; indicates that a displacement is a 16-bit address rather than the default 32-bit size
operand size	0 or 1	value 66_{16} if present; indicates that a memory operand is 16-bit if in 32-bit mode or 32-bit if in 16-bit mode
segment override	0 or 1	indicates that an operand is in a segment other than the default segment
opcode	1 or 2	operation code
mod-reg-r/m	0 or 1	indicates register or memory operand, encodes register(s)
scaled index base byte	0 or 1	additional scaling and register information
displacement	0 to 4	an address
immediate	0 to 4	an immediate value

Figure 9.2   80x86 instruction fields

When an **address size byte** of 67_{16} is coded, a two-byte rather than a four-byte displacement is used in the displacement field. This prefix byte will not appear in machine code generated from the assembly language code shown in this book.

On the other hand, the **operand size byte** has frequently been generated from this book's assembly language code. The 80x86 CPU has a status bit that determines whether operands are 16-bit or 32-bit. With the assembly and linking options we have used, that bit is always set to indicate 32-bit operands. Each time you code a word-size operand, the generated instruction includes the 66_{16} prefix byte to indicate the 16-bit operand. Other assembly and linking options—not used in this book—cause the default operand size to be 16-bit; in this case a 66_{16} prefix byte indicates a 32-bit operand.

What indicates a byte-size operand? A different opcode. Why don't 16-bit and 32-bit operands use distinct opcodes? This design decision was made by Intel. The original 8086 processor design had 16-bit registers and used separate opcodes for 8-bit and 16-bit operand sizes; no instruction used 32-bit operands. When the 80386 was designed with 32-bit registers, the choice was made to "share" opcodes for 16-bit and 32-bit operand sizes rather than to introduce many new opcodes.

The *mod-reg-r/m* byte has different uses for different instructions. When present it always has three fields, a two-bit *mod* field (for "mode"), a three-bit *reg* field (for "register," but sometimes used for other purposes), and a 3-bit *r/m* field (for "register/memory"). The *mod-reg-r/m* byte is examined below.

The opcode field completely identifies many instructions, but some require additional information—for example, to determine the type of operand or even to determine the operation itself. You have previously seen the latter situation. For example, each of the instructions add, or, adc, sbb, and, sub, xor, and cmp having a byte-size operand in a register or memory and an immediate operand uses the opcode 80. Which of these eight instructions is determined by the *reg* field of the *mod-reg-r/m* byte. For the particular case of the 80 opcode, the *reg* field is 000 for add, 001 for or, 010 for adc, 011 for sbb, 100 for and, 101 for sub, 110 for xor, and 111 for cmp.

The opcode 80 is one of twelve in which the *reg* field of the *mod-reg-r/m* byte actually determines the instruction. The others are 81, 82, 83, D0, D1, D2, D3, F6, F7, FE, and FF. The table in Fig. 9.3 gives *reg* field information for the most common instructions.

Each two-operand, nonimmediate 80x86 instruction has at least one register operand. The *reg* field contains a code for this register. Figure 9.4 shows how the eight possible register codes are assigned. The meaning of a *reg* code varies with the operand size and with the instruction, so that, for example, the same code is used for ECX and

		reg field							
Opcode		000	001	010	011	100	101	110	111
	80, 81, 82, 83	ADD	OR	ADC	SBB	AND	SUB	XOR	CMP
	D0, D1, D2, D3	ROL	ROR	RCL	RCR	SHL	SHR		SAR
	F6, F7	TEST		NOT	NEG	MUL	IMUL	DIV	IDIV
	FE, FF	INC	DEC					PUSH	

Figure 9.3   *reg* field for specified opcodes

reg code	register 32	register 16	register 8	segment register
000	EAX	AX	AL	ES
001	ECX	CX	CL	CS
010	EDX	DX	DL	SS
011	EBX	BX	BL	DS
100	ESP	SP	AH	FS
101	EBP	BP	CH	GS
110	ESI	SI	DH	
111	EDI	DI	BH	

Figure 9.4 80x86 register codes

CL. These codes are used any time information about a register is encoded in an instruction, whether in the *reg* field or other places.

The *mod* field is also used to determine the type of operands an instruction has. Often the same opcode is used for an instruction that has two register operands or one register operand and one memory operand. The choice *mod*=11 means that the instruction is a register-to-register operation or an immediate-to-register operation. For a register-to-register operation, the destination register is coded in the *reg* field and the source register is coded in the *r/m* field. Both use the register codes shown in Fig. 9.4. For an immediate-to-register operation, the operation is coded as shown in Fig. 9.3 and the destination register is coded in the *r/m* field. The situation is complicated for the other possible *mod* values and depends on the *r/m* field as well as the *mod* field. For *r/m*=100, it also depends on the scaled index base (*SIB*) byte.

The *SIB* byte consists of three fields, a two-bit scaling field, a three-bit index register field, and a three-bit base register field.

> The scale values are 00 for 1, 01 for 2, 10 for 4, and 11 for 8.

The index and base register encodings are as shown in Fig. 9.4, except that 100 cannot appear in the index register field since ESP cannot be an index register. Figure 9.5 shows the different encodings. The *mod* field in these formats tells how many bytes there are in the displacement. A value of 00 means that there is no displacement in the machine code, except when *r/m*=101 when there is *only* a displacement. This special case is for direct memory addressing, so is frequently used. A *mod* value of 01 means

mod	r/m	base from SIB	operand (scale and index from SIB)
00	000		DS:[EAX]
	001		DS:[ECX]
	010		DS:[EDX]
	011		DS:[EBX]
	100	000	DS:[EAX + (*scale*index*)]
	(use *SIB*)	001	DS:[ECX + (*scale*index*)]
		010	DS:[EDX + (*scale*index*)]
		011	DS:[EBX + (*scale*index*)]
		100	SS:[ESP + (*scale*index*)]
		101	DS:[*displacement32* + (*scale*index*)]
		110	DS:[ESI + (*scale*index*)]
		111	DS:[EDI + (*scale*index*)]
	101		DS:*displacement32*
	110		DS:[ESI]
	111		DS:[EDI]
01	000		DS:[EAX + *displacement8*]
	001		DS:[ECX + *displacement8*]
	010		DS:[EDX + *displacement8*]
	011		DS:[EBX + *displacement8*]
	100	000	DS:[EAX + (*scale*index*) + *displacement8*]
	(use *SIB*)	001	DS:[ECX + (*scale*index*) + *displacement8*]
		010	DS:[EDX + (*scale*index*) + *displacement8*]
		011	DS:[EBX + (*scale*index*) + *displacement8*]
		100	SS:[ESP + (*scale*index*) + *displacement8*]
		101	SS:[EBP + (*scale*index*) + *displacement8*]
		110	DS:[ESI + (*scale*index*) + *displacement8*]
		111	DS:[EDI + (*scale*index*) + *displacement8*]
	101		SS:[EBP + *displacement8*]
	110		DS:[ESI + *displacement8*]
	111		DS:[EDI + *displacement8*]

(continued)

Figure 9.5   80x86 instruction encodings

mod	r/m	base from SIB	operand (scale and index from SIB)
10	000		DS:[EAX + *displacement32*]
	001		DS:[ECX + *displacement32*]
	010		DS:[EDX + *displacement32*]
	011		DS:[EBX + *displacement32*]
	100	000	DS:[EAX + (*scale*index*) + *displacement32*]
	(use *SIB*)	001	DS:[ECX + (*scale*index*) + *displacement32*]
		010	DS:[EDX + (*scale*index*) + *displacement32*]
		011	DS:[EBX + (*scale*index*) + *displacement32*]
		100	SS:[ESP + (*scale*index*) + *displacement32*]
		101	SS:[EBP + (*scale*index*) + *displacement32*]
		110	DS:[ESI + (*scale*index*) + *displacement32*]
		111	DS:[EDI + (*scale*index*) + *displacement32*]
	101		SS:[EBP + *displacement32*]
	110		DS:[ESI + *displacement32*]
	111		DS:[EDI + *displacement32*]

mod	reg	r/m	operands
11	dest	source	source register, destination register
	operation	dest	destination register, immediate operand

Figure 9.5 *(continued)*

that there is a displacement *byte* in the machine code; this byte is treated as a signed number and is extended to a doubleword before it is added to the value from the base register and/or index register. A value of 10 means that there is a displacement *double-word* in the machine code; this doubleword is added to the value that comes from the base register and/or scaled index register. The scaling factor is multiplied times the value in the index register.

It is time for some examples. The first example shows the kind of instruction seen frequently in this book.

```
add ecx, value
```

Suppose that at execution time *value* references the memory doubleword at address 1B27D48C. From Fig. 4.5 or Appendix D, this `add` instruction has opcode 03. The direct address consists only of the 32-bit displacement—there is no index register or base register used. Therefore the components of the *mod-reg-r/m* byte are *mod*=00, *reg*=001 (for ECX), and *r/m*=101 (for direct addressing), giving 00 001 101 or 0D after regrouping and converting to hexadecimal. The final part of the instruction is the displacement, so the entire instruction is encoded as 03 0D 1B27D48C (where the bytes of the address will actually be stored backwards).

Now consider the instruction

```
add ecx, eax
```

This instruction also has opcode 03. The *mod* field is 11 since there are two register operands. The *reg* field specifies the destination register, 001 for ECX. The *r/m* field gives the source register, 000 for EAX. The *mod-reg-r/m* byte of the instruction is therefore 11 001 000, or C8 in hex. The machine code for the instruction is 03 C8.

Next consider the instruction

```
mov edx, [ebx]
```

Figure 4.3 or Appendix D gives the opcode as 8B. Since the operand [ebx] is indirect addressing using no displacement, the *mod* field is 00. The *reg* field contains 010, the code for EDX. The fourth line of the *mod*=00 group shows address DS:[EBX], that is, register indirect addressing in the data segment using the address in EBX. Therefore the *r/m* field is 011. Putting these fields together gives a *mod-reg-r/m* byte of 00 010 011 or 13, and the entire instruction assembles to 8B 13.

Now look at

```
xor ecx, [edx+2]
```

Figure 8.2 or Appendix D gives the opcode of this instruction as 33. The memory operand uses indirect addressing and a displacement of 2, small enough to encode in a single byte 02. Therefore the *mod* field is 01. The *reg* field contains 001 for ECX. Figure 9.5 gives the *r/m* field as 010. Putting this together gives a *mod-reg-r/m* byte of 01 001 010 or 4A, so this instruction has machine code 33 4A 02.

Next consider an instruction that uses scaling.

```
add eax, [ebx + 4*ecx]
```

This type of instruction is useful to process an array almost as in a high level language. You can store the starting address of the array in EBX, and the array index in ECX (assuming that indexing starts at 0). The index is multiplied by the scaling factor 4 (the size of a doubleword), and added to the base address to get the address of the array element. Figure 4.5 gives the opcode as 03. The *mod-reg-r/m* byte is 00 000 100 or 04 for no displacement, destination register EAX, and *SIB* byte used. The *SIB* byte is required since the instruction includes both base and index registers. Its fields are *scale*=10 for 4, *index*=001 for ECX, and *base*=011 for EBX, giving a *SIB* byte of 10 001 011 or 8B. The object code is therefore 03 04 8B.

Next we look at

```
sub ecx, value[ebx + 2*edi]
```

where *value* references an address in the data segment. The opcode for this sub instruction is 2B. This address is treated as a 32-bit displacement, and there is both a base and an index register. Therefore *mod*=10, *reg*=001 (for ECX), and *r/m*=100 (for *SIB* needed). The fields of the *SIB* byte are 01 (for scaling factor 2), 111 (for index register EDI), and 011 (for base register EBX). The displacement doubleword will contain the run-time address of value. The machine code is therefore 2B 8C 7B xxxxxxxx, where the x's represent the address of *value*.

If the second operand in the last example is changed to value[EBX+2*EDI+10], then the displacement/address (represented above by xxxxxxxx) is simply 10 larger. That is, the assembler combines the displacement 10 and the displacement corresponding to *value*.

You may have noticed that the first group in Fig. 9.5 does not show how to encode the operand [ebp]. It is encoded as [ebp+0], using a byte-size displacement. For example

```
mov eax, [ebp]
```

is encoded as 8B 45 00, opcode 8B, *mod-reg-r/m* byte 01 000 101 (1-byte displacement, destination EAX, base register EBP), and displacement 00.

Figure 9.5 points out again that indirect addresses using ESP and EBP are in the stack segment, not the data segment. One would rarely want to override this. However, you might want to reference data in, say, the extra segment. To do this, you might code an instruction like

```
cmp ax, WORD PTR es:[edx + 2*esi + 512]
```

This example has been chosen to involve almost all of the possible components of an 80x86 instruction. It uses operand size prefix since word-size operands are being used. It uses a segment override prefix for ES. It uses base and index registers and a 32-bit dis-

Prefix	Segment
2E	CS
3E	DS
26	ES
36	SS
64	FS
65	GS

Figure 9.6   Segment override prefixes

placement. The code generated is 66 26 3B 84 72 00000200, operand size prefix 66, segment override 26 (for ES), opcode 3B, *mod-reg-r/m byte* 84, *SIB* 72, and displacement 00000200. The possible segment override bytes are in Fig. 9.6.

While it may seem that opcode assignments are completely random, there are actually several patterns. For example, given a doubleword operand referenced by *value*, the opcode for the memory-to-register instruction mov eax,value is A1 and the opcode for the register-to-memory instruction mov value,eax is A3. In binary, these differ only in bit position 1, the next-to-last bit. Bit 1 often serves as a **direction bit**, having value 1 when the first operand is in memory and 0 when the first operand is in a register.

Similarly, corresponding instructions with doubleword operands and byte-size operands often have opcodes that differ only in bit position 0, the last bit. For example, given a byte referenced by *bVal* and a doubleword referenced by *dVal*, then the opcode for cmp bVal,dl is 38 and for cmp dVal,edx is 39. Bit 0 often serves as a **size bit**, having value 1 for doubleword (or word) operands and value 0 for byte operands.

Another set of patterns occurs in some single byte instructions where the same instruction is available for each of the registers—the opcode ends in the appropriate register code. For instance, the inc instructions for *register32* operands (Fig. 4.6) have opcodes 40 through 47, and the last three bits are 000 through 111, the register codes for the registers to be incremented. Another way of looking at this is that the opcodes for this class of inc instructions are obtained by adding 40 and the register code.

Exercises 9.2

1. Why can no 80x86 assembly language instruction specify two memory operands?

2. Find the machine code for each of the following instructions. Make the following assumptions:

```
dbl   DWORD   ?      ; run-time location 1122AABB
wrd   WORD    ?      ; run-time location 3344CCDD
byt   BYTE    ?      ; run-time location 5566EEFF
```

(a) add   dbl, ecx
(b) add   wrd, cx
(c) add   byt, cl
(d) add   edx, ebx
(e) add   dx, bx
(f) add   dl, bh
(g) push ebp
(h) cmp   ecx, dbl
(i) cmp   al, byt
(j) inc   ecx
(k) inc   cx
(l) pop   eax
(m) push dbl
(n) or   al, 35
(o) sub   dbl, 2 (byte-size immediate operand)
(p) and   ebx, 0ff000000h (doubleword-size immediate operand)
(q) xchg ebx, ecx
(r) xchg eax, ecx (note accumulator operand)
(s) cwd
(t) shl   edx, 1
(u) neg   WORD PTR [EBX]
(v) imul ch
(w) div   dbl
(x) dec   DWORD PTR [ebx+esi]
(y) and   ecx, [ebx+4*edi]
(z) sub   ebx, dbl[4*eax]

Programming Exercises 9.2

1. Assuming that *arr*[0..nbr] contains a collection of doublewords in increasing order. The following design describes a **binary search** for *keyValue*, returning the index of *keyValue* if it is present in the array and −1 if it is absent.

```
procedure binarySearch(arr : array, nbr: integer, keyValue : integer) : integer
topIndex := nbr;
bottomIndex := 0;
while (bottomIndex ≤ topIndex) loop
    midIndex := (bottomIndex + topIndex) div 2;
    if (keyValue = arr[midIndex])
    then
            return midIndex;
    elseif (keyValue < arr[midIndex])
    then
            topIndex := midIndex—1;
    else
            bottomIndex := midIndex + 1;
    end if;
end loop;
return −1;
```

Implement this design as an 80x86 NEAR32 procedure *binarySearch* with three parameters, (1) the address of an array of doublewords, (2) a doubleword *nbr*, and (3) a doubleword *keyValue*. Return the appropriate result in EAX. The procedure will change no register other than EAX, and it will be responsible for removing parameters from the stack. Use scaled and indexed addressing appropriately to address array elements. Write a short test driver program to test your procedure *binarySearch*.

2. The first *nbrElts* values in an array a[*1..maxIndex*] can be sorted into increasing order using the **selection sort** algorithm.

```
procedure selectionSort(arr : array, nbr: integer)
for position := 1 to nbrElts−1 loop
    smallSpot := position;
    smallValue := a[position];
    for i := position+1 to nbrElts loop
            if a[i] < smallValue
            then
                    smallSpot := i;
                    smallValue := a[i];
            end if;
```

```
        end for;
        a[smallSpot] := a[position];
        a[position] := smallValue;
    end for;
```

Implement this algorithm in a NEAR32 procedure *selectionSort* with two parameters: (1) the address of an array *a* of doubleword integers, and (2) a doubleword *nbrElts*. The procedure will change no register and it will be responsible for removing parameters from the stack. Use scaled and indexed addressing appropriately to address array elements, noting that the algorithm as written starts with index 1, not index 0. Write a short test driver program to test your procedure.

3. The **quick sort** algorithm sorts an array slice *a[leftEnd..rightEnd]* into increasing order by identifying a middle value in the array and moving elements of the array so that all elements on the left are smaller than the middle value and all on the right are larger than the middle value. Then the procedure is recursively called to sort the left and right sides. The recursion terminates when the portion to be sorted has one or fewer elements. Here is a design.

```
procedure quickSort(a:array, leftEnd:integer, rightEnd:integer)
if leftEnd < rightEnd
then
    left := leftEnd;
    right := rightEnd;

    while left < right loop
        while (left < right) and (a[left] ≤ a[right]) loop
            add 1 to left;
        end while;
        swap a[left] and a[right];

        while (left < right) and (a[left] ≤ a[right]) loop
            subtract 1 from right;
        end while;
```

        swap a[left] and a[right];
    end while;

    quickSort(a, leftEnd, left−1);
    quickSort(a, right+1, rightEnd);
end if;

Implement this algorithm in a `NEAR32` procedure *quickSort* with three parameters: (1) the address of an array *a* of doubleword integers, (2) a doubleword *leftEnd,* and (3) a doubleword *rightEnd*. The procedure will change no register and it will be responsible for removing parameters from the stack. Use scaled and indexed addressing appropriately to address array elements. Write a short test driver program to test your procedure.

9.3   Macro Definition and Expansion

A macro was defined in Chapter 3 as a statement that is shorthand for a sequence of other statements. The assembler expands a macro to the statements it represents, and then assembles these new statements. Many previous chapters have made extensive use of macros defined in the file IO.H. This section explains how to write macro definitions and tells how MASM uses these definitions to expand macros into other statements.

      A macro definition resembles a procedure definition in a high-level language. The first line gives the name of the macro being defined and a list of parameters; the main part of the definition consists of a collection of statements that describe the action of the macro in terms of the parameters. A macro is called much like a high-level language procedure, too; the name of the macro is followed by a list of arguments.

      These similarities are superficial. A procedure call in a high-level language is generally compiled into a sequence of instructions to push parameters on the stack followed by a `call` instruction, whereas a macro call actually expands into statements given in the macro, with the arguments substituted for the parameters used in the macro definition. Code in a macro is repeated every time a macro is called, but there is just one copy of the code for a procedure. Macros often execute more rapidly than procedure calls since there is no overhead for passing parameters or for `call` and `ret` instructions, but this is usually at the cost of more bytes of object code.

Every macro definition is bracketed by `MACRO` and `ENDM` directives. The format of a macro definition is

> *name*   MACRO   *list of parameters*
>   *assembly language statements*
>   ENDM

The parameters in the `MACRO` directive are ordinary symbols, separated by commas. The assembly language statements may use the parameters as well as registers, immediate operands, or symbols defined outside the macro. These statements may even include macro calls.

A macro definition can appear anywhere in an assembly language source code file as long as the definition comes before the first statement that calls the macro. It is good programming practice to place macro definitions near the beginning of a source file.

The remainder of this section gives several examples of macro definitions and macro calls. Suppose that a program design requires several pauses where the user is prompted to press the [Enter] key. Rather than write this code every time or use a proce-dure, a macro *pause* can be defined. Figure 9.7 gives such a definition.

The *pause* macro has no parameter, so a call expands to almost exactly the same statements as are in the definition. If the statement

> pause

```
pause    MACRO
; prompt user and wait for [Enter] to be pressed
         output pressMsg    ; "Press [Enter]"
         input  stringIn,5  ; input
         ENDM
```

Figure 9.7   *pause* **macro**

is included in subsequent source code, then the assembler expands this macro call into the statements

```
output pressMsg     ; "Press [Enter]"
input  stringIn,5   ; input
```

Of course, each of these statements is itself a macro call and will expand to additional statements. Notice that the *pause* macro is not self-contained; it references two fields in the data segment:

```
pressMsg BYTE "Press [Enter] to continue", 0
stringIn BYTE 5 DUP (?)
```

Note again that the definition and expansion for the pause macro contain no ret statement. Although macros look much like procedures, they generate in-line code when the macro call is expanded at assembly time.

Figure 9.8 gives a definition of a macro *add2* that finds the sum of two parameters, putting the result in the EAX register. The parameters used to define the macro are *nbr1* and *nbr2*. These labels are local to the definition. The same names could be used for other purposes in the program, although some human confusion might result.

The statements to which *add2* expands depends on the arguments used in a call. For example, the macro call

```
add2   value, 30   ; value + 30
```

expands to

```
; put sum of two doubleword parameters in EAX
mov    eax, value
add    eax, 30
```

```
add2     MACRO  nbr1, nbr2
; put sum of two doubleword parameters in EAX
        mov     eax, nbr1
        add     eax, nbr2
        ENDM
```

Figure 9.8   **Macro to add two integers**

The statement

```
add2   value1, value2    ; value1 + value2
```

expands to

```
; put sum of two doubleword parameters in EAX
mov    eax, value1
add    eax, value2
```

The macro call

```
add2   eax, ebx      ; sum of two values
```

expands to

```
; put sum of two doubleword parameters in EAX
mov    eax, eax
add    eax, ebx
```

The instruction mov eax, eax is legal, even if it accomplishes nothing.

In each of these examples, the first argument is substituted for the first parameter *nbr1* and the second argument is substituted for the second parameter *nbr2*. Each macro results in two mov instructions, but since the types of arguments differ, the object code will vary.

If one of the parameters is missing the macro will still be expanded. For instance, the statement

```
add2   value
```

expands to

```
; put sum of two doubleword parameters in EAX
mov    eax, value
add    eax,
```

The argument *value* replaces *nbr1* and an empty string replaces *nbr2*. The assembler will report an error, but it will be for the illegal add instruction that results from the macro expansion, not directly because of the missing argument.

Similarly, the macro call

```
add    , value
```

expands to

```
; put sum of two doubleword parameters in EAX
mov     eax,
add     eax, value
```

The comma in the macro call separates the first missing argument from the second argument *value*. An empty argument replaces the parameter *nbr1*. The assembler will again report an error, this time for the illegal mov instruction.

Figure 9.9 shows the definition of a macro *swap* that will exchange the contents of two doublewords in memory. It is very similar to the 80x86 xchg instruction that will not work with two memory operands.

As with the *add2* macro, the code generated by calling the *swap* macro depends on the arguments used. For example, the call

```
swap    [ebx], [ebx+4]     ; swap adjacent words in array
```

expands to

```
; exchange two doublewords in memory
        push    eax
        mov     eax, [ebx]
        xchg    eax, [ebx+4]
        mov     [ebx], eax
        pop     eax
```

```
swap    MACRO   dword1, dword2
; exchange two doublewords in memory
        push    eax
        mov     eax, dword1
        xchg    eax, dword2
        mov     dword1, eax
        pop     eax
        ENDM
```

Figure 9.9   Macro to swap two memory words

```
min2      MACRO  first, second
          LOCAL  endIfMin
; put smaller of two doublewords in the EAX register
          mov    eax, first
          cmp    eax, second
          jle    endIfMin
          mov    eax, second
endIfMin:
          ENDM
```

Figure 9.10 Macro to find smaller of two memory words

It might not be obvious to the user that the swap macro uses the EAX register, so the push and pop instructions in the macro protect the user from accidentally losing the contents of this register.

Figure 9.10 gives a definition of a macro *min2*, which finds the minimum of two doubleword signed integers, putting the smaller in the EAX register. The code for this macro must implement a design with an *if* statement, and this requires at least one assembly language statement with a label. If an ordinary label were used, then it would appear every time a *min2* macro call was expanded and the assembler would produce error messages because of duplicate labels. The solution is to use a LOCAL directive to define a symbol *endIfMin* that is local to the *min2* macro.

The LOCAL directive is used only within a macro definition and must be the first statement after the MACRO directive. (Not even a comment can separate the MACRO and LOCAL directives.) It lists one or more symbols, separated by commas, which are used within the macro definition. Each time the macro is expanded and one of these symbols is needed, it is replaced by a symbol starting with two question marks and ending with four hexadecimal digits (??0000, ??0001, etc.) The same *??dddd* symbol replaces the local symbol each place the local symbol is used in one particular expansion of a macro call. The same symbols may be listed in LOCAL directives in different macro definitions or may be used as regular symbols in code outside of macro definitions.

The macro call

```
min2   [ebx], ecx   ; find smaller of two values
```

might expand to the code

```
LOCAL   endIfMin
; put smaller of two doublewords in the EAX register
        mov     eax, [ebx]
        cmp     eax, ecx
        jle     ??000C
        mov     eax, ecx
??000C:
```

Here *endIfMin* has been replaced the two places it appears within the macro definition by ??000C in the expansion. Another expansion of the same macro would use a different number after the question marks.

The MASM assembler has several directives that control how macros and other statements are shown in .LST files. The most useful are

- `.LIST` that causes statements to be included in the listing file
- `.NOLIST` that completely suppresses the listing of all statements, and
- `.NOLISTMACRO` that selectively suppresses macro expansions while allowing the programmer's original statements to be listed

The file IO.H ends starts with a `.NOLIST` directive so that macro definitions do not clutter the listing. Similarly IO.H ends with `.NOLISTMACRO` and `.LIST` directives so that macro expansion listings do not obscure the programmer's code, but original statements are listed.

Exercises 9.3

1. Using the macro definition for *add2* given in Fig. 9.8, show the sequence of statements to which each of the following macro calls expands.
   (a) `add2   25, ebx`
   (b) `add2   ecx, edx`
   (c) `add2                  ; no argument`
   (d) `add2   value1, value2, value3`
   (Hint: the third argument is ignored since it has no matching parameter.)

2. Using the macro definition for *swap* given in Fig. 9.9, show the sequence of statements to which each of the following macro calls expands.
   (a) `swap   value1, value2`
   (b) `swap   temp, [ebx]`
   (c) `swap   value`

3. Using the macro definition for *min2* given in Fig. 9.10, show the sequence of statements to which each of the following macro calls expands.

   (a) `min2   value1, value2`

   (Assume the local symbol counter is at 000A)

   (b) `min2   cx, value`

   (Assume the local symbol counter is at 0019)

Programming Exercises 9.3

1. Write a definition of a macro *add3* that has three doubleword integer parameters and puts the sum of the three numbers in the EAX register.

2. Write a definition of a macro *max2* that has two doubleword integer parameters and puts the maximum of the two numbers in the EAX register.

3. Write a definition of a macro *min3* that has three doubleword integer parameters and puts the minimum of the three numbers in the EAX register.

4. Write a definition of a macro *toUpper* with one parameter, the address of a byte in memory. The code generated by the macro will examine the byte, and if it is the ASCII code for a lowercase letter, will replace it by the ASCII code for the corresponding uppercase letter.

9.4   Conditional Assembly

The Microsoft Macro Assembler can observe various conditions that can be tested at assembly time and alter how the source code is assembled on the basis of these conditions. For instance, a block of code may be assembled or skipped based on the definition of a constant. This ability to do **conditional assembly** is especially useful in macro definitions. For example, two macros using the same mnemonic may be expanded into different sequences of statements based on the number of operands present. This section describes some of the ways that conditional assembly can be used.

Figure 9.11 shows a definition for a macro *addAll* that will add one to five doubleword integers, putting the sum in the EAX register. It employs the conditional assembly directive `IFNB` ("if not blank"). This directive is most often used in macro definitions, although it is legal in **open code**, that is, regular code outside a macro. When an *addAll*

```
addAll MACRO  nbr1, nbr2, nbr3, nbr4, nbr5
; add up to 5 doubleword integers, putting sum in EAX
        mov    eax, nbr1    ; first operand
        IFNB   <nbr2>
        add    eax, nbr2    ; second operand
        ENDIF
        IFNB   <nbr3>
        add    eax, nbr3    ; third operand
        ENDIF
        IFNB   <nbr4>
        add    eax, nbr4    ; fourth operand
        ENDIF
        IFNB   <nbr5>
        add    eax, nbr5    ; fifth operand
        ENDIF
        ENDM
```

Figure 9.11   addAll **macro using conditional assembly**

macro call is expanded and one of its IFNB directives is encountered, MASM examines the value of the macro parameter whose name is enclosed between < and >. If that parameter has a corresponding argument passed to it, then it is "not blank" and the add instruction for that argument is included in the expansion of the macro. If a parameter does not have a corresponding argument, the add instruction is not assembled.

Given the macro call

```
addAll  ebx, ecx, edx, number, 1
```

each of the five macro parameters has a corresponding argument, so the macro expands to

```
        mov    eax, ebx     ; first operand
        add    eax, ecx     ; second operand
        add    eax, edx     ; third operand
        add    eax, number    ; fourth operand
        add    eax, 1     ; fifth operand
```

The macro call

```
addAll  ebx, ecx, 45          ; value1 + value2 + 45
```

has only three arguments. The argument `ebx` becomes the value for parameter *nbr1*, `ecx` is substituted for *nbr2*, and 45 will be used for *nbr3*, but the parameters *nbr4* and *nbr5* will be blank. Therefore the macro expands to the statements

```
mov    eax, ebx     ; first operand
add    eax, ecx     ; second operand
add    eax, 45      ; third operand
```

Although it would be unusual to do so, arguments other than trailing ones can be omitted. For example, the macro call

```
addAll  ebx, ,ecx
```

has `ebx` corresponding to *nbr1* and `ecx` matched to *nbr3*, but all other parameters will be blank. Therefore the macro expands to

```
mov    eax, ebx     ; first operand
add    eax, ecx     ; third operand
```

If the first argument is omitted in an *addAll* macro call, the macro will still be expanded. However, the resulting statement sequence will contain a `mov` instruction with a missing operand, and this statement will cause MASM to issue an error message. For example, the macro call

```
addAll  , value1, value2
```

expands to

```
mov    eax,       ; first operand
add    eax, value1    ; second operand
add    eax, value2    ; third operand
```

An unusual use of the *addAll* macro is illustrated by the call

```
addAll  value, eax, eax, value, eax     ; 10 * value
```

that expands to

```
mov    eax, value    ; first operand
add    eax, eax      ; second operand
add    eax, eax      ; third operand
add    eax, value    ; fourth operand
add    eax, eax      ; fifth operand
```

The comment "10 * value" explains the purpose of this call.

The Microsoft assembler provides several conditional assembly directives. The `IFNB` directive has a companion `IFB` ("if blank") that checks if a macro parameter *is* blank.

The `IF` and `IFE` directives examine an expression whose value can be determined at assembly time. For `IF`, MASM assembles conditional code if the value of the expression is not zero. For `IFE`, MASM includes conditional code if the value is zero.

The `IFDEF` and `IFNDEF` are similar to `IF` and `IFE`. They examine a symbol and MASM assembles conditional code depending on whether or not the symbol has previously been defined in the program.

Each conditional assembly block is terminated by the `ENDIF` directive. `ELSEIF` and `ELSE` directives are available to provide alternative code. In general, blocks of conditional assembly code look like

```
IF...   [operands]
statements
ELSEIF ...
statements
ELSE
statements
ENDIF
```

Operands vary with the type of IF and are not used with all types. The ELSEIF directive and statements following it are optional, as are the ELSE directive and statements following it. There can be more than one ELSEIF directive, but at most one ELSE directive.

The above syntax strongly resembles what appears in many high-level languages. It is important to realize, however, that these directives are used at *assembly* time, not at *execution* time. That is, they control assembly of statements that are later executed, not the order of statement execution.

The `EXITM` directive can be used to make some macro definitions simpler to write and understand. When MASM is processing a macro call and finds an EXITM directive, it immediately stops expanding the macro, ignoring any statements following EXITM in the macro definition. The design

---

if condition

then

  process assembly language statements for condition;

else

  process statements for negation of condition;

end if;

---

and the alternative design

---

if condition

then

  process assembly language statements for condition;

  terminate expansion of macro;

end if;

---

process statements for negation of condition;

are equivalent, assuming that no macro definition statements follow those sketched in the designs. These alternative designs can be implemented using

```
IF... [operands]
assembly language statements for condition
ELSE
assembly language statements for negation of condition
ENDIF
```

and

```
IF... [operands]
assembly language statements for condition
EXITM
ENDIF
assembly language statements for negation of condition
```

Notice that the EXITM directive is not needed when the ELSE directive is used. A macro definition using EXITM appears in Fig. 9.12 on the next page.

```
min2      MACRO  value1,value2,extra
          LOCAL  endIfLess
; put smaller of value1 and value2 in EAX


          IFB    <value1>
          .ERR   <first argument missing in min2 macro>
          EXITM
          ENDIF


          IFB    <value2>
          .ERR   <second argument missing in min2 macro>
          EXITM
          ENDIF


          IFNB   <extra>
          .ERR   <more than two arguments in min2 macro>
          EXITM
          ENDIF


          mov  eax, value1   ;; first value to EAX
          cmp  eax, value2   ;; value1 <= value2?
          jle  endIfLess     ;; done if so
          mov  eax, value2   ;; otherwise value2 smaller
endIfLess:
          ENDM
```

Figure 9.12 Improved *min2* macro

Examples in the previous section showed macro calls that expanded to illegal statements as a result of missing arguments. Such illegal statements are detected by MASM during subsequent assembly rather than as the macro is expanded. The designer of a macro definition may wish to include safeguards to ensure that the correct number of arguments is included in a macro call, or that the call is valid in other ways. Conditional assembly directives make this possible. If, however, assembly errors are eliminated by avoiding generation of illegal statements, a user may not know when a macro call is faulty. It requires additional effort to inform the user of an error.

One way to do this is with the `.ERR` directive. This directive generates a **forced error** at assembly time, resulting in a message to the console and a message to the listing file, if any. It also ensures that no .obj file is produced for the assembly. The `.ERR` directive is often followed by a string enclosed by < and >. This string is included in the error message.

The *min2* macro definition in Fig. 9.12 incorporates safeguards to ensure that the macro is called with the correct number of parameters. The conditional block

```
IFB    <value1>
.ERR   <first argument missing in min2 macro>
EXITM
ENDIF
```

examines the first argument. If it is missing, then the `.ERR` directive displays the message "first argument missing in min2 macro." Note that the conditional block ends with an `EXITM` directive, so that if the first argument is missing, no further expansion of the macro is done. An alternative way to suppress additional macro expansion would be to nest the rest of the macro definition between an `ELSE` directive and the `ENDIF` directive for this first conditional block.

The conditional block

```
IFB    <value2>
.ERR   <second argument missing in min2 macro>
EXITM
ENDIF
```

examines the second argument, generating an error if it is missing. The conditional block

```
IFNB   <extra>
.ERR   <more than two arguments in min2 macro>
EXITM
ENDIF
```

tells MASM to check to see if a third argument was listed in the macro call that is being expanded. Since there should be no third argument, an error is generated if the argument is not blank.

Exercises 9.4

1. Using the macro definition for *min2* given in Fig. 9.12, show the sequence of statements to which each of the following macro calls expands.

    (a) `min2  nbr1, nbr2`

    (Assume the local symbol counter is at 0004.)

    (b) `min2  , value`

    (Assume the local symbol counter is at 0011.)

    (c) `min2  ecx`

    (Assume the local symbol counter is at 000B.)

    (d) `min2  nbr1, nbr2, nbr3`

    (Assume the local symbol counter is at 01D0.)

Programming Exercises 9.4

1. Rewrite the macro definition for *swap* from Fig. 9.9, so that a *swap* macro call must have exactly two arguments; use .ERR with appropriate messages if there are missing or extra arguments.

2. Write a definition of a macro *min3* that has exactly three doubleword integer parameters and that puts the minimum of the three numbers in the EAX register. Use .ERR with appropriate messages if there are missing or extra arguments in a *min3* call.

9.5 Macros in IO.H

Macros in the file IO.H are designed to provide simple, safe access to standard input and output devices. Figure 9.13 shows the contents of IO.H and the remainder of the section discusses the directives and macros in the file.

Most of the file IO.H consists of macro definitions that, when used, generate code to call external procedures. However, the file does contain other directives. It begins with a .NOLIST directive; this suppresses the listing of all source code, in particular the contents of IO.H. It then has EXTRN directives that identify the external procedures called by the macros. The file ends with a .NOLISTMACRO directive to suppress listing of any macro expansions and an .LIST directive so that the user's statements following the directive INCLUDE io.h will again be shown in the listing file.

```
; IO.H — header file for I/O macros
; 32-bit version for flat memory model
; R. Detmer   last revised 8/2000
.NOLIST    ; turn off listing
.386


           EXTRN  itoaproc:near32, atoiproc:near32
           EXTRN  dtoaproc:near32, atodproc:near32
           EXTRN  inproc:near32, outproc:near32

itoa       MACRO  dest,source,xtra    ;; convert integer to ASCII string

           IFB    <source>
           .ERR <missing operand(s) in ITOA>
           EXITM
           ENDIF


           IFNB   <xtra>
           .ERR <extra operand(s) in ITOA>
           EXITM
           ENDIF


           push   ebx                 ;; save EBX
           mov    bx, source
           push   bx                  ;; source parameter
           lea    ebx,dest            ;; destination address
           push   ebx                 ;; destination parameter
           call   itoaproc            ;; call itoaproc(source,dest)
           pop    ebx                 ;; restore EBX
           ENDM

atoi       MACRO  source,xtra         ;; convert ASCII string to integer in AX
                                      ;; offset of terminating character in ESI


           IFB    <source>
           .ERR <missing operand in ATOI>
           EXITM
           ENDIF


           IFNB   <xtra>
           .ERR <extra operand(s) in ATOI>
           EXITM
           ENDIF
```

(continued)

Figure 9.13 IO.H

```
                push    ebx                 ;; save EBX
                lea     ebx,source          ;; source address to EBX
                push    ebx                 ;; source parameter on stack
                call    atoiproc            ;; call atoiproc(source)
                pop     ebx                 ;; parameter removed by ret
                ENDM

dtoa            MACRO   dest,source,xtra    ;; convert double to ASCII string

                IFB     <source>
                .ERR    <missing operand(s) in DTOA>
                EXITM
                ENDIF

                IFNB    <xtra>
                .ERR    <extra operand(s) in DTOA>
                EXITM
                ENDIF

                push    ebx                 ;; save EBX
                mov     ebx, source
                push    ebx                 ;; source parameter
                lea     ebx,dest            ;; destination address
                push    ebx                 ;; destination parameter
                call    dtoaproc            ;; call dtoaproc(source,dest)
                pop     ebx                 ;; restore EBX
                ENDM

atod            MACRO   source,xtra         ;; convert ASCII string to integer in EAX
                                            ;; offset of terminating character in ESI

                IFB     <source>
                .ERR    <missing operand in ATOD>
                EXITM
                ENDIF

                IFNB    <xtra>
                .ERR    <extra operand(s) in ATOD>
                EXITM
                ENDIF

                lea     eax,source          ;; source address to EAX
                push    eax                 ;; source parameter on stack
```

(continued)

Figure 9.13   *(continued)*

```
                call    atodproc            ;; call atodproc(source)
                                            ;; parameter removed by ret
                ENDM

output          MACRO   string,xtra         ;; display string

                IFB     <string>
                .ERR    <missing operand in OUTPUT>
                EXITM
                ENDIF

                IFNB    <xtra>
                .ERR    <extra operand(s) in OUTPUT>
                EXITM
                ENDIF

                push    eax                 ;; save EAX
                lea     eax,string          ;; string address
                push    eax                 ;; string parameter on stack
                call    outproc             ;; call outproc(string)
                pop     eax                 ;; restore EAX
                ENDM

input           MACRO   dest,length,xtra    ;; read string from keyboard

                IFB     <length>
                .ERR    <missing operand(s) in INPUT>
                EXITM
                ENDIF

                IFNB    <xtra>
                .ERR    <extra operand(s) in INPUT>
                EXITM
                ENDIF

                push    ebx                 ;; save EBX
                lea     ebx,dest            ;; destination address
                push    ebx                 ;; dest parameter on stack
                mov     ebx,length          ;; length of buffer
                push    ebx                 ;; length parameter on stack
                call    inproc              ;; call inproc(dest,length)
                pop     ebx                 ;; restore EBX
                ENDM

.NOLISTMACRO ; suppress macro expansion listings
.LIST        ; begin listing
```

Figure 9.13 *(continued)*

The bulk of the file IO.H consists of definitions for *itoa, atoi, dtoa, atod, output*, and *input* macros. These definitions have similar structures. Each uses IFB and IFNB directives to check that a macro call has the correct number of arguments. If not, .ERR directives are used to generate forced errors and appropriate messages. Actually, the checks are not quite complete.

Assuming that its arguments are correct, an input/output macro call expands to a sequence of instructions that call the appropriate external procedure, for instance *itoaproc* for the macro *itoa*. Parameters are passed on the stack, but some code sequences use a register to temporarily contain a value, with push and pop instructions to ensure that these registers are not changed following a macro call.

Exercises 9.5

1. Notice that *itoa* has only one error message that is used if either or both argument is missing. Rewrite the definition of *itoa* to provide complete argument checking. That is, check separately for missing *source* and *dest* arguments, generating specific messages for each missing argument. Allow for the possibility that both are missing.

Chapter Summary

This chapter has discussed the assembly process. A typical two-pass assembler scans an assembly language program twice, using a location counter to construct a symbol table during the first pass, and completing assembly during the second pass. The symbol table contains information about each identifier used in the program, including its type, size, and location. Assembly can be done in a single pass if the object code is "fixed up" when forward references are resolved.

A machine instruction may have one or more prefix bytes. However, the main byte of machine code for each 80x86 instruction is its opcode. Some instructions are a single byte long, but most consist of multiple bytes. The next byte often has the format *mod reg r/m* where *reg* indicates a source or destination register, and the other two fields combine to describe the addressing mode. Other instruction bytes contain additional addressing information, immediate data, or the address of a memory operand.

Macros are defined using MACRO and ENDM directives. Macros may use parameters that are associated with corresponding arguments in macro calls. A call is expanded at assembly time. The statements in the expansion of a macro call appear in the macro definition, with arguments substituted for parameters. A macro definition may declare local labels that MASM expands to different symbols for different macro calls.

Conditional assembly may be used in regular code or in macro definitions to generate different statements, based on conditions that can be checked at assembly time. The IFB and IFNB directives are used in macros to check for the absence or presence of arguments. Several other conditional assembly directives are also available, including IF, IFE, IFDEF, and IFNDEF. An ELSE directive may be used to provide two alternative blocks of code, and the ENDIF directive ends a conditional assembly block.

If the assembler encounters an EXITM directive when expanding a macro definition, it immediately terminates expansion of the macro. The .ERR directive triggers a forced error so that MASM displays an error message and produces no .OBJ file for the assembly.

The file IO.H contains definitions for a collection of input/output macros, and a few directives. These macro definitions use conditional assembly to check for missing or extra arguments and generate code that calls external procedures.

10

Floating-Point Arithmetic

This book has concentrated on integer representations of numbers, primarily 2's complement since all 80x86 microprocessors have a variety of instructions to manipulate 2's complement numbers. Many 80x86 microprocessor systems—including all Pentium systems, systems with a 486DX, and other systems equipped with a floating-point coprocessor—also have the capability to manipulate numbers stored in floating-point format.

Section 1.5 described the IEEE format used to store floating-point values in 32 bits. The MASM assembler has directives that accept decimal operands and initialize storage using the IEEE format. There are two ways to do floating-point arithmetic with a PC. If you have a microprocessor with a floating-point unit built in or a floating-point coprocessor, then you can simply use the floating-point instructions. Otherwise, you can employ a collection of procedures that implement arithmetic operations such as addition and multiplication.

Section 10.1 describes the 80x86 floating-point architecture. Section 10.2 describes how to convert floating-point values to and from other formats, including ASCII. Section 10.3 shows floating-point emulation routines of addition, subtraction, multiplication, division, negation, and comparison operations—these routines are useful for floating-point operations on an 80x86 system without built-in floating-point instructions. The procedures in this section serve as examples of assembly language implementation of moderately complex, useful algorithms and also illustrate some techniques not covered earlier in this book. Section 10.4 gives a brief introduction into using in-line assembly code in C++ code, with C++ for input/output operations, and assembly language for floating-point operations. In-line assembly code is not restricted to floating-point instructions, however.

10.1 80x86 Floating-Point Architecture

As stated above, some 80x86 microprocessors do not have built-in floating point capability, depending instead on a floating-point coprocessor chip to execute floating-point instructions. Even with the ones that do, the floating-point unit (FPU) of the chip is almost independent of the rest of the chip. It has its own internal registers, completely separate from the familiar 80x86 registers. It executes instructions to do floating-point arithmetic operations, including commonplace operations such as addition or multiplication, and more complicated operations such as evaluation of some transcendental functions. Not only can it transfer floating-point operands to or from memory, it can also transfer integer or BCD operands to or from the coprocessor. Nonfloating formats are always converted to floating point when moved to a floating-point register; a number in internal floating-point format can be converted to integer or BCD format as it is moved to memory.

The FPU has eight data registers, each 80 bits long. A ten-byte floating-point format (also specified by IEEE standards) is used for values stored in these registers. The registers are basically organized as a stack; for example, when the `fld` (floating load) instruction is used to transfer a value from memory to the floating point unit, the value is loaded into the register at the top of the stack, and data stored in the stack top and other registers are pushed down one register. However, some instructions can access any of the eight registers, so that the organization is not a "pure" stack.

Mnemonic	Operand	Action
fld	memory (real)	real value from memory pushed onto stack
fild	memory (integer)	integer value from memory converted to floating point and pushed onto stack
fbld	memory (BCD)	BCD value from memory converted to floating point and pushed onto stack
fld	st (*num*)	contents of floating-point register pushed onto stack
fld1	(none)	1.0 pushed onto stack
fldz	(none)	0.0 pushed onto stack
fldpi	(none)	π (pi) pushed onto stack
fldl2e	(none)	$\log_2(e)$ pushed onto stack
fldl2t	(none)	$\log_2(10)$ pushed onto stack
fldlg2	(none)	$\log_{10}(2)$ pushed onto stack
fldln2	(none)	$\log_e(2)$ pushed onto stack

Figure 10.1 Floating-point load instructions

The names of the eight floating-point registers are

- ST, the stack top, also called ST(0),
- ST(1), the register just below the stack top,
- ST(2), the register just below ST(1),
- ST(3), ST(4), ST(5), ST(6), and
- ST(7), the register at the bottom of the stack.

In addition to the eight data registers, the floating-point unit has several 16-bit control registers. Some of the **status word** bits are assigned values by floating-point comparison instructions, and these bits must be examined in order for the 80x86 to execute conditional jump instructions based on floating-point comparison. Bits in the FPU **control word** must sometimes be set to ensure certain modes of rounding.

Before considering the floating-point instructions, a few notes are in order. Each floating-point mnemonic starts with the letter *F*, a letter that is not used as the first character of any nonfloating instruction. Most floating-point instructions act on the stack top ST and one other operand in another floating-point register or in memory. No floating-point instruction can transfer data between an 80x86 general register (such as EAX) and a floating-point register—transfers must be made using a memory location for intermediate storage. (There are, however, instructions to store the status word or the control word in AX.)

The floating-point instructions will be examined in groups, starting with instructions to push operands onto the stack. Figure 10.1 lists these mnemonics.

Some examples illustrate how these instructions work. Suppose that the floating-point register stack contains

1.0	ST
2.0	ST(1)
3.0	ST(2)
	ST(3)
	ST(4)
	ST(5)
	ST(6)
	ST(7)

with values shown in decimal rather than in IEEE floating-point format. If the data segment contains

```
fpValue    REAL4   10.0
intValue   DWORD   20
bcdValue   TBYTE      30
```

then the values assembled will be 41200000 for *fpValue*, 00000014 for *intValue*, and 00000000000000000030 for *bcdValue*. If the instruction `fld  fpValue` is executed, the register stack will contain

10.0	ST
1.0	ST(1)
2.0	ST(2)
3.0	ST(3)
	ST(4)
	ST(5)
	ST(6)
	ST(7)

The original values have all been pushed down one register position on the stack. Starting with these values, if the instruction `fld st(2)` is executed, the register stack will contain

2.0	ST
10.0	ST(1)
1.0	ST(2)
2.0	ST(3)
3.0	ST(4)
	ST(5)
	ST(6)
	ST(7)

Notice that the value 2.0 from ST(2) has been pushed onto the top of the stack, but not removed from the stack. Starting with these values, assume that the instruction `fild intValue` is executed. The new contents of the register stack will be

20.0	ST
2.0	ST(1)
10.0	ST(2)
1.0	ST(3)
2.0	ST(4)
3.0	ST(5)
	ST(6)
	ST(7)

What is not obvious here is that the 32-bit value 00000014 is converted to an 80-bit floating-point value. An integer operand must be word length, doubleword length, or quadword length—byte length integer operands are allowed. This chapter does not show opcodes for floating-point instructions.

If the instruction `fbld bcdValue` is now executed, the stack values will become

30.0	ST
20.0	ST(1)
2.0	ST(2)
10.0	ST(3)
1.0	ST(4)
2.0	ST(5)
3.0	ST(6)
	ST(7)

where the 80 bit BCD value is converted to the very different 80 bit floating-point format. Finally, if the instruction `fldz` is executed, the register stack will contain

0.0	ST
30.0	ST(1)
20.0	ST(2)
2.0	ST(3)
10.0	ST(4)
1.0	ST(5)
2.0	ST(6)
3.0	ST(7)

The stack is now full. No further value can be pushed onto the stack unless some value is popped from the stack, or the stack is cleared. The instruction `finit` initializes the floating-point unit and clears the contents of all eight registers. Often a program that uses the floating-point unit will include the statement

```
finit      ; initialize the math processor
```

near the beginning of the code. It may be desirable to reinitialize the floating-point unit at points in the code, but normally this is not required since values will be popped from the stack, not allowed to accumulate on the stack.

You can trace floating-point operations using Windbg. Figure 10.2 shows a screen dump following execution of the code on the left pane. A floating-point window is shown in the right pane.

Figure 10.3 lists the floating-point instructions that are used to copy data from the stack top to memory or to another floating-point register. These instructions are mostly paired: One instruction of each pair simply copies ST to its destination while the other instruction is identical except that it copies ST to its destination and also pops ST off the register stack.

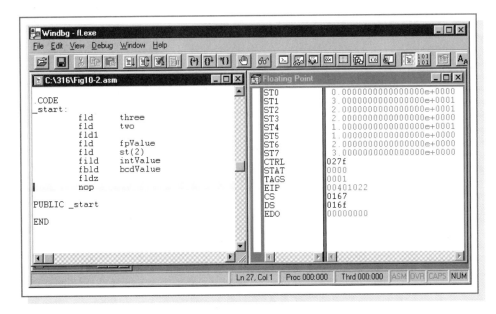

Figure 10.2   Windbg view of floating point execution

Mnemonic	Operand	Action
fst	st (*num*)	replaces contents of ST(*num*) by copy of value from ST; only ST(*num*) is affected
fstp	st (*num*)	replaces contents of ST(*num*) by copy of value from ST; ST popped off the stack
fst	memory (real)	copy of ST stored as real value in memory; the stack is not affected
fstp	memory (real)	copy of ST stored as real value in memory; ST popped off the stack
fist	memory (integer)	copy of ST converted to integer and stored in memory
fistp	memory (integer)	copy of ST converted to integer and stored in memory; ST popped off the stack
fbstp	memory (BCD)	copy of ST converted to BCD and stored in memory; ST popped off the stack

Figure 10.3   Floating-point data store instructions

A few examples illustrate the actions of and the differences between these instructions. Assume that the directive

```
intValue   DWORD ?
```

is coded in the data segment. Suppose that the floating-point register stack contains

10.0	ST
20.0	ST(1)
30.0	ST(2)
40.0	ST(3)
	ST(4)
	ST(5)
	ST(6)
	ST(7)

The left diagram below shows the resulting stack if `fist  intValue` is executed and the right diagram shows the resulting stack if `fistp  intValue` is executed. In both cases, the contents of *intValue* will be 0000000A, the doubleword length 2's complement integer version of the floating-point number 10.0.

10.0	ST	20.0	ST
20.0	ST(1)	30.0	ST(1)
30.0	ST(2)	40.0	ST(2)
40.0	ST(3)		ST(3)
	ST(4)		ST(4)
	ST(5)		ST(5)
	ST(6)		ST(6)
	ST(7)		ST(7)

The situation is a bit more confusing when the destination is one of the floating-point registers. Suppose that at execution time the floating register stack contains

1.0	ST
2.0	ST(1)
3.0	ST(2)
4.0	ST(3)
	ST(4)
	ST(5)
	ST(6)
	ST(7)

The left diagram below shows the resulting stack if `fst st(2)` is executed and the right diagram shows the resulting stack if `fstp st(2)` is executed. In the first case, a copy of ST has been stored in ST(2). In the second case, the copy has been made, and then the stack has been popped.

1.0	ST
2.0	ST(1)
1.0	ST(2)
4.0	ST(3)
	ST(4)
	ST(5)
	ST(6)
	ST(7)

2.0	ST
1.0	ST(1)
4.0	ST(2)
	ST(3)
	ST(4)
	ST(5)
	ST(6)
	ST(7)

In addition to the load and store instructions listed above, the floating-point unit has an `fxch` instruction that will exchange the contents of two floating-point registers. With no operand,

```
fxch            ; exchange ST and ST(1)
```

will exchange the contents of the stack top and ST(1) just below ST on the stack. With a single operand, for example,

```
fxch  st(3)   ; exchange ST and ST(3)
```

will interchange ST with the specified register.

Figure 10.4 shows the floating-point addition instructions. There are versions for adding the contents of ST to another register, contents of any register to ST, a real number from memory to ST, or an integer number from memory to ST. No version uses a BCD number. The `faddp` instruction pops the stack top after adding it to another register, so that both operands are destroyed.

A few examples illustrate how the floating-point addition instructions work. Suppose that the data segment contains the directives

```
fpValue   REAL4   5.0
intValue  DWORD   1
```

Mnemonic	Operand	Action
fadd	(none)	pops both ST and ST(1); adds these values; pushes sum onto the stack
fadd	st(*num*), st	adds ST(*num*) and ST; replaces ST(*num*) by the sum
fadd	st,st(*num*)	adds ST and ST(*num*); replaces ST by the sum
fadd	memory (real)	adds ST and real number from memory; replaces ST by the sum
fiadd	memory (integer)	adds ST and integer from memory; replaces ST by the sum
faddp	st(*num*),st	adds ST(*num*) and ST; replaces ST(*num*) by the sum; pops ST from stack

Figure 10.4   Floating-point addition instructions

and that the floating-point register stack contains

10.0	ST
20.0	ST(1)
30.0	ST(2)
40.0	ST(3)
	ST(4)
	ST(5)
	ST(6)
	ST(7)

After the instruction

```
fadd    st,st(3)
```

is executed, the stack contains

50.0	ST
20.0	ST(1)
30.0	ST(2)
40.0	ST(3)
	ST(4)
	ST(5)
	ST(6)
	ST(7)

Starting with these stack values, after the two instructions

```
fadd    fpValue
fiadd   intValue
```

are executed, the contents of the stack are

56.0	ST
20.0	ST(1)
30.0	ST(2)
40.0	ST(3)
	ST(4)
	ST(5)
	ST(6)
	ST(7)

Finally, if the instruction

```
faddp   st(2),st
```

is executed, the stack will contain

20.0	ST
86.0	ST(1)
40.0	ST(2)
	ST(3)
	ST(4)
	ST(5)
	ST(6)
	ST(7)

Subtraction instructions are displayed in Fig. 10.5. The first six instructions are very similar to the corresponding addition instructions. The second six subtraction instructions are the same except that the operands are subtracted in the opposite order. This is convenient since subtraction is not commutative.

Mnemonic	Operand	Action
fsub	(none)	pops ST and ST(1); calculates ST(1) − ST; pushes difference onto the stack
fsub	st(num), st	calculates ST(num) − ST; replaces ST(num) by the difference
fsub	st, st(num)	calculates ST − ST(num); replaces ST by the difference
fsub	memory (real)	calculates ST − real number from memory; replaces ST by the difference
fisub	memory (integer)	calculates ST − integer from memory; replaces ST by the difference
fsubp	st(num), st	calculates ST(num) − ST; replaces ST(num) by the difference; pops ST from the stack
fsubr	(none)	pops ST and ST(1); calculates ST − ST(1); pushes difference onto the stack
fsubr	st(num), st	calculates ST − ST(num); replaces ST(num) by the difference
fsubr	st, st(num)	calculates ST(num) − ST; replaces ST by the difference
fsubr	memory (real)	calculates real number from memory − ST; replaces ST by the difference
fisubr	memory (integer)	calculates integer from memory − ST; replaces ST by the difference
fsubpr	st(num), st	calculates ST − ST(num); replaces ST(num) by the difference; pops ST from the stack

Figure 10.5   **Floating-point subtraction instructions**

An example illustrates the difference between the parallel subtraction instructions. Suppose that the floating-point register stack contains

15.0	ST
25.0	ST(1)
35.0	ST(2)
45.0	ST(3)
55.0	ST(4)
	ST(5)
	ST(6)
	ST(7)

The two diagrams below show the results after executing the instructions `fsub st,st(3)` and `fsubr st,st(3)`.

after
`fsub st,st(3)`

−30.0	ST
25.0	ST(1)
35.0	ST(2)
45.0	ST(3)
55.0	ST(4)
	ST(5)
	ST(6)
	ST(7)

after
`fsubr st,st(3)`

30.0	ST
25.0	ST(1)
35.0	ST(2)
45.0	ST(3)
55.0	ST(4)
	ST(5)
	ST(6)
	ST(7)

Multiplication and division instructions are listed in Figs. 10.6 and 10.7, respectively. Multiplication instructions have the same forms as the addition instructions in Fig. 10.4. Division instructions have the same forms as subtraction instructions in Fig. 10.5, that is, the *R* versions reverse the operands' dividend and divisor roles.

Mnemonic	Operand	Action
fmul	(none)	pops ST and ST(1); multiplies these values; pushes product onto the stack
fmul	st(*num*), st	multiplies ST(*num*) and ST; replaces ST(*num*) by the product
fmul	st, st(*num*)	multiplies ST and ST(*num*); replaces ST by the product
fmul	memory (real)	multiplies ST and real number from memory; replaces ST by the product
fimul	memory (integer)	multiplies ST and integer from memory; replaces ST by the product
fmulp	st(*num*), st	multiplies ST(*num*) and ST; replaces ST(*num*) by the product; pops ST from stack

Figure 10.6 Floating-point multiplication instructions

Mnemonic	Operand	Action
fdiv	(none)	pops ST and ST(1); calculates ST(1) / ST; pushes quotient onto the stack
fdiv	st(*num*), st	calculates ST(*num*) / ST; replaces ST(*num*) by the quotient
fdiv	st, st(*num*)	calculates ST / ST(*num*); replaces ST by the quotient
fdiv	memory (real)	calculates ST / real number from memory; replaces ST by the quotient
fidiv	memory (integer)	calculates ST / integer from memory; replaces ST by the quotient
fdivp	st(*num*), st	calculates ST(*num*) / ST; replaces ST(*num*) by the quotient; pops ST from the stack
fdivr	(none)	pops ST and ST(1); calculates ST / ST(1); pushes quotient onto the stack
fdivr	st(*num*), st	calculates ST / ST(*num*); replaces ST(*num*) by the quotient
fdivr	st, st(*num*)	calculates ST(*num*) / ST; replaces ST by the quotient
fdivr	memory (real)	calculates real number from memory / ST; replaces ST by the quotient
fidivr	memory (integer)	calculates integer from memory / ST; replaces ST by the quotient
fdivpr	st(*num*), st	calculates ST / ST(*num*); replaces ST(*num*) by the quotient; pops ST from the stack

Figure 10.7 Floating-point division instructions

Mnemonic	Operand	Action
fabs	(none)	ST := | ST | (absolute value)
fchs	(none)	ST := − ST (change sign)
frndint	(none)	rounds ST to an integer value
fsqrt	(none)	replace the contents of ST by its square root

Figure 10.8　Additional floating-point instructions

Figure 10.8 describes four additional floating-point instructions. Additional instructions that calculate tangent, arctangent, exponent, and logarithm functions are not covered in this book.

The floating-point unit provides a collection of instructions to compare the stack top ST to a second operand. These are listed in Fig. 10.9. Recall that the floating point has a 16-bit control register called the status word. The comparison instructions

Mnemonic	Operand	Action
fcom	(none)	compares ST and ST(1)
fcom	st (num)	compares ST and ST(num)
fcom	memory (real)	compares ST and real number in memory
ficom	memory (integer)	compares ST and integer in memory
ftst	(none)	compares ST and 0.0
fcomp	(none)	compares ST and ST(1); then pops stack
fcomp	st (num)	compares ST and ST(num); then pops stack
fcomp	memory (real)	compares ST and real number in memory; then pops stack
ficomp	memory (integer)	compares ST and integer in memory; then pops stack
fcompp	(none)	compares ST and ST(1); then pops stack twice

Figure 10.9　Floating-point comparison instructions

Mnemonic	Operand	Action
fstsw	memory word	copies status register to memory word
fstsw	AX	copies status register to AX
fstcw	memory word	copies control word register to memory word
fldcw	memory word	copies memory word to control word register

Figure 10.10 Miscellaneous floating-point instructions

assign values to bits 14, 10, and 8 in the status word; these "condition code" bits are named C3, C2, and C0, respectively. These flags are set as follows:

result of comparison	C3	C2	C0
ST > second operand	0	0	0
ST < second operand	0	0	1
ST = second operand	1	0	0

Another possibility is that the operands are not comparable. This can occur if one of the operands is the IEEE representation for infinity or NaN (not a number). In this case, all three bits are set to 1.

If a comparison is made in order to determine program flow, simply setting flags in the status word is no help. Conditional jump instructions look at bits in the flag register in the 80x86, not the status word in the floating-point unit. Consequently, the status word must be copied to memory or to the AX register before its bits can be examined by an 80x86 instruction, perhaps with a test instruction. The floating-point unit has two instructions to store the status word; these are summarized in Fig. 10.10. This table also shows the instructions for storing or setting the control word.

The 80x86 floating-point and integer units can actually execute instructions concurrently. Under certain circumstances this requires special care in assembly language programming. However, these techniques are not discussed in this book.

Exercises 10.1

1. Suppose that a program's data segment contains

```
fpValue    REAL4    0.5
intValue   DWORD    6
```

and that code executed so far by the program has not changed these values. Suppose also that the floating-point register stack contains

9.0	ST
12.0	ST(1)
23.0	ST(2)
24.0	ST(3)
35.0	ST(4)
	ST(5)
	ST(6)
	ST(7)

Assume that these values are correct before each instruction below is executed; do *not* use the "after" state of one problem as the "before" state of the next problem. Give the contents of the floating-point register stack of *fpValue* and of *intValue* following execution of the instruction.

(a) fld   st(2)

(b) fld   fpValue

(c) fild   intValue

(d) fldpi

(e) fst   st(4)

(f) fstp   st(4)

(g) fst   fpValue

(h) fistp   intValue

(i) fxch   st(3)

(j) fadd

(k) fadd   st(3),st

(l) fadd   st,st(3)

(m) faddp   st(3),st

(n) fsub   fpValue

(o) fisub   intValue

(p) fisubr   intValue

    (q) fsubp   st(3),st

    (r) fmul   st, st(4)

    (s) fmul

    (t) fmul   fpValue

    (u) fdiv

    (v) fdivr

    (w) fidiv intValue

    (x) fdivp st(2),st

    (y) fchs

    (z) fsqrt

2.   Suppose that a program's data segment contains

    fpValue   REAL4   1.5
    intValue   DWORD   9

    and that code executed so far by the program has not changed these values. Suppose also that the floating-point register stack contains

9.0	ST
12.0	ST(1)
23.0	ST(2)
24.0	ST(3)
35.0	ST(4)
	ST(5)
	ST(6)
	ST(7)

    Assume that these values are correct before each instruction below is executed. Give the contents of the status word flags C3, C2, and C0 following execution of the instruction.

    (a) fcom

    (b) fcom   st(3)

    (c) fcom   fpValue

    (d) ficom intValue

For the next two parts, also give the contents of the stack following execution of the instructions.

(e) `fcomp`

(f) `fcompp`

10.2 Programming with Floating-Point Instructions

This section gives three examples of coding with floating-point instructions. The first is a program that calculates the square root of the sum of the squares of two numbers. Although we do not yet have any procedures to facilitate input/output of floating-point values, FPU operations can be viewed through Windbg. The second and third examples show procedure to facilitate input/output of floating-point numbers.

Figure 10.11 has a listing of the first example. Floating-point values are assembled at *value1* and *value2*. The first instruction copies *value1* from memory to ST. The second instruction copies it from ST to ST, pushing down the first stack entry to ST(1). The third instruction gives *value1*value1* in ST, with "nothing" in ST(1). (Of course, there is always some value in each floating-point register.) The same sequence of instructions is repeated for *value2*. Figure 10.12 shows Windbg's view of the CPU just before the second `fmul` is executed. At this point, there are copies of *value2* in both ST and ST(1) and *value1*value1* in ST(2). After the result is calculated in ST, it is stored in *sqrt* and popped from the stack, leaving the stack in its original state.

```
; find the sum of the squares of two floating-point numbers
; Author:   R. Detmer
; Date:     4/98

.386
.MODEL FLAT

.STACK  4096                ; reserve 4096-byte stack

.DATA                       ; reserve storage for data
value1  REAL4   0.5
value2  REAL4   1.2
sqrt    REAL4   ?

                                                    (continued)
```

Figure 10.11 Floating-point computations

```
.CODE
_start:
        fld     value1    ; value1 in ST
        fld     st        ; value1 in ST and ST(1)
        fmul              ; value1*value1 in ST
        fld     value2    ; value2 in ST (value1*value1 in ST(1))
        fld     st        ; value2 in ST and ST(1)
        fmul              ; value2*value2 in ST
        fadd              ; sum of squares in ST
        fsqrt             ; square root of sum of squares in ST
        fstp    sqrt      ; store result

PUBLIC _start
END
```

Figure 10.11 *(continued)*

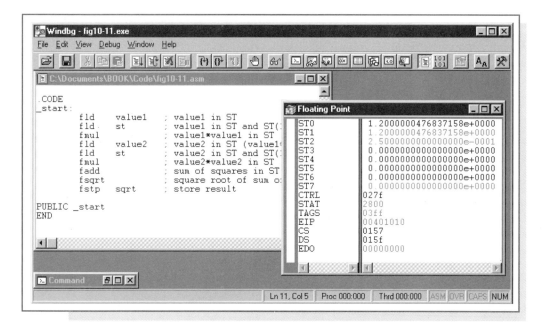

Figure 10.12   Execution of floating-point example

Notice that the value 1.2 is shown in Fig. 10.12 as 1.2000000476837158e+0000. The reason that there are nonzero digits after the decimal point is that 1.2 does not have an exact representation as a floating point number. The approximation used by the 32-bit REAL4 directive translates back to the number shown in 17-decimal-digit precision. You can get a better approximation by using a REAL8 or a REAL10 directive, but at the cost of extra bytes of storage.

The second example is an implementation of a simple ASCII to floating-point conversion algorithm. This algorithm, given in Fig. 10.13, is similar to the one used by

```
value := 0.0;
divisor := 1.0;
point := false;
minus := false;

point at first character of source string;
if source character = '-'
then
      minus := true;
      point at next character of source string;
end if;

while (source character is a digit or a decimal point) loop
      if source character = '.'
      then
            point := true;
      else
            convert ASCII digit to 2's complement digit;
            value := 10*value + float(digit);
            if point
            then
                  multiply divisor by 10;
                  end if;
      end if;
      point at next character of source string;
end while;

value := value/divisor;

if minus
then
      value := – value;
end if;
```

Figure 10.13   ASCII to floating-point algorithm

the *atoi* and *atod* macros—it scans memory at the address given by its parameter, inter-preting the characters as a floating point.

This algorithm is implemented in a NEAR32 procedure *atofproc*. This procedure has one parameter—the address of the string. It returns the floating-point value in ST. No flags are set to indicate illegal conditions, such as multiple minus signs or decimal points. The code appears in Fig. 10.14.

```
; ASCII to floating-point code
; author:  R. Detmer
; revised:  4/98

.386
.MODEL FLAT

PUBLIC atofproc

false      EQU  0
true       EQU  1

.DATA
ten        REAL4  10.0
point      BYTE   ?
minus      BYTE   ?
digit      WORD   ?

.CODE

atofproc  PROC NEAR32   ; convert ASCII string to floating-point number
; Parameter passed on the stack:  address of ASCII source string
; After an optional leading minus sign, only digits 0-9 and a decimal
; point are accepted — the scan terminates with any other character.
; The floating-point value is returned in SP.

        push ebp                ; establish stack frame
        mov  ebp, esp
        push eax                ; save registers
        push ebx
        push esi

        fld1                    ; divisor := 1.0
        fldz                    ; value := 0.0
        mov  point, false       ; no decimal point found yet
        mov  minus, false       ; no minus sign found yet
```

(continued)

Figure 10.14   ASCII to floating-point conversion

```
            mov  esi, [ebp+8]      ; address of first source character

            cmp  BYTE PTR [esi], '-'    ; leading minus sign?
            jne  endifMinus        ; skip if not
            mov  minus, true       ; minus sign found
            inc  esi               ; point at next source character
endifMinus:

whileOK:  mov  bl, [esi]           ; get next character
          cmp  bl, '.'             ; decimal point?
          jne  endifPoint          ; skip if not
          mov  point, true         ; found decimal point
          jmp  nextChar
endifPoint:
            cmp  bl, '0'           ; character a digit?
            jl   endwhileOK        ; exit if lower than '0'
            cmp  bl, '9'
            jg   endwhileOK        ; exit if higher than '9'
            and  bx, 000fh         ; convert ASCII to integer value
            mov  digit, bx         ; put integer in memory
            fmul ten               ; value := value * 10
            fiadd digit            ; value := value + digit
            cmp  point, true       ; already found a decimal point?
            jne  endifDec          ; skip if not
            fxch                   ; put divisor in ST and value in ST(1)
            fmul ten               ; divisor := divisor * 10
            fxch                   ; value back to ST; divisor back to ST(1)
endifDec:
nextChar: inc  esi                 ; point at next source character
          jmp  whileOK
endwhileOK:

            fdivr                  ; value := value / divisor
            cmp  minus, true       ; was there a minus sign?
            jne  endifNeg
            fchs                   ; value := -value
endifNeg:
            pop  esi               ; restore registers
            pop  ebx
            pop  eax
            pop  ebp
            ret  4
atofproc  ENDP
          END
```

Figure 10.14   (continued)

This implementation of the ASCII to floating-point algorithm uses ST(1) for *divisor* and ST for *value* except for one short segment where they are reversed in order to modify *divisor*. After the procedure entry code, the instructions

```
fld1            ; divisor := 1.0
fldz            ; value := 0.0
```

initialize these two variables. Note that the value 1.0 for *divisor* ends up in ST(1) since it is pushed down by the `fldz` instruction.

The design element

```
value := 10*value + float(digit);
```

is implemented by the code

```
fmul ten        ; value := value * 10
fiadd digit     ; value := value + digit
```

Note that a word-length 2's complement integer version of *digit* is stored in memory. The floating-point unit takes care of converting it to floating point as part of the `fiadd` instruction.

To implement "multiply divisor by 10," the number to be multiplied must be in ST. The instructions

```
fxch            ; put divisor in ST and value in ST(1)
fmul ten        ; divisor := divisor * 10
fxch            ; value back to ST; divisor back to ST(1)
```

take care of swapping *divisor* and *value*, carrying out the multiplication in ST, and then swapping back.

When it is time to execute "*value := value / divisor*" the instruction

```
fdivr           ; value := value / divisor
```

pops *value* from ST and *divisor* from ST(1), computes the quotient, and pushes it back to ST. Notice that the `fdiv` version of this instruction would incorrectly compute "*divisor/value*." After the division instruction, ST(1) is no longer in use by this procedure. The instruction `fchs` changes the sign of *value* if a leading minus sign was noted in the ASCII string.

You can test *atofproc* with a simple test driver program such as the one shown in Fig. 10.15. The "output" of the procedure can be viewed using Windbg.

```
; test driver for atofproc
; Author:  R. Detmer
; Date:    4/98

.386
.MODEL FLAT

ExitProcess PROTO NEAR32 stdcall, dwExitCode:DWORD
EXTRN atofproc:NEAR32
.STACK  4096                 ; reserve 4096-byte stack

.DATA                        ; reserve storage for data
String      BYTE    "435.75", 0

.CODE                                ; program code

_start:
          pushd  NEAR32 PTR String
          call   atofproc
          INVOKE ExitProcess, 0
PUBLIC _start
END
```

Figure 10.15   Test driver for atofproc

Finally we come to a procedure to convert a floating-point parameter to "E notation." The procedure generates a 12-byte long ASCII string consisting of

- a leading minus sign or a blank
- a digit
- a decimal point
- five digits
- the letter *E*
- a plus sign or a minus sign
- two digits

This string represents the number in base 10 scientific notation. For example, for the decimal value 145.8798, the procedure would generate the string *b*1.45880E+02, where *b* represents a blank. Notice that the ASCII string has a rounded value.

Figure 10.16 displays the design for the floating to ASCII procedure. After the leading space or minus sign is generated, most of the work necessary to get the remaining characters is done before they are actually produced. The value is repeatedly multiplied or divided by 10 until it is at least 1.0 but less than 10.0. Multiplication is used if the

```
point at first destination byte;

if value ≥ 0
then
        put blank in destination string;
else
        put minus in destination string;
        value := –value;
end if;
point at next destination byte;

exponent := 0;
if value ≠ 0
then
        if value > 10
        then
                until value < 10 loop
                        divide value by 10;
                        add 1 to exponent;
                end until;
        else
                while value < 1 loop
                        multiply value by 10;
                        subtract 1 from exponent;
                end while;
        end if;
end if;
```

(continued)

Figure 10.16 Floating-point to ASCII conversion algorithm

```
add 0.000005 to value;   { for rounding }
if value > 10
then
        divide value by 10;
        add 1 to exponent;
end if;

digit := int(value);       { truncate to integer }
convert digit to ASCII and store in destination string;
point at next destination byte;
store "." in destination string;
point at next destination byte;

for i := 1 to 5 loop
        value := 10 * (value – float(digit));
        digit := int(value);
        convert digit to ASCII and store in destination string;
        point at next destination byte;
end for;
store E in destination string;
point at next destination byte;
if exponent ≥ 0
then
        put + in destination string;
else
        put – in destination string;
        exponent := –exponent;
end if;
point at next destination byte;

convert exponent to two decimal digits;
convert two decimal digits of exponent to ASCII;
store characters of exponent in destination string;
```

Figure 10.16   *(continued)*

value is initially less than 1; the number of multiplications gives the negative power of 10 required for scientific notation. Division is used if the value is initially 10.0 or more; the number of divisions gives the positive power of 10 required for scientific notation.

Only five digits are going to be displayed after the decimal point. The value between 1.0 and 10.0 is rounded by adding 0.000005; if the sixth digit after the decimal point is 5 or greater, this will be reflected in the digits that are actually displayed. It is possible that this addition gives a sum of 10.0 or more; if this happens, the value is divided by 10 again and the exponent is incremented.

With a value at least 1.0 but under 10.0, truncating to an integer gives the digit to go before the decimal point. This digit and the decimal point are generated. Then the remaining five digits can be generated by repeatedly subtracting the whole part from the value, multiplying the remaining fraction by 10, and truncating the new value to an integer.

After the "fraction" of the ASCII string is generated, the letter E, a plus or minus sign for the exponent, and the exponent digits are generated. The exponent will contain at most two digits—the single IEEE notation provides for numbers as large as 2^{128}, which is less than 10^{39}.

Figure 10.17 shows this design implemented in a procedure named *ftoaproc*. The procedure has two parameters: first, the floating-point value to be converted and second, the address of the destination string.

The program opens with directives that make it easy to refer to the control bits by name. The 1's for C3, C2, and C0 are in positions 14, 10, and 8 respectively.

```
C3 EQU 0100000000000000b
C2 EQU 0000010000000000b
C0 EQU 0000000100000000b
```

After normal procedure entry code, the FPU control word is copied to memory and then pushed on the stack so that it can be restored at the end of the procedure. Bits 10 and 11 of the control word are used for rounding control. The next two instructions set them to 11 so that a floating point to integer store will result in chopping of the fractional part of the number.

```
fstcw controlWd        ; get control word
push controlWd         ; save control word
or   controlWd, 0000110000000000b
fldcw controlWd        ; set control to chop
```

```
; floating point to ASCII code
; author:  R. Detmer
; revised:  4/98

.386
.MODEL FLAT

PUBLIC ftoaproc

C3 EQU 0100000000000000b
C2 EQU 0000010000000000b
C0 EQU 0000000100000000b

.DATA
value      REAL4   ?
ten        REAL4   10.0
one        REAL4   1.0
round      REAL4   0.000005
digit      WORD    ?
exponent   WORD    ?
controlWd  WORD    ?
byteTen    BYTE    10

.CODE
ftoaproc  PROC NEAR32   ; convert floating-point number to ASCII string
; Parameters passed on the stack:
;    (1) 32-bit floating point value
;    (2) address of ASCII destination string
; ASCII string with format [blank/-]d.dddddE[+/-]dd is generated.
; (The string is always 12 characters long.)
          push ebp                 ; establish stack frame
          mov  ebp, esp
          push eax                 ; save registers
          push ebx
          push ecx
          push edi

          fstcw controlWd          ; get control word
          push controlWd           ; save control word
          or    controlWd, 0000110000000000b
          fldcw controlWd          ; set control to chop
```

(continued)

Figure 10.17   Floating point to ASCII conversion procedure

```
                mov  edi, [ebp+8]       ; destination string address
                mov  eax, [ebp+12]      ; value to convert
                mov  exponent, 0        ; exponent := 0
                mov  value, eax         ; value to ST via memory
                fld  value
                ftst                    ; value >= 0?
                fstsw  ax               ; status word to AX
                and  ax, C0             ; check C0
                jnz  elseNeg            ; skip if set (value negative)
                mov  BYTE PTR [edi], ' '  ; blank for positive
                jmp  endifNeg
elseNeg:        mov  BYTE PTR [edi], '-'  ; minus for negative
                fchs                    ; make number positive
endifNeg:
                inc  edi                ; point at next destination byte

                mov  exponent, 0        ; exponent := 0
                ftst                    ; value = 0?
                fstsw ax                ; status word to AX
                and  ax, C3             ; check C3
                jne  endifZero          ; skip if zero
                fcom ten                ; value > 10?
                fstsw ax                ; status word to AX
                and  ax, C3 or C2 or C0   ; check for all C3=C2=C0=0
                jnz  elseLess           ; skip if value not > 10
untilLess:
                fdiv ten                ; value := value/10
                inc  exponent           ; add 1 to exponent
                fcom ten                ; value < 10
                fstsw ax                ; status word to AX
                and  ax, C0             ; check C0
                jnz  untilLess          ; continue until value < 10
                jmp  endifBigger        ; exit if
elseLess:
whileLess:
                fcom one                ; value < 1
                fstsw ax                ; status word to AX
                and  ax, C0             ; check C0
                jz   endwhileLess       ; exit if not less
                fmul ten                ; value := 10*value
                dec  exponent           ; subtract 1 from exponent
                jmp  whileLess          ; continue while value < 1
```

(continued)

Figure 10.17   *(continued)*

```
endwhileLess:
endifBigger:
endifZero:

        fadd round               ; add rounding value
        fcom ten                 ; value > 10?
        fstsw ax                 ; status word to AX
        and  ax, C3 or C2 or C0  ; C3=C2=C0=0? (value > 10?)
        jnz  endifOver           ; skip if not
        fdiv ten                 ; value := value/10
        inc  exponent            ; add 1 to exponent
endifOver:

; at this point 1.0 <= value < 10.0
        fist digit               ; store integer part
        mov  bx, digit           ; copy integer to BX
        or   bx, 30h             ; convert digit to character
        mov  BYTE PTR [edi], bl  ; store character in destination
        inc  edi                 ; point at next destination byte
        mov  BYTE PTR [edi], '.'     ; decimal point
        inc  edi                 ; point at next destination byte

        mov  ecx, 5              ; count of remaining digits
forDigit: fisub digit            ; subtract integer part
        fmul ten                 ; multiply by 10
        fist digit               ; store integer part
        mov  bx, digit           ; copy integer to BX
        or   bx, 30h             ; convert digit to character
        mov  BYTE PTR [edi], bl  ; store character in destination
        inc  edi                 ; point at next destination byte
        loop forDigit            ; repeat 5 times

        mov  BYTE PTR [edi], 'E'  ; exponent indicator
        inc  edi                 ; point at next destination byte
        mov  ax, exponent        ; get exponent
        cmp  ax, 0               ; exponent >= 0 ?
        jnge NegExp
        mov  BYTE PTR [edi], '+'  ; non-negative exponent
        jmp  endifNegExp
NegExp: mov  BYTE PTR [edi], '-'  ; negative exponent
        neg  ax                  ; change exponent to positive
```

(continued)

Figure 10.17   *(continued)*

```
endifNegExp:
        inc   edi                ; point at next destination byte

        div   byteTen            ; convert exponent to 2 digits
        or    ax, 3030h          ; convert both digits to ASCII
        mov   BYTE PTR [edi+1], ah  ; store characters in destination
        mov   BYTE PTR [edi], al

        pop   controlWd          ; restore control word
        fldcw controlWd
        pop   edi                ; restore registers
        pop   ecx
        pop   ebx
        pop   eax
        pop   ebp
        ret   8
ftoaproc ENDP
        END
```

Figure 10.17   *(continued)*

Most of the code in the procedure is a straightforward implementation of the design. However, the floating-point comparisons need some explanation. The first sequence is

```
ftst                    ; value >= 0?
fstsw  ax               ; status word to AX
and    ax, C0           ; check C0
jnz    elseNeg          ; skip if set (value negative)
```

The ftst instruction compares *value* to 0, setting the flags in the status word. To test these bits, the status word is copied to AX. The C0 flag is set only when ST < 0. The and instruction masks all bits but the one corresponding to C0, and the jnz instruction branches if the remaining bit is nonzero, that is, the value is negative.

A similar but more complicated check comes when "*value* > 10" is implemented with

```
fcom ten                ; value > 10?
fstsw ax                ; status word to AX
and   ax, C3 or C2 or C0   ; check for all C3=C2=C0=0
jnz   elseLess          ; skip if value not > 10
```

Since ST > *operand* results in all C3 = C2 = C0 = 0, all three control bits must be zero. The program masks with `C3 or C2 or C0`, a descriptive way of writing 0100010100000000. This `or` operation combines operands at assembly time, not at execution time.

Conversion of the exponent to two ASCII characters uses a slightly new technique. The exponent in AX is non-negative and less than 40 when the following code is executed.

```
div   byteTen            ; convert exponent to 2 digits
or    ax, 3030h          ; convert both digits to ASCII
mov   BYTE PTR [edi+1], ah  ; store characters in destination
mov   BYTE PTR [edi], al
```

Dividing by 10 puts the quotient (the high-order base ten digit) in AL and the remainder (the low-order digit) in AH. These are simultaneously converted to ASCII by the `or` instruction, and are then stored in the destination string.

Programming Exercises 10.2

1. Write a complete program that will prompt for and input a decimal value for the radius of a circle and will calculate and display (appropriately labeled) the circumference and the area of the circle. Use the *input* and *output* macros to input and output character strings, the *atofproc* and *ftoaoproc* procedures to convert between floating point and ASCII, and FPU instructions for floating-point operations.

2. Write a NEAR32 procedure *ftoaproc1* that will convert a floating-point number to an ASCII string in fixed point format. Specifically, the procedure must have four parameters pushed on the stack:

    *   a 32-bit floating point value
    *   the address of the destination string
    *   a word containing the total number *n* of characters in the string to be generated
    *   a word containing the number of digits *d* to be generated after the decimal point

    The output string will consist of a leading blank or minus sign, the integer part of the value in *n*-*d*-2 positions (with leading blanks as needed), a decimal point, and the fractional part of the value rounded to *d* positions. The procedure will preserve all registers and will remove parameters from the stack.

3. The following algorithm approximates the cube root of a real number *x*

   ```
   root := 1.0;
   until (|root – oldRoot| < smallValue) loop
       oldRoot := root;
       root := (2.0*root + x/(root*root)) / 3.0;
   end until;
   ```

   Implement this design in a NEAR32 procedure *cuberoot*, using 0.001 for *smallValue*. Assume there is one parameter passed on the stack, the value of *x*. Return the result in ST. The procedure will preserve all registers and will remove parameters from the stack.

   Write a short test driver for your procedure, viewing the results with WinDbg.

10.3 Floating-Point Emulation

Some 80x86 computer systems have no floating-point unit. Such a system can still do floating-point arithmetic. However, floating-point operations must be performed by software routines using memory and the general purpose registers, rather than by a floating-point unit. This section describes procedures for multiplication and for addition of floating-point numbers. These could be useful for floating-point emulation, and they also provide a better understanding of the floating-point representation.

The procedures in this section manipulate floating-point values in the IEEE single format. Recall from Section 1.5 that this scheme includes the pieces that describe a number in "base two scientific notation":

- a leading sign bit for the entire number, 0 for positive and 1 for negative
- an 8-bit biased exponent (or **characteristic**). This is the actual exponent plus a bias of 127_{10}
- 23 bits that are the fraction (or **mantissa**) expressed with the leading 1 removed

This is the format produced by the REAL4 directive.

Each procedure combines the components of its parameters to yield a result in the structure fp3. Often this result is not normalized; that is, there are not exactly 24 significant fraction bits. The NEAR procedure *normalize* adjusts the fraction and exponent to recover the standard format.

Notice that there is a problem representing the number 0.0 using the normal IEEE scheme. There is no "binary scientific notation" zero with a 1 bit preceding the binary point of the fraction. The best that can be done is 1.0×2^{-127}, which is small, but nonzero. According to the rules given previously, this value would have an IEEE representation consisting of 32 zero bits. However, the two bit patterns that end with 31 zeros are considered special cases, and each is interpreted as 0.0 instead of plus or minus 1.0×2^{-127}. These special cases will be considered in the following multiplication and addition code.

In addition to a special bit pattern to represent 0.0, the IEEE standard describes three other distinctive situations. The pattern

```
s 11111111 00000000000000000000000
```

(sign bit s, biased exponent 255, and fraction 0) represents plus or minus infinity. These values are used, for example, as quotients when a nonzero number is divided by zero. Another special case is called NaN (not a number) and is represented by any bit pattern with a biased exponent of 255 and a nonzero fraction. The quotient 0/0 should result in NaN, for example. The final special case is a denormalized number; when the biased exponent is zero and the fraction is nonzero, then no leading 1 is assumed for the fraction. This allows for representation of extra small numbers. Code in this section's floating-point procedures looks for the special zero representations wherever needed. However, other special number forms are ignored.

We will frequently need to extract the sign, exponent, and fraction of a floating-point number. For this purpose we will use a macro *expand*. This macro will have four parameters

1. a 32-bit floating point number

2. a byte to hold the sign (0 for positive, 1 for negative)

3. a word to hold the unbiased (actual) exponent

4. a doubleword to hold the fraction, including the leading 1 for a nonzero number.

Code for the macro *expand* appears in Fig. 10.18.

The expand macro code illustrates how useful the bit manipulation operations can be. The sign bit is isolated by rotating it left to bit position 0, saving the byte con-

```
expand    MACRO   source, sign, exponent, fraction
LOCAL   addOne, endAddOne
; take the 32-bit floating-point value source and expand it into
; separate pieces:
;    sign: byte
;    exponent: word (bias removed)
;    fraction: doubleword (with leading 1)
          push eax              ; save EAX
          mov   eax, source     ; get source
          rol   eax, 1          ; sign to bit 0
          mov   sign, 0         ; clear sign
          mov   sign, al        ; get byte with sign bit
          and   sign, 1         ; mask all but sign bit
          rol   eax, 8          ; shift exponent to bits 0-7
          mov   exponent, ax    ; get word with biased exponent
          and   exponent, 0ffh  ; mask all but exponent
          sub   exponent, 127   ; subtract bias
          shr   eax, 9          ; shift fraction to right
          test eax, eax         ; is fraction zero?
          jnz   addOne          ; add leading 1 bit if nonzero
          cmp   exponent, -127  ; was original exponent 0?
          je    endAddOne       ; if so, leave fraction at zero
AddOne:   or    eax, 800000h    ; add leading 1 bit
endAddOne:
          mov   fraction, eax   ; store fraction
          pop   eax             ; restore EAX
          ENDM
```

Figure 10.18 *expand* **macro**

taining it, and then masking by 1 (=00000001b) to zero all bits except the sign bit. Then the additional eight exponent bits are rotated to the right end of EAX and saved as a word before the leading bits are masked off. The bias of 127 is subtracted to get the true signed exponent. Finally the fraction is shifted back to the right of EAX. Before it is saved, a check for the IEEE 0.0 representation is made. If the original number was not 0.0, then the leading 1 bit of the scientific notation is inserted with the or operation.

```
combine  MACRO  destination, sign, exponent, fraction
LOCAL  endZero
; take the separate pieces:
;   sign: byte
;   exponent: word (bias removed)
;   fraction: doubleword (with leading 1)
; of a floating-point value and combine them into a 32-bit
; IEEE result at destination
        push eax                ; save EAX
        push ebx                ;    and EBX
        mov  eax, 0             ; zero result
        cmp  fraction, 0        ; zero value?
        je   endZero            ; skip if so
        mov  al, sign           ; get sign
        ror  eax, 1             ; rotate sign into position
        mov  bx, exponent       ; get exponent
        add  bx, 127            ; add bias
        shl  ebx, 23            ; shift to exponent position
        or   eax, ebx           ; combine with sign
        mov  ebx, fraction      ; get fraction
        and  ebx, 7fffffh       ; remove leading 1 bit
        or   eax, ebx           ; combine with sign and exponent
endZero:
        mov  destination, eax ;store result
        pop  ebx                ; restore registers
        pop  eax
        ENDM
```

Figure 10.19 *combine* **macro**

The plan is to take floating-point numbers apart into their sign-fraction-exponent forms, implement an operation by manipulating the parts, and then combine the resulting sign-fraction-exponent pieces back into a floating-point result. The combine operation will also be done with a macro, called *combine*. Code for this macro appears in Fig. 10.19.

The design for the *combine* macro assumes that each of the pieces of representing a floating-point value is legal, with a zero fraction the only special case considered. With these assumptions, the fraction will be **normalized**; that is, bit 24 will be the one and no bit to the left will be one. The operations that we will do with floating-point representations may leave a non-normalized result. We need a third macro, this one to normalize a floating-point representation. The code is in Fig. 10.20. It implements the following design:

---

if the fraction is zero then exit; end if;
while there is a non-zero bit in the left-hand byte of the fraction loop
　　shift fraction bits one position to the right;
　　add 1 to exponent;
end loop;
while bit 23 is not 1 loop
　　shift fraction bits one position to the left;
　　subtract one from exponent;
end loop;

```
normalize  MACRO sign, exponent, fraction
LOCAL  endZero, while1, while2, endWhile1, endWhile2
; Normalize floating-point number represented by separate pieces:
;    sign: byte
;    exponent: word (bias removed)
;    fraction: doubleword (with leading 1)
           push eax           ; save EAX
           cmp  fraction, 0   ; zero fraction?
           je   endZero       ; exit if so
while1:    mov  eax, fraction ; copy fraction
           and  eax, 0ff000000h ; nonzero leading byte?
           jz   endWhile1     ; exit if zero
           shr  fraction, 1   ; shift fraction bits right
           inc  exponent      ; subtract 1 from exponent
           jmp  while1        ; repeat
endWhile1:
while2:    mov  eax, fraction ; copy fracton
           and  eax, 800000h  ; check bit 23
           jnz  endWhile2     ; exit if 1
           shl  fraction, 1   ; shift fraction bits left
           dec  exponent      ; subtract 1 from exponent
           jmp  while2        ; repeat
endWhile2:
endZero:
           pop  eax           ; restore EAX
           ENDM
```

Figure 10.20　*normalize* **macro**

Multiplication is the easiest floating-point operation to implement. It is based on the usual method of multiplying numbers in scientific notation:

- multiply the fractions to get the fraction of the result
- add the exponents to get the exponent of the result
- follow customary rules of signs to get the sign of the result

This method is implemented in the code displayed in Fig. 10.21. The procedure *fMult-Proc* has three parameters pushed on the stack—the two operands and the address for

```
; procedure fMultProc(Operand1, Operand2 : float;
;                     Result : address of float)
; parameters are passed in doublewords on the stack
; parameters are removed by the procedure
; author:  R. Detmer  4/98

.DATA
sign1       BYTE   ?
exponent1   WORD   ?
fraction1   DWORD  ?
sign2       BYTE   ?
exponent2   WORD   ?
fraction2   DWORD  ?
sign3       BYTE   ?
exponent3   WORD   ?
fraction3   DWORD  ?

.CODE
fMultProc   PROC NEAR32
            push    ebp             ; save base pointer
            mov     ebp,esp         ; copy stack pointer
            push    eax             ; save registers
            push    edx

            expand  [ebp+16], sign1, exponent1, fraction1
            expand  [ebp+12], sign2, exponent2, fraction2
            mov     al, sign1       ; combine signs
            xor     al, sign2
            mov     sign3, al       ; and save
            mov     ax, exponent1   ; add exponents
            add     ax, exponent2
            mov     exponent3, ax   ; and save
```

(continued)

Figure 10.21   *fMultProc* procedure

```
           mov      eax, fraction1 ; multiply fractions
           mul      fraction2
           shrd     eax, edx, 23   ; discard extra bits
           mov      fraction3, eax ; and save

           normalize sign3, exponent3, fraction3
           mov      edx, [ebp+8]   ; address for result
           combine [edx], sign3, exponent3, fraction3

           pop      edx                 ; restore registers
           pop      eax
           pop      ebp                 ; restore base pointer
           ret      12                  ; return, removing parameters
fMultProc  ENDP
```

Figure 10.21 *(continued)*

the result. The sign is computed with using an exclusive or of the operands' signs. Addition of the exponents is straightforward. Multiplication of the fractions is followed by shifting off the low-order 23 bits; recall that each fraction is logically a 1, followed by a binary point, followed by 23 binary fraction bits. Multiplying two such fractions gives 46 fraction bits, and the extra 23 must be discarded.

The macros used by *fMultProc* are shown in previous figures. Although macros are convenient here, note that there are some dangers. You could not, for instance, use the statements

```
mov      eax, [ebp+8]   ; address for result
combine [eax], sign3, exponent3, fraction3
```

to combine the result pieces. The reason is that the combine macro uses the EAX register internally. It would have been safer to implement each of *expand*, *combine*, and *normalize* as procedures rather than macros.

Next we implement an algorithm for floating-point addition. This is somewhat more difficult than multiplication, but again follows the same sort of procedure that you would use to add two numbers in scientific notation, namely to adjust them to have the same exponent, and then add the fractions. One additional complication is that for a negative number, the fraction must be negated prior to adding it to the other fraction. The following algorithm is implemented in the code in Fig. 10.22.

```
; procedure fAddProc(Operand1, Operand2 : float;
;                       Result : address of float)
; parameters are passed in doublewords on the stack
; parameters are removed by the procedure
; author: R. Detmer   4/98

.DATA
sign1       BYTE   ?
exponent1   WORD   ?
fraction1   DWORD  ?
sign2       BYTE   ?
exponent2   WORD   ?
fraction2   DWORD  ?
sign3       BYTE   ?
exponent3   WORD   ?
fraction3   DWORD  ?

.CODE
fAddProc    PROC NEAR32
            push   ebp             ; save base pointer
            mov    ebp,esp         ; copy stack pointer
            push   eax             ; save registers
            push   edx
            expand [ebp+16], sign1, exponent1, fraction1
            expand [ebp+12], sign2, exponent2, fraction2
            mov    ax, exponent1   ; copy exponent1
while1:     cmp    ax, exponent2   ; exponent1 < exponent2?
            jnl    endWhile1       ; exit if not
            inc    ax              ; add 1 to exponent1
            shr    fraction1,1     ; shift fraction1 1 bit right
            jmp    while1          ; repeat
endWhile1:  mov    exponent1, ax   ; put fraction1 back in memory
            mov    ax, exponent2   ; copy exponent2
while2:     cmp    ax, exponent1   ; exponent2 < exponent1?
            jnl    endWhile2       ; exit if not
            inc    ax              ; add 1 to exponent1
            shr    fraction2,1     ; shift fraction2 1 bit right
            jmp    while2          ; repeat
endWhile2:  mov    exponent2, ax   ; put fraction2 back in memory
            mov    exponent3, ax   ; save common exponent
            cmp    sign1, 1        ; sign1 = minus?
            jne    notNeg1         ; skip if not
            neg    fraction1       ; negate fraction1
```

(continued)

Figure 10.22   *fAddProc* procedure

```
notNeg1:
            cmp     sign2, 1        ; sign1 = minus?
            jne     notNeg2         ; skip if not   ·
            neg     fraction2       ; negate fraction2
notNeg2:
            mov     eax, fraction1 ; add fractions
            add     eax, fraction2
            mov     fraction3, eax ; and save
            mov     sign3, 0        ; plus
            cmp     eax, 0          ; fraction3 < 0?
            jnl     notNegResult    ; skip if not
            mov     sign3, 1        ; minus
            neg     fraction3       ; make fraction3 positive
notNegResult:
            normalize sign3, exponent3, fraction3
            mov     edx, [ebp+8]    ; address for result
            combine [edx], sign3, exponent3, fraction3
            pop     edx             ; restore registers
            pop     eax
            pop     ebp             ; restore base pointer
            ret     12              ; return, removing parameters
fAddProc    ENDP
```

Figure 10.22 *(continued)*

expand each number into sign, exponent, and fraction components;
while exponent1 < exponent2 loop
    add 1 to exponent1;
    shift fraction1 one bit right;
end while;
while exponent2 < exponent1 loop
    add 1 to exponent2;
    shift fraction2 one bit right;
end while;
exponent3 := exponent1; {the exponents are equal}
if sign1 = minus then negate fraction1; end if;
if sign2 = minus then negate fraction2; end if;
fraction3 := fraction1 + fraction2;
sign3 := plus;

if fraction3 < 0
then
      sign3 := minus;
      negate fraction3;
end if;
normalize sign3, exponent3, fraction3;
combine sign3, exponent3, fraction3 into result;

Programming Exercises 10.3

Each of the exercises below are to be programmed without using float-ing-point instructions.

1. Write a NEAR32 procedure *fDivProc* that has three parameters, *Operand1*, *Operand2*, and *Result*. Each of the operands is a 32-bit float-ing point value and *Result* gives the address for a 32-bit floating-point result. If *Operand2* ≠ 0.0, put the value of *Operand1/Operand2* in the address given by *Result*. If the second operand is zero, then use the IEEE representation for plus or minus infinity as the result (plus or minus will depend on the sign of *Operand1*). The procedure will remove parameters from the stack and will change no register.

2. Write a NEAR32 procedure *fSubProc* that has three parameters, *Operand1*, *Operand2*, and *Result*. Each of the operands is a 32-bit float-ing-point value and *Result* gives the address for a 32-bit floating-point result. Put the value of *Operand1—Operand2* in the address given by *Result*. The procedure will remove parameters from the stack and will change no register. (Although you could do this by calling *fAddProc*, write a complete procedure instead.)

3. Write a NEAR32 procedure *fNegProc* that has two parameters, *Operand* and *Result*. *Operand* is a 32-bit floating-point value and *Result* gives the address for a 32-bit floating-point result. Put the value of −*Operand1* in the address given by *Result*. The procedure will remove parameters from the stack and will change no register.

4. Write a NEAR32 procedure *fCmpProc* that has two parameters, *Operand1* and *Operand2*. Each of the operands is a 32-bit floating-point value. This procedure will compare the values of *Operand1* and

Operand2 and will return 0 in EAX if they are equal, -1 if *Operand1* < *Operand2*, and $+1$ if *Operand1* > *Operand2*. The procedure will remove parameters from the stack and will change no register other than EAX.

10.4   Floating-Point and In-line Assembly

High-level language compilers sometimes have the ability to translate a program that includes **in-line assembly code**. This permits most of a program to be written in the high-level language, while a few parts are written in assembly language. These parts may need critical optimization or may implement low-level algorithms that would be difficult or impossible to code in the high-level language.

This section contains a single example of a program that compiles using Microsoft Visual C++. It performs the same computations as does the code in Fig. 10.11, namely to find the square root of the sum of the squares of two floating-point values, However, this version provides for input of the values and output of the results, with the input and output done in C++. The code is shown in Fig. 10.23.

Notice that for this compiler the in-line assembly language code is preceded by the _ _asm keyword that begins with two underscores, and that braces surround the

```
// square root of sum of squares of two values
#include <iostream.h>
void main()
{
  float value1;
  float value2;
  float sum;

  cout << "First value? ";
  cin >> value1;
  cout << "Second value? ";
  cin >> value2;

  __asm
  {
    fld     value1
    fld     st
```

(continued)

Figure 10.23   **In-line assembly code**

```
    fmul
    fld    value2
    fld    st
    fmul
    fadd
    fsqrt
    fstp   sum
  }
    cout << "The sum is " << sum << endl;
}
```

Figure 10.23   *(continued)*

assembly language statements. Notice also that the assembly language statements can reference variables declared in C++ statements. Finally, although these assembly language statements are floating-point instructions, almost any statements can appear in in-line assembly language, including those with labels.

Programming Exercises 10.4

1. Write a complete program that will prompt for and input a decimal value for the radius of a circle and will calculate and display (appropriately labeled) the circumference and the area of the circle. Do the input and output with C++ and the floating-point calculations with floating-point instructions in in-line assembly.

2. The following algorithm approximates the cube root of a real number x

   root := 1.0;
   until (|root − oldRoot| < smallValue) loop
       oldRoot := root;
       root := (2.0*root + x/(root*root)) / 3.0;
   end until;

   Write a C++ program to declare variables, input a value for x, and display root. Implement the cube root algorithm with in-line assembly code, using 0.001 for *smallValue*.

Chapter Summary

The Intel 80x86 floating-point unit (FPU) contains eight data 80-bit data registers, organized as a stack. It executes a variety of instructions from load and store to arithmetic to complex transcendental functions. Comparison instructions set bits in a FPU status register; this status word must be copied to AX or to memory to check the outcome of a comparison.

Conversion between floating point and ASCII representations is similar to that previously done for integers. The easiest ASCII format to scan is a simple decimal format. The simplest ASCII format to produce is E-notation.

Floating-point instructions can be emulated without a floating-point unit. The basic techniques involve separating floating-point representations into sign, exponent, and fraction components, manipulating these components, and then combining the resulting components back into a floating-point representation.

Some high-level language compilers translate in-line assembly code. One application of this is with floating-point instructions, doing input/output in a language like C++ and computations in assembly language. However, in-line assembly is also useful in other critical or difficult-to-implement applications.

Decimal Arithmetic

Section 1.5 contained a brief introduction to the integer representation systems known as binary coded decimal (BCD). BCD representations are especially useful for storing integers with many digits, such as might be needed for financial records. BCD values are easier than 2's complement values to convert to or from ASCII format, but only a few 80x86 instructions are available to facilitate arithmetic with BCD numbers.

Chapter 11 describes BCD representation schemes and the 80x86 instructions that are used with BCD numbers. It includes code to convert BCD representations for numbers to and from corresponding ASCII representations and some procedures for BCD arithmetic.

11.1 Packed BCD Representations

The two major classifications of BCD schemes are packed and unpacked, and many variations with respect to the number of bytes used and how the sign of a value is represented. This section and Section 11.2 discuss packed BCD numbers. Section 11.3 tells about unpacked BCD numbers.

Packed BCD representations store two decimal digits per byte, one in the high-order four bits and one in the low-order four bits. For example, the bit pattern 01101001 represents the decimal number 69, using 0110 for 6 and 1001 for 9. One confusing thing about packed BCD is that this same bit pattern is written 69 in hexadecimal; however, this just means that if 01101001 is thought of as a BCD number, it represents the decimal value 69, but if it is viewed as a signed or unsigned binary integer, the corresponding decimal value is 105. This again makes the point that a given pattern of bits can have multiple numeric interpretations, as well as nonnumeric meanings.

If single bytes were used for packed BCD representations, then decimal numbers from 0 to 99 could be stored. This would not be very useful, so typically several bytes are used to store a single number. Many schemes are possible; some use a fixed number of bytes and some have variable length, incorporating a field for length as part of the representation. The bit pattern for a number often includes one or more bits to indicate the sign of the number.

As mentioned in Chapter 10, the Microsoft Macro Assembler provides a DT directive that can be used to define a 10 byte packed decimal number. Although other representation systems are equally valid, this book concentrates on this scheme. The directive

```
DT 123456789
```

reserves ten bytes of storage with initial values (in hex)

```
89 67 45 23 01 00 00 00 00 00
```

Notice that the bytes are stored backward, low order to high order, but within each byte the individual decimal digits are stored forward. This is consistent with the way that high-order and low-order bytes are reversed in 2's complement integers. The tenth byte in this representation is used to indicate the sign of the entire number. This byte is 00 for a positive number and 80 for a negative number. Therefore the DT directive

```
DT  -1469
```

produces

      69 14 00 00 00 00 00 00 00 80

Notice that only the sign indicator changes for a negative number; other digits of the representation are the same as they would be for the corresponding positive number.

Since an entire byte is used for the sign indicator, only nine bytes remain to store decimal digits. Therefore the packed BCD scheme used by the DT directive stores a signed number up to decimal 18 digits long. With MASM 6.11, extra digits are truncated without warning.

Although DT directives can be used to initialize packed BCD numbers in an assembly language program and arithmetic can be done on these numbers with the aid of the instructions covered in the next section, packed BCD numbers are of little service unless they can be displayed for human use. Figure 11.1 gives the source code for a procedure *ptoaProc* that converts a packed BCD number to the corresponding ASCII string. This procedure does the same job for packed BCD numbers as *itoaProc* and *dtoaProc* do for 2's complement integers.

The procedure *ptoaProc* has two parameters: a 10-byte-long packed BCD source and a 19-byte-long ASCII destination string, each passed by location. The destination is 19 bytes long to allow for a sign and 18 digits. The sign will be a space for a positive number and a minus sign for a negative number. For the digits, leading zeros rather than spaces are produced. The procedure implements the following design:

---

copy source address to ESI;
copy destination address to EDI;
add 18 to EDI to point at last byte of destination string;

for count := 9 down to 1 loop { process byte containing two digits }
     copy next source byte to AL;
     duplicate source byte in AH;
     mask out high-order digit in AL;
     convert low-order digit in AL to ASCII code;
     store ASCII code for low-order digit in destination string;
     decrement EDI to point at next destination byte to left;
     shift AH 4 bits to right to get only high-order digit;
     convert high-order digit in AH to ASCII code;
     store ASCII code for high-order digit in destination string;
     decrement EDI to point at next destination byte to left;

```
ptoaProc  PROC NEAR
; convert 10-byte BCD number to a 19-byte-long ASCII string
; parameter 1:  address of BCD number
; parameter 2:  destination address
; author:  R. Detmer      revised: 5/98
          push ebp         ; establish stack frame
          mov  ebp, esp
          push esi         ; save registers
          push edi
          push eax
          push ecx
          mov  esi, [ebp+12]  ; source address
          mov  edi, [ebp+8]   ; destination address
          add  edi, 18     ; point to last byte of destination
          mov  ecx, 9      ; count of bytes to process
for1:     mov  al, [esi] ; byte with two bcd digits
          mov  ah, al      ; copy to high-order byte of AX
          and  al, 00001111b       ; mask out higher-order digit
          or   al, 30h   ; convert to ASCII character
          mov  [edi], al ; save lower-order digit
          dec  edi         ; point at next destination byte to left
          shr  ah, 4       ; shift out lower-order digit
          or   ah, 30h   ; convert to ASCII
          mov  [edi], ah ; save higher-order digit
          dec  edi         ; point at next destination byte to left
          inc  esi         ; point at next source byte
          loop for1        ; continue for 9 bytes

          mov  BYTE PTR [edi], ' '  ; space for positive number
          and  BYTE PTR [esi], 80h  ; check sign byte
          jz   nonNeg               ; skip if not negative
          mov  BYTE PTR [edi], '-'  ; minus sign
nonNeg:
          pop  ecx         ; restore registers
          pop  eax
          pop  esi
          pop  edi
          pop  ebp
          ret 8            ; return, removing parameters
ptoaProc  ENDP
```

Figure 11.1   Packed BCD to ASCII conversion

      increment ESI to point at next source digit to right;

end for;

move space to first byte of destination string;

if source number is negative

then

      move minus sign to first byte of destination string;

end if;

The most interesting part of the design and code is the portion that splits a single source byte into two destination bytes. Two copies of the source byte are made, one in AL and one in AH. The byte in AL is converted to the ASCII code for the low-order digit using an and instruction to mask the left four bits and an or instruction to put 0011 (hex 3) in their place. The high-order digit is processed similarly. A shr instruction discards the low-order digit in AH, moves the high-order digit to the right four bits and zeros the left four bits. Another or instruction produces the ASCII code for the high-order digit.

Once a packed BCD number is converted to an ASCII string it can be displayed using the *output* macro or by some other means. Since BCD numbers are often used for financial calculations, some other ASCII representation may be more desirable than that generated by *ptoaProc*. Some exercises at the end of this section specify alternatives.

Sometimes it is necessary to convert an ASCII string to a corresponding packed BCD value. Figure 11.2 shows a procedure *atopProc* that accomplishes this task in a

```
atopProc   PROC NEAR32
; Convert ASCII string at to 10-byte BCD number
; parameter 1: ASCII string address    parameter 2: BCD number address
; null-terminated source string consists only of ASCII codes for digits,
; author:  R. Detmer     revised: 5/98
           push ebp         ; establish stack frame
           mov  ebp, esp
           push esi                     ; save registers
           push edi
           push eax
           push ecx
           mov  esi, [ebp+12]           ; source address
```
(continued)

Figure 11.2 ASCII to packed BCD conversion

```
                mov   edi, [ebp+8]         ; destination address
                mov   DWORD PTR [edi], 0   ; zero BCD destination
                mov   DWORD PTR [edi+4], 0
                mov   WORD PTR [edi+8], 0
; find length of source string and move ESI to trailing null
                mov   ecx, 0               ; count := 0
while1:         cmp   BYTE PTR [esi], 0    ; while not end of string (null)
                jz    endwhile1
                inc   ecx                  ; add 1 to count of characters
                inc   esi                  ; point at next character
                jmp   while1               ; check again
endwhile1:
; process source characters a pair at a time
while2:         cmp   ecx, 0               ; while count > 0
                jz    endwhile2
                dec   esi                  ; point at next ASCII byte from right
                mov   al, BYTE PTR [esi]    ; get byte
                and   al, 00001111b        ; convert to BCD digit
                mov   BYTE PTR [edi], al    ; save BCD digit
                dec   ecx                  ; decrement count
                jz    endwhile2            ; exit loop if out of source digits
                dec   esi                  ; point at next ASCII byte from right
                mov   al, BYTE PTR [esi]    ; get byte
                shl   al, 4                ; shift to left and convert to digit
                or    BYTE PTR [edi], al    ; combine with other BCD digit
                dec   ecx                  ; decrement count
                inc   edi                  ; point at next destination byte
                jmp   while2               ; repeat for all source characters
endwhile2:
                pop   ecx                  ; restore registers
                pop   eax
                pop   esi
                pop   edi
                pop   ebp
                ret   8                    ; return, removing parameters
atopProc        ENDP
```

Figure 11.2   (continued)

restricted setting. The procedure has two parameters, the addresses of an ASCII source string and a 10 byte BCD destination string. The ASCII source string is very limited. It can consist only of ASCII codes for digits terminated by a null byte; no sign, no space, nor any other character code is permitted.

The design of procedure *atopProc* is quite different from *atodProc* (Fig. 8.9) that produces a doubleword integer from an ASCII string. The ASCII-to-doubleword routine scans source characters left to right one at a time, but the ASCII-to-packed BCD procedure scans the source string right to left, two characters at a time, in order to pack two decimal digits into one byte. The procedure must begin by locating the right end of the string. If there is an odd number of source characters, then only one character will contribute to the last BCD byte. The design for *atopProc* appears below.

```
copy source address to ESI;
copy destination address to EDI;
initialize all 10 bytes of destination, each to 00;
counter := 0;
while ESI is not pointing at trailing null byte of ASCII source loop
        add 1 to counter;
        increment ESI to point at next byte of source string;
end while;
while counter > 0 loop
        decrement ESI to point at next source byte from right;
        copy source byte to AL;
        convert ASCII code to digit by zeroing leftmost 4 bits;
        save low-order digit in destination string;
        subtract 1 from counter;
        if counter = 0
        then
                exit loop;
        end if;
        decrement ESI to point at next source byte from right;
        copy source byte to AL;
        shift AL 4 bits left to get digit in high order 4 bits;
        or AL with destination byte to combine with low-order digit;
        subtract 1 from counter;
        increment EDI to point at next destination byte;
end while;
```

The first *while* loop in the design simply scans the source string left to right, counting digits preceding the trailing null byte. Although this design allows only ASCII codes for digits, an extra loop could be included to skip leading blanks and a leading minus or plus (− or +) could be noted. (These and other enhancements are specified in programming exercises.)

The second *while* loop processes the ASCII codes for digits that have been counted in the first loop. Two digits, if available, must be packed into a single destination byte. At least one source byte is there each time through the loop, so the first is loaded into AL, changed from an ASCII code to a digit, and stored in the destination string. (An alternative way to convert the ASCII code to a digit would be to subtract 30_{16}.) If source characters are exhausted, then the *while* loop is exited. Otherwise a second ASCII character is loaded into AL, a left shift instruction converts it to a digit in the left four bits of AL, and an `or` combines it with the right digit already stored in memory in the destination string.

The *atopProc* procedure could be used to convert a string obtained from the *input* macro. If some other method were used, one would have to ensure that the string has a trailing null byte.

Exercises 11.1

1. Find the initial values that MASM will generate for each DT directive below:

   (a) `DT 123456`
   (b) `DT -123456`
   (c) `DT 345`
   (d) `DT -345`
   (e) `DT 102030405060708090`
   (f) `DT -102030405060708090`

2. Explain how you could use floating-point instructions to convert a number stored as a 2's complement doubleword integer to a 10-byte packed decimal equivalent value. From packed BCD to doubleword integer?

3. Define a macro *ptoa* similar to the *itoa* macro described in Section 9.5. Use two parameters, *dest* and *source*, *dest* referencing a 19-byte-long ASCII string and *source* referencing a 10-byte packed BCD string in memory. Include safeguards to ensure that the correct number of arguments is used in a call. Code in the macro will call *ptoaProc*.

Programming Exercises 11.1

1. Modify the code for the *ptoaProc* procedure so that it produces leading spaces instead of zeros, and so that the minus sign, if any, is placed to the immediate left of the first nonzero digit. If the value of the entire number is zero, the units-position (rightmost) zero is not replaced by a space. The total string length will remain 19 characters. The procedure will remove parameters from the stack.

2. Modify the code for the *ptoaProc* procedure so that it produces a 22-byte-long ASCII string giving a monetary representation of the source value. Use leading spaces instead of leading zeros (if any) in the first 16 positions. Character 17 is always a decimal point. Characters 18 and 19 are always digits, even if they have value zero. Character 20 is a space. Characters 21 and 22 are ASCII codes for "CR" if the value is positive and "DB" if the value is negative. The procedure will remove parameters from the stack.

3. (a) Modify the code for the *atopProc* procedure so that it will skip leading spaces in the source string, accept a leading plus or minus (+ or −) immediately before the first digit, and terminate scanning when any nondigit (rather than only a null byte) is encountered in the string. If a minus sign is encountered, the sign byte of the BCD representation is set to 80_{16}. The procedure will remove parameters from the stack.

    (b) Define a macro *atop* similar to the *atoi* macro described in Section 9.5. Use two parameters, *dest* and *source*, *dest* referencing a 10-byte packed BCD string in memory and *source* referencing a 19-byte-long ASCII string. Include safeguards to ensure that the correct number of arguments is used in a call. Code in the macro will call the modified *atopProc* from part (a).

4. Write a procedure *editProc* that has two parameters, (1) the address of a pattern string and (2) the address of a 10-byte packed BCD value. The procedure selectively replaces some characters in the pattern string by spaces or by ASCII codes for digits extracted from the BCD value. Except for a terminating null byte, the only allowable characters in a pattern string are a pound sign (#), a comma (,) and a period (.). A period is always unchanged. Each # is replaced by a digit. There will be

at most 18 pound signs and if there are fewer than 18, then lower-order digits from the BCD value are used. Leading zeros in the resulting string are changed to spaces unless they follow a period, in which case they remain zeros. A comma is unchanged unless it is adjacent to a space; such a comma is changed to a space. The following examples (with *b* indicating a space) illustrate how *editProc* works. Note that the original pattern is destroyed by the procedure. The procedure will remove parameters from the stack.

Before *pattern*	*BCD value*	*After* *pattern*
##,###.##	123456	*b*1,234.56
##,###.##	12345	*bbb*123.45
##,###.##	1	*bbbbbb*.01

11.2   Packed BCD Instructions

Addition and subtraction operations for packed BCD numbers are similar to those for multicomponent 2's complement numbers (Section 4.5). Corresponding bytes of the two operands are added, and the carry-from-one addition is added to the next pair of bytes. BCD operands have no special addition instruction; the regular add and adc instructions are used. However, these instructions are designed for binary values, not BCD values, so for many operands they give the wrong sums.

The 80x86 architecture includes a daa (decimal adjust after addition) instruction used after an addition instruction to correct the sum. This section explains the operation of the daa instruction and its counterpart das for subtraction. Procedures for addition and subtraction of non-negative 10-byte packed BCD numbers are developed; then a general addition procedure is given.

A few examples illustrate the problem with using binary addition for BCD operands. The AF column gives the value of the auxiliary carry flag, the significance of which is discussed below.

Before		*After* add al,bl		
AL	*BL*	*AL*	*AF*	*CF*
34	25	59	0	0
37	25	5C	0	0
93	25	B8	0	0
28	39	61	1	0
79	99	12	1	1

Although each answer is correct as the sum of two unsigned binary integers, only the first result is correct as a BCD value. The second and third sums contain bit patterns that are not used in BCD representations, C_{16} in the second example and B_{16} in the third. The last two sums contain no invalid digit—they are simply wrong as decimal sums.

The daa instruction is used after an addition instruction to convert a binary sum into a packed BCD sum. The instruction has no operand; the sum to be converted must be in the AL register. A daa instruction examines and sets both the carry flag CF and the auxiliary carry flag AF (bit 4 of the EFLAGS register). Recall that the carry flag is set to 1 during addition of two eight bit numbers if there is a carry out of the leftmost position. The AF flag similarly is set to 1 by add or adc instructions if there is a carry resulting from addition of the low-order four bits of the two operands. One way of thinking of this is that the sum of the two low-order hex digits is greater than F_{16}.

A daa instruction first examines the right hex digit of the binary sum in AL. If this digit is over 9 (that is, A through F), then 6 is added to the entire sum and AF is set to 1. Notice that this would correct the result in the second example above since 5C + 6 = 62, the correct packed BCD sum of 37 and 25. The same correction is applied if AF=1 when the daa instruction is executed. Thus in the fourth example, 61 + 6 = 67.

After correcting the right digit, daa examines the left digit in AL. The action is similar: If the left digit is over 9 or CF=1, then 60_{16} is added to the entire sum. The carry flag CF is set to 1 if this correction is applied. In the third example, B8 + 60 = 18 with a carry of 1.

Both digits must be corrected in the last example, 12 + 6 = 18 and 18 + 60 = 78 (since CF=1). The chart below completes the above examples, assuming that both of the following instructions are executed.

```
add   al, bl
daa
```

Before	*After* add	*After* daa
AL: 34	AL: 59	AL: 59
BL: 25	AF: 0 CF: 0	AF: 0 CF: 0
AL: 37	AL: 5C	AL: 62
BL: 25	AF: 0 CF: 0	AF: 1 CF: 0
AL: 93	AL: B8	AL: 18
BL: 25	AF: 0 CF: 0	AF: 0 CF: 1
AL: 28	AL: 61	AL: 67
BL: 39	AF: 1 CF: 0	AF: 1 CF: 0
AL: 79	AL: 12	AL: 78
BL: 99	AF: 1 CF: 1	AF: 1 CF: 1

The das instruction (decimal adjust after subtraction) is used after a sub or sbb instruction. It acts like the daa except that 6 or 60_{16} is subtracted from rather than added to the value in AL. The following examples show how das works following sub al,bl. In the first example, both CF and AF are set to 1 since the subtraction requires borrows in both digit positions. When 6 and 60_{16} are subtracted from BC, the result is 56, and both CF and AF remain set to 1. This is the correct answer since 25 − 69 = 56 (borrowing 1 to change 25 into 125.)

Before	*After* sub	*After* das
AL: 25	AL: BC	AL: 56
BL: 69	AF: 1 CF: 1	AF: 1 CF: 1
AL: 37	AL: 12	AL: 12
BL: 25	AF: 0 CF: 0	AF: 0 CF: 0
AL: 93	AL: 6E	AL: 68
BL: 25	AF: 1 CF: 0	AF: 1 CF: 1
AL: 92	AL: 59	AL: 53
BL: 39	AF: 1 CF: 0	AF: 1 CF: 0
AL: 79	AL: E4	AL: 84
BL: 95	AF: 0 CF: 1	AF: 0 CF: 1

Each of the daa and das instructions encodes in a single byte. The daa instruction has opcode 27 and the das instruction has opcode 2F. Each requires three clock cycles to execute on a Pentium. In addition to modifying AF and CF, the SF, ZF and PF flags are set or reset by daa or das instructions to correspond to the final value in AL. The overflow flag OF is undefined and other flags are not affected.

The first BCD arithmetic procedure in this section adds two non-negative 10-byte numbers. This procedure will have two parameters, addresses of destination and source values, respectively. Each will serve as an operand, and the destination will be replaced by the sum, consistent with the way that ordinary addition instructions use the destination operand. We will not be concerned about setting flags; the exercises specify a more complete procedure that assigns appropriate values to SF, ZF, and CF. A design for the procedure is given below. This design is implemented in the procedure *addBcd1* (see Fig. 11.3).

point at first source and destination bytes;
for count := 1 to 9 loop
    copy destination byte to AL;
    add source byte to AL;

use `daa` to convert sum to BCD;

save AL in destination;

point at next source and destination bytes;

end for;

```
addBcd1    PROC NEAR32
; add two non-negative 10 byte packed BCD numbers
; parameter1:  address of operand1 (and destination)
; parameter2:  address of operand2
; author:  R. Detmer      revised: 5/98
           push ebp              ; establish stack frame
           mov  ebp, esp
           push esi              ; save registers
           push edi
           push ecx
           push eax
           mov  edi, [ebp+12]    ; destination address
           mov  esi, [ebp+8]     ; source address

           clc                   ; clear carry flag for first add
           mov  ecx, 9           ; count of bytes to process
forAdd:    mov  al, [edi]        ; get one operand byte
           adc  al, [esi]        ; add other operand byte
           daa                   ; adjust to BCD
           mov  [edi], al        ; save sum
           inc  edi              ; point at next operand bytes
           inc  esi
           loop forAdd           ; repeat for all 9 bytes

           pop  eax              ; restore registers
           pop  ecx
           pop  edi
           pop  esi
           pop  ebp
           ret  8                ; return to caller

addBcd1    ENDP
```

Figure 11.3   Addition of non-negative packed BCD numbers

A subtraction procedure for 10-byte packed BCD numbers is more difficult. Even with the operands restricted to non-negative values, subtracting the source value (address in parameter 2) from the destination (address in parameter 1) will produce a negative result if the source is larger than the destination. A design for the procedure is below.

---

point at first source and destination bytes;
for count := 1 to 9 loop
     copy destination byte to AL;
     subtract source byte from AL;
     use das to convert difference to BCD;
     save AL in destination string;
     point at next source and destination bytes;
end for;

if source > destination
then
     point at first destination byte;
     for count := 1 to 9 loop
          put 0 in AL;
          subtract destination byte from AL;
          use das to convert difference to BCD;
          save AL in destination string;
          increment DI;
     end for;
     move sign byte 80 to destination string;
end if;

The first part of this design is almost the same as the design for addition. The condition *(source > destination)* is true if the carry flag is set after the first loop, and the difference is corrected by subtracting it from zero. If this were not done, then, for example, 3 − 7 would produce 999999999999999996 instead of −4. This design is implemented as procedure *subBcd1* in Fig. 11.4.

```
subBcd1    PROC NEAR32
; subtract 2 non-negative 10 byte packed BCD numbers
; parameter1:  address of operand1 (and destination)
; parameter2:  address of operand2
; operand1 - operand2  stored at destination
; author:  R. Detmer     revised: 5/98
           push ebp                ; establish stack frame
           mov  ebp, esp
           push esi  .             ; save registers
           push edi
           push ecx
           push eax
           mov  edi, [ebp+12] ; destination address (operand 1)
           mov  esi, [ebp+8]  ; source address (operand 2)
           clc                     ; clear carry flag
           mov  ecx, 9             ; count of bytes to process
forSub:    mov  al, [edi]          ; get one operand byte
           sbb  al, [esi]          ; subtract other operand byte
           das                     ; adjust to BCD
           mov  [edi], al          ; save difference
           inc  edi                ; point at next operand bytes
           inc  esi
           loop forSub             ; repeat for all 9 bytes

           jnc  endIfBigger        ; done if destination >= source
           sub  edi, 9             ; point at beginning of destination
           mov  ecx, 9             ; count of bytes to process
forSub1:   mov  al, 0              ; subtract destination from zero
           sbb  al, [edi]
           das
           mov  [edi], al
           inc  edi                ; next byte
           loop forSub1
           mov  BYTE PTR [edi], 80h    ; negative result
endIfBigger:
           pop  eax                ; restore registers
           pop  ecx
           pop  edi
           pop  esi
           pop  ebp
           ret  8                  ; return to caller
subBcd1    ENDP
```

Figure 11.4 Subtraction of non-negative packed BCD numbers

Once you have the *addBcd1* and *subBcd1* procedures that combine non-negative operands, it is not too difficult to construct the general packed BCD addition and subtraction procedures. The design for addition is

```
if operand1 ≥ 0
then
        if operand2 ≥ 0
        then
                addBcd1(operand1, operand2);
        else
                subBcd1(operand1, operand2);
        end if;
else {operand1 < 0}
        if (operand2 < 0)
        then
                addBcd1(operand1, operand2);
        else
                change sign byte of operand1;
                subBcd1(operand1, operand2);
                change sign byte of operand1;
        end if;
end if;
```

The design for negative *operand1* is a little tricky. When *operand2* is also negative, the result will be negative. Since *addBcd1* does not affect the sign byte of the destination (*operand1*), the result after adding *operand2* will be negative with no special adjustment required. Adding a non-negative *operand2* can result in either a positive or negative result. The reader should verify that this design and corresponding code produces the correct sign for the result. This design is implemented in procedure *addBcd*, shown in Fig. 11.5. A general procedure for subtraction is left as an exercise.

```
addBcd     PROC NEAR32
; add two arbitrary 10 byte packed BCD numbers
; parameter1:  address of operand1 (and destination)
; parameter2:  address of operand2
; author:  R. Detmer      revised: 5/98
           push ebp                 ; establish stack frame
           mov  ebp, esp
           push esi                 ; save registers
           push edi
           mov  edi, [ebp+12]   ; destination address
           mov  esi, [ebp+8]    ; source address
           push edi                 ; parameter1 for next call
           push esi                 ; parameter2 for next call
           cmp  BYTE PTR [edi+9], 80h   ; operand1 >= 0?
           je   op1Neg
           cmp  BYTE PTR [esi+9], 80h   ; operand2 >= 0?
           je   op2Neg
           call addBcd1             ; add (>=0, >=0)
           jmp  endIfOp2Pos
op2Neg:    call subBcd1             ; sub (>=0, <0)
endIfOp2Pos:
           jmp  endIfOp1Pos     ; done
op1Neg:    cmp  BYTE PTR [esi+9], 80h    ; operand2 < 0 ?
           jne  op2Pos
           call addBcd1             ; add (<0, <0)
           jmp  endIfOp2Neg
op2Pos:    xor  BYTE PTR [edi+9], 80h  ; change sign byte
           call subBcd1             ; sub (<0, >=0)
           xor  BYTE PTR [edi+9], 80h  ; change sign byte
endIfOp2Neg:
endIfOp1Pos:
           pop  edi                 ; restore registers
           pop  esi
           pop  ebp
           ret  8                   ; return to caller

addBcd     ENDP
```

Figure 11.5 General BCD addition procedure

Exercises 11.2

1. In each part below, assume that the instructions

   ```
   add   al, bl
   daa
   ```

   are executed. Give the values in the AL register, carry flag CF, and auxiliary flag AF: (1) after the add and before the daa and (2) after the daa.
   (a) AL: 35 BL: 42
   (b) AL: 27 BL: 61
   (c) AL: 35 BL: 48
   (d) AL: 47 BL: 61
   (e) AL: 35 BL: 92
   (f) AL: 27 BL: 69
   (g) AL: 75 BL: 46
   (h) AL: 00 BL: 61
   (i) AL: 85 BL: 82
   (j) AL: 89 BL: 98
   (k) AL: 76 BL: 89
   (l) AL: 27 BL: 00

2. Repeat the parts of Exercise 1 for the instructions

   ```
   sub   al, bl
   das
   ```

Programming Exercises 11.2

1. Modify the *addBcd* procedure to set SF, ZF, and CF. The sign flag will be set according to the sign of the sum, and ZF will be set for a zero result. The carry flag CF will be set if there are more than 18 digits in the sum.

2. Design and code a general subtraction procedure *subBcd* with two parameters: (1) the address of *operand1* and (2) the address of *operand2*. The difference *operand1—operand2* will be stored at the address of *operand1*. The procedure will remove parameters from the stack.

11.3   Unpacked BCD Representations and Instructions

Unpacked BCD numbers differ from packed representations by storing one decimal digit per byte instead of two. The bit pattern in the left half of each byte is 0000. This section describes how to define unpacked BCD numbers, how to convert this representation to and from ASCII, and how to use 80x86 instructions to do some arithmetic operations with unpacked BCD numbers.

Unpacked BCD representations have no standard length. In this book each value will be stored in eight bytes, with high-order digits on the left and low-order digits on the right (opposite to the way a DT directive stores packed BCD numbers). No sign byte will be used, so only non-negative numbers will be represented. An ordinary BYTE directive can be used to initialize an unpacked BCD value. For example, the statement

```
BYTE 0,0,0,5,4,3,2,8
```

reserves eight bytes of storage containing 00 00 00 05 04 03 02 08, the unpacked BCD representation for 54328. The directive

```
BYTE 8 DUP (?)
```

establishes an eight-byte-long area that can be used to store an unpacked BCD value.

It is simple to convert an unpacked BCD value to or from ASCII. Suppose that the data segment of a program includes the directives

```
ascii      DB   8 DUP (?)
unpacked   DB   8 DUP (?)
```

If *unpacked* already contains an unpacked BCD value, the following code fragment will produce the corresponding ASCII representation at *ascii*.

```
        lea   edi, ascii          ; destination
        lea   esi, unpacked       ; source
        mov   ecx, 8              ; bytes to process
for8:   mov   al, [esi]           ; get digit
        or    al, 30h             ; convert to ASCII
        mov   [edi], al           ; store ASCII character
        inc   edi                 ; increment pointers
        inc   esi
        loop  for8                ; repeat for all bytes
```

Converting from an ASCII string to an unpacked BCD representation is equally easy. The same loop structure can be used with the roles of EDI and ESI reversed, and with the or instruction replaced by

```
        and   al, 0fh       ; convert ASCII to unpacked BCD
```

Instruction	Mnemonic	Number of bytes	Opcode	Clocks (Pentium)
ASCII adjust after addition	aaa	1	37	3
ASCII adjust for subtraction	aas	1	3F	3
ASCII adjust after multiplication	aam	2	D4 0A	18
ASCII adjust before division	aad	2	D5 0A	10

Figure 11.6 Unpacked BCD instructions

to mask the high-order four bits. Conversions between ASCII and unpacked BCD are even simpler if they are done "in place" (see Exercise 3).

The 80x86 architecture includes four instructions to facilitate arithmetic with unpacked BCD representations. Each mnemonic begins with "aa" for "ASCII adjust"— Intel uses the word ASCII to describe unpacked BCD representations, even though the ASCII representation for a digit has 0011 in the left half byte and the unpacked representation has 0000. The four instructions are aaa, aas, aam, and aad. Information about these instructions is given in Fig. 11.6.

The aaa and aas instructions are similar to their packed BCD counterparts daa and das. For addition, bytes containing unpacked BCD operands are combined using an add or adc instruction, yielding a sum in the AL register. An aaa instruction then corrects the value in AL if necessary. An aaa instruction sets flags and may also affect AH; recall that a daa affects only AL and flags. The following algorithm describes how aaa works.

```
if (right digit in AL > 9) or (AF=1)
then
        add 6 to AL;
        increment AH;
        AF := 1;
end if;

CF := AF;
left digit in AL := 0;
```

The action of an `aas` instruction is similar. The first two operations inside the *if* are replaced by

> subtract 6 from AL;
>
> decrement AH;

The OF, PF, SF, and ZF flags are left undefined by `aaa` and `aas` instructions.

Here are some examples of showing how `add` and `aaa` work together. In each example, assume that the following pair of instructions is executed.

```
add   al, ch
aaa
```

Before	*After* add	*After* aaa
AX: 00 04	AX: 00 07	AX: 00 07
CH: 03	AF: 0	AF: 0 CF: 0
AX: 00 04	AX: 00 0B	AX: 01 01
CH: 07	AF: 0	AF: 1 CF: 1
AX: 00 08	AX: 00 11	AX: 01 07
CH: 09	AF: 1	AF: 1 CF: 1
AX: 05 05	AX: 05 0C	AX: 06 02
CH: 07	AF: 0	AF: 1 CF: 1

Another set of examples illustrates how `sub` and `aas` find differences of single byte unpacked BCD operands. This time assume that the following instructions are executed.

```
sub   al, dl
aas
```

Before	*After* sub	*After* aas
AX: 00 08	AX: 00 05	AX: 00 05
DL: 03	AF: 0	AF: 0 CF: 0
AX: 00 03	AX: 00 FC	AX: FF 06
DL: 07	AF: 1	AF: 1 CF: 1
AX: 05 02	AX: 05 F9	AX: 04 03
DL: 09	AF: 1	AF: 1 CF: 1

Figure 11.7 displays a procedure *addUnp* that adds two eight-byte unpacked BCD numbers whose addresses are passed as parameters. This procedure is simpler

```
addUnp     PROC NEAR32
; add two 8-byte unpacked BCD numbers
; parameter 1:  operand1 and destination address
; parameter 2:  operand2 address
; author:  R. Detmer    revised:  5/98
           push ebp              ; establish stack frame
           mov  ebp, esp
           push esi              ; save registers
           push edi
           push eax
           push ecx
           mov  edi, [ebp+12]    ; destination address
           mov  esi, [ebp+8]     ; source address
           add  esi, 8           ; point at byte after source
           add  edi, 8           ; byte after destination
           clc                   ; clear carry flag
           mov  ecx, 8           ; count of bytes to process
forAdd:    dec  edi              ; point at operand bytes to left
           dec  esi
           mov  al, [edi]        ; get one operand byte
           adc  al, [esi]        ; add other operand byte
           aaa                   ; adjust to unpacked BCD
           mov  [edi], al        ; save sum
           loop forAdd           ; repeat for all 8 bytes
           pop  ecx              ; restore registers
           pop  eax
           pop  edi
           pop  esi
           pop  ebp
           ret  8               ; return, discarding paramters
addUnp     ENDP
```

Figure 11.7 Addition of two 8-byte unpacked BCD numbers

than the similar *addBcd1* procedure in Fig. 11.3. No effort is made to produce significant flag values. Since low-order digits are stored to the right, the bytes are processed right to left. (Programming Exercise 1 specifies the corresponding procedure for subtraction.)

One interesting feature of the procedure *addUnp* is that it will give the correct unpacked BCD sum of eight byte ASCII (not unpacked BCD) numbers—Intel's use of

"ASCII" in the unpacked BCD mnemonics is not as unreasonable as it first seems. The procedure is successful for ASCII strings since the action of the aaa instruction depends only on what add does with low-order digits, and aaa always sets the high-order digit in AL to zero. However, even if the operands are true ASCII character strings, the sum is not ASCII; it is unpacked BCD.

Two single byte unpacked BCD operands are multiplied using an ordinary mul instruction, resulting in a product in the AX register. Of course, this product will be correct as a binary number, not usually as a BCD value. The aam instruction converts the product in AX to two unpacked BCD digits in AH and AL. In effect, an aam instruction divides the number in AL by 10, putting the quotient in AH and the remainder in AL. The following examples assume that the instructions

```
mul   bh
aam
```

are executed.

Before	After mul	After aam
AX: 00 09	AX: 00 51	AX: 08 01
BH: 06		
AX: 00 05	AX: 00 1E	AX: 03 00
BH: 06		
AX: 00 06	AX: 00 2A	AX: 04 02
BH: 07		

Some flags are affected by an aam instruction. The PF, SF, and ZF flags are given values corresponding to the final value in AX; the AF, CF, and OF flags are undefined.

Multiplication of single-digit numbers is not very useful. Figure 11.8 gives a procedure *mulUnp1* to multiply an eight-byte unpacked BCD number by a single-digit unpacked BCD number. The procedure has three parameters: (1) the destination address, (2) the address of the BCD source, and (3) a word containing the single-digit unpacked BCD number as its low-order byte.

The algorithm implemented is essentially the same one as used by grade school children. The single digit is multiplied times the low-order digit of the multi-digit number, the units digit is stored, and the tens digit is recorded as a carry to add to the next product. All eight products can be treated the same by initializing a *last-Carry* variable to zero prior to beginning a loop. Here is the design that is actually implemented.

```
mulUnp1    PROC NEAR32
; multiply 8 byte and 1 byte unpacked BCD numbers
; parameter 1:  destination address
; parameter 2:  address of 8 byte unpacked BCD number
; parameter 3:  word w/ low-order byte containing 1-digit BCD nbr
           push ebp              ; establish stack frame
           mov  ebp, esp
           push esi              ; save registers
           push edi
           push eax
           push ebx
           push ecx
           mov  edi, [ebp+14]   ; destination address
           mov  esi, [ebp+10]   ; source address
           mov  bx, [ebp+8]     ; multiplier
           add  esi, 8          ; point at byte after source
           add  edi, 8          ; byte after destination
           mov  bh, 0           ; lastCarry := 0
           mov  ecx, 8          ; count of bytes to process
forMul:    dec  esi             ; point at operand byte to left
           dec  edi             ; and at destination byte
           mov  al, [esi]       ; digit from 8 byte number
           mul  bl              ; multiply by single byte
           aam                  ; adjust to unpacked BCD
           add  al, bh          ; add lastCarry
           aaa                  ; adjust to unpacked BCD
           mov  [edi], al       ; store units digit
           mov  bh, ah          ; store lastCarry
           loop forMul          ; repeat for all 8 bytes
           pop  ecx             ; restore registers
           pop  ebx
           pop  eax
           pop  edi
           pop  esi
           pop  ebp
           ret  10              ; return, discarding paramters
mulUnp1    ENDP
```

Figure 11.8 Multiplication of unpacked BCD numbers

{ multiply $X_7X_6X_5X_4X_3X_2X_1X_0$ times Y giving $Z_7Z_6Z_5Z_4Z_3Z_2Z_1Z_0$}
lastCarry := 0;
for i := 0 to 7 loop
        multiply X_i times Y;
        add lastCarry;
        Z_i := units digit;
        lastCarry := tens digit;
end for;

In the code for *mulUnp1*, the value for *lastCarry* is stored in the BH register. After a digit from the eight-byte BCD value is multiplied by the single digit in BL, the product is adjusted to unpacked BCD and *lastCarry* is added. It is then necessary to adjust the sum to unpacked BCD.

The `aad` instruction essentially reverses the action of the `aam` instruction. It combines a two-digit unpacked BCD value in AH and AL into a single binary value in AX, multiplying the digit in AH by 10 and adding the digit in AL. The AH register is always cleared to 00. The PF, SF, and ZF flags are given values corresponding to the result; AF, CF, and OF are undefined.

The `aad` instruction is used *before* a `div` instruction, contrary to the other ASCII adjust instructions that are used after the corresponding arithmetic instructions. The examples below assume that the instructions

```
    aad
    div   dh
```

are executed.

Before	After aad	After div
AX: 07 05	AX: 00 4B	AX: 03 09
DH: 08	DH: 08	
AX: 06 02	AX: 00 3E	AX: 02 0F
DH: 04	DH: 04	
AX: 09 03	AX: 00 5D	AX: 01 2E
DH: 02	DH: 02	

In the first example, the quotient and remainder are in BCD format in AL and AH, respectively, following the `div` instruction. However, the second and third examples show that this is not always the case. The remainder is correct in AH because it is a binary remainder following division by a number 9 or smaller. The remainder must be 0 through 8, and for numbers in this range a single byte binary value agrees with the unpacked BCD representation. The quotient in AL is obviously a binary number, not a BCD representation. To convert it to unpacked BCD, an aam instruction needs to follow the div. In the second example, this would change AX to 01 05, the correct quotient for 62 ÷ 4. In the third example, aam would yield 0406 in AX, again the correct quotient. Notice that the remainder from the division is lost, so if it is needed, it must be copied from AH before aam is executed.

Notice that the problems illustrated by the previous examples cannot occur when the original digit in AH is smaller than the divisor in DH. The elementary school algorithm for dividing a single digit into a multidigit number works left to right through the dividend, dividing a two digit number by the divisor. The first of the two digits is the remainder from the previous division, which must be smaller than the divisor. The following design formalizes the grade school algorithm.

{ divide $X_7X_6X_5X_4X_3X_2X_1X_0$ by Y giving $Z_7Z_6Z_5Z_4Z_3Z_2Z_1Z_0$ }
lastRemainder := 0;
for i := 7 downto 0 loop
      dividend := 10*lastRemainder + X_i;
      divide dividend by Y getting quotient & lastRemainder;
      Z_i := quotient;
end for;

Code that implements this design is given in Fig. 11.9. The AH register is ideally suited to store *lastRemainder* since that is where the remainder ends up following division of a 16-bit binary number by an 8-bit number.

▨▨▨ **Exercises 11.3**

1. In each part below, assume that the instructions

   ```
   add    al, bl
   aaa
   ```

   are executed. Give the values in the AX register, carry flag CF, and auxiliary flag AF: (1) after the add and before the aaa and (2) after the aaa.
   (a) AX: 00 05 BL: 02
   (b) AX: 02 06 BL: 03

```
divUnp1    PROC NEAR32
; parameter 1: destination address
; parameter 2: address of 8 byte unpacked BCD number
; parameter 3: word w/ 1-digit BCD number as low-order byte
; author:  R. Detmer    revised:  5/98
           push ebp              ; establish stack frame
           mov  ebp, esp
           push esi              ; save registers
           push edi
           push eax
           push ebx
           push ecx
           mov  edi, [ebp+14]  ; destination address
           mov  esi, [ebp+10]  ; source address
           mov  bx, [ebp+8]    ; divisor
           mov  ah, 0          ; lastRemainder := 0
           mov  ecx, 8         ; count of bytes to process
forDiv:    mov  al, [esi]      ; digit from 8 byte number
           aad                 ; adjust to binary
           div  bl             ; divide by single byte
           mov  [edi], al      ; store quotient
           inc  esi            ; point at next digit of dividend
           inc  edi            ; and at next destination byte
           loop forDiv         ; repeat for all 8 bytes
           pop  ecx            ; restore registers
           pop  ebx
           pop  eax
           pop  edi
           pop  esi
           pop  ebp
           ret  10             ; return, discarding paramters
divUnp1    ENDP
```

Figure 11.9   Division of unpacked BCD numbers

   (c) AX: 03 05 BL: 08

   (d) AX: 00 07 BL: 06

   (e) AX: 00 09 BL: 08

   (f) AX: 02 07 BL: 09

   (g) AX: 04 01 BL: 09

   (h) AX: 00 00 BL: 01

2. Repeat the parts of Exercise 1 for the instructions

```
sub   al, bl
aas
```

3. Both parts of this problem assume the definition

```
value   BYTE   8 DUP(?)
```

   (a) Assume that *value* contains ASCII codes for digits 0 through 9. Write a code fragment to replace these bytes "in place" (without copying bytes to another location) by the corresponding unpacked BCD values.

   (b) Assume that *value* contains an eight-byte-long unpacked BCD value. Write a code fragment to replace these bytes in place by the corresponding ASCII codes for digits 0 through 9.

4. In each part below, assume that the instructions

```
mul   ch
aam
```

   are executed. Give the values in the AX register: (1) after the mul and before the aam and (2) after the aam.

   (a) AL: 05 CH: 02

   (b) AL: 06 CH: 03

   (c) AL: 03 CH: 08

   (d) AL: 07 CH: 06

   (e) AL: 09 CH: 08

   (f) AL: 07 CH: 09

   (g) AL: 04 CH: 09

   (h) AL: 08 CH: 01

5. In each part below, assume that the instructions

    aad
    div   dl
    aam

    are executed. Give the values in the AX register: (1) after the aad and
    before the div, (2) after the div and before the aam, and (3) after the aam.
    (a) AX: 07 05 DL: 08
    (b) AX: 05 06 DL: 09
    (c) AX: 02 07 DL: 08
    (d) AX: 04 07 DL: 06
    (e) AX: 05 09 DL: 06
    (f) AX: 03 07 DL: 07
    (g) AX: 07 04 DL: 03
    (h) AX: 05 00 DL: 04

Programming Exercises 11.3

1. Write a procedure *subUnp* to find the difference of two eight-byte
    unpacked BCD numbers. The procedure will have two parameters: (1)
    the address of *operand1* and *destination* and (2) the address of
    operand2. The value of *operand1* − *operand2* will be stored at *destina-
    tion*. The procedure will set CF to 1 if the source is larger than the desti-
    nation and clear it to 0 otherwise. Other flag values will not be changed.
    The procedure will remove parameters from the stack.

2. Here is one possible variable-length representation for multibyte
    unpacked BCD numbers. An unsigned binary value in the first byte tells
    how many decimal digits are in the number. Then digits are stored right
    to left (low order to high order). For example, the decimal number
    1234567890 could be stored 0A 00 09 08 07 06 05 04 03 02 01. This sys-
    tem allows for decimal numbers up to 255 digits long to be stored.

    Write a procedure *addVar* that adds two unpacked BCD numbers
    stored in this variable length format. The procedure will have two
    parameters: (1) the address of *operand1* and *destination* and (2) the
    address of *operand2*. The value of *operand1* + *operand2* will be stored at
    destination. The two numbers are not necessarily the same length. The

sum may be the same length as the longer operand, or one byte longer. Assume that sufficient space has been reserved in the destination field for the sum, even if *operand1* is the shorter operand. The procedure will remove parameters from the stack.

11.4 Other Architectures: VAX Packed Decimal Instructions

Since the 80x86 architecture provides very limited support for packed decimal operations, a large procedure library is necessary to use packed decimal types. Some other architectures provide extensive hardware support for packed decimal. This section briefly examines packed decimal instructions defined in the VAX architecture, although not necessarily implemented in all VAX machines.

The VAX architecture defines a packed decimal string by its length and starting address. The length gives the number of decimal digits stored in the string, not the number of bytes. The last four bits (half byte) are always a sign indicator, normally C_{16} for positive and D_{16} for negative. Since decimal digits are packed two per byte, the length (in bytes) of a packed decimal string is approximately half the number of digits. More precisely, for n decimal digits it is $(n + 1)/2$ if n is odd and $(n + 2)/2$ if n is even.

The VAX architecture includes a complete set of instructions for performing packed decimal arithmetic: ADDP (add packed), DIVP (divide packed), MULP (multiply packed), and SUBP (subtract packed). Each of these has at least four operands to specify the length and address of each of the packed decimal strings involved. When just two strings are specified, one serves both as a source and the destination. All also have six-operand formats where the sources are specified separately from the destination. (MULP and DIVP have only the six-operand formats.) The MOVP (move packed) instruction copies a packed decimal string from one address to another. The CMPP (compare packed) instruction compares two packed decimal strings, setting condition codes (flags).

Recall the difficulty of converting packed decimal to or from other formats. The VAX architecture provides six different instructions for this purpose. There are functions to convert between packed decimal strings and 32-bit 2's complement integers, and others to convert between packed decimal and numeric strings (including ASCII). There is also an EDIT instruction that converts a packed decimal string to a character string, performing many possible editing operations during the conversions. (Programming Exercises 11.1, #4, describes a similar, but much simpler, editing job.)

The COBOL language directly supports packed decimal types and operations. If you were writing a COBOL compiler for a VAX, then the packed decimal instructions would greatly simplify the job. The resulting compiler would yield much more compact and efficient code than if each packed decimal operation were emulated by a software procedure.

Chapter Summary

Integers may be stored in a computer in binary coded decimal form instead of unsigned or 2's complement binary form. There are two basic BCD systems, packed and unpacked. Packed BCD values store two decimal digits per byte, and unpacked BCD values store a single decimal digit per byte.

Binary representations are much more compact than BCD representations and the 80x86 processor has more instructions for doing arithmetic with binary numbers. However, BCD representations can easily store very large integers and are simple to convert to or from ASCII.

BCD systems may use a variable or a fixed number of bytes and may or may not store a sign indicator. The MASM assembler provides a DT directive that can produce a ten byte signed, packed BCD number. Unpacked BCD numbers can be initialized using BYTE directives.

Arithmetic is done with BCD numbers by combining pairs of bytes from two operands using ordinary binary arithmetic instructions. The binary results are then adjusted to BCD. Packed decimal representations use daa (decimal adjust for addition) and das (decimal adjust for subtraction) instructions. Using these instructions along with binary arithmetic instructions, arithmetic procedures for packed BCD numbers can be developed.

Four instructions are used for unpacked BCD arithmetic: aaa (ASCII adjust for addition), aas (ASCII adjust for subtraction), aam (ASCII adjust for multiplication), and aad (ASCII adjust for division). The aad instruction is different from the others in that it is applied to a BCD result to convert it to binary before applying a div instruction.

Some other architectures provide a much more complete set of packed decimal instructions. In particular, the VAX architecture includes arithmetic, data movement, comparison, and conversion instructions.

CHAPTER 12

Input/Output

Programs in previous chapters have used the *input* macro to input data from the PC console keyboard and the *output* macro to output data to the console display. Input and output from an assembly language program have been limited to the keyboard and the monitor. This chapter examines the underlying operating system calls that are used by the *input* and *output* macros. It then examines similar operating system calls that make it possible to read and write sequential files to secondary storage. Next it looks at the 80x86 instructions that actually do input and output and discusses alternative I/O schemes, including memory-mapped and interrupt-driven I/O.

12.1 Console I/O Using the Kernel32 Library

Figure 12.1 shows a simple example illustrating how kernel32 functions can write a simple message. This example is similar to many of those seen previously in the book in its overall structure. However, it is missing the "standard" directive INCLUDE io.h. In addition to the familiar prototype for the *ExitProcess* function, it contains two new function prototypes. These functions are needed to write to the console.

The Windows 95/98/NT operating systems are similar to many others in that they treat input/output devices and disk files in a uniform manner. Note that in Fig. 12.1, a *WriteFile* call is used to display a message on the console. This same function can be used to write to a disk file. The device or file used for I/O is identified by its *handle*, a doubleword value in an assembly language program. The handle value must be obtained before the *WriteFile* call is made. There is more than one way to do this for a console file; *GetStandardHandle* provides an easy method.

Any *GetStdHandle* call has a single parameter; a numeric value, distinct from the handle, indicates the particular device. There are three standard devices: one for input, one for output, and one to report errors (normally the same as the standard output device). Each device number is usually equated to a symbol, and these symbols are used in code. We will only use the input and output devices; their numbers and names appear in Fig. 12.2. *GetStdHandle* is a function, returning in EAX a handle for the standard I/O device. The handle value is usually stored in memory to be available later. In the sample program, the returned value is immediately copied to the doubleword referenced by *hStdOut*.

With five parameters, a *WriteFile* call is more complicated. The first is the handle that identifies the file—this handle is returned by GetStdHandle, not the device number. The second parameter is the address of the string—note the use of the NEAR32 PTR operator in the example to tell the assembler to use the address of *OldProg* rather than the value stored there. The third parameter is a doubleword containing the number of bytes to be displayed. The next parameter is used to return a value to the calling program. This value indicates how many bytes were actually written. In the case of output to the console, this will be the length of the message unless an error occurs. The fifth and final parameter will always be 0 in this book's examples. It can be used to indicate non-sequential access to some files, but we are going to deal only with sequential access.

Console input is almost as easy as output. Figure 12.3 shows a program that inputs a string of characters, converts each uppercase letter to lowercase, and displays the resulting string.

The new function in this example is *Readfile*. It is very similar to *WriteFile* except that the second parameter has the address of an input buffer, the third parameter

```
; Program to display a simple message
; Author:  R. Detmer
; Date:     6/98

.386
.MODEL FLAT

ExitProcess PROTO NEAR32 stdcall, dwExitCode:DWORD

GetStdHandle PROTO NEAR32 stdcall,
    nStdHandle:DWORD

WriteFile PROTO NEAR32 stdcall,
    hFile:DWORD, lpBuffer:NEAR32, nNumberOfCharsToWrite:DWORD,
    lpNumberOfBytesWritten:NEAR32, lpOverlapped:NEAR32

STD_OUTPUT EQU -11

cr       EQU     0dh     ; carriage return character
Lf       EQU     0ah     ; line feed

.STACK
.DATA

OldProg BYTE    "Old programmers never die.", cr, lf
        BYTE    "They just lose their byte.", cr, lf
msgLng  DWORD   56    ; number of characters in above message
written DWORD   ?
hStdOut DWORD   ?

.CODE
_start:
        INVOKE GetStdHandle,     ; get handle for console output
          STD_OUTPUT
        mov    hStdOut, eax

        INVOKE WriteFile,
          hStdOut,                ; file handle for screen
          NEAR32 PTR OldProg,     ; address of string
          msgLng,                 ; length of string
          NEAR32 PTR written,     ; bytes written
          0                       ; overlapped mode

        INVOKE  ExitProcess, 0 ; exit with return code 0

PUBLIC _start
END
```

Figure 12.1   Console output using kernel32 functions

Mnemonic	Equated Value
STD_INPUT	−10
STD_OUTPUT	−11

Figure 12.2 Standard device numbers

gives the maximum number of characters to read, and the fourth parameter returns the number of characters actually read.

The number of characters read will normally be smaller than the size of the buffer to receive the characters. If it is larger, values in memory following the input buffer may be destroyed. An additional consideration with console input is that carriage return and linefeed characters are added to the characters that you key in. That is, if you type six characters and then press Enter, eight characters will actually be stored in the input buffer—the six characters plus the carriage return and linefeed.

In the program from Fig. 12.3, there is a blank line of output before the line of lowercase characters, which is because of the CR/LF that is in memory before the input buffer. The starting address for output includes these two additional characters and the character count has been increased by two to include these characters. Because the original character count includes the CR/LF at the end of the characters read in, there will also be a skip to a new line after the characters are displayed.

The *input* and *output* macros that you have used in most of this book expand into procedure calls that use the kernel32 console input/output functions. The relevant portion of the file IO.ASM is shown in Fig. 12.4.

```
; Program to input a message and echo it in lowercase
; Author:   R. Detmer
; Date:     6/98

.386
.MODEL FLAT

ExitProcess PROTO NEAR32 stdcall, dwExitCode:DWORD

GetStdHandle PROTO NEAR32 stdcall,
    nStdHandle:DWORD
```
(continued)

Figure 12.3 Console I/O using kernel32 functions

```
ReadFile PROTO NEAR32 stdcall,
    hFile:DWORD, lpBuffer:NEAR32, nNumberOfCharsToRead:DWORD,
    lpNumberOfBytesRead:NEAR32, lpOverlapped:NEAR32

WriteFile PROTO NEAR32 stdcall,
    hFile:DWORD, lpBuffer:NEAR32, nNumberOfCharsToWrite:DWORD,
    lpNumberOfBytesWritten:NEAR32, lpOverlapped:NEAR32

STD_INPUT  EQU -10
STD_OUTPUT EQU -11

.STACK
.DATA

prompt  BYTE    "String to convert? "
CrLf    BYTE    0ah, 0dh
StrIn   BYTE    80 DUP (?)
read    DWORD   ?
written DWORD   ?
hStdIn  DWORD   ?
hStdOut DWORD   ?

.CODE
_start:
        INVOKE GetStdHandle,    ; get handle for console output
          STD_OUTPUT
        mov    hStdOut, eax

        INVOKE WriteFile,
          hStdOut,              ; file handle for screen
          NEAR32 PTR prompt,    ; address of prompt
          19,                   ; length of prompt
          NEAR32 PTR written,   ; bytes written
          0                     ; overlapped mode

        INVOKE GetStdHandle,    ; get handle for console input
          STD_INPUT
        mov    hStdIn, eax

        INVOKE ReadFile,
          hStdIn,               ; file handle for keyboard
          NEAR32 PTR StrIn,     ; address of string
```

(continued)

Figure 12.3 *(continued)*

```
            80,                     ; maximum number to read
            NEAR32 PTR read,        ; bytes read
            0                       ; overlapped mode

        mov    ecx, read           ; set up loop to convert
        lea    ebx, StrIn          ; starting address
forCh:  cmp    BYTE PTR [ebx], 'A'  ; char < 'A' ?
        jl     endIfUpper          ; skip if so
        cmp    BYTE PTR [ebx], 'Z'  ; char > 'Z' ?
        jg     endIfUpper          ; skip if so
        add    BYTE PTR [ebx], 'a' - 'A'  ; convert to lower
endIfUpper:
        inc    ebx                 ; point at next character
        loop   forCh               ; repeat

        mov    ecx, read           ; get length to write
        add    ecx, 2              ; for leading CR and LF

        INVOKE WriteFile,
           hStdOut,                ; file handle for screen
           NEAR32 PTR crLf,        ; start with
           ecx,                    ; length of output
           NEAR32 PTR written,     ; bytes written
           0                       ; overlapped mode

        INVOKE  ExitProcess, 0  ; exit with return code 0

PUBLIC _start
END
```

Figure 12.3   (continued)

```
STD_OUTPUT EQU -11
STD_INPUT  EQU -10

GetStdHandle PROTO NEAR32 stdcall,
    nStdHandle:DWORD

ReadFile PROTO NEAR32 stdcall,
    hFile:DWORD, lpBuffer:NEAR32, nNumberOfCharsToRead:DWORD,
    lpNumberOfBytesRead:NEAR32, lpOverlapped:NEAR32

WriteFile PROTO NEAR32 stdcall,
    hFile:DWORD, lpBuffer:NEAR32, nNumberOfCharsToWrite:DWORD,
    lpNumberOfBytesWritten:NEAR32, lpOverlapped:NEAR32

.DATA

written    DWORD   ?
read       DWORD   ?
strAddr    DWORD   ?
strLength  DWORD   ?
hStdOut    DWORD   ?
hStdIn     DWORD   ?

.CODE

; outproc(source)
; Procedure to display null-terminated string
; No registers are changed; flags are not affected.

outproc     PROC    NEAR32
            push    ebp                 ; save base pointer
            mov     ebp, esp            ; establish stack frame
            pushad
            pushfd                      ; save flags

            mov     esi,[ebp+8]         ; source address
            mov     strAddr, esi

; find string length
            mov     strLength, 0        ; initialize string length
WhileChar:  cmp     BYTE PTR [esi], 0   ; character = null?
            jz      EndWhileChar        ; exit if so
```

(continued)

Figure 12.4 Input/output procedures in IO.ASM

```
                inc     strLength           ; increment character count
                inc     esi                 ; point at next character
                jmp     WhileChar
EndWhileChar:

                INVOKE GetStdHandle,         ; get handle for console output
                  STD_OUTPUT
                mov     hStdOut, eax

                INVOKE WriteFile,
                  hStdOut,                   ; file handle for screen
                  strAddr,                   ; address of string
                  strLength,                 ; length of string
                  NEAR32 PTR written,        ; bytes written
                  0                          ; overlapped mode

                popfd                        ; restore flags
                popad                        ; restore registers
                pop     ebp
                ret     4                    ;exit, discarding parameter
outproc     ENDP

; inproc(dest,length)
; Procedure to input a string from keyboard.
; The string will be stored at the address given by dest.
; The length parameter gives the size of the user's buffer.  It is
; assumed that there will be room for the string and a null byte.
; The string will be terminated by a null character (00h).
; Flags are unchanged.

inproc      PROC    NEAR32
            push    ebp                      ; save base pointer
            mov     ebp, esp                 ; establish stack frame
            pushad                           ; save all registers
            pushfd                           ; save flags

            INVOKE GetStdHandle,             ; get handle for console
              STD_INPUT
            mov     hStdIn, eax
```

(continued)

Figure 12.4   *(continued)*

```
            mov    ecx, [ebp+8]          ; string length
            mov    strLength, ecx

            mov    esi, [ebp+12]         ; source address
            mov    strAddr, esi

            INVOKE ReadFile,
              hStdIn,                    ; file handle for keyboard
              strAddr,                   ; address of string
              strLength,                 ; length of string
              NEAR32 PTR read,           ; bytes read
              0                          ; overlapped mode

            mov    ecx, read             ; number of bytes read
            mov    BYTE PTR [esi+ecx-2],0 ; replace CR/LF by trailing null

            popfd                        ; restore flags
            popad                        ; restore registers
            pop    ebp
            ret    8                     ; exit, discarding parameters
inproc      ENDP
```

Figure 12.4 *(continued)*

At this point there is nothing surprising in the input/output code in IO.ASM. It starts with the same directives that appeared in the previous two examples. The data area does not include an input buffer since this will be in the user's calling program. It does have the variable *strAddr* to locally store the input or output buffer address that is passed as a parameter. The output procedure *outproc* expects this to be the address of a null-terminated string. After standard procedure entry code, it computes the length of that string. It then gets the handle for the console and writes to the console, exactly as in the earlier example in Fig. 12.1.

The input procedure *inproc* is also simple. After standard procedure entry code, it gets the handle for the console and copies the two parameters (length and string address) to local variables. A *ReadFile* call does the actual input. The only complication is that the *inproc* procedure promises a null-terminated string, and the string read by *ReadFile* is terminated by the CR/LF. The code

```
mov     ecx, read
mov     BYTE PTR [esi+ecx-2],0
```

places a null byte at the end of the string, actually replacing the carriage return character by a null. It works because the starting address of the string is in ESI, so that when the character count is put in ECX, ESI+ECX–2 points to the address of the next-to-last character in the input buffer.

This is an appropriate time to repeat the warning from Section 6.1: some Microsoft operating system functions may require that the stack be doubleword-aligned. When these functions are used in procedures, you must only push doubleword values onto the stack. This is, for instance, why the code in Fig. 12.4 contains a `pushfd` instruction even though a `pushf` would save all the flag values that are meaningful to most programs.

Programming Exercises 12.1

1. Using only functions from kernel32—and without using the book's I/O package—write a program that will prompt for and input a name from the console in the form *last, first* (that is, last name, comma, first name) and display it with an appropriate label in the format *first last* (that is, first name, space, last name).

2. Using only functions from kernel32—and without using the book's I/O package—write a program that will prompt for and input a phrase from the console and will report whether or not it is a palindrome (that is, exactly the same string when reversed).

12.2 Sequential File I/O Using the Kernel32 Library

File processing applications generally involve opening the file, reading from or writing to the file, and finally closing the file. At the level of the kernel32 library, opening the file means to obtain a handle for it. Closing the file that has been read may be important to free it up for access by another user. Closing a file that has been written may be necessary to force the operating systems to save the final characters. In this section we investigate how to do some of these operations for sequential disk files. File operations like these are usually more appropriately done using a high-level language, so the primary purpose of this section is to give you a sense of what is "under the hood" of a high-level language.

Figure 12.5 shows a program that prompts for inputs the name of a file and then displays the contents of the file on the console. It includes two new kernel32 function prototypes, *CreateFileA* and *CloseHandle*. In spite of its name, *CreateFileA* is used both to open an existing file or to create a new file. *CloseHandle* is used to close a file.

```
; Read sequential file and display on console
; Author:  R. Detmer
; Date:  6/98

.386
.MODEL FLAT

ExitProcess PROTO NEAR32 stdcall, dwExitCode:DWORD

STD_OUTPUT     EQU  -11
STD_INPUT      EQU  -10
GENERIC_READ   EQU  80000000h
OPEN_EXISTING EQU  3

GetStdHandle PROTO NEAR32 stdcall,
    nStdHandle:DWORD

ReadFile PROTO NEAR32 stdcall,
    hFile:DWORD, lpBuffer:NEAR32, nNumberOfCharsToRead:DWORD,
    lpNumberOfBytesRead:NEAR32, lpOverlapped:NEAR32

WriteFile PROTO NEAR32 stdcall,
    hFile:DWORD, lpBuffer:NEAR32, nNumberOfCharsToWrite:DWORD,
    lpNumberOfBytesWritten:NEAR32, lpOverlapped:NEAR32

CreateFileA PROTO NEAR32 stdcall,
    lpFileName:NEAR32, access:DWORD, shareMode:DWORD,
    lpSecurity:NEAR32, creation:DWORD, attributes:DWORD, copyHandle:DWORD

CloseHandle PROTO NEAR32 stdcall,
    fHandle:DWORD

.DATA
```

(continued)

Figure 12.5 Sequential file input using kernel32 functions

```
written     DWORD   ?
read        DWORD   ?
fileName    BYTE    60 DUP (?)
hStdOut     DWORD   ?
hStdIn      DWORD   ?
hFile       DWORD   ?
buffer      BYTE    64 DUP (?)
prompt      BYTE    "File name?  "

.CODE
_start:
            INVOKE GetStdHandle,        ; handle for console output
              STD_OUTPUT
            mov    hStdOut, eax

            INVOKE GetStdHandle,        ; handle for console input
              STD_INPUT
            mov    hStdIn, eax

            INVOKE WriteFile,
              hStdOut,                  ; file handle for screen
              NEAR32 PTR prompt,        ; address of prompt
              12,                       ; length of prmpt
              NEAR32 PTR written,       ; bytes written
              0                         ; overlapped mode

            INVOKE ReadFile,
              hStdIn,                   ; file handle for keyboard
              NEAR32 PTR fileName,      ; address for name
              60,                       ; maximum length
              NEAR32 PTR read,          ; bytes read
              0                         ; overlapped mode

            mov    ecx, read            ; number of bytes read
            mov    BYTE PTR fileName[ecx-2],0 ; add trailing null

            INVOKE CreateFileA,         ; open file
              NEAR32 PTR fileName,      ; file name
              GENERIC_READ,             ; access
              0,                        ; no sharing
              0,                        ; no predefined security
              OPEN_EXISTING,            ; open only if file exists
```

(continued)

Figure 12.5 *(continued)*

```
                0,                          ; no special attributes
                0                           ; no copied handle
        mov     hFile, eax                  ; handle for file

readLoop:   INVOKE ReadFile,
            hFile,                          ; file handle
            NEAR32 PTR buffer,              ; address for input
            64,                             ; buffer length
            NEAR32 PTR read,                ; bytes read
            0                               ; overlapped mode

        INVOKE WriteFile,
            hStdOut,                        ; file handle for screen
            NEAR32 PTR buffer,              ; address for output
            read,                           ; write same number as read
            NEAR32 PTR written,             ; bytes written
            0                               ; overlapped mode

        cmp     read, 64                    ; were 64 characters read?
        jnl     readLoop                    ; continue if so

        INVOKE  CloseHandle,                ; close file handle
            hfile

        INVOKE  ExitProcess, 0              ; exit with return code 0
PUBLIC _start                               ; make entry point public
END                                         ; end of source code
```

Figure 12.5   *(continued)*

CreateFileA returns the handle of a file that it opens or creates, or returns −1 (FFFFFFFF$_{16}$) if the operation fails. It has seven parameters

1. The address of a null-terminated string giving the name of the file

2. A doubleword giving the desired access. We will only use GENERIC_READ (80000000$_{16}$) and GENERIC_WRITE (40000000$_{16}$).

3. A doubleword indicating how the file can be shared. We will use 0 to indicate that it cannot be shared.

4. This parameter is used to indicate whether this file can be used by child processes. We will use 0 to indicate that it cannot.

5. A doubleword containing flags indicating what to do if the file does not exist. We will use OPEN_EXISTING (3) when opening an existing file; the *CreateFileA* function will fail if the file does not exist. We will use CRE-ATE_NEW (1) when creating a new file; the *CreateFileA* function will fail if the file already exists. In other applications, CREATE_ALWAYS (2) may be appropriate; this creates a new file if one does not exist and over-writes an existing file if it does exist.

6. This parameter is used to set various file attributes. We will use a value of 0 to indicate no special attributes.

7. The final parameter can be used to indicate the handle of a template file whose attributes will be used for the newly created file. We will always use 0 to indicate no template.

As we will use *CreateFileA*, we will specify parameters 1, 2 and 5, and supply zeros for the other four.

The *CloseHandle* function is very simple. It has a single parameter, the handle of the file to be closed.

The main read loop in Fig. 12.5 uses *ReadFile* to read 64 characters at a time from the source file. End of file is detected by comparing the number of characters actually read to 64. If it is smaller, then the end of the file has been reached. However, note that the characters read are displayed first, so that you don't lose the last partial buffer.

In this example, there is nothing special about the number 64 except that it is a power of two. Most operating systems maintain their own buffers for disk file access, and since the size of such a buffer is almost always a power of two, it makes sense to have the program's buffer a size that is comparable.

Figure 12.6 shows a program that will create a disk file from console input. It first prompts for and inputs the name of the file. It creates that file, fails if it already exists, and copies lines from the console keyboard to the file until the user begins a line with %%, a character combination chosen to be unlikely to appear at the beginning of a line in ordinary text.

There is very little new in this example. The call to *CreateFileA* uses GENERIC_WRITE and CREATE_NEW for creation of a new file. The main loop reads a string of up to 128 characters from the keyboard and writes the string to the file. Loop control is accomplished by checking the first two characters of the string before writing it to the file.

```
; Create sequential file from console input
; Author:  R. Detmer
; Date:  6/98

.386
.MODEL FLAT

ExitProcess PROTO NEAR32 stdcall, dwExitCode:DWORD

STD_OUTPUT    EQU  -11
STD_INPUT     EQU  -10
GENERIC_WRITE EQU  40000000h
CREATE_NEW    EQU  1

GetStdHandle PROTO NEAR32 stdcall,
    nStdHandle:DWORD

ReadFile PROTO NEAR32 stdcall,
    hFile:DWORD, lpBuffer:NEAR32, nNumberOfCharsToRead:DWORD,
    lpNumberOfBytesRead:NEAR32, lpOverlapped:NEAR32

WriteFile PROTO NEAR32 stdcall,
    hFile:DWORD, lpBuffer:NEAR32, nNumberOfCharsToWrite:DWORD,
    lpNumberOfBytesWritten:NEAR32, lpOverlapped:NEAR32

CreateFileA PROTO NEAR32 stdcall,
    lpFileName:NEAR32, access:DWORD, shareMode:DWORD,
    lpSecurity:NEAR32, creation:DWORD, attributes:DWORD,
copyHandle:DWORD

CloseHandle PROTO NEAR32 stdcall,
    fHandle:DWORD

.DATA

written      DWORD   ?
read         DWORD   ?
fileName     BYTE    60 DUP (?)
hStdOut      DWORD   ?
hStdIn       DWORD   ?
```

(continued)

Figure 12.6   Create a file from console input

```
hFile      DWORD  ?
buffer     BYTE   128 DUP (?)
prompt1    BYTE   "File name?  "
prompt2    BYTE   "Enter text.  Start a line with %% to stop", 0dh, 0ah

.CODE
_start:
        INVOKE GetStdHandle,        ; handle for console output
          STD_OUTPUT
        mov    hStdOut, eax

        INVOKE GetStdHandle,        ; handle for console input
          STD_INPUT
        mov    hStdIn, eax

        INVOKE WriteFile,
          hStdOut,                  ; file handle for screen
          NEAR32 PTR prompt1,       ; address of prompt
          12,                       ; length of prompt
          NEAR32 PTR written,       ; bytes written
          0                         ; overlapped mode

        INVOKE ReadFile,
          hStdIn,                   ; file handle for keyboard
          NEAR32 PTR fileName,      ; address for name
          60,                       ; maximum length
          NEAR32 PTR read,          ; bytes read
          0                         ; overlapped mode

        mov    ecx, read            ; number of bytes read
        mov    BYTE PTR fileName[ecx-2],0 ; add trailing null

        INVOKE CreateFileA,         ; open file
          NEAR32 PTR fileName,      ; file name
          GENERIC_WRITE,            ; access
          0,                        ; no sharing
          0,                        ; no predefined security
          CREATE_NEW,               ; open if file doesn't exist
          0,                        ; no special attributes
          0                         ; no copied handle
        mov    hFile, eax           ; handle for file
```

(continued)

Figure 12.6 *(continued)*

```
            INVOKE  WriteFile,
               hStdOut,               ; file handle for screen
               NEAR32 PTR prompt2,    ; address of prompt
               43,                    ; length of prompt
               NEAR32 PTR written,    ; bytes written
               0                      ; overlapped mode

readLoop:   INVOKE  ReadFile,
               hStdIn,                ; read from console
               NEAR32 PTR buffer,     ; address for input
               128,                   ; buffer length
               NEAR32 PTR read,       ; bytes read
               0                      ; overlapped mode

            cmp     buffer, "%"        ; first character %?
            jne     continue           ; continue if not
            cmp     buffer+1, "%"      ; second character %?
            je      endRead            ; quit if so
continue:
            INVOKE  WriteFile,
               hfile,                 ; file handle
               NEAR32 PTR buffer,     ; address for output
               read,                  ; write same number as read
               NEAR32 PTR written,    ; bytes written
               0                      ; overlapped mode

            jmp     readLoop           ; continue if so
endRead:

            INVOKE  CloseHandle,       ; close file handle
               hfile

            INVOKE  ExitProcess, 0     ; exit with return code 0

PUBLIC  _start                         ; make entry point public
END                                    ; end of source code
```

Figure 12.6 *(continued)*

Exercises 12.2

1. The examples in this section do not check to be sure that the file open
   is successful. Why does the code in Fig. 12.5 "work" even if the file is
   not successfully opened? How do you modify the code in Fig. 12.5 to
   display a warning message and exit if the file is not opened?

2. The examples in this section do not check to be sure that the file open is successful. What happens when you run the program in Fig. 12.6, specifying an output file that already exists? How do you modify the code in Fig. 12.6 to display a warning message and exit if the file is not opened?

Programming Exercises 12.2

1. A file dump program displays each byte of a file as a two-character hexadecimal code and the corresponding printable character, if any. Using only the kernel32 library (not IO.ASM), write a file dump program that will input the name of a file and then dump it to the console display using the following format:

Show 16 characters per line, first in hex with a space after each hex pair so that this takes a total of 48 positions, then as ordinary characters, substituting a period for a nonprintable character, with no spaces between. A typical line will look like

```
50 72 6F 67 72 61 6D 6D 69 6E 67 20 0D 0A 69 73  Programming ..is
```

After 20 lines are displayed on the console, prompt the user with "m[ore] or q[uit]?" and either continue with the next 20 lines or exit the program based on the response.

2. Write a program to copy a source file to a destination file. Specifically, the program must prompt for the source file name, attempt to open the source file and exit with an error message if it cannot do so. If the source file is opened successfully, then the user will be prompted for the destination file name. If the destination file exists, which can be determined by attempting to open it with CREATE_NEW, the user should be asked if the old file is to be destroyed with CREATE_ALWAYS, and the program should terminate if the answer is negative. If the destination file does not exist, no warning is needed before making the file copy. Use only input/output functions from the kernel32 library, not macros from IO.H.

3. Write a program that will copy a source file to a destination file, changing all uppercase letters to lowercase letters, leaving other characters unchanged. The program must prompt for both file names. It is not necessary to warn the user if the destination file exists before wiping it out with the copy. Use only input/output functions from the kernel32 library, not macros from IO.H.

4. Write a program that will process a collection of fixed format records from the file RECORDS.DAT. Each line of the file will consist of ASCII data with

   - a person's name in columns 1–20
   - an integer right-justified in columns 21–25

   Each line of the file will be terminated by a carriage return and a line-feed character so that the total line length is 27 characters. Such a file can be produced by a standard text editor. The program must echo the lines of data and then report

   - the number of records
   - the sum of the numbers
   - the person with the largest number

   Use only input/output functions from the kernel32 library, not macros from IO.H. The *atod* and *dtoa* macros from IO.H may be used.

12.3 Lower-Level Input/Output

Earlier in this book input and output have been done using macros in IO.H. In this chapter, input and output have been done using function calls from the kernel32 library, a somewhat lower-level approach. You have probably also done higher-level I/O using high-level programming languages. This section discusses I/O at a level lower than that offered by the kernel32 library, covering the Intel 80x86 and other architectures. Since low-level I/O is increasingly restricted to the operating system, this section does not show actual code.

As discussed in Chapter 2, the Intel 80x86 architecture has memory addresses from 00000000_{16} to $FFFFFFFF_{16}$. It also has a separate I/O address space, with **port** addresses ranging from 0000_{16} to $FFFF_{16}$. Memory addresses have been used by many of the instructions covered in this book. However, port addresses are used by only a few instructions, the most common of which are the in and out instructions that move data from the addressed port to or from the accumulator (e.g., AL, AX, or EAX). In this sense, they are like limited mov instructions.

In an IBM-compatible PC, common I/O devices normally have standard port assignments. For example, the parallel printer port known as LPT1 uses three port addresses: 0378, 0379, and 037A. The first of these ports is used to send characters to a printer, the second to determine its status, and the third to send control information to the printer. Serial ports are usually controlled by a serial input/output (SIO) chip, which will also require several port addresses.

One of the options in the 80x86 architecture is to use **memory-mapped I/O**. With memory-mapped I/O, some of the ordinary memory addresses are assigned for input/output purposes and regular data movement instructions are used to transfer data to or from external devices. The hardware designer chooses whether to use memory-mapped I/O or the separate I/O address space when building the system. Other architectures, for example the Motorola 680x0 designs, use only memory-mapped I/O.

Regardless of how I/O devices are addressed, there is the separate issue of how to know when the device has a character ready for the program, or conversely, how to ensure that the device is ready to receive a character from the program. We will look at the situation of sending a character to an old-fashioned, slow, mechanical printer. Obviously the computer can generate characters to be printed much more rapidly than the printer can print them. One technique is to use **polling**—that is, the program repeatedly checks a status port on the device until it gets a report that the device is able to accept a character, then it transmits the character. The design looks like

```
forever
        get status from status port;
        if clear to send character, then exit loop;
end loop;
transmit character to data port;
```

The loop in this design is called a **busy-waiting loop** for obvious reasons. Unless the computer is otherwise set up for multitasking, it can do no useful work while waiting for the device to accept the character.

Interrupt-driven I/O relies on hardware interrupts to inform the CPU of a device's change in status. An **interrupt** is a hardware signal generated by the device and received by the CPU. When the CPU receives such a signal, it normally finishes executing the current instruction, and then transfers control to an **interrupt procedure**. This is very similar to a regular procedure call.

An Intel 80x86 system provides for up to 256 different interrupts. The address for an interrupt procedure comes from a table of addresses in the very bottom of memory. Memory locations 0 to 1024_{10} contain 256 addresses corresponding to interrupt levels 0 through 255. In general, for interrupt type t, the interrupt procedure's address is stored at address $4*t$.

A computer system may be designed to generate an interrupt when a key on the keyboard is pressed. The associated interrupt procedure would capture the character and store it in a buffer for later processing before returning, allowing the computer to go back to whatever it was doing.

The 80x86 architecture includes an `int` instruction that enables a program to invoke an interrupt procedure. Not all interrupt types are used by hardware devices, and some operating systems, notably Microsoft DOS, use `int` instructions to call operating system functions.

80x86 interrupts 0 and 4 are always preassigned. Interrupt type 0 is automatically called by the 80x86 CPU when division by zero is attempted. A simple program containing the instruction `int  0` also calls the divide by zero interrupt handler, showing how a particular 80x86 system is set up to handle division errors without actually doing a division.

The handler for interrupt type 4 also has an assigned purpose, namely to handle overflow conditions that result from instructions. This interrupt handler is not called automatically by the 80x86. It can be called using `int  4` but is more commonly invoked by the `into` (interrupt on overflow) instruction. This is a conditional call: The overflow interrupt handler is called if the overflow flag OF is set, but otherwise execution continues with the next instruction. Typically an `into` instruction would follow an instruction that might cause overflow to occur.

Exercises 12.3

1. What are the advantages of memory-mapped I/O? What are the advantages of using a separate address space for I/O?

2. What address contains the interrupt procedure address for interrupt 15_{10} in an 80x86 system?

Chapter Summary

Input and output can be done at many levels, from high-level language procedures down to `in` and `out` instructions. The kernel32 library illustrates the operating-system level example of I/O. This library has functions for getting a file or device handle, reading from a file or device, writing to a file or device, and releasing the file or device.

At the hardware level, I/O may either use separate port addresses for external devices or it may use memory-mapped I/O, with a portion of the regular memory space assigned to external devices rather than memory.

Devices may be accessed by polling or—more efficiently—by using interrupt-driven I/O. The 80x86 architecture provides for up to 256 different interrupts, although these are often assigned other uses than servicing I/O requests.

APPENDIX A

Hexadecimal/ASCII conversion

00	NUL	(null)	20	space	
01	SOH		21	!	
02	STX		22	"	
03	ETX		23	#	
04	EOT		24	$	
05	ENQ		25	%	
06	ACK		26	&	
07	BEL	(bell)	27	'	
08	BS	(backspace)	28	(	
09	HT	(tab)	29	)	
0A	LF	(line feed)	2A	*	
0B	VT		2B	+	
0C	FF	(form feed)	2C	,	
0D	CR	(return)	2D	-	
0E	SO		2E	.	
0F	SI		2F	/	
10	DLE		30	0	
11	DC1		31	1	
12	DC2		32	2	
13	DC3		33	3	
14	DC4		34	4	
15	NAK		35	5	
16	SYN		36	6	
17	ETB		37	7	
18	CAN		38	8	
19	EM		39	9	
1A	SUB		3A	:	
1B	ESC	("escape")	3B	;	
1C	FS		3C	<	
1D	GS		3D	=	
1E	RS		3E	>	
1F	US		3F	?	

40	@		60	`
41	A		61	a
42	B		62	b
43	C		63	c
44	D		64	d
45	E		65	e
46	F		66	f
47	G		67	g
48	H		68	h
49	I		69	i
4A	J		6A	j
4B	K		6B	k
4C	L		6C	l
4D	M		6D	m
4E	N		6E	n
4F	O		6F	o
50	P		70	p
51	Q		71	q
52	R		72	r
53	S		73	s
54	T		74	t
55	U		75	u
56	V		76	v
57	W		77	w
58	X		78	x
59	Y		79	y
5A	Z		7A	z
5B	[		7B	{
5C	\		7C	|
5D	]		7D	}
5E	^		7E	~
5F	_		7F	DEL

Useful MS-DOS Commands

MS-DOS (and Windows) uses a hierarchical file structure like Unix. In MS-DOS files are identified by a drive (C:, A:, etc.), followed by a path that identifies directories (folders) and finally a file name itself. An example of a complete file name is A:\asm\project1\example.asm. The symbol \ is used as the separator between path components and as the name of the root (top-level) directory. Most MS-DOS systems are set up to display the current drive and path as part of the prompt (e.g., C:\WINDOWS>).

Default refers to the drive or directory that is used if you don't specify a drive or directory in a path. To change the default (current) drive, simply type the new drive letter and a colon.

To change the default (current) directory, use the CD command. The symbol .. is shorthand for the parent of the current directory. For example, if the current directory is \WINDOWS\Desktop, then CD .. will change the current directory to \WINDOWS. (Note: MS-DOS is not case-sensitive – cd works just as well.)

The MD command creates a new directory. To create a new directory in the current directory, use MD *directoryName*.

The DIR command displays a directory of files in the current folder. Alternatively, you can give the path of the directory in which you want, like DIR C:\projects. You can use * as a wildcard character. For example DIR s*.* finds all file names beginning with the letter s.

The COPY command copies a file from one directory to another. The format is COPY *source destination*. If you don't specify a name for the destination file, then the name of the original file will be used. You can use the COPY command to create a duplicate of a file in the same directory, but with a different name. The COPY command allows use of the wildcard character * to copy a group of files.

The EDIT command is used to create or modify a text file. EDIT *filename* invokes a simple text editor opening filename if it exists or creating it if it doesn't. EDIT has its own help system with more information than you need about this editor.

The REN command is used to rename files. Its format is REN *oldName newName*.

The DOSKEY command loads an extension to the command processor that allows you to use the up-arrow key to recall a previous command, which then can be executed again or edited.

You can get more information about most commands by typing *command* /?

Note: Just because you are doing some work in MS-DOS doesn't mean that you can't use other Windows tools. It is fine to use My Computer or Explorer to create directories, copy files, rename files, etc. You can use Notepad to edit files, but be careful since Notepad likes to put a TXT extension on every file name. (You can end up with crazy names like program.asm.txt.) In general you should avoid using a word processor to edit text files such as assembly language source code files.

MASM 6.11 Reserved Words

AAA	BTR	COMM	DUP
AAD	BTS	COMMENT	DWORD
AAM	BX	COMMON	DX
AAS	BYTE	CONST	EAX
ABS	CALL	.CONTINUE	EBP
ADC	CARRY?	@Cpu	EBX
ADD	CASEMAP	.CREF	ECHO
AH	CATSTR	CS	ECX
AL	@CatStr	@CurSeg	EDI
ALIGN	CBW	CWD	EDX
.ALPHA	CDQ	CWDE	ELSE
AND	CH	CX	ELSEIF
AND	CL	DAA	ELSEIFDIF
ARPL	CLC	DAS	ELSEIFIDN
ASSUME	CLD	.DATA	EMULATOR
AT	CLI	@data	END
AX	CLTS	.DATA?	ENDIF
BH	CMC	@DataSize	.ENDIF
BL	CMP	@Date	ENDM
BOUND	CMPS	DEC	ENDP
BP	CMPSB	DH	ENDS
.BREAK	CMPSD	DI	ENDW
BSF	CMPSW	DIV	ENTER
BSR	CMPXCHG	DL	@Environment
BSWAP	.CODE	.DOSSEG	EPILOGUE
BT	@code	DOTNAME	EQ
BTC	@CodeSize	DS	EQU

ERR	FDECSTP	FMULP	FSTENVD
.ERRB	FDISI	FNCLEX	FSTENVW
ERRDEF	FDIV	FNDISI	FSTP
.ERRDIF	FDIVP	FNENI	FSTSW
.ERRE	FDIVR	FNINIT	FSUB
.ERRIDN	FDIVRP	FNOP	FSUBP
.ERRNB	FENI	FNSAVE	FSUBR
ERRNDEF	FFREE	FNSAVED	FSUBRP
.ERRNZ	FIADD	FNSAVEW	FTST
ESI	FICOM	FNSTCW	FUCOM
ES	FICOMP	FNSTENV	FUCOMP
ESP	FIDIV	FNSTENVD	FUCOMPP
EVEN	FIDIVR	FNSTENVW	FWAIT
.EXIT	FILD	FNSTSW	FWORD
EXITM	@FileCur	FOR	FXAM
EXPORT	@FileName	FORC	FXCH
EXPR16	FIMUL	FORCEFRAME	FXTRACT
EXPR32	FINCSTP	FPATAN	FYL2X
EXTERN	FINIT	FPREM	FYL2XP1
EXTERNDEF	FIST	FPREM1	GE
@F	FISTP	FPTAN	GOTO
F2XM1	FISUB	FRNDINT	GROUP
FABS	FISUBR	FRSTOR	GS
FADD	FLAT	FRSTORD	GT
FADDP	FLD	FRSTORW	HIGH
FARDATA	FLD1	FS	HIGHWORD
@fardata	FLDCW	FSAVE	HLT
FARDATA?	FLDENV	FSAVED	IDIV
@fardata?	FLDENVD	FSAVEW	IF
FBLD	FLDENVW	FSCALE	.IF
FBSTP	FLDL2E	FSETPM	IFB
FCHS	FLDL2T	FSIN	IFDEF
FCLEX	FLDLG2	FSINCOS	IFDIF
FCOM	FLDLN2	FSQRT	IFDIFI
FCOMP	FLDPI	FST	IFE
FCOMPP	FLDZ	FSTCW	IFIDN
FCOS	FMUL	FSTENV	IFIDNI

IFNB	JNC	LLDT	.NOCREF
IFNDEF	JNE	LMSW	NODOTNAME
IMUL	JNG	LOADDS	NOKEYWORD
IN	JNGE	LOCAL	.NOLIST
INC	JNL	LOCK	.NOLISTIF
INCLUDE	JNLE	LODS	.NOLISTMACRO
INCLUDELIB	JNO	LODSB	NOLJMP
INS	JNP	LODSD	NOM510
INSB	JNS	LODSW	NOP
INSD	JNZ	LOOP	NOREADONLY
INSTR	JO	LOOPD	NOSCOPED
@InStr	JP	LOOPW	NOSIGNEXTEND
INSW	JPE	LOW	NOT
INT	JPO	LOWWORD	OFFSET
INTO	JS	LROFFSET	OPTION
INVD	JZ	LSL	OR
INVLPG	LABEL	LSS	ORG
INVOKE	LAHF	LT	OUT
IRET	LANGUAGE	LTR	OUTS
IRETD	LAR	M510	OUTSB
JA	LDS	MACRO	OUTSD
JAE	LE	MASK	OUTSW
JB	LEA	MEMORY	OVERFLOW?
JBE	LEAVE	MOD	PAGE
JC	LENGTHOF	.MODEL	PARA
JCXZ	LES	@Model	PARITY?
JE	LFS	MOV	POP
JECXZ	LGDT	MOVS	POPA
JG	LGS	MOVSB	POPAD
JGE	LIDT	MOVSD	POPCONTEXT
JL	@Line	MOVSW	POPF
JLE	.LIST	MOVSX	POPFD
JMP	.LISTALL	MOVZX	PRIVATE
JNA	.LISTIF	MUL	PROC
JNAE	.LISTMACRO	NE	PROLOGUE
JNB	.LISTMACROALL	NEG	PROTO
JNBE	LJMP	.NO87	PTR

PUBLIC	ROL	SIGN?	TEST
PURGE	ROR	SIZEOF	TEXTEQU
PUSH	SAHF	SIZESTR	.TFCOND
PUSHA	SAL	@SizeStr	THIS
PUSHAD	SAR	SLDT	@Time
PUSHCONTEXT	SBB	SMSW	TITLE
PUSHD	SBYTE	SP	TYPE
PUSHF	SCAS	SS	TYPEDEF
PUSHFD	SCASB	.STACK	UNION
PUSHW	SCASD	@stack	.UNTIL
QWORD	SCASW	.STARTUP	USE16
.RADIX	SCOPED	STC	USE32
RCL	SDWORD	STD	USES
RCR	SEG	STDCALL	VERR
READONLY	SEGMENT	STI	@Version
REAL10	.SEQ	STOS	VERW
REAL4	SET	STOSB	WAIT
REAL8	.SETIF2	STOSD	WBINVD
RECORD	SGDT	STOSW	WHILE
REP	SHL	STR	.WHILE
REPE	SHL	STRUCT	WIDTH
REPEAT	SHLD	SUB	WORD
REPNE	SHORT	SUBSTR	@WordSize
REPNZ	SHR	@SubStr	XADD
REPZ	SHR	SUBTITLE	XCHG
RET	SHRD	SWORD	XLAT
RETF	SI	SYSCALL	XOR
RETN	SIDT	TBYTE	ZERO?

80x86 Instructions (by Mnemonic)

Mnemonic	Operand(s)	Flags affected	Opcode	Number of Bytes	Timing 386	Timing 486	Timing Pentium
aaa	none	AF,CF SF,ZF,OF,PF ?	37	1	4	3	3
aad	none	SF,ZF,PF OF,AF,CF ?	D5 0A	2	19	14	10
aam	none	SF,ZF,PF OF,AF,CF ?	D4 0A	2	17	15	18
aas	none	AF,CF SF,ZF,OF,PF ?	3F	1	4	3	3
adc	AL,imm8	SF,ZF,OF,CF,PF,AF	14	2	2	1	1
adc	AX,imm16 EAX,imm32	SF,ZF,OF,CF,PF,AF	15	3 5	2	1	1
adc	reg8,imm8	SF,ZF,OF,CF,PF,AF	80	3	2	1	1
adc	reg16,imm16 reg32,imm32	SF,ZF,OF,CF,PF,AF	81	4 6	2	1	1
adc	reg16,imm8 reg32,imm8	SF,ZF,OF,CF,PF,AF	83	3	2	1	1
adc	mem8,imm8	SF,ZF,OF,CF,PF,AF	80	3+	7	3	3
adc	mem16,imm16 mem32,imm32	SF,ZF,OF,CF,PF,AF	81	4+ 6+	7	3	3
adc	mem16,imm8 mem32,imm8	SF,ZF,OF,CF,PF,AF	83	3+	7	3	3

Mnemonic	Operand(s)	Flags affected	Opcode	Number of Bytes	Timing 386	Timing 486	Timing Pentium
adc	reg8,reg8	SF,ZF,OF,CF,PF,AF	12	2	2	1	1
adc	reg16,reg16 reg32,reg32	SF,ZF,OF,CF,PF,AF	13	2	2	1	1
adc	reg8,mem8	SF,ZF,OF,CF,PF,AF	12	2+	6	2	2
adc	reg16,mem16 reg32,mem32	SF,ZF,OF,CF,PF,AF	13	2+	6	2	2
adc	mem8,reg8	SF,ZF,OF,CF,PF,AF	10	2+	7	3	3
adc	mem16,reg16 mem32,reg32	SF,ZF,OF,CF,PF,AF	11	2+	7	3	3
add	AL,imm8	SF,ZF,OF,CF,PF,AF	04	2	2	1	1
add	AX,imm16 EAX,imm32	SF,ZF,OF,CF,PF,AF	05	3 5	2	1	1
add	reg8,imm8	SF,ZF,OF,CF,PF,AF	80	3	2	1	1
add	reg16,imm16 reg32,imm32	SF,ZF,OF,CF,PF,AF	81	4 6	2	1	1
add	reg16,imm8 reg32,imm8	SF,ZF,OF,CF,PF,AF	83	3	2	1	1
add	mem8,imm8	SF,ZF,OF,CF,PF,AF	80	3+	7	3	3
add	mem16,imm16 mem32,imm32	SF,ZF,OF,CF,PF,AF	81	4+ 6+	7	3	3
add	mem16,imm8 mem32,imm8	SF,ZF,OF,CF,PF,AF	83	3+	7	3	3
add	reg8,reg8	SF,ZF,OF,CF,PF,AF	02	2	2	1	1
add	reg16,reg16 reg32,reg32	SF,ZF,OF,CF,PF,AF	03	2	2	1	1
add	reg8,mem8	SF,ZF,OF,CF,PF,AF	02	2+	6	2	2
add	reg16,mem16 reg32,mem32	SF,ZF,OF,CF,PF,AF	03	2+	6	2	2
add	mem8,reg8	SF,ZF,OF,CF,PF,AF	00	2+	7	3	3
add	mem16,reg16 mem32,reg32	SF,ZF,OF,CF,PF,AF	01	2+	7	3	3
and	AL,imm8	SF,ZF,OF,CF,PF,AF	24	2	2	1	1

Mnemonic	Operand(s)	Flags affected	Opcode	Number of Bytes	Timing 386	Timing 486	Timing Pentium
and	AX,imm16 EAX,imm32	SF,ZF,OF,CF,PF,AF	25	3 5	2	1	1
and	reg8,imm8	SF,ZF,OF,CF,PF,AF	80	3	2	1	1
and	reg16,imm16 reg32,imm32	SF,ZF,OF,CF,PF,AF	81	4 6	2	1	1
and	reg16,imm8 reg32,imm8	SF,ZF,OF,CF,PF,AF	83	3	2	1	1
and	mem8,imm8	SF,ZF,OF,CF,PF,AF	80	3+	7	3	3
and	mem16,imm16 mem32,imm32	SF,ZF,OF,CF,PF,AF	81	4+ 6+	7	3	3
and	mem16,imm8 mem32,imm8	SF,ZF,OF,CF,PF,AF	83	3+	7	3	3
and	reg8,reg8	SF,ZF,OF,CF,PF,AF	22	2	2	1	1
and	reg16,reg16 reg32,reg32	SF,ZF,OF,CF,PF,AF	23	2	2	1	1
and	reg8,mem8	SF,ZF,OF,CF,PF,AF	22	2+	6	2	2
and	reg16,mem16 reg32,mem32	SF,ZF,OF,CF,PF,AF	23	2+	6	2	2
and	mem8,reg8	SF,ZF,OF,CF,PF,AF	20	2+	7	3	3
and	mem16,reg16 mem32,reg32	SF,ZF,OF,CF,PF,AF	21	2+	7	3	3
call	rel32	none	E8	5	7+	3	1
call	reg32 (near indirect)	none	FF	2	7+	5	2
call	mem32 (near indirect)	none	FF	2+	10+	5	2
call	far direct	none	9A	7	17+	18	4
call	far indirect	none	FF	6	22+	17	5
cbw	none	none	98	1	3	3	3
cdq	none	none	99	1	2	3	2
clc	none	CF	F8	1	2	2	2
cld	none	DF	FC	1	2	2	2
cmc	none	CF	F5	1	2	2	2

Mnemonic	Operand(s)	Flags affected	Opcode	Number of Bytes	Timing 386	Timing 486	Timing Pentium
cmp	AL,imm8	SF,ZF,OF,CF,PF,AF	3C	2	2	1	1
cmp	AX,imm16 EAX,imm32	SF,ZF,OF,CF,PF,AF	3D	3 5	2	1	1
cmp	reg8,imm8	SF,ZF,OF,CF,PF,AF	80	3	2	1	1
cmp	reg16,imm16 reg32,imm32	SF,ZF,OF,CF,PF,AF	81	4 6	2	1	1
cmp	reg16,imm8 reg32,imm8	SF,ZF,OF,CF,PF,AF	83	3	2	1	1
cmp	mem8,imm8	SF,ZF,OF,CF,PF,AF	80	3+	5	2	2
cmp	mem16,imm16 mem32,imm32	SF,ZF,OF,CF,PF,AF	81	4+ 6+	5	2	2
cmp	mem16,imm8 mem32,imm8	SF,ZF,OF,CF,PF,AF	83	3+	5	2	2
cmp	reg8,reg8	SF,ZF,OF,CF,PF,AF	38	2	2	1	1
cmp	reg16,reg16 reg32,reg32	SF,ZF,OF,CF,PF,AF	3B	2	2	1	1
cmp	reg8,mem8	SF,ZF,OF,CF,PF,AF	3A	2+	6	2	2
cmp	reg16,mem16 reg32,mem32	SF,ZF,OF,CF,PF,AF	3B	2+	6	2	2
cmp	mem8,reg8	SF,ZF,OF,CF,PF,AF	38	2+	5	2	2
cmp	mem16,reg16 mem32,reg32	SF,ZF,OF,CF,PF,AF	39	2+	5	2	2
cmpsb	none	none	A6	1	10	8	5
cmpsw cmpsd	none	none	A7	1	10	8	5
cwd	none	none	99	1	2	3	2
cwde	none	none	98	1	3	3	3
daa	none	SF,ZF,PF,AF OF ?	27	1	4	2	3
das	none	SF,ZF,PF,AF OF ?	2F	1	4	2	3
dec	reg8		FE	2	2	1	1

Mnemonic	Operand(s)	Flags affected	Opcode	Number of Bytes	Timing 386	Timing 486	Timing Pentium
dec	AX EAX	SF,ZF,OF,PF,AF	48	1	2	1	1
dec	CX ECX	SF,ZF,OF,PF,AF	49	1	2	1	1
dec	DX EDX	SF,ZF,OF,PF,AF	4A	1	2	1	1
dec	BX EBX	SF,ZF,OF,PF,AF	4B	1	2	1	1
dec	SP ESP	SF,ZF,OF,PF,AF	4C	1	2	1	1
dec	BP EBP	SF,ZF,OF,PF,AF	4D	1	2	1	1
dec	SI ESI	SF,ZF,OF,PF,AF	4E	1	2	1	1
dec	DI EDI	SF,ZF,OF,PF,AF	4F	1	2	1	1
dec	mem8	SF,ZF,OF,PF,AF	FE	2+	6	3	3
dec	mem16 mem32	SF,ZF,OF,PF,AF	FF	2+	6	3	3
div	reg8	SF,ZF,OF,PF,AF ?	F6	2	14	16	17
div	reg16 reg32	SF,ZF,OF,PF,AF ?	F7	2	22 38	24 40	25 41
div	mem8	SF,ZF,OF,PF,AF ?	F6	2+	17	16	17
div	mem16 mem32	SF,ZF,OF,PF,AF ?	F7	2+	25 41	24 40	25 41
idiv	reg8	SF,ZF,OF,PF,AF ?	F6	2	19	19	22
idiv	reg16 reg32	SF,ZF,OF,PF,AF ?	F7	2	27 43	27 43	30 48
idiv	mem8	SF,ZF,OF,PF,AF ?	F6	2+	22	20	22
idiv	mem16 mem32	SF,ZF,OF,PF,AF ?	F7	2+	30 46	28 44	30 48
imul	reg8	OF,CF SF,ZF, PF,AF ?	F6	2	9-14	13-18	11

Mnemonic	Operand(s)	Flags affected	Opcode	Number of Bytes	Timing 386	Timing 486	Timing Pentium
imul	reg16 reg32	OF,CF SF,ZF, PF,AF ?	F7	2	9-22 9-38	13-26 13-42	11 10
imul	mem8	OF,CF SF,ZF, PF,AF ?	F6	2+	12-17	13-18	11
imul	mem16 mem32	OF,CF SF,ZF, PF,AF ?	F7	2+	12-25 12-41	13-26 13-42	11 10
imul	reg16,reg16 reg32,reg32	OF,CF SF,ZF, PF,AF ?	0F AF	3	9-22 9-38	13-26 13-42	11 10
imul	reg16,mem16 reg32,mem32	OF,CF SF,ZF, PF,AF ?	0F AF	3+	12-25 12-41	13-26 13-42	11 10
imul	reg16,imm8 reg32,imm8	OF,CF SF,ZF, PF,AF ?	6B	3	9-14	13-18	10
imul	mem16 mem32	OF,CF SF,ZF, PF,AF ?	F7	4 6	9-22 9-38	13-26 13-42	11 10
imul	reg16,reg16,imm8 reg32,reg32,imm8	OF,CF SF,ZF, PF,AF ?	6B	3	9-14	13-18	10
imul	reg16,reg16,imm16 reg32,reg32,imm32	OF,CF SF,ZF, PF,AF ?	69	4 6	9-22 9-38	13-26 13-42	10 10
imul	reg16,mem16,imm8 reg32,mem32,imm8	OF,CF SF,ZF, PF,AF ?	6B	3+	9-17	13-18	10
imul	reg16,mem16,imm16 reg32,mem32,imm32	OF,CF SF,ZF, PF,AF ?	69	4+ 6+	12-25 12-41	13-26 13-42	10 10
inc	reg8	SF,ZF,OF,PF,AF	FE	2	2	1	1
inc	AX EAX	SF,ZF,OF,PF,AF	40	1	2	1	1
inc	CX ECX	SF,ZF,OF,PF,AF	41	1	2	1	1
inc	DX EDX	SF,ZF,OF,PF,AF	42	1	2	1	1
inc	BX EBX	SF,ZF,OF,PF,AF	43	1	2	1	1
inc	SP ESP	SF,ZF,OF,PF,AF	44	1	2	1	1
inc	BP EBP	SF,ZF,OF,PF,AF	45	1	2	1	1

Mnemonic	Operand(s)	Flags affected	Opcode	Number of Bytes	Timing 386	Timing 486	Timing Pentium
inc	SI ESI	SF,ZF,OF,PF,AF	47	1	2	1	1
inc	DI EDI	SF,ZF,OF,PF,AF	48	1	2	1	1
inc	mem8	SF,ZF,OF,PF,AF	FE	2+	6	3	3
inc	mem16 mem32	SF,ZF,OF,PF,AF	FF	2+	6	3	3
ja jnbe	rel8	none	77	7+,3	3,1	1	2
ja jnbe	rel32	none	0F 87	7+,3	3,1	1	6
jae jnb	rel8	none	73	7+,3	3,1	1	2
jae jnb	rel32	none	0F 83	7+,3	3,1	1	6
jb jnae	rel8	none	72	7+,3	3,1	1	2
jb jnae	rel32	none	0F 82	7+,3	3,1	1	6
jbe jna	rel8	none	76	7+,3	3,1	1	2
jbe jna	rel32	none	0F 86	7+,3	3,1	1	6
jc	rel8	none	72	7+,3	3,1	1	2
jc	rel32	none	0F 82	7+,3	3,1	1	6
je jz	rel8	none	74	7+,3	3,1	1	2
je jz	rel32	none	0F 84	7+,3	3,1	1	6
jecxz	rel8	none	E3			6,5	2
jg jnle	rel8	none	7F	7+,3	3,1	1	2
jg jnle	rel32	none	0F 8F	7+,3	3,1	1	6

Mnemonic	Operand(s)	Flags affected	Opcode	Number of Bytes	Timing 386	Timing 486	Timing Pentium
jge jnl	rel8	none	7D	7+,3	3,1	1	2
jge jnl	rel32	none	0F 8D	7+,3	3,1	1	6
jl jnge	rel8	none	7C	7+,3	3,1	1	2
jl jnge	rel32	none	0F 8C	7+,3	3,1	1	6
jle jng	rel8	none	7E	7+,3	3,1	1	2
jle jng	rel32	none	0F 8E	7+,3	3,1	1	6
jmp	rel8	none	EB	2	7+	3	1
jmp	rel32	none	E9	5	7+	3	1
jmp	reg32	none	FF	2	10+	5	2
jmp	mem32	none	FF	2+	10+	5	2
jnc	rel8	none	73	7+,3	3,1	1	2
jnc	rel32	none	0F 83	7+,3	3,1	1	6
jne jnz	rel8	none	75	7+,3	3,1	1	2
jne jnz	rel32	none	0F 85	7+,3	3,1	1	6
jno	rel8	none	71	7+,3	3,1	1	2
jno	rel32	none	0F 81	7+,3	3,1	1	6
jnp jpo	rel8	none	7B	7+,3	3,1	1	2
jnp jpo	rel32	none	0F 8B	7+,3	3,1	1	6
jns	rel8	none	79	7+,3	3,1	1	2
jns	rel32	none	0F 89	7+,3	3,1	1	6
jo	rel8	none	70	7+,3	3,1	1	2
jo	rel32	none	0F 80	7+,3	3,1	1	6
jp jpe	rel8	none	7A	7+,3	3,1	1	2

Mnemonic	Operand(s)	Flags affected	Opcode	Number of Bytes	Timing 386	Timing 486	Timing Pentium
jp jpe	rel32	none	0F 8A	7+,3	3,1	1	6
js	rel8	none	78	7+,3	3,1	1	2
js	rel32	none	0F 88	7+,3	3,1	1	6
lea	reg32,mem32	none	8D	2+	2	1	1
lodsb	none	none	AC	1	5	5	2
lodsw lodsd	none	none	AD	1	5	5	2
loop	none	none	E2	11+	6,7	5,6	2
loope loopz	none	none	E1	11+	6,9	7,8	2
loopne loopnz	none	none	E0	11+	6,9	7,8	2
mov	AL, imm8	none	B0	2	2	1	1
mov	CL, imm8	none	B1	2	2	1	1
mov	DL, imm8	none	B2	2	2	1	1
mov	BL, imm8	none	B3	2	2	1	1
mov	AH, imm8	none	B4	2	2	1	1
mov	CH, imm8	none	B5	2	2	1	1
mov	DH, imm8	none	B6	2	2	1	1
mov	BH, imm8	none	B7	2	2	1	1
mov	AX, imm16 EAX, imm32	none	B8	3 5	2	1	1
mov	CX, imm16 ECX, imm32	none	B9	3 5	2	1	1
mov	DX, imm16 EDX, imm32	none	BA	3 5	2	1	1
mov	BX, imm16 EBX, imm32	none	BB	3 5	2	1	1
mov	SP, imm16 ESP, imm32	none	BC	3 5	2	1	1
mov	BP, imm16 EPB, imm32	none	BD	3 5	2	1	1

Mnemonic	Operand(s)	Flags affected	Opcode	Number of Bytes	Timing 386	Timing 486	Timing Pentium
mov	SI, imm16 ESI, imm32	none	BE	3 5	2	1	1
mov	DI, imm16 EDI, imm32	none	BF	3 5	2	1	1
mov	mem8, imm8	none	C6	3+	2	1	1
mov	mem16,imm16 mem32,imm32	none	C7	4+ 6+	2	1	1
mov	reg8,reg8	none	8A	2	2	1	1
mov	reg16,reg16 reg32,reg32	none	8B	2	2	1	1
mov	AL, direct	none	A0	5	4	1	1
mov	AX, direct EAX, direct	none	A1	5	4	1	1
mov	reg8,mem8	none	8A	2+	4	1	1
mov	reg16,mem16 reg32,mem32	none	8B	2+	4	1	1
mov	mem8,reg8	none	88	2+	2	1	1
mov	mem16,reg16 mem32,reg32	none	89	2+	2	1	1
mov	direct ,AL	none	A2	5	2	1	1
mov	direct, AX direct, EAX	none	A3	5	2	1	1
mov	sreg, reg16	none	8E	2	2	3	1
mov	reg16, sreg	none	8C	2	2	3	1
mov	sreg,mem16	none	8E	2+	2	3*	2*
mov	mem16,sreg	none	8C	2+	2	3	1
movsb	none	none	A4	1	7	7	4
movsw movsd	none	none	A5	1	7	7	4
movsx	reg16,reg8 reg32,reg8	none	0F BE	3	3	3	3
movsx	reg16,mem8 reg32,mem8	none	0F BE	3+	6	3	3

Mnemonic	Operand(s)	Flags affected	Opcode	Number of Bytes	Timing 386	Timing 486	Timing Pentium
movsx	reg32,reg16	none	0F BF	3	3	3	3
movsx	reg32,mem16	none	0F BF	3+	6	3	3
movzx	reg16,reg8 reg32,reg8	none	0F B6	3	3	3	3
movzx	reg16,mem8 reg32,mem8	none	0F B6	3+	6	3	3
movzx	reg32,reg16	none	0F B7	3	3	3	3
movzx	reg32,mem16	none	0F B7	3+	6	3	3
mul	reg8	OF,CF SF,ZF, PF,AF ?	F6	2	9-14	13-18	11
mul	reg16 reg32	OF,CF SF,ZF, PF,AF ?	F7	2	9-22 9-38	13-26 13-42	11 10
mul	mem8	OF,CF SF,ZF, PF,AF ?	F6	2+	12-17	13-18	11
mul	mem16 mem32	OF,CF SF,ZF, PF,AF ?	F7	2+	12-25 12-41	13-26 13-42	11 10
neg	reg8	SF,ZF,OF,CF,PF,AF	F6	2	2	1	1
neg	reg16 reg32	SF,ZF,OF,CF,PF,AF	F7	2	2	1	1
neg	mem8	SF,ZF,OF,CF,PF,AF	F6	2+	2	1	1
neg	mem16 mem32	SF,ZF,OF,CF,PF,AF	F7	2+	2	1	1
not	reg8	none	F6	2	2	1	1
not	reg16 reg32	none	F7	2	2	1	1
not	mem8	none	F6	2+	6	3	3
not	mem16 mem32	none	F7	2+	6	3	3
or	AL,imm8	SF,ZF,OF,CF,PF,AF	0C	2	2	1	1
or	AX,imm16 EAX,imm32	SF,ZF,OF,CF,PF,AF	0D	3 5	2	1	1
or	reg8,imm8	SF,ZF,OF,CF,PF,AF	80	3	2	1	1
or	reg16,imm16 reg32,imm32	SF,ZF,OF,CF,PF,AF	81	4 6	2	1	1

Mnemonic	Operand(s)	Flags affected	Opcode	Number of Bytes	Timing 386	Timing 486	Timing Pentium
or	reg16,imm8 reg32,imm8	SF,ZF,OF,CF,PF,AF	83	3	2	1	1
or	mem8,imm8	SF,ZF,OF,CF,PF,AF	80	3+	7	3	3
or	mem16,imm16 mem32,imm32	SF,ZF,OF,CF,PF,AF	81	4+ 6+	7	3	3
or	mem16,imm8 mem32,imm8	SF,ZF,OF,CF,PF,AF	83	3+	7	3	3
or	reg8,reg8	SF,ZF,OF,CF,PF,AF	0A	2	2	1	1
or	reg16,reg16 reg32,reg32	SF,ZF,OF,CF,PF,AF	0B	2	2	1	1
or	reg8,mem8	SF,ZF,OF,CF,PF,AF	0A	2+	6	2	2
or	reg16,mem16 reg32,mem32	SF,ZF,OF,CF,PF,AF	0B	2+	6	2	2
or	mem8,reg8	SF,ZF,OF,CF,PF,AF	08	2+	7	3	3
or	mem16,reg16 mem32,reg32	SF,ZF,OF,CF,PF,AF	09	2+	7	3	3
pop	AX EAX	none	58	1	4	1	1
pop	CX ECX	none	59	1	4	1	1
pop	DX EDX	none	5A	1	4	1	1
pop	BX EBX	none	5B	1	4	1	1
pop	SP ESP	none	5C	1	4	1	1
pop	BP EBP	none	5D	1	4	1	1
pop	SI ESI	none	5E	1	4	1	1
pop	DI EDI	none	5F	1	4	1	1
pop	DS	none	1F	1	7	3	3
pop	ES	none	07	1	7	3	3

Mnemonic	Operand(s)	Flags affected	Opcode	Number of Bytes	Timing 386	Timing 486	Timing Pentium
pop	SS	none	17	1	7	3	3
pop	FS	none	0F A1	2	7	3	3
pop	GS	none	0F A9	2	7	3	3
pop	mem16 mem32	none	8F	2+	5	6	3
popa popad	none	none	61	1	24	9	5
popf popfd	none	none	9D	1	5	9	4
push	AX EAX	none	50	1	2	1	1
push	CX ECX	none	51	1	2	1	1
push	DX EDX	none	52	1	2	1	1
push	BX EBX	none	53	1	2	1	1
push	SP ESP	none	54	1	2	1	1
push	BP EBP	none	55	1	2	1	1
push	SI ESI	none	56	1	2	1	1
push	DI EDI	none	57	1	2	1	1
push	CS	none	0E	1	2	3	1
push	DS	none	1E	1	2	3	1
push	ES	none	06	1	2	3	1
push	SS	none	16	1	2	3	1
push	FS	none	0F A0	2	2	3	1
push	GS	none	0F A8	2	2	3	1
push	mem16 mem32	none	FF	2+	5	4	2

Mnemonic	Operand(s)	Flags affected	Opcode	Number of Bytes	Timing 386	Timing 486	Timing Pentium
push	imm8	none	6A	2	2	1	1
push	imm16 imm32	none	68	3 5	2	1	1
pusha pushad	none	none	60	1	18	11	5
pushf pushfd	none	none	9C	1	4	4	3
rep repz repe	none (string instruction prefix)	none	F3	1			
rep movsb	none	none	F3 A4	2	7+4n	12+3n	13+4n
rep movsw rep movsd	none	none	F3 A5	2	7+4n	12+3n	13+4n
rep stosb	none	none	F3 A6	2	5+5n	7+4n	9n
rep stosw rep stosd	none	none	F3 A7	2	5+5n	7+4n	9n
repe cmpsb	none	none	F3 A6	2	5+9n	7+7n	9+4n
repe cmpsw repe cmpsd	none	none	F3 A7	2	5+9n	7+7n	9+4n
repe scasb	none	none	F3 AE	2	5+8n	7+5n	9+4n
repe scasw repe scasd	none	none	F3 AF	2	5+8n	7+5n	9+4n
repne cmpsb	none	none	F2 A6	2	5+9n	7+7n	9+4n
repne cmpsw repne cmpsd	none	none	F2 A7	2	5+9n	7+7n	9+4n

Mnemonic	Operand(s)	Flags affected	Opcode	Number of Bytes	Timing 386	Timing 486	Timing Pentium
repne scasb	none	none	F2 AE	2	5+8n	7+5n	9+4n
repne scasw repne scasd	none	none	F2 AF	2	5+8n	7+5n	9+4n
repnz repne	none (string instruction prefix)	none	F2	1			
ret (far)	none	none	CB	1	18+	13	4
ret (far)	imm16	none	CA	3	18+	14	4
ret (near)	none	none	C3	1	10+	5	2
ret (near)	imm16	none	C2	3	10+	5	3
rol ror	reg8	SF,ZF,OF,CF,PF AF ?	D0	2	3	3	1
rol ror	reg16 reg32	SF,ZF,OF,CF,PF AF ?	D1	2	3	3	1
rol ror	mem8	SF,ZF,OF,CF,PF AF ?	D0	2+	7	4	3
rol ror	reg16 reg32	SF,ZF,OF,CF,PF AF ?	D1	2+	7	4	3
rol ror	reg8, imm8	SF,ZF,OF,CF,PF AF ?	C0	3	3	2	1
rol ror	reg16,imm8 reg32,imm8	SF,ZF,OF,CF,PF AF ?	C1	3	3	2	1
rol ror	mem8, imm8	SF,ZF,OF,CF,PF AF ?	C0	3+	7	4	3
rol ror	mem16,imm8 mem32,imm8	SF,ZF,OF,CF,PF AF ?	C1	3+	7	4	3
rol ror	reg8, CL	SF,ZF,OF,CF,PF AF ?	D2	2	3	2	1
rol ror	reg16,CL reg32,CL	SF,ZF,OF,CF,PF AF ?	D3	2	3	2	1
rol ror	mem8, CL	SF,ZF,OF,CF,PF AF ?	D2	2+	7	4	4

Mnemonic	Operand(s)	Flags affected	Opcode	Number of Bytes	Timing 386	Timing 486	Timing Pentium
rol ror	mem16,CL mem32,CL	SF,ZF,OF,CF,PF AF ?	D3	2+	7	4	4
sbb	AL,imm8	SF,ZF,OF,CF,PF,AF	1C	2	2	1	1
sbb	AX,imm16 EAX,imm32	SF,ZF,OF,CF,PF,AF	1D	3 5	2	1	1
sbb	reg8,imm8	SF,ZF,OF,CF,PF,AF	80	3	2	1	1
sbb	reg16,imm16 reg32,imm32	SF,ZF,OF,CF,PF,AF	81	4 6	2	1	1
sbb	reg16,imm8 reg32,imm8	SF,ZF,OF,CF,PF,AF	83	3	2	1	1
sbb	mem8,imm8	SF,ZF,OF,CF,PF,AF	80	3+	7	3	3
sbb	mem16,imm16 mem32,imm32	SF,ZF,OF,CF,PF,AF	81	4+ 6+	7	3	3
sbb	mem16,imm8 mem32,imm8	SF,ZF,OF,CF,PF,AF	83	3+	7	3	3
sbb	reg8,reg8	SF,ZF,OF,CF,PF,AF	1A	2	2	1	1
sbb	reg16,reg16 reg32,reg32	SF,ZF,OF,CF,PF,AF	1B	2	2	1	1
sbb	reg8,mem8	SF,ZF,OF,CF,PF,AF	1A	2+	6	2	2
sbb	reg16,mem16 reg32,mem32	SF,ZF,OF,CF,PF,AF	1B	2+	6	2	2
sbb	mem8,reg8	SF,ZF,OF,CF,PF,AF	18	2+	7	3	3
sbb	mem16,reg16 mem32,reg32	SF,ZF,OF,CF,PF,AF	19	2+	7	3	3
scasb	none	none	AE	1	7	6	4
scasw scasd	none	none	AE	1	7	6	4
shl/sal shr sar	reg8,1	SF,ZF,OF,CF,PF AF ?	D0	2	3	3	1
shl/sal shr sar	reg16,1 reg32,1	SF,ZF,OF,CF,PF AF ?	D1	2	3	3	1

Mnemonic	Operand(s)	Flags affected	Opcode	Number of Bytes	Timing 386	Timing 486	Timing Pentium
shl/sal shr sar	mem8,1	SF,ZF,OF,CF,PF AF ?	D0	2+	7	4	3
shl/sal shr sar	reg16,1 reg32,1	SF,ZF,OF,CF,PF AF ?	D1	2+	7	4	3
shl/sal shr sar	reg8, imm8	SF,ZF,OF,CF,PF AF ?	C0	3	3	2	1
shl/sal shr sar	reg16,imm8 reg32,imm8	SF,ZF,OF,CF,PF AF ?	C1	3	3	2	1
shl/sal shr sar	mem8, imm8	SF,ZF,OF,CF,PF AF ?	C0	3+	7	4	3
shl/sal shr sar	mem16,imm8 mem32,imm8	SF,ZF,OF,CF,PF AF ?	C1	3+	7	4	3
shl/sal shr sar	reg8, CL	SF,ZF,OF,CF,PF AF ?	D2	2	3	2	1
shl/sal shr sar	reg16,CL reg32,CL	SF,ZF,OF,CF,PF AF ?	D3	2	3	2	1
shl/sal shr sar	mem8, CL	SF,ZF,OF,CF,PF AF ?	D2	2+	7	4	4
shl/sal shr sar	mem16,CL mem32,CL	SF,ZF,OF,CF,PF AF ?	D3	2+	7	4	4
shld	reg16,reg16,imm8 reg32,reg32,imm8	SF,ZF,CF,PF OF,AF ?	0F 04	4	3	2	4
shld	mem16,reg16,imm8 mem32,reg32,imm8	SF,ZF,CF,PF OF,AF ?	0F 04	4+	7	4	4
shld	reg16,reg16,CL reg32,reg32,CL	SF,ZF,CF,PF OF,AF ?	0F 05	3	3	3	4

Mnemonic	Operand(s)	Flags affected	Opcode	Number of Bytes	Timing 386	Timing 486	Timing Pentium
shld	mem16,reg16,CL mem32,reg32,CL	SF,ZF,CF,PF OF,AF ?	0F 05	3+	7	4	5
shrd	reg16,reg16,imm8 reg32,reg32,imm8	SF,ZF,CF,PF OF,AF ?	0F AC	4	3	2	4
shrd	mem16,reg16,imm8 mem32,reg32,imm8	SF,ZF,CF,PF OF,AF ?	0F AC	4+	7	4	4
shrd	reg16,reg16,CL reg32,reg32,CL	SF,ZF,CF,PF OF,AF ?	0F AD	3	3	3	4
shrd	mem16,reg16,CL mem32,reg32,CL	SF,ZF,CF,PF OF,AF ?	0F AD	3+	7	4	5
stc	none	CF	F9	1	2	2	2
std	none	DF	FD	1	2	2	2
stosb	none	none	AA	1	4	5	3
stosw stosd	none	none	AB	1	4	5	3
sub	AL,imm8	SF,ZF,OF,CF,PF,AF	2C	2	2	1	1
sub	AX,imm16 EAX,imm32	SF,ZF,OF,CF,PF,AF	2D	3 5	2	1	1
sub	reg8,imm8	SF,ZF,OF,CF,PF,AF	80	3	2	1	1
sub	reg16,imm16 reg32,imm32	SF,ZF,OF,CF,PF,AF	81	4 6	2	1	1
sub	reg16,imm8 reg32,imm8	SF,ZF,OF,CF,PF,AF	83	3	2	1	1
sub	mem8,imm8	SF,ZF,OF,CF,PF,AF	80	3+	7	3	3
sub	mem16,imm16 mem32,imm32	SF,ZF,OF,CF,PF,AF	81	4+ 6+	7	3	3
sub	mem16,imm8 mem32,imm8	SF,ZF,OF,CF,PF,AF	83	3+	7	3	3
sub	reg8,reg8	SF,ZF,OF,CF,PF,AF	2A	2	2	1	1
sub	reg16,reg16 reg32,reg32	SF,ZF,OF,CF,PF,AF	2B	2	2	1	1
sub	reg8,mem8	SF,ZF,OF,CF,PF,AF	2A	2+	6	2	2
sub	reg16,mem16 reg32,mem32	SF,ZF,OF,CF,PF,AF	2B	2+	6	2	2

Mnemonic	Operand(s)	Flags affected	Opcode	Number of Bytes	Timing 386	Timing 486	Timing Pentium
sub	mem8,reg8	SF,ZF,OF,CF,PF,AF	28	2+	7	3	3
sub	mem16,reg16 mem32,reg32	SF,ZF,OF,CF,PF,AF	29	2+	7	3	3
test	AL,imm8	SF,ZF,OF,CF,PF,AF	A8	2	2	1	1
test	AX,imm16 EAX,imm32	SF,ZF,OF,CF,PF,AF	A9	3 5	2	1	1
test	reg8,imm8	SF,ZF,OF,CF,PF,AF	F6	3	2	1	1
test	reg16,imm16 reg32,imm32	SF,ZF,OF,CF,PF,AF	F7	4 6	2	1	1
test	mem8,imm8	SF,ZF,OF,CF,PF,AF	F6	3+	5	2	2
test	mem16,imm16 mem32,imm32	SF,ZF,OF,CF,PF,AF	F7	4+ 6+	5	2	2
test	reg8,reg8	SF,ZF,OF,CF,PF,AF	84	2	2	1	1
test	reg16,reg16 reg32,reg32	SF,ZF,OF,CF,PF,AF	85	2	2	1	1
test	mem8,reg8	SF,ZF,OF,CF,PF,AF	84	2+	5	2	2
test	mem16,reg16 mem32,reg32	SF,ZF,OF,CF,PF,AF	85	2+	5	2	2
xchg	AX, CX EAX, ECX	none	91	1	3	3	2
xchg	AX, DX EAX, EDX	none	92	1	3	3	2
xchg	AX, BX EAX, EBX	none	93	1	3	3	2
xchg	AX, SP EAX, ESP	none	94	1	3	3	2
xchg	AX, BP EAX, EBP	none	95	1	3	3	2
xchg	AX, SI EAX, ESI	none	96	1	3	3	2
xchg	AX, DI EAX, EDI	none	97	1	3	3	2
xchg	reg8,reg8	none	86	2	3	3	3

Mnemonic	Operand(s)	Flags affected	Opcode	Number of Bytes	Timing 386	Timing 486	Timing Pentium
xchg	reg8,mem8	none	86	2+	5	5	3
xchg	reg16,reg16 reg32,mem32	none	87	2	3	3	3
xchg	reg16,mem16 reg32,mem32	none	87	2+	5	5	3
xlat	none	none	D7	1	5	4	4
xor	AL,imm8	SF,ZF,OF,CF,PF,AF	34	2	2	1	1
xor	AX,imm16 EAX,imm32	SF,ZF,OF,CF,PF,AF	35	3 5	2	1	1
xor	reg8,imm8	SF,ZF,OF,CF,PF,AF	80	3	2	1	1
xor	reg16,imm16 reg32,imm32	SF,ZF,OF,CF,PF,AF	81	4 6	2	1	1
xor	reg16,imm8 reg32,imm8	SF,ZF,OF,CF,PF,AF	83	3	2	1	1
xor	mem8,imm8	SF,ZF,OF,CF,PF,AF	80	3+	7	3	3
xor	mem16,imm16 mem32,imm32	SF,ZF,OF,CF,PF,AF	81	4+ 6+	7	3	3
xor	mem16,imm8 mem32,imm8	SF,ZF,OF,CF,PF,AF	83	3+	7	3	3
xor	reg8,reg8	SF,ZF,OF,CF,PF,AF	32	2	2	1	1
xor	reg16,reg16 reg32,reg32	SF,ZF,OF,CF,PF,AF	33	2	2	1	1
xor	reg8,mem8	SF,ZF,OF,CF,PF,AF	32	2+	6	2	2
xor	reg16,mem16 reg32,mem32	SF,ZF,OF,CF,PF,AF	33	2+	6	2	2
xor	mem8,reg8	SF,ZF,OF,CF,PF,AF	30	2+	7	3	3
xor	mem16,reg16 mem32,reg32	SF,ZF,OF,CF,PF,AF	31	2+	7	3	3

* timing varies

80x86 Instructions (by Opcode)

Opcode	Mnemonic	Operand(s)	Flags affected	Number of bytes	Timing 386	Timing 486	Timing Pentium
00	add	mem8,reg8	SF,ZF,OF,CF,PF,AF	2+	7	3	3
01	add	mem16,reg16 mem32,reg32	SF,ZF,OF,CF,PF,AF	2+	7	3	3
02	add	reg8,reg8	SF,ZF,OF,CF,PF,AF	2	2	1	1
02	add	reg8,mem8	SF,ZF,OF,CF,PF,AF	2+	6	2	2
03	add	reg16,reg16 reg32,reg32	SF,ZF,OF,CF,PF,AF	2	2	1	1
03	add	reg16,mem16 reg32,mem32	SF,ZF,OF,CF,PF,AF	2+	6	2	2
04	add	AL,imm8	SF,ZF,OF,CF,PF,AF	2	2	1	1
05	add	AX,imm16 EAX,imm32	SF,ZF,OF,CF,PF,AF	3 5	2	1	1
06	push	ES	none	1	2	3	1
07	pop	ES	none	1	7	3	3
08	or	mem8,reg8	SF,ZF,OF,CF,PF,AF	2+	7	3	3
09	or	mem16,reg16 mem32,reg32	SF,ZF,OF,CF,PF,AF	2+	7	3	3
0A	or	reg8,reg8	SF,ZF,OF,CF,PF,AF	2	2	1	1
0A	or	reg8,mem8	SF,ZF,OF,CF,PF,AF	2+	6	2	2
0B	or	reg16,reg16 reg32,reg32	SF,ZF,OF,CF,PF,AF	2	2	1	1
0B	or	reg16,mem16 reg32,mem32	SF,ZF,OF,CF,PF,AF	2+	6	2	2

Opcode	Mnemonic	Operand(s)	Flags affected	Number of bytes	Timing 386	Timing 486	Timing Pentium
0C	or	AL,imm8	SF,ZF,OF,CF,PF,AF	2	2	1	1
0D	or	AX,imm16 EAX,imm32	SF,ZF,OF,CF,PF,AF	3 5	2	1	1
0E	push	CS	none	1	2	3	1
0F 04	shld	reg16,reg16,imm8 reg32,reg32,imm8	SF,ZF,CF,PF OF,AF ?	4	3	2	4
0F 04	shld	mem16,reg16,imm8 mem32,reg32,imm8	SF,ZF,CF,PF OF,AF ?	4+	7	4	4
0F 05	shld	reg16,reg16,CL reg32,reg32,CL	SF,ZF,CF,PF OF,AF ?	3	3	3	4
0F 05	shld	mem16,reg16,CL mem32,reg32,CL	SF,ZF,CF,PF OF,AF ?	3+	7	4	5
0F 80	jo	rel32	none	7+,3	3,1	1	6
0F 81	jno	rel32	none	7+,3	3,1	1	6
0F 82	jb jnae	rel32	none	7+,3	3,1	1	6
0F 82	jc	rel32	none	7+,3	3,1	1	6
0F 83	jae jnb	rel32	none	7+,3	3,1	1	6
0F 83	jnc	rel32	none	7+,3	3,1	1	6
0F 84	je jz	rel32	none	7+,3	3,1	1	6
0F 85	jne jnz	rel32	none	7+,3	3,1	1	6
0F 86	jbe jna	rel32	none	7+,3	3,1	1	6
0F 87	ja jnbe	rel32	none	7+,3	3,1	1	6
0F 88	js	rel32	none	7+,3	3,1	1	6
0F 89	jns	rel32	none	7+,3	3,1	1	6
0F 8A	jp jpe	rel32	none	7+,3	3,1	1	6
0F 8B	jnp jpo	rel32	none	7+,3	3,1	1	6
0F 8C	jl jnge	rel32	none	7+,3	3,1	1	6

Opcode	Mnemonic	Operand(s)	Flags affected	Number of bytes	Timing 386	Timing 486	Timing Pentium
0F 8D	jge jnl	rel32	none	7+,3	3,1	1	6
0F 8E	jle jng	rel32	none	7+,3	3,1	1	6
0F 8F	jg jnle	rel32	none	7+,3	3,1	1	6
0F A0	push	FS	none	2	2	3	1
0F A1	pop	FS	none	2	7	3	3
0F A8	push	GS	none	2	2	3	1
0F A9	pop	GS	none	2	7	3	3
0F AC	shrd	reg16,reg16,imm8 reg32,reg32,imm8	SF,ZF,CF,PF OF,AF ?	4	3	2	4
0F AC	shrd	mem16,reg16,imm8 mem32,reg32,imm8	SF,ZF,CF,PF OF,AF ?	4+	7	4	4
0F AD	shrd	reg16,reg16,CL reg32,reg32,CL	SF,ZF,CF,PF OF,AF ?	3	3	3	4
0F AD	shrd	mem16,reg16,CL mem32,reg32,CL	SF,ZF,CF,PF OF,AF ?	3+	7	4	5
0F AF	imul	reg16,reg16 reg32,reg32	OF,CF SF,ZF, PF,AF ?	3	9-22 9-38	13-26 13-42	11 10
0F AF	imul	reg16,mem16 reg32,mem32	OF,CF SF,ZF, PF,AF ?	3+	12-25 12-41	13-26 13-42	11 10
0F B6	movzx	reg16,reg8 reg32,reg8	none	3	3	3	3
0F B6	movzx	reg16,mem8 reg32,mem8	none	3+	6	3	3
0F B7	movzx	reg32,reg16	none	3	3	3	3
0F B7	movzx	reg32,mem16	none	3+	6	3	3
0F BE	movsx	reg16,reg8 reg32,reg8	none	3	3	3	3
0F BE	movsx	reg16,mem8 reg32,mem8	none	3+	6	3	3
0F BF	movsx	reg32,reg16	none	3	3	3	3
0F BF	movsx	reg32,mem16	none	3+	6	3	3
10	adc	mem8,reg8	SF,ZF,OF,CF,PF,AF	2+	7	3	3

Opcode	Mnemonic	Operand(s)	Flags affected	Number of bytes	Timing 386	Timing 486	Timing Pentium
11	adc	mem16,reg16 mem32,reg32	SF,ZF,OF,CF,PF,AF	2+	7	3	3
12	adc	reg8,reg8	SF,ZF,OF,CF,PF,AF	2	2	1	1
12	adc	reg8,mem8	SF,ZF,OF,CF,PF,AF	2+	6	2	2
13	adc	reg16,reg16 reg32,reg32	SF,ZF,OF,CF,PF,AF	2	2	1	1
13	adc	reg16,mem16 reg32,mem32	SF,ZF,OF,CF,PF,AF	2+	6	2	2
14	adc	AL,imm8	SF,ZF,OF,CF,PF,AF	2	2	1	1
15	adc	AX,imm16 EAX,imm32	SF,ZF,OF,CF,PF,AF	3 5	2	1	1
16	push	SS	none	1	2	3	1
17	pop	SS	none	1	7	3	3
18	sbb	mem8,reg8	SF,ZF,OF,CF,PF,AF	2+	7	3	3
19	sbb	mem16,reg16 mem32,reg32	SF,ZF,OF,CF,PF,AF	2+	7	3	3
1A	sbb	reg8,reg8	SF,ZF,OF,CF,PF,AF	2	2	1	1
1A	sbb	reg8,mem8	SF,ZF,OF,CF,PF,AF	2+	6	2	2
1B	sbb	reg16,reg16 reg32,reg32	SF,ZF,OF,CF,PF,AF	2	2	1	1
1B	sbb	reg16,mem16 reg32,mem32	SF,ZF,OF,CF,PF,AF	2+	6	2	2
1C	sbb	AL,imm8	SF,ZF,OF,CF,PF,AF	2	2	1	1
1D	sbb	AX,imm16 EAX,imm32	SF,ZF,OF,CF,PF,AF	3 5	2	1	1
1E	push	DS	none	1	2	3	1
1F	pop	DS	none	1	7	3	3
20	and	mem8,reg8	SF,ZF,OF,CF,PF,AF	2+	7	3	3
21	and	mem16,reg16 mem32,reg32	SF,ZF,OF,CF,PF,AF	2+	7	3	3
22	and	reg8,reg8	SF,ZF,OF,CF,PF,AF	2	2	1	1
22	and	reg8,mem8	SF,ZF,OF,CF,PF,AF	2+	6	2	2
23	and	reg16,reg16 reg32,reg32	SF,ZF,OF,CF,PF,AF	2	2	1	1

Opcode	Mnemonic	Operand(s)	Flags affected	Number of bytes	Timing 386	Timing 486	Timing Pentium
23	and	reg16,mem16 reg32,mem32	SF,ZF,OF,CF,PF,AF	2+	6	2	2
24	and	AL,imm8	SF,ZF,OF,CF,PF,AF	2	2	1	1
25	and	AX,imm16 EAX,imm32	SF,ZF,OF,CF,PF,AF	3 5	2	1	1
27	daa	none	SF,ZF,PF,AF OF ?	1	4	2	3
28	sub	mem8,reg8	SF,ZF,OF,CF,PF,AF	2+	7	3	3
29	sub	mem16,reg16 mem32,reg32	SF,ZF,OF,CF,PF,AF	2+	7	3	3
2A	sub	reg8,reg8	SF,ZF,OF,CF,PF,AF	2	2	1	1
2A	sub	reg8,mem8	SF,ZF,OF,CF,PF,AF	2+	6	2	2
2B	sub	reg16,reg16 reg32,reg32	SF,ZF,OF,CF,PF,AF	2	2	1	1
2B	sub	reg16,mem16 reg32,mem32	SF,ZF,OF,CF,PF,AF	2+	6	2	2
2C	sub	AL,imm8	SF,ZF,OF,CF,PF,AF	2	2	1	1
2D	sub	AX,imm16 EAX,imm32	SF,ZF,OF,CF,PF,AF	3 5	2	1	1
2F	das	none	SF,ZF,PF,AF OF ?	1	4	2	3
30	xor	mem8,reg8	SF,ZF,OF,CF,PF,AF	2+	7	3	3
31	xor	mem16,reg16 mem32,reg32	SF,ZF,OF,CF,PF,AF	2+	7	3	3
32	xor	reg8,reg8	SF,ZF,OF,CF,PF,AF	2	2	1	1
32	xor	reg8,mem8	SF,ZF,OF,CF,PF,AF	2+	6	2	2
33	xor	reg16,reg16 reg32,reg32	SF,ZF,OF,CF,PF,AF	2	2	1	1
33	xor	reg16,mem16 reg32,mem32	SF,ZF,OF,CF,PF,AF	2+	6	2	2
34	xor	AL,imm8	SF,ZF,OF,CF,PF,AF	2	2	1	1
35	xor	AX,imm16 EAX,imm32	SF,ZF,OF,CF,PF,AF	3 5	2	1	1
37	aaa	none	AF,CF SF,ZF,OF,PF ?	1	4	3	3

Opcode	Mnemonic	Operand(s)	Flags affected	Number of bytes	Timing 386	Timing 486	Timing Pentium
38	cmp	reg8,reg8	SF,ZF,OF,CF,PF,AF	2	2	1	1
38	cmp	mem8,reg8	SF,ZF,OF,CF,PF,AF	2+	5	2	2
39	cmp	mem16,reg16 mem32,reg32	SF,ZF,OF,CF,PF,AF	2+	5	2	2
3A	cmp	reg8,mem8	SF,ZF,OF,CF,PF,AF	2+	6	2	2
3B	cmp	reg16,reg16 reg32,reg32	SF,ZF,OF,CF,PF,AF	2	2	1	1
3B	cmp	reg16,mem16 reg32,mem32	SF,ZF,OF,CF,PF,AF	2+	6	2	2
3C	cmp	AL,imm8	SF,ZF,OF,CF,PF,AF	2	2	1	1
3D	cmp	AX,imm16 EAX,imm32	SF,ZF,OF,CF,PF,AF	3 5	2	1	1
3F	aas	none	AF,CF SF,ZF,OF,PF ?	1	4	3	3
40	inc	AX EAX	SF,ZF,OF,PF,AF	1	2	1	1
41	inc	CX ECX	SF,ZF,OF,PF,AF	1	2	1	1
42	inc	DX EDX	SF,ZF,OF,PF,AF	1	2	1	1
43	inc	BX EBX	SF,ZF,OF,PF,AF	1	2	1	1
44	inc	SP ESP	SF,ZF,OF,PF,AF	1	2	1	1
45	inc	BP EBP	SF,ZF,OF,PF,AF	1	2	1	1
47	inc	SI ESI	SF,ZF,OF,PF,AF	1	2	1	1
48	dec	AX EAX	SF,ZF,OF,PF,AF	1	2	1	1
48	inc	DI EDI	SF,ZF,OF,PF,AF	1	2	1	1
49	dec	CX ECX	SF,ZF,OF,PF,AF	1	2	1	1
4A	dec	DX EDX	SF,ZF,OF,PF,AF	1	2	1	1

Opcode	Mnemonic	Operand(s)	Flags affected	Number of bytes	Timing 386	Timing 486	Timing Pentium
4B	dec	BX EBX	SF,ZF,OF,PF,AF	1	2	1	1
4C	dec	SP ESP	SF,ZF,OF,PF,AF	1	2	1	1
4D	dec	BP EBP	SF,ZF,OF,PF,AF	1	2	1	1
4E	dec	SI ESI	SF,ZF,OF,PF,AF	1	2	1	1
4F	dec	DI EDI	SF,ZF,OF,PF,AF	1	2	1	1
50	push	AX EAX	none	1	2	1	1
51	push	CX ECX	none	1	2	1	1
52	push	DX EDX	none	1	2	1	1
53	push	BX EBX	none	1	2	1	1
54	push	SP ESP	none	1	2	1	1
55	push	BP EBP	none	1	2	1	1
56	push	SI ESI	none	1	2	1	1
57	push	DI EDI	none	1	2	1	1
58	pop	AX EAX	none	1	4	1	1
59	pop	CX ECX	none	1	4	1	1
5A	pop	DX EDX	none	1	4	1	1
5B	pop	BX EBX	none	1	4	1	1
5C	pop	SP ESP	none	1	4	1	1
5D	pop	BP EBP	none	1	4	1	1

Opcode	Mnemonic	Operand(s)	Flags affected	Number of bytes	Timing 386	Timing 486	Timing Pentium
5E	pop	SI ESI	none	1	4	1	1
5F	pop	DI EDI	none	1	4	1	1
60	pusha pushad	none	none	1	18	11	5
61	popa popad	none	none	1	24	9	5
68	push	imm16 imm32	none	3 5	2	1	1
69	imul	reg16,reg16,imm16 reg32,reg32,imm32	OF,CF SF,ZF, PF,AF ?	4 6	9-22 9-38	13-26 13-42	10 10
69	imul	reg16,mem16,imm16 reg32,mem32,imm32	OF,CF SF,ZF, PF,AF ?	4+ 6+	12-25 12-41	13-26 13-42	10 10
6A	push	imm8	none	2	2	1	1
6B	imul	reg16,imm8 reg32,imm8	OF,CF SF,ZF, PF,AF ?	3	9-14	13-18	10
6B	imul	reg16,reg16,imm8 reg32,reg32,imm8	OF,CF SF,ZF, PF,AF ?	3	9-14	13-18	10
6B	imul	reg16,mem16,imm8 reg32,mem32,imm8	OF,CF SF,ZF, PF,AF ?	3+	9-17	13-18	10
70	jo	rel8	none	7+,3	3,1	1	2
71	jno	rel8	none	7+,3	3,1	1	2
72	jb jnae	rel8	none	7+,3	3,1	1	2
72	jc	rel8	none	7+,3	3,1	1	2
73	jae jnb	rel8	none	7+,3	3,1	1	2
73	jnc	rel8	none	7+,3	3,1	1	2
74	je jz	rel8	none	7+,3	3,1	1	2
75	jne jnz	rel8	none	7+,3	3,1	1	2
76	jbe jna	rel8	none	7+,3	3,1	1	2
77	ja jnbe	rel8	none	7+,3	3,1	1	2

Opcode	Mnemonic	Operand(s)	Flags affected	Number of bytes	Timing 386	Timing 486	Timing Pentium
78	js	rel8	none	7+,3	3,1	1	2
79	jns	rel8	none	7+,3	3,1	1	2
7A	jp jpe	rel8	none	7+,3	3,1	1	2
7B	jnp jpo	rel8	none	7+,3	3,1	1	2
7C	jl jnge	rel8	none	7+,3	3,1	1	2
7D	jge jnl	rel8	none	7+,3	3,1	1	2
7E	jle jng	rel8	none	7+,3	3,1	1	2
7F	jg jnle	rel8	none	7+,3	3,1	1	2
80	adc	reg8,imm8	SF,ZF,OF,CF,PF,AF	3	2	1	1
80	adc	mem8,imm8	SF,ZF,OF,CF,PF,AF	3+	7	3	3
80	add	reg8,imm8	SF,ZF,OF,CF,PF,AF	3	2	1	1
80	add	mem8,imm8	SF,ZF,OF,CF,PF,AF	3+	7	3	3
80	and	reg8,imm8	SF,ZF,OF,CF,PF,AF	3	2	1	1
80	and	mem8,imm8	SF,ZF,OF,CF,PF,AF	3+	7	3	3
80	cmp	reg8,imm8	SF,ZF,OF,CF,PF,AF	3	2	1	1
80	cmp	mem8,imm8	SF,ZF,OF,CF,PF,AF	3+	5	2	2
80	or	reg8,imm8	SF,ZF,OF,CF,PF,AF	3	2	1	1
80	or	mem8,imm8	SF,ZF,OF,CF,PF,AF	3+	7	3	3
80	sbb	reg8,imm8	SF,ZF,OF,CF,PF,AF	3	2	1	1
80	sbb	mem8,imm8	SF,ZF,OF,CF,PF,AF	3+	7	3	3
80	sub	reg8,imm8	SF,ZF,OF,CF,PF,AF	3	2	1	1
80	sub	mem8,imm8	SF,ZF,OF,CF,PF,AF	3+	7	3	3
80	xor	reg8,imm8	SF,ZF,OF,CF,PF,AF	3	2	1	1
80	xor	mem8,imm8	SF,ZF,OF,CF,PF,AF	3+	7	3	3
81	adc	reg16,imm16 reg32,imm32	SF,ZF,OF,CF,PF,AF	4 6	2	1	1
81	adc	mem16,imm16 mem32,imm32	SF,ZF,OF,CF,PF,AF	4+ 6+	7	3	3

Opcode	Mnemonic	Operand(s)	Flags affected	Number of bytes	Timing 386	TIming 486	Timing Pentium
81	add	reg16,imm16 reg32,imm32	SF,ZF,OF,CF,PF,AF	4 6	2	1	1
81	add	mem16,imm16 mem32,imm32	SF,ZF,OF,CF,PF,AF	4+ 6+	7	3	3
81	and	reg16,imm16 reg32,imm32	SF,ZF,OF,CF,PF,AF	4 6	2	1	1
81	and	mem16,imm16 mem32,imm32	SF,ZF,OF,CF,PF,AF	4+ 6+	7	3	3
81	cmp	reg16,imm16 reg32,imm32	SF,ZF,OF,CF,PF,AF	4 6	2	1	1
81	cmp	mem16,imm16 mem32,imm32	SF,ZF,OF,CF,PF,AF	4+ 6+	5	2	2
81	or	reg16,imm16 reg32,imm32	SF,ZF,OF,CF,PF,AF	4 6	2	1	1
81	or	mem16,imm16 mem32,imm32	SF,ZF,OF,CF,PF,AF	4+ 6+	7	3	3
81	sbb	reg16,imm16 reg32,imm32	SF,ZF,OF,CF,PF,AF	4 6	2	1	1
81	sbb	mem16,imm16 mem32,imm32	SF,ZF,OF,CF,PF,AF	4+ 6+	7	3	3
81	sub	reg16,imm16 reg32,imm32	SF,ZF,OF,CF,PF,AF	4 6	2	1	1
81	sub	mem16,imm16 mem32,imm32	SF,ZF,OF,CF,PF,AF	4+ 6+	7	3	3
81	xor	reg16,imm16 reg32,imm32	SF,ZF,OF,CF,PF,AF	4 6	2	1	1
81	xor	mem16,imm16 mem32,imm32	SF,ZF,OF,CF,PF,AF	4+ 6+	7	3	3
83	adc	reg16,imm8 reg32,imm8	SF,ZF,OF,CF,PF,AF	3	2	1	1
83	adc	mem16,imm8 mem32,imm8	SF,ZF,OF,CF,PF,AF	3+	7	3	3
83	add	reg16,imm8 reg32,imm8	SF,ZF,OF,CF,PF,AF	3	2	1	1
83	add	mem16,imm8 mem32,imm8	SF,ZF,OF,CF,PF,AF	3+	7	3	3
83	and	reg16,imm8 reg32,imm8	SF,ZF,OF,CF,PF,AF	3	2	1	1

Opcode	Mnemonic	Operand(s)	Flags affected	Number of bytes	Timing 386	Timing 486	Timing Pentium
83	and	mem16,imm8 mem32,imm8	SF,ZF,OF,CF,PF,AF	3+	7	3	3
83	cmp	reg16,imm8 reg32,imm8	SF,ZF,OF,CF,PF,AF	3	2	1	1
83	cmp	mem16,imm8 mem32,imm8	SF,ZF,OF,CF,PF,AF	3+	5	2	2
83	or	reg16,imm8 reg32,imm8	SF,ZF,OF,CF,PF,AF	3	2	1	1
83	or	mem16,imm8 mem32,imm8	SF,ZF,OF,CF,PF,AF	3+	7	3	3
83	sbb	reg16,imm8 reg32,imm8	SF,ZF,OF,CF,PF,AF	3	2	1	1
83	sbb	mem16,imm8 mem32,imm8	SF,ZF,OF,CF,PF,AF	3+	7	3	3
83	sub	reg16,imm8 reg32,imm8	SF,ZF,OF,CF,PF,AF	3	2	1	1
83	sub	mem16,imm8 mem32,imm8	SF,ZF,OF,CF,PF,AF	3+	7	3	3
83	xor	reg16,imm8 reg32,imm8	SF,ZF,OF,CF,PF,AF	3	2	1	1
83	xor	mem16,imm8 mem32,imm8	SF,ZF,OF,CF,PF,AF	3+	7	3	3
84	test	reg8,reg8	SF,ZF,OF,CF,PF,AF	2	2	1	1
84	test	mem8,reg8	SF,ZF,OF,CF,PF,AF	2+	5	2	2
85	test	reg16,reg16 reg32,reg32	SF,ZF,OF,CF,PF,AF	2	2	1	1
85	test	mem16,reg16 mem32,reg32	SF,ZF,OF,CF,PF,AF	2+	5	2	2
86	xchg	reg8,reg8	none	2	3	3	3
86	xchg	reg8,mem8	none	2+	5	5	3
87	xchg	reg16,reg16	none	2	3	3	3
87	xchg	reg16,mem16	none	2+	5	5	3
88	mov	mem8,reg8	none	2+	2	1	1
89	mov	mem16,reg16 mem32,reg32	none	2+	2	1	1
8A	mov	reg8,reg8	none	2	2	1	1
8A	mov	reg8,mem8	none	2+	4	1	1

Opcode	Mnemonic	Operand(s)	Flags affected	Number of bytes	Timing 386	Timing 486	Timing Pentium
8B	mov	reg16,reg16 reg32,reg32	none	2	2	1	1
8B	mov	reg16,mem16 reg32,mem32	none	2+	4	1	1
8C	mov	reg16, sreg	none	2	2	3	1
8C	mov	mem16,sreg	none	2+	2	3	1
8D	lea	reg32,mem32	none	2+	2	1	1
8E	mov	sreg, reg16	none	2	2	3	1
8E	mov	sreg,mem16	none	2+	2	3*	2*
8F	pop	mem16 mem32	none	2+	5	6	3
91	xchg	AX, CX EAX, ECX	none	1	3	3	2
92	xchg	AX, DX EAX, EDX	none	1	3	3	2
93	xchg	AX, BX EAX, EBX	none	1	3	3	2
94	xchg	AX, SP EAX, ESP	none	1	3	3	2
95	xchg	AX, BP EAX, EBP	none	1	3	3	2
96	xchg	AX, SI EAX, ESI	none	1	3	3	2
97	xchg	AX, DI EAX, EDI	none	1	3	3	2
98	cbw	none	none	1	3	3	3
98	cwde	none	none	1	3	3	3
99	cdq	none	none	1	2	3	2
99	cwd	none	none	1	2	3	2
9A	call	far direct	none	7	17+	18	4
9C	pushf pushfd	none	none	1	4	4	3
9D	popf popfd	none	none	1	5	9	4
A0	mov	AL, direct	none	5	4	1	1

Opcode	Mnemonic	Operand(s)	Flags affected	Number of bytes	Timing 386	Timing 486	Timing Pentium
A1	mov	AX, direct EAX, direct	none	5	4	1	1
A2	mov	direct ,AL	none	5	2	1	1
A3	mov	direct, AX direct, EAX	none	5	2	1	1
A4	movsb	none	none	1	7	7	4
A5	movsw movsd	none	none	1	7	7	4
A6	cmpsb	none	none	1	10	8	5
A7	cmpsw cmpsd	none	none	1	10	8	5
A8	test	AL,imm8	SF,ZF,OF,CF,PF,AF	2	2	1	1
A9	test	AX,imm16 EAX,imm32	SF,ZF,OF,CF,PF,AF	3 5	2	1	1
AA	stosb	none	none	1	4	5	3
AB	stosw stosd	none	none	1	4	5	3
AC	lodsb	none	none	1	5	5	2
AD	lodsw lodsd	none	none	1	5	5	2
AE	scasb	none	none	1	7	6	4
AE	scasw scasd	none	none	1	7	6	4
B0	mov	AL, imm8	none	2	2	1	1
B1	mov	CL, imm8	none	2	2	1	1
B2	mov	DL, imm8	none	2	2	1	1
B3	mov	BL, imm8	none	2	2	1	1
B4	mov	AH, imm8	none	2	2	1	1
B5	mov	CH, imm8	none	2	2	1	1
B6	mov	DH, imm8	none	2	2	1	1
B7	mov	BH, imm8	none	2	2	1	1
B8	mov	AX, imm16 EAX, imm32	none	3 5	2	1	1
B9	mov	CX, imm16 ECX, imm32	none	3 5	2	1	1

Opcode	Mnemonic	Operand(s)	Flags affected	Number of bytes	Timing 386	Timing 486	Timing Pentium
BA	mov	DX, imm16 EDX, imm32	none	3 5	2	1	1
BB	mov	BX, imm16 EBX, imm32	none	3 5	2	1	1
BC	mov	SP, imm16 ESP, imm32	none	3 5	2	1	1
BD	mov	BP, imm16 EPB, imm32	none	3 5	2	1	1
BE	mov	SI, imm16 ESI, imm32	none	3 5	2	1	1
BF	mov	DI, imm16 EDI, imm32	none	3 5	2	1	1
C0	rol ror	reg8, imm8	SF,ZF,OF,CF,PF AF ?	3	3	2	1
C0	rol ror	mem8, imm8	SF,ZF,OF,CF,PF AF ?	3+	7	4	3
C0	shl/sal shr sar	reg8, imm8	SF,ZF,OF,CF,PF AF ?	3	3	2	1
C0	shl/sal shr sar	mem8, imm8	SF,ZF,OF,CF,PF AF ?	3+	7	4	3
C1	rol ror	reg16,imm8 reg32,imm8	SF,ZF,OF,CF,PF AF ?	3	3	2	1
C1	rol ror	mem16,imm8 mem32,imm8	SF,ZF,OF,CF,PF AF ?	3+	7	4	3
C1	shl/sal shr sar	reg16,imm8 reg32,imm8	SF,ZF,OF,CF,PF AF ?	3	3	2	1
C1	shl/sal shr sar	mem16,imm8 mem32,imm8	SF,ZF,OF,CF,PF AF ?	3+	7	4	3
C2	ret (near)	imm16	none	3	10+	5	3
C3	ret (near)	none	none	1	10+	5	2
C6	mov	mem8, imm8	none	3+	2	1	1
C7	mov	mem16,imm16 mem32,imm32	none	4+ 6+	2	1	1

Opcode	Mnemonic	Operand(s)	Flags affected	Number of bytes	Timing 386	Timing 486	Timing Pentium
CA	ret (far)	imm16	none	3	18+	14	4
CB	ret (far)	none	none	1	18+	13	4
D0	rol ror	reg8	SF,ZF,OF,CF,PF AF ?	2	3	3	1
D0	rol ror	mem8	SF,ZF,OF,CF,PF AF ?	2+	7	4	3
D0	shl/sal shr sar	reg8	SF,ZF,OF,CF,PF AF ?	2	3	3	1
D0	shl/sal shr sar	mem8	SF,ZF,OF,CF,PF AF ?	2+	7	4	3
D1	rol ror	reg16 reg32	SF,ZF,OF,CF,PF AF ?	2	3	3	1
D1	rol ror	reg16 reg32	SF,ZF,OF,CF,PF AF ?	2+	7	4	3
D1	shl/sal shr sar	reg16 reg32	SF,ZF,OF,CF,PF AF ?	2	3	3	1
D1	shl/sal shr sar	reg16 reg32	SF,ZF,OF,CF,PF AF ?	2+	7	4	3
D2	rol ror	reg8, CL	SF,ZF,OF,CF,PF AF ?	2	3	2	1
D2	rol ror	mem8, CL	SF,ZF,OF,CF,PF AF ?	2+	7	4	4
D2	shl/sal shr sar	reg8, CL	SF,ZF,OF,CF,PF AF ?	2	3	2	1
D2	shl/sal shr sar	mem8, CL	SF,ZF,OF,CF,PF AF ?	2+	7	4	4
D3	rol ror	reg16,CL reg32,CL	SF,ZF,OF,CF,PF AF ?	2	3	2	1
D3	rol ror	mem16,CL mem32,CL	SF,ZF,OF,CF,PF AF ?	2+	7	4	4
D3	shl/sal shr sar	reg16,CL reg32,CL	SF,ZF,OF,CF,PF AF ?	2	3	2	1

Opcode	Mnemonic	Operand(s)	Flags affected	Number of bytes	Timing 386	Timing 486	Timing Pentium
D3	shl/sal shr sar	mem16,CL mem32,CL	SF,ZF,OF,CF,PF AF ?	2+	7	4	4
D4 0A	aam	none	SF,ZF,PF OF,AF,CF ?	2	17	15	18
D5 0A	aad	none	SF,ZF,PF OF,AF,CF ?	2	19	14	10
D7	xlat	none	none	1	5	4	4
E0	loopne loopnz	none	none	11+	6,9	7,8	2
E1	loope loopz	none	none	11+	6,9	7,8	2
E2	loop	none	none	11+	6,7	5,6	2
E3	jecxz	rel8	none			6,5	2
E8	call	rel32	none	5	7+	3	1
E9	jmp	rel32	none	5	7+	3	1
EB	jmp	rel8	none	2	7+	3	1
F2	repnz repne	none (string instruction prefix)	none	1			
F2 A6	repne cmpsb	none	none	2	5+9n	7+7n	9+4n
F2 A7	repne cmpsw repne cmpsd	none	none	2	5+9n	7+7n	9+4n
F2 AE	repne scasb	none	none	2	5+8n	7+5n	9+4n
F2 AF	repne scasw repne scasd	none	none	2	5+8n	7+5n	9+4n
F3	rep repz repe	none (string instruction prefix)	none	1			
F3 A4	rep movsb	none	none	2	7+4n	12+3n	13+4n

Opcode	Mnemonic	Operand(s)	Flags affected	Number of bytes	Timing 386	Timing 486	Timing Pentium
F3 A5	rep movsw rep movsd	none	none	2	7+4n	12+3n	13+4n
F3 A6	rep stosb	none	none	2	5+5n	7+4n	9n
F3 A6	repe cmpsb	none	none	2	5+9n	7+7n	9+4n
F3 A7	rep stosw rep stosd	none	none	2	5+5n	7+4n	9n
F3 A7	repe cmpsw repe cmpsd	none	none	2	5+9n	7+7n	9+4n
F3 AE	repe scasb	none	none	2	5+8n	7+5n	9+4n
F3 AF	repe scasw repe scasd	none	none	2	5+8n	7+5n	9+4n
F5	cmc	none	CF	1	2	2	2
F6	div	reg8	SF,ZF,OF,PF,AF ?	2	14	16	17
F6	div	mem8	SF,ZF,OF,PF,AF ?	2+	17	16	17
F6	idiv	reg8	SF,ZF,OF,PF,AF ?	2	19	19	22
F6	idiv	mem8	SF,ZF,OF,PF,AF ?	2+	22	20	22
F6	imul	reg8	OF,CF SF,ZF, PF,AF ?	2	9-14	13-18	11
F6	imul	mem8	OF,CF SF,ZF, PF,AF ?	2+	12-17	13-18	11
F6	mul	reg8	OF,CF SF,ZF, PF,AF ?	2	9-14	13-18	11
F6	mul	mem8	OF,CF SF,ZF, PF,AF ?	2+	12-17	13-18	11
F6	neg	reg8	SF,ZF,OF,CF,PF,AF	2	2	1	1
F6	neg	mem8	SF,ZF,OF,CF,PF,AF	2+	2	1	1
F6	not	reg8	none	2	2	1	1
F6	not	mem8	none	2+	6	3	3
F6	test	reg8,imm8	SF,ZF,OF,CF,PF,AF	3	2	1	1
F6	test	mem8,imm8	SF,ZF,OF,CF,PF,AF	3+	5	2	2

Opcode	Mnemonic	Operand(s)	Flags affected	Number of bytes	Timing 386	Timing 486	Timing Pentium
F7	div	reg16 reg32	SF,ZF,OF,PF,AF ?	2	22 38	24 40	25 41
F7	div	mem16 mem32	SF,ZF,OF,PF,AF ?	2+	25 41	24 40	25 41
F7	idiv	reg16 reg32	SF,ZF,OF,PF,AF ?	2	27 43	27 43	30 48
F7	idiv	mem16 mem32	SF,ZF,OF,PF,AF ?	2+	30 46	28 44	30 48
F7	imul	reg16 reg32	OF,CF SF,ZF, PF,AF ?	2	9-22 9-38	13-26 13-42	11 10
F7	imul	mem16 mem32	OF,CF SF,ZF, PF,AF ?	2+	12-25 12-41	13-26 13-42	11 10
F7	imul	mem16 mem32	OF,CF SF,ZF, PF,AF ?	4 6	9-22 9-38	13-26 13-42	11 10
F7	mul	reg16 reg32	OF,CF SF,ZF, PF,AF ?	2	9-22 9-38	13-26 13-42	11 10
F7	mul	mem16 mem32	OF,CF SF,ZF, PF,AF ?	2+	12-25 12-41	13-26 13-42	11 10
F7	neg	reg16 reg32	SF,ZF,OF,CF,PF,AF	2	2	1	1
F7	neg	mem16 mem32	SF,ZF,OF,CF,PF,AF	2+	2	1	1
F7	not	reg16 reg32	none	2	2	1	1
F7	not	mem16 mem32	none	2+	6	3	3
F7	test	reg16,imm16 reg32,imm32	SF,ZF,OF,CF,PF,AF	4 6	2	1	1
F7	test	mem16,imm16 mem32,imm32	SF,ZF,OF,CF,PF,AF	4+ 6+	5	2	2
F8	clc	none	CF	1	2	2	2
F9	stc	none	CF	1	2	2	2
FC	cld	none	DF	1	2	2	2
FD	std	none	DF	1	2	2	2
FE	dec	reg8		2	2	1	1
FE	dec	mem8	SF,ZF,OF,PF,AF	2+	6	3	3

Opcode	Mnemonic	Operand(s)	Flags affected	Number of bytes	Timing 386	Timing 486	Timing Pentium
FE	inc	reg8	SF,ZF,OF,PF,AF	2	2	1	1
FE	inc	mem8	SF,ZF,OF,PF,AF	2+	6	3	3
FF	call	reg32 (near indirect)	none	2	7+	5	2
FF	call	mem32 (near indirect)	none	2+	10+	5	2
FF	call	far indirect	none	6	22+	17	5
FF	dec	mem16 mem32	SF,ZF,OF,PF,AF	2+	6	3	3
FF	inc	mem16 mem32	SF,ZF,OF,PF,AF	2+	6	3	3
FF	jmp	reg32	none	2	10+	5	2
FF	jmp	mem32	none	2+	10+	5	2
FF	push	mem16 mem32	none	2+	5	4	2

* timing varies

INDEX